"This book delivers exciting research focused exclusively on the vital first year of language study. Its four thematic sections – Language Competence, Intercultural Competence, Technology, and Assessment and Evaluation – will be immensely useful to all language instructors, regardless of language taught."

Jason Merrill, *Professor of Russian, Michigan State University; Director of the Middlebury College, Kathryn Wasserman Davis School of Russian, USA*

"This book presents critical research findings and practical recommendations focused on language instruction at the elementary level in colleges and universities. I recommend this well-organized volume to all those working to encourage these language learners in their efforts to become effective communicators in today's globalized world."

Marilyn S. Severson, *Professor Emerita, Seattle Pacific University, USA*

"With a thoughtful collection of empirical studies on a range of critical issues in the field of foreign language education, this volume fills in the gap of research devoted to novice level adult language learners in college and university programs. I highly recommend this reference book for professionals looking for research ideas and pedagogical recommendations in program design and curriculum innovation."

Yilin Sun, *Professor, Seattle Colleges-South Seattle College; President of TESOL International Association (2014–2015), USA*

ENHANCING BEGINNER-LEVEL FOREIGN LANGUAGE EDUCATION FOR ADULT LEARNERS

This book is an authoritative text that explores best classroom practices for engaging adult learners in beginner-level foreign language courses.

Built around a diverse range of international research studies and conceptual articles, the book covers four key issues in teaching language to novice students: development of linguistic skills, communicative and intercultural competence, evaluation and assessment, and the use of technology. Each chapter includes teaching insights that are supported by critical research and can be practically applied across languages to enhance instructional strategies and curriculum designs. The text also aims to build intercultural competence, harness technology, and design assessment to stimulate effective learning in formal instructional settings, including colleges, universities, and specialist language schools.

With its broad coverage of language pedagogy at the novice level, this book is a must read for graduate students, scholars, researchers, and practitioners in the fields of language education, second language acquisition, language teaching and learning, and applied linguistics.

Ekaterina Nemtchinova is Professor of Linguistics at Seattle Pacific University, USA, where she was named "Professor of the Year" in 2018. Her research interests include teacher education and technology in language teaching. She has previously authored a number of articles and textbooks in these areas.

Routledge Research in Language Education

The *Routledge Research in Language Education* series provides a platform for established and emerging scholars to present their latest research and discuss key issues in Language Education. This series welcomes books on all areas of language teaching and learning, including but not limited to language education policy and politics, multilingualism, literacy, L1, L2 or foreign language acquisition, curriculum, classroom practice, pedagogy, teaching materials, and language teacher education and development. Books in the series are not limited to the discussion of the teaching and learning of English only.

Books in the series include:

Pluricentric Languages and Language Education
Pedagogical Implications and Innovative Approaches to Language Teaching
Edited by Marcus Callies and Stefanie Hehner

The Acquisition of English Grammar and Phonology by Cantonese ESL Learners
Challenges, Causes and Pedagogical Insights
Alice Yin Wa Chan

Using Digital Portfolios to Develop Students' Writing
A Practical Guide for Language Teachers
Ricky Lam and Benjamin Luke Moorhouse

Enhancing Beginner-Level Foreign Language Education for Adult Learners
Language Instruction, Intercultural Competence, Technology, and Assessment
Edited by Ekaterina Nemtchinova

For more information about the series, please visit www.routledge.com/Routledge-Research-in-Language-Education/book-series/RRLE

ENHANCING BEGINNER-LEVEL FOREIGN LANGUAGE EDUCATION FOR ADULT LEARNERS

Language Instruction, Intercultural Competence, Technology, and Assessment

Edited by Ekaterina Nemtchinova

NEW YORK AND LONDON

First published 2023
by Routledge
605 Third Avenue, New York, NY 10158

and by Routledge
4 Park Square, Milton Park, Abingdon, Oxon, OX14 4RN

Routledge is an imprint of the Taylor & Francis Group, an informa business

© 2023 selection and editorial matter, Ekaterina Nemtchinova; individual chapters, the contributors

The right of Ekaterina Nemtchinova to be identified as the author of the editorial material, and of the authors for their individual chapters, has been asserted in accordance with sections 77 and 78 of the Copyright, Designs and Patents Act 1988.

All rights reserved. No part of this book may be reprinted or reproduced or utilised in any form or by any electronic, mechanical, or other means, now known or hereafter invented, including photocopying and recording, or in any information storage or retrieval system, without permission in writing from the publishers.

Trademark notice: Product or corporate names may be trademarks or registered trademarks, and are used only for identification and explanation without intent to infringe.

Library of Congress Cataloging-in-Publication Data
Names: Nemtchinova, Ekaterina, editor.
Title: Enhancing beginner-level foreign language education for adult learners : language instruction, intercultural competence, technology, and assessment / edited by Ekaterina Nemtchinova.
Description: New York, NY : Routledge, 2023. | Series: Routledge research in language education | Includes bibliographical references and index. | Summary: "This book is an authoritative text that explores best classroom practices for engaging adult learners in beginner-level foreign language courses"-- Provided by publisher.
Identifiers: LCCN 2022036621 (print) | LCCN 2022036622 (ebook) | ISBN 9780367528010 (hardback) | ISBN 9781032422381 (paperback) | ISBN 9781003058441 (ebook)
Subjects: LCSH: Language and languages--Study and teaching. | Adult education. | LCGFT: Essays.
Classification: LCC P51 .E526 2023 (print) | LCC P51 (ebook) | DDC 418.0071--dc23/eng/20221012
LC record available at https://lccn.loc.gov/2022036621
LC ebook record available at https://lccn.loc.gov/2022036622

ISBN: 978-0-367-52801-0 (hbk)
ISBN: 978-1-032-42238-1 (pbk)
ISBN: 978-1-003-05844-1 (ebk)

DOI: 10.4324/9781003058441

Typeset in Bembo
by SPi Technologies India Pvt Ltd (Straive)

Ancillary materials for chapters of this book are openly available on Google Drive at https://tinyurl.com/22n582v4

CONTENTS

Foreword by Benjamin Rifkin   x
Acknowledgments   xiv
List of contributors   xv

1 Introduction: Enhancing beginner-level foreign language education for adult learners   1
   Ekaterina Nemtchinova

PART I
Teaching language competence   9

2 Postsecondary language learners' ideal L2 self in a beginning Chinese, French, and Spanish classrooms   11
   Yan Xie and Laura Ziebart

3 Experience with application of usage-based model of language to beginning L2 instruction   26
   Serafima Gettys

4 Enhancing grammar acquisition among beginner-level learners of Chinese using the flipped learning model   42
   Hongying Xu

5 Building beginning Spanish language learners' linguistic and cultural competence through online task-based instruction 58
Lina Lee

PART II
Teaching intercultural competence 75

6 Integrating culture in language curriculum from beginning to intermediate level in a blended learning environment: A design-based empirical study 77
Shenglan Zhang

7 Intercultural competence in elementary-level language classes in higher education 95
Islam Karkour

8 The culture portfolio: Assessing growth toward intercultural competence 113
Julianne Bryant

9 Employing concept maps in teaching foreign language culture 131
Elmira Gerfanova

PART III
Teaching with technology 147

10 Pathways to digital L2 literacies for text-based telecollaboration at the beginning level 149
Maria Bondarenko and Liudmila Klimanova

11 Student satisfaction and engagement in a beginning Ukrainian blended-learning course: Debunking fears of blending and lessons learned 167
Alla Nedashkivska

12 Data-driven learning in a low-level language classroom 185
Katya Goussakova

13 Поехали! Training Russian prefixed verbs of motion in virtual reality 200
Kristin Bidoshi and Ekaterina Nemtchinova

PART IV
Assessment and evaluation   **215**

14 An exploration of beginner-level Korean learners'
    perceptions and participation in collaborative writing
    tasks for learning-oriented assessment   217
    Yunjung Nam and Hakyoon Lee

15 Feminist assessment in elementary world language courses   235
    Veta Chitnev

16 Assessment of the relationship between derivational
    morphological awareness and second language reading
    comprehension   254
    Anna Shur

Index   *270*

FOREWORD

Benjamin Rifkin

FAIRLEIGH DICKINSON UNIVERSITY

Research conducted in the United States on the instructed acquisition of a second (or third) language by college-age learners tends to focus on the acquisition of English by immigrants and international students and American-born learners of Spanish, in part, no doubt, because in any one institution, the largest number of research subjects are students of these precise groups. It is difficult, however, to generalize from such studies since the diversity of human language is much greater than English and Spanish, and the instructional practices in any one classroom may differ significantly from the instructional practices in any other classroom. This volume, with chapters focusing on the acquisition of very different languages in a variety of instructional settings, is very promising in that it provides readers with insights that may well be generalizable to the learning and teaching of target languages in a variety of institutional contexts.

Our understanding of the learning and teaching dynamic in world language education rests on a foundation of four key issues at play in different ways in each instructional setting. The first of these is the issue of time: how much time do students have in the classroom and how much time are they expected to devote to outside-of-class activities, including homework, and with what learning outcomes? Some institutions teach a first-year course with three contact hours per week, others with six or more. Time is not a sufficient variable for the acquisition of proficiency in a language, but time on task is a prerequisite of acquisition. The second issue has to do with students' intersectional identities, which they do not surrender as they log in or walk into the classroom. We have to consider the intersectional identities of the students (heritage or foreign language learners, Black, white, Hispanic, or Asian, LGBTQ+ or straight, from what socioeconomic background, able-bodied or with a disability, among other factors), the instructors (all of the previously mentioned identities and whether they are native speakers of the target culture), the target culture itself and the ways in which that target culture seems to welcome and embrace those who study it in this particular classroom, the representation of the target culture in the instructional materials as welcoming or not, and the institutional culture (for instance, a historically Black college or university or a predominantly white institution, a women's college or a co-educational college, a public institution in an urban setting or a private institution in a suburban or rural setting). The third of these issues is the motivation that learners bring to the learning enterprise and the degree to which instructors have designed and delivered a curriculum that matches learner motivations and interests, as well as the degree to which instructors can enhance learner motivation. The fourth issue is one of values and metrics: in what ways are students' learning outcomes measured (by performance on a grammar test, by performance in a communicative interaction, or by some other means), and how do those metrics compare to the values instructors (and administrators) articulate for the given language program? If a program director says that the program values communicative success, how is that measured in course assessment instruments from the beginning of the course of study to the end, and how are those learning outcomes documented? Each of these four issues brings into play cognitive, affective, and metacognitive variables for both learners and instructors, and therefore have a direct bearing on persistence in the language learning enterprise and in students' learning outcomes, as we will see in all the chapters in this volume.

Powerful learning outcomes (as demonstrated by high levels of proficiency) are unattainable without persistence in the language learning enterprise. Programs and instructors must retain students from the first year of instruction to continue into the second and beyond, and yet Modern Language Association surveys of enrollments in world language instruction at the postsecondary level consistently show decreasing enrollment in language classes from the first-year level to more advanced levels of instruction. In other words, regardless of language, and almost regardless of institution, more students begin a course of study in a world language than continue this study into the second year or beyond. Given that time on task is a prerequisite for the attainment of higher levels of proficiency, regardless of the language studied, all world language instructors must consider the importance of learner persistence in language study and construct curricula that motivate students to continue their language learning journeys. This means that every language learning classroom must be a place where every learner feels welcome, every learner feels included, and every learner feels that they belong. For many world language educators, this means not only ensuring that the classroom environment is respectful, supportive, and inclusive but also that instructional materials and classroom activities are inclusive. There is no world culture that does not have individuals who identify as LGBTQ+ or individuals with disabilities. Why, then, do we have textbooks that do not include or represent people from these communities in America or the target culture? It is not possible for many instructors to choose the textbooks they use, and even for those who can choose their textbooks, for some languages, there may be no textbook that depicts individuals from historically excluded backgrounds. However, every instructor can supplement the textbook (if they use one at all) with materials in which students' intersectional identities (as well as the identities of individuals who are not represented in the current classroom) are recognized and included. This enhances students' sense of belonging and may well encourage students to continue their learning journey beyond the first year. We cannot expect students to embrace the learning of a second or third language and culture, for the goal of attaining intercultural competence as described in the chapters of the second section of this volume, if their own identities are not respected in their language learning classroom.

Students' motivations and beliefs about language learning are critically important for every aspect of the learning experience. The design of classroom, technology-mediated, and other at-home activities that engage students deeply in the learning process is critically important for encouraging persistence in the language learning journey. When students *want to know* how a short story ends, who in their class will win a game, how to tell a story themselves to the public using digital media, they will want to persist in their language learning experience, whether from one day to the next or one year to the next. The nature of the design and delivery of instruction, what students are assigned to do, whether in a face-to-face classroom, online, or in individual at-home exercises, must be aligned with students' motivations and beliefs.

The fourth key issue for the learning and teaching of world languages is the question of values and metrics for the assessment of learning outcomes. Far too often, we count those indicators that are most easily counted (for instance, spelling or grammatical errors in student writing, or correct responses to a multiple-choice question), even though those indicators are not aligned with what we value most dearly in the learning and teaching dynamic. In close collaboration with their colleagues both in their own postsecondary programs and the K–12 institutions that are their most important "feeder schools," university-level world language educators must articulate what they value most in the language learning enterprise. What is most important for students to be able to *do* in the target language when they walk across the stage at commencement and receive their diplomas? With those values explicitly articulated, instructors should then plan backward for *what* to assess and *how* to assess as milestones along the way toward that ultimate "commencement day" goal. In doing so, instructors will align the metrics of assessment with the values of the learning enterprise. We must count what we value because by default, we are only valuing what we count. The final section in this volume makes important contributions to our understanding of assessment in the language learning curriculum.

As you read the chapters in this volume, you will embark on your own journey in which you will question many of the assumptions that have been the foundation of world language education for decades, despite the evolution of proficiency- and standards-based instruction. This is precisely the function of the best research: in consideration of the findings shared in this volume, you may ultimately revisit some of your own assumptions and restructure some aspects of your own curricula. This is how things ought to be: we should not limit ourselves to teaching only in the ways in which we ourselves were taught. Most of our students will not seek a doctoral degree in our fields and approach their language learning journey differently than we approached ours; there are also many other ways in which our students, and the times in which they are enrolled in bachelor's degree programs, are very different from us and the times in which we were undergraduates. I wish you a thoughtful and productive journey as you read the chapters in this volume.

ACKNOWLEDGMENTS

The idea for this volume became a reality thanks to many people, and I would like to acknowledge those who helped me on the way.

I am indebted to the authors whose voices made this book possible and whose research studies are furthering world language learning in the first-year classroom. Their commitment to teaching low-level courses is sure to increase the status of language programs all over the world.

My heartfelt thanks go to the reviewers who were very generous with their time and suggestions. Although they will remain anonymous, their helpful feedback and professional wisdom are greatly valued.

I would like to thank the two anonymous reviewers who provided excellent comments on the book proposal. I am extremely grateful to Alice Salt, my editor at Routledge, and Sophie Ganesh and Khyati Sanger, my editorial assistants, for their expertise and patience as they answered my many questions. I am also grateful to the Routledge staff for their vital editorial work on this volume.

My biggest thanks and love go to my family in the U.S. and Russia who encouraged, cheered, and supported me through every step of the process.

Finally, my deepest respect and admiration go to all novice-level adult language learners whose diligence, enthusiasm, and commitment inspired this volume.

CONTRIBUTORS

Kristin Bidoshi is a Professor of Russian and Director of the Russian and East European Studies Program at Union College, USA, where she teaches courses in Russian language, literature, and culture. She conducts fieldwork in Eastern Europe and publishes on subjects including the use of the oral tradition in literary works and Russian language pedagogy. Her current research focuses on language acquisition in virtual environments.

Maria Bondarenko (PhD in cultural studies) has been teaching the Russian language at the University of Montreal (Canada) and in different intensive summer language programs in the USA since 2011. Her research interests focus on such aspects of second language (L2) acquisition as content-based L2 instruction for beginners, neuroeducational approach to L2 teaching and learning, and telecollaboration at low proficiency levels. She is the author of three volumes of a Russian language textbook for beginners.

Julianne Bryant is an Associate Professor of Spanish and Chair of the Modern Languages Department at Biola University, USA, where she teaches elementary language courses, as well as Hispanic linguistics, teaching pedagogy, Caribbean culture and Community Spanish. Her research interests include language and identity, heritage language acquisition, bilingualism, the intersection of language and culture, and Caribbean cultural studies.

Veta Chitnev is the Director of Undergraduate Studies (Russian) at the University of British Columbia, Canada. Her areas of specialization are Russian as a second language, pedagogy, and curriculum development and design. Her research interests center around assessment in higher education, critical feminist pedagogy, intercultural studies, and educational psychology.

Elmira Gerfanova is an Assistant Professor at Astana IT University, Kazakhstan. Her academic interests include intercultural education, linguocultural aspect of foreign language teaching, and English as a Foreign Language textbook analysis. She is a senior researcher in the project "Development and Popularization of the Kazakh Language and Culture in the Context of Intercultural Education" (2020–2022) under the Ministry of Education and Science of the Republic of Kazakhstan.

Serafima Gettys is an Associate Professor, instructor of Russian language, and director of the foreign language program at Lewis University, USA, where she has been teaching for 16 years. Serafima has published about 30 works, including *Learning to Teach Russian: Effective Classroom Techniques* (Berkeley Slavic Specialties, 1998).

Katya Goussakova is a Professor of English for Academic Purposes at Seminole State College of Florida, USA. Over the years, she has taught Intensive English, Second Language Acquisition, English to Speakers of Other Languages, and English for Academic Purposes courses and has been active with local, state, and international teacher organizations. Her current research interests include corpus linguistics, heritage language maintenance, grammar and vocabulary instruction, and instructional technology.

Islam Karkour teaches at the University of New Hampshire, USA. His research interests include intercultural competence, foreign language education, and curriculum design and development. Dr. Karkour has published several articles related to his work on foreign language education and curriculum design.

Liudmila Klimanova is an Assistant Professor of Second Language Acquisition and Technology at the University of Arizona, USA, and a faculty member in the doctoral program in Second Language Acquisition and Teaching. Her research focuses on social and psychological aspects of multimodal identity representation in multilingual online chats and telecollaboration. Dr. Klimanova's recent projects examine the role of digital experience in cultural learning within the framework of digital humanistic pedagogy.

Hakyoon Lee is an Assistant Professor in the Department of World Languages and Cultures at Georgia State University, USA, and the Director of Center for Urban Language Teaching and Research (CULTR). She has been teaching Korean and coordinating the Korean program at GSU since 2013. Her research interests are at the intersection of sociolinguistics, Korean language education, bilingualism/multilingualism, and immigrant education.

Lina Lee (PhD, University of Texas-Austin) is a Professor of Spanish at the University of New Hampshire, USA, where she teaches courses in L2 acquisition, applied linguistics, and foreign language methodology. She has conducted research and published articles on language pedagogy, computer-mediated communication, and discourse analysis.

Yunjung Nam (Eunice) has recently completed a PhD degree in the Department of Applied Linguistics and English as a Second Language at Georgia State University, USA. Her research interests include classroom-based assessment, language assessment literacy, stakeholder perceptions in language assessment, and language teacher education.

Alla Nedashkivska is a Professor of Slavic applied linguistics in the department of Modern Languages and Cultural Studies and a former Director of the Ukrainian Language Education Centre at the Canadian Institute of Ukrainian Studies at the University of Alberta. She publishes in the areas of Slavic linguistics, discourse analysis, political and media language, and language ideologies, as well as Ukrainian language pedagogy and L2 acquisition.

Ekaterina Nemtchinova (Katya) is a professor of linguistics at Seattle Pacific University, USA, where she was named "Professor of the Year" in 2018. Her research interests include teacher education and technology in language teaching. In addition to articles and book chapters, she published a Russian language textbook, *Listen Up!* (University Press of the South, 2011) and *Teaching Listening* (TESOL 2011; 2020).

Anna Shur has recently gotten a PhD in curriculum and instruction with a concentration in literacy education from the University of Wyoming. Dr. Shur taught ESL and EFL classes in various social and educational contexts in the U.S. and Russia. She is a researcher at Saratov State University (Russia) and an EFL instructor at Present Perfect, the online language school.

Yan Xie is a Professor of Chinese and the Director of the Chinese Program at the Department of Modern Languages at Liberty University, USA. She is an American Council on the Teaching of Foreign Languages–certified OPI-Mandarin Chinese Tester (Full). Her research interests include L2 motivation and acquisition of Mandarin basic vowels and Chinese characters.

Hongying Xu is an Associate Professor and the Director of the Chinese Program at the University of Wisconsin-La Crosse, USA. Her research interests include language acquisition and language pedagogy, especially on using technology in instruction to enhance language learning.

Shenglan Zhang is an Associate Professor in the Department of World Languages and Cultures at Iowa State University, USA, where she is the coordinator for the Multi-Section Lower Division Chinese courses. Her research interests include Computer-Assisted Language Learning, designing for online learning, and self-regulated learning.

Laura Ziebart is a senior undergraduate student at Liberty University, USA. She is studying psychology, with a focus on Chinese and French, and is a research assistant to Dr. Yan Xie. Some of her research interests involve L2 learning, student motivation, and effective teaching strategies.

1

INTRODUCTION

Enhancing beginner-level foreign language education for adult learners

Ekaterina Nemtchinova

An introduction: Teaching beginner-level adults in a world language classroom

"Why do you study a foreign language? Are you going to continue into the second year?" At the end of their first year of college Russian study, my students usually respond to the first of these questions with "love the language," "want to live in the country," "will help me with my career," "appreciate the culture," "enjoy the class." They often give a resolute "Yes" to the second. While our students may have different goals – from passing their college's language requirement to finding a job in a country in which their chosen language is spoken, the first year of language learning is the first step along a challenging path to building proficiency in a new language.

This book aims to draw attention to a wide range of critical research issues emerging from the adult beginning-level language classroom in a formal instructional setting such as colleges, universities, and specialized language schools. Beginning courses are paramount for successful language learning and ensuring continuing enrollment in college language programs. And yet they do not enjoy the same prestige as upper-level courses in language, literature, cultural studies, and linguistics. Moreover, beginning-level courses are often staffed with part-time faculty or teaching assistants who may or may not have the necessary preparation, training, experience, or motivation to inspire their students' language exploration (Halcrow & Olson, 2008; Lacorte & Canabal, 2003). Considering the added challenges of shrinking language class size and the resulting reduction in course offerings (a common theme in many chapters of the volume), we need to facilitate teaching to try and reverse the trend. It is hoped that instructional strategies and curriculum designs investigated in the volume will help increase

DOI: 10.4324/9781003058441-1

the number of students learning a foreign language. Striving to strike a balance between second language (L2) teaching research and practice, the international team of classroom practitioners presents empirical analysis of novice language learner data and discusses pedagogical implications of their studies. Given the relative scarcity of materials targeting adult low-level instruction, the research findings and practical recommendations contained in the book will strengthen the novice curriculum as they appeal to various learning styles, build learners' confidence, and help stimulate language production.

This volume focuses on the novice language classroom at the postsecondary level and the theoretical and practical issues emerging from teaching adult beginning language learners. *Adult* in this context refers to students enrolled in college or university foreign language courses to study a new language; while coming from a variety of regional, social, and economic backgrounds, they are at least 18 years old and have secondary education. The term *beginning* is frequently associated with children learning an L2; teaching beginner adults receives less attention from researchers and practitioners. This is likely because most foreign language instruction worldwide happens in elementary and secondary schools (Ur, 2012). And yet, there is a total of 1,158,562 students enrolled in introductory (first- and second-year) foreign language courses in higher-education institutions in the U.S. alone (Looney & Lusin, 2019). World languages including English as a second or foreign language (ESL/EFL) are taught all over the world in two- and four-year colleges, universities, and specialized language schools off- and online, testifying to a considerable increase in the number of adults taking part in different language programs (Illeris, 2004).

Adolescents and older learners in a college or a university setting bring a distinctive set of learner characteristics to the task of learning a new language. Their cognitive maturity and developed conceptual, analytical, and processing capabilities allow them to approach language in a deliberate way by applying rules, forming associations, and engaging in intentional practice. Adults have a better memory for vocabulary, a longer attention span, and a conscious knowledge of the first language (L1). They are aware of their learning style and enjoy greater autonomy in learning, which tends to be goal-oriented and relevant to their academic, personal, and professional lives (Strong, 2009). In fact, when compared with children who are commonly known to absorb a new language from their surroundings with little effort, older learners have proved to acquire language faster in the initial stages of learning and achieve greater success in formal instructional settings (Saville-Troike & Barto, 2017).

A formal instructional setting of a college or university language classroom offers advantages that support and enhance adults' learning processes and cannot be achieved in out-of-class environments, such as an immersive experience in a country or independent practice online. As language is presented in a sequence of steps that follows natural acquisition processes from basic to more complex structures, all language skills are learned together with one reinforcing the other.

The presence of a teacher ensures instant feedback in the form of explanations, corrections, praise, encouragement, and support. Typical classroom activities such as practice exercises, home assignments, and tests provide a sense of discipline and structure, which may be difficult to maintain when learning a language independently. The social context – a group of classmates with similar goals and challenges – often creates additional motivation and provides opportunities for personal contact. While classroom interaction may lack in variety of input and discourse types of natural acquisition settings, it usually seems less threatening than direct contact with native speakers, particularly for beginners (Saville-Troike & Barto, 2017). Together, these cognitive, social, and motivational characteristics of in-class experience stimulate adult learners in the beginning language classroom.

The beginning stage of language proficiency in this book covers American Council on the Teaching of Foreign Languages Proficiency Guidelines novice low, mid, and high levels (American Council on the Teaching of Foreign Languages, 2012) or levels A1–A2 of Common European Framework of Reference for Languages Global Scale (Council of Europe, 2001) and refers to the level of ability that can be achieved by completing a sequence of first-year semester or quarter-length language courses at the postsecondary level, or roughly 150–200 hours of instructional time in a college, university, or a specialized language school. The book uses the terms *beginner*, *beginning*, *elementary*, *low-level*, and *novice* interchangeably. Although performance outcomes vary from language to language depending on the writing system, degree of similarity to L1, and one's individual investment into learning, language students at this level of ability can be expected to understand the gist of a simple reading text and slow, deliberate speech on familiar subjects related to them and their immediate environment. They can ask rehearsed questions and use memorized words, phrases, and occasional sentences to respond in speech and writing. They can sustain a short conversation on everyday topics, discuss their likes and dislikes, say that they don't understand the speaker or ask to speak slower. They should be aware of the basic target culture symbols and norms. These are remarkable feats considering the difficulty of learning a foreign language and the time it takes.

As novice learners acquire basic grammar and vocabulary while developing reading, writing, listening, and speaking skills in a new language, they are challenged by a new linguistic system, often with a different alphabet, and an unfamiliar way of expressing thoughts shaped by a novel culture. Their instructors, meanwhile, face a challenge of their own: while students' proficiency level does not allow them to articulate complex ideas or engage in lengthy conversations, any type of communication beyond basic topics and simple exchanges is beyond their reach. There is a lot of recycling and repetition of language, and the progress seems slow. How does one teach language in a way that sustains interest, confidence, and motivation, and is accessible for beginners? The research studies presented in this book address facilitation of linguistic, communicative, and cultural competence in an elementary language classroom. The volume contributors study the impact of new approaches and techniques on the learning process by analyzing student motivation and attitudes and addressing learning outcomes in the light of classroom performance. While the studies were conducted in different settings and with different target languages, the research conclusions are applicable to other educational settings at the beginning level. Drawing on their research findings, the volume contributors provide a host of innovative materials and techniques, describe successful instructional strategies and collaborative projects, and offer specific classroom suggestions on teaching target language and culture, using information and communication technology, and assessing learners' performance.

This volume was coming together during the COVID-19 pandemic. As colleges and universities shifted their operations and activities to online mode, the language educators who contributed to this volume had to adapt their teaching to on-screen delivery amid an unprecedented amount of stress and pedagogical and personal upheavals. The pandemic and new teaching mode also impacted the research methodology and sample size of many studies. Despite all the strain, it is my hope that the studies in the volume offer new insights into beginning-level language instruction and help widen the learners' path toward higher target language proficiency.

The volume

This volume presents empirical studies investigating various aspects of second or foreign language instruction to adults at the novice level. While the scholarly interest has largely been concerned with English as a second, foreign, or global language or Spanish contexts, mirroring the prevalence of the languages in language education worldwide (Guo et al., 2021; Jurisevic, 2013), this volume brings together practitioners from a variety of world language classrooms who offer a research-based approach to teaching adult beginners. Rather than focusing on a single language, the chapters in the collection deal with many different foreign languages taught in colleges and universities. The book will appeal to academic audiences such as postgraduate students, scholars, and researchers interested in issues related to instructed L2 acquisition, exploration of knowledge and practice, the process of learning, and language pedagogy. The book can also be used as supplementary reading for advanced undergraduate and graduate degrees and endorsements in world language education, language teaching, bilingual education, teaching English language learners, applied linguistics, etc. A useful reference for recent research on language teaching as well as classroom ideas, the volume will also appeal to teacher educators, supervisors, and program administrators who would like to provide professional development opportunities to teachers and teaching assistants and substantiate instruction with research. A professional audience will find examples of innovative beginning-level language activities suitable for any language.

Although in a real-life classroom teaching target language and culture skills, using technology, and assessing linguistic and intercultural competence are often inextricable from each other, these aspects of foreign language instruction are presented separately in the book for organizational purposes. The book consists of four sections. The first section, "Teaching Language Competence," offers an analysis of innovative approaches to curricular instruction that ensure effective skill development on a variety of topics, for different purposes, and in different situations. Known as competencies, together these skills ultimately lead to world-readiness through sustained meaningful oral and written communication in a wide range of contexts. Yan Xie and Laura Ziebart, in the first chapter in this section, address elementary language learners' ideal L2 self, i.e., their desired achievements in learning the four language skills. By comparing the goals and motivational self-systems of learners of three different languages, the study provides suggestions that will benefit elementary-level language courses. Serafima Gettys, in the second chapter, draws the link between the usage-based linguistics that still receives little attention in the practitioners' world and the foreign language classroom practice. The results of the action research indicate the effectiveness of a usage-based instruction focusing on more implicit, construction-based learning rather than grammar drills and vocabulary lists that many scholars find ineffective. In the next chapter, Hongying Xu examines whether, compared to traditional instruction, the flipped learning model can better facilitate the acquisition of grammar patterns among beginner-level Chinese learners. She offers a quantitative analysis of learners' gains in comprehension and production language tasks, examines student experiences through a semi-open survey, and provides specific guidelines for implementing the model in actual teaching practice. In the last chapter in this section, Lina Lee explores the benefits of task-based instruction (TBI) in a fully online beginning Spanish class. The results of her study support such affordances of TBI as noticing linguistic forms and independent and collaborative learning that facilitate the development of beginning students' linguistic and cultural competence.

The chapters in the second section, "Teaching Intercultural Competence," explore key issues in developing intercultural competence (IC) in lower-level classes. While the question of IC becomes ever more important today, many instructors struggle to alight their teaching with *World-Readiness Standards* (National Standards Collaborative, 2015) and devote class time to intercultural goals, a challenge reiterated in the section's chapters. Students can and should progress in their intercultural skills as they study a world language, but the integration of linguistic and cultural objectives requires a skillful embedding of cultural activities at the curricular level and appropriate assessment measures. Comparison and reflective activities in particular can further students' ability to understand, respect, and empathize with the target culture, as well as express themselves in a culturally appropriate way. The chapters in this section provide valuable insights into various aspects of IC development. Thus, in the first chapter, Shenglan Zhang analyzes the integration of language and culture instruction at the curricular level. She describes the five consecutive steps that allow students to explore culture through different channels and offers research data to support the effectiveness of this approach. Islam Karkour's study presented in the second chapter measures intercultural sensitivity of beginning-level students in different world language classes over one semester of language study. He argues that intercultural development is affected by a particular instructional approach and supports the effectiveness of reflection for intercultural learning. Next, Julianne Bryant explores students' gains in IC in a culture-centered (as opposed to language-centered) curriculum. She concludes that while culture-forward materials and required conversational practice with target language speakers augment IC development, process-oriented tasks such as cultural portfolio are detrimental to perceptible IC growth. In the next chapter, Elmira Gerfanova focuses on concept maps, i.e., graphic organizers that represent relationships between concepts and ideas, as a means of teaching culture. Her study analyzes the effectiveness of concept mapping in a Kazakhstani first-year language classroom from student and instructors' points of view.

The next section, *Teaching with technology*, investigates novel ways in which different media can impact language development while engaging students in learning tasks and offering multiple opportunities for language practice in real-life context and meaningful communication, ultimately making learning more enjoyable. Maria Bondarenko and Liudmila Klimanova present a conceptual reflection on the role of digital literacies. Based on the results of research focusing on text-based telecollaboration projects, they explore the digital media affordances and discuss their culture-of-use in the context of a low-level language classroom. Next, Alla Nedashkivska examines the impact of the blended-learning model (i.e., the combination of face-to-face and online teaching) on the level of student engagement and satisfaction in a beginning Ukrainian classroom. The results of her study are meant to dispel some of the instructors' fears associated with the blended-learning format. In the following chapter, Katya Goussakova describes the use of corpus linguistics as a means of providing contextualized and individualized instruction, allowing low-level students to learn the most frequent lexico-grammatical structures and collocations, and increasing learner autonomy, motivation, and active learning. Kristin Bidoshi and Ekaterina Nemtchinova's study in the last chapter of this section highlights the benefits of using virtual reality and gaming software to teach a challenging grammatical concept. The survey of student experiences shows that aural, visual, and motion features of technology considerably increase beginning students' comprehension and production of new language.

The section on "Assessment and Evaluation" focuses on the key component of a language learning program that informs instructors and administrators about student progress and helps shape and implement subsequent instruction. The chapters in this section invite us to rethink traditional assessment formats such as fill-in-the-blank and write a dialogue. Although easier to design and grade, these individual assessments fail to capture the authentic and collaborative nature of language use in the real world. Yunjung Nam and Hakyoon Lee explore students' perceptions and patterns of interactions in collaborative writing assessments in the beginning Korean class – a level of proficiency that has not been widely discussed in the literature on L2 writing – and discuss ways of enhancing the collaborative aspect of writing tasks in an elementary language classroom. Next, Veta Chitnev's study adopts a critical feminist pedagogy approach to compare summative and formative assessment measures in the first-year world language class. She emphasizes the value of the feminist view of assessment as it helps minimize competition between students as well as power disparity between students and teachers. Anna Shur, in the last chapter of the section, examines the cross-linguistic transfer of derivational morphological awareness (DMA) in groups of beginning German and Russian adult learners of English in the context of assessment of vocabulary and reading comprehension skills. While one group showed evidence of cross-linguistic DMA transfer and the other did not, the two groups' reading comprehension scores were not different, which may suggest that DMA has influence on the development of L2 reading comprehension.

Concluding remarks

The goal of this volume is to call attention to elementary-level language courses by identifying and examining critical research issues arising from teaching adult beginners in colleges and universities. Successful introductory courses are crucial for a foreign language program, as they lay a foundation for further language and culture study, instill a love for language, and populate upper-level courses with students. One way to ensure that the pursuit of the language continues beyond the first year is to sustain learners' interest, confidence, and motivation from the start by supporting language instruction with empirical research findings. The chapters included in the book highlight the adult college language learner with their widely ranging learning characteristics and goals and offer a contribution to evidence-based research on L2 teaching and learning. By examining issues of language and IC development, the use of technology, and assessment, this volume seeks to foster a better understanding of the complexities involved in introducing adults to a new language. It is my hope that research findings and classroom implications presented in the book will inform novice-level language instruction and ultimately help learners advance on the path to becoming effective communicators in today's globalized world.

References

American Council on the Teaching of Foreign Languages (ACTFL). (2012). ACTFL proficiency guidelines 2012. http://www.actfl.org/publications/guidelines-and-manuals/actfl-proficiency-guidelines-2012

Council of Europe. (2001). *Common European framework of reference for languages (CEFR): Learning, teaching, assessment*. Cambridge University Press. https://rm.coe.int/1680459f97

Guo, Q., Zhou, X., & Gao, X. (2021). Research on learning and teaching of languages other than English in System. *System*, 100. https://doi.org/10.1016/j.system.2021.102541

Halcrow, C., & Olson, M.R. (2008). ADJUNCT FACULTY: Valued resource or cheap labor? *Focus on Colleges, Universities, and Schools*, 2(1). https://www.semanticscholar.org/paper/ADJUNCT-FACULTY%3A-Valued-Resource-or-Cheap-Labor-Halcrow-Olson/2905e8593ea72021b7e916585542e232ca51ba26

Illeris, K. (2004). *Adult education and adult learning*. Roskilde University Press.

Jurisevic, D. (2013). Voice from the field: Examining the role of foreign language teaching in the community college. *Research in Comparative and International Education*, 8(2). www.wwwords.co.uk/RCIE

Lacorte, M., & Canabal, E. (2003). Interaction with heritage language learners in foreign language classrooms. https://files.eric.ed.gov/fulltext/ED481792.pdf

Looney, D., & Lusin, N. (2019). Enrollments in languages other than English in United States institutions of higher education, summer 2016 and fall 2016: Final report. *Modern Language Association*. https://www.mla.org/content/download/110154/2406932/2016-Enrollments-Final-Report.pdf

National Standards Collaborative Board. (2015). *World-readiness for learning languages*. https://www.actfl.org/sites/default/files/publications/standards/World-ReadinessStandardsforLearningLanguages.pdf

Saville-Troike, M., & Barto, K. (2017). *Introducing second language acquisition*. Cambridge University Press.

Strong, G. (2009). Adult language learners: An overview. In Smith, A. F. V., & Strong, G. (Eds.), *Adult language learners: Context and innovation* (pp. 1–9). Teaching English to Speakers of Other Languages (TESOL).

Ur, P. (2012). *A course in English language teaching*. Cambridge University Press.

PART I
Teaching language competence

2
POSTSECONDARY LANGUAGE LEARNERS' IDEAL L2 SELF IN A BEGINNING CHINESE, FRENCH, AND SPANISH CLASSROOMS

Yan Xie and Laura Ziebart

While speaking and listening skills have an immediate effect on real-world spoken communication for second language (L2) learners, reading and writing competence determines how far they can advance in learning the language. At lower levels, emphasizing oral/aural skills can quickly instill a sense of authentic communication in learners, which undoubtedly increases learning enjoyment and motivation. However, reading and writing skills are equally important. Introducing written language in the beginning classroom prepares students for more advanced language learning; otherwise, they will feel unprepared and may not consider taking upper-level courses. Although higher-level course enrollments usually decrease since many students do not need language credits for graduation, the decline can be prevented by integrating listening, speaking, reading, and writing skills from the onset of instruction so that together they create context for language use and increase students' confidence. Nowadays, digital literacy is becoming the fifth language skill because of the rapid expansion of technology. Thus, establishing both pen and digital literacy along with other language skills is necessary to prepare learners for the challenges of higher-level language study, as well as for the demands of the real world.

To develop a comprehensive skills curriculum, instructors need to understand learners' goals for each skill. A useful notion that displays learners' goals is ideal L2 self: a motivational component that represents learners' personal desires, aspirations, and ideals concerning language learning (Dörnyei, 2005). For example, an ideal L2 self of speaking can be living in a target language environment and fluently communicating with the locals. Many studies (e.g., Dörnyei & Ushioda, 2009) investigated learners' speaking goals by assessing their ideal L2 self, while research exploring learners' ideal self in other language skills is scant. The present study explores Chinese, French, and Spanish language learners' views of ideal

L2 self in speaking, listening, reading, pen writing, and digital writing. The three languages were chosen because, for native (first language (L1)) English-speaking college students in the U.S., French and Spanish are cognate languages (i.e., having a common etymological origin with English), while Chinese is not. The writing systems are also different (alphabetical French and Spanish vs. logographic Chinese). The quantitative and qualitative study findings reveal the learners' ideal self as seen through their language learning goals, which can facilitate differentiation of instruction and address individual students' challenges. This study shows how understanding the student ideal L2 self in various language skills can balance skill development in the beginning classroom, motivate students to keep learning the language, and empower language teaching.

Literature review

Ideal L2 self

Foreign/second language learner motivation has received much research attention, especially in connection with learning outcomes, learning perseverance, attitudes toward language and cultures, self-identity, goal setting, etc. From the socio-educational model (Gardner, 1985), which approaches L2 motivation from the perspective of learners' attitudes toward L2 and L2 communication, to the L2 motivational self-system (Dörnyei, 2005), motivational theories presented various perspectives advancing the understanding of learner motivation. Thus, Dörnyei (2005) proposed the L2 motivational self-system, suggesting that the motivation for learning another language originates from the need to advance from a current level of L2 proficiency to a desired proficiency, or a desired L2 self, which has two dimensions: ideal L2 self and ought-to L2 self. Ideal L2 self refers to an idealized image that learners want to achieve based on their inner desires, goals, and beliefs about L2 learning, while ought-to L2 self is shaped by others' expectations of the learner. Researchers believe that learners' L2 ideal self is associated with their proficiency level and thus affects their intrinsic, integrative, and instrumental motivation (Noels, 2009; Taguchi et al., 2009; Xie, 2014, 2018). A low level of one's ideal self can explain a lack of motivation to learn a new language (Dörnyei, 2014). Taguchi et al. (2009), investigating nearly 5,000 English as a second language learners in China, Japan, and Iran, stated that instrumentality can be either ideal or ought-to L2 self, depending on the degree of internalization of extrinsic motives. Xie (2014) reported that ideal L2 self, rather than ought-to L2 self, is a salient motivational component for non-heritage language learners. Similarly, Xie (2018) investigated Chinese language learners in an American university to show that world globalization made career demands for intercultural and cross-language communications an internal part of ideal L2 self, even though this need is also attached to utilitarian ends.

Despite the value of the concept of ideal L2 self for interpreting learner motivation, most studies exclusively examined speaking skills. Campbell and

Storch (2011) interviewed eight English L1 Chinese learners at a large Australian university and reported that their ideal L2 self was related to the goal of speaking Chinese in an international, multilingual workplace. Kong et al. (2018), investigating 1,296 Korean college foreign language learners, including 638 learning commonly taught and 658 learning less commonly taught languages, found that their ideal L2 self in speaking skills was influenced by their attitudes toward the target language, culture, and society. Oakes (2013) extended the focus to the other skills, studying French and Spanish language learners in the U.K.'s monolingual English culture and found that the desire for language proficiency in descending order is speaking, listening, reading, and writing. Although the study did not address specifically the ideal L2 self while investigating learner motivation, it suggested that ideal L2 self was a considerable incentive because of its strong correlation to the top motivation factor, which was language proficiency. Mendoza and Phung (2019) synthesized 30 studies, published between 2005 and 2018, that adopted the framework of the L2 motivational self-system to probe learner motivation of languages other than English. The study concluded that ideal L2 self was consistently a strong motivation factor, while ought-to L2 self was not. However, the study claimed that learners in Asia demonstrated a stronger ought-to L2 self than those in inner circle English-speaking countries. Existing literature shows that ideal L2 self is a strong motivation for foreign/second language learning and has been investigated primarily in speaking skills, but not in literacy skills.

Four language skills

Given the prevalence of speaking in daily communication, it is unsurprising that communicative language teaching (CLT) was and is still prominent in teaching practices, emphasizing spoken communication in realistic, meaningful situations. In the same vein, most influential CLT research concentrated on analyzing oral skills rather than literacy (e.g., Littlewood and William, 1981; Rao, 2018; Richards, 2005) with studies investigating ideal L2 self following the trend (e.g., Dörnyei & Ushioda, 2009). And yet, as real-life communication involves reading and writing as well as listening and speaking, all four skills must be addressed by motivation research and the inquiry into ideal L2 to fully understand the skill interaction in overall L2 proficiency.

The fundamental relationship between speaking, listening, reading, and writing skills has been noticed by researchers. Thus, Nan (2018) reported a strong impact between the four skills upon one another, stating that an effective way to develop language proficiency is to capitalize on the positive transfer between the skills and the interaction and coordination among them. Dash and Dash (2007) described how listening leads to speaking, which leads to reading, which leads to writing, and the skills facilitate one another. A failure in one skill will cause a failure in learning the language. They stated that receptive skills (listening and reading) are less demanding than productive skills (speaking and writing) and proposed a sequential order to teach the four skills: listening, speaking, reading, and then writing, while pointing out that the order did not mean neglecting any one of the skills. Cohen and Cowen (2007), on the other hand, commented that the four skills are reciprocal and interdependent, and that developing all skills simultaneously is critical for mastering successful communication. Therefore, it is important to integrate all four skills at an early stage of learning.

Given the wide use of digital devices in social communication, developing digital literacy is pertinent for developing L2 literacy. Dahlström and Boström (2017) found that writing on tablets instead of paper led to increased text length and better spelling, structure, and content for Swedish L2 middle schoolers. However, students from different backgrounds may have different attitudes toward digital writing. For example, Hsu (2013) reported that adult EFL learners from different Asian countries and regions differed in their attitudes toward mobile-assisted language learning. The use and production of digital information impact individuals' daily situations, so L2 digital writing capabilities will determine learners' roles in cross-cultural and cross-language interactions, and lead to career success. Discovering learners' attitudes toward digital writing will help language educators teach literacy.

In summary, the existing studies exploring L2 motivation from the perspective of ideal L2 self focus almost exclusively on speaking proficiency. Given that all language skills are interdependent, the ideal L2 selves of those skills should influence one another. Thus, a study on the relationships between the ideal L2 selves of the four skills will allow a better understanding of learner motivation. The present study seeks to discover the ideal L2 self of Chinese, French and Spanish language learners in speaking, listening, reading, pen writing, and digital writing; it also probes the intergroup differences and intragroup relationships among the ideal L2 selves of these skills. This study was guided by the following questions:

1. What ideal L2 self in speaking, listening, reading, pen writing, and digital writing skills do Chinese and French/Spanish learners desire to achieve? Are there significant differences between the two groups?
2. How strong are relationships among the ideal L2 self of speaking, listening, reading, pen writing, and digital writing in each group?
3. Is ideal L2 self different in pen writing and digital writing for each group? If so, what are the differences?

The study

Participants

Seventy-four Chinese and 83 French/Spanish (34 and 49, respectively) beginning-level language learners (first and second semester) at a U.S. university participated in the study. The Chinese language learners include 30 males and 44 females with an average age of 20.38; the French/Spanish learners include 27 males and

56 females with an average age of 19.64. All participants were undergraduate students from a variety of majors: government, computer, business, music, education, global studies, history, psychology, nursing, religion, aviation, etc.

Setting

The three languages were taught by one instructor each, all using CLT methods emphasizing speaking and listening skills. The students received more practice in reading and writing in the second semester. Handwriting and typewriting started in the first semester, but the former had more assignments. Each instructor used similar materials, curriculum, and pedagogy of their language to teach beginning-level sessions and made every effort to use the target language in their classrooms.

Instrument

The survey developed by Taguchi et al. (2009) was used to investigate ideal L2 self by asking learners to imagine what they will be able to do in the future by speaking the target language. In this study, the words "speaking/speak" was replaced by the words "listening/listen," "reading/read," or "writing/write" to determine the students' ideal selves relative to each skill.[1] The survey consisted of three parts. The first part collected general information; the second part included 30 items (six items for each skill) that were rated on a Likert-type scale. In the third part of the survey, the participants were asked to compute points for their self-ratings and compare their needs for each of the skills. Participants' comments were used to corroborate the quantitative data. Cronbach's Alpha for this instrument shows a high reliability for each category: speaking ($\alpha = 0.836$), listening ($\alpha = 0.843$), reading ($\alpha = 0.821$), pen writing ($\alpha = 0.846$), and digital writing ($\alpha = 0.915$).

Procedures

The researcher contacted the Chinese, French, and Spanish instructors about the possibility of inviting their students to complete the survey. Upon receiving their agreement, the researcher emailed them a survey link. The survey contained the letter of consent, which informed the students that their participation was voluntary, and the data would be collected anonymously and stored confidentially. The survey was completed online during regular class time in the fall semester of 2019.

Research design and data analysis

The research was nonexperimental since the independent (language groups) and dependent variables (ideal L2 selves) were preexisting facts. To answer the research questions, the study implemented a quantitative method to explore the ideal L2 self of the five skills and conducted the intergroup and intragroup comparisons, as well as correlational analysis. Open-ended questions were used to collect qualitative data for a deeper analysis and interpretation of the findings. Two open-ended questions asked the students to interpret the total points of each skill's ideal L2 self and compare their needs for different skills.

Data were scanned for inconsistencies and outliers before conducting analyses. Additionally, normality of distribution was assessed using a Shapiro-Wilk test ($p < 0.01$). The data distribution in the Chinese classroom was not normal in speaking (0.008), listening (0.003), or digital writing (0.001), but was normal in reading (0.051) and pen writing (0.083). The data distribution in the French/Spanish classes was normal in all skills ($p = 0.04-0.242$). To answer the first research question concerning the ideal L2 self the learners desire to achieve, the researchers first resorted to descriptive data to present the strength level of the ideal L2 self in the five skills and then compared the two groups in speaking, listening, and digital writing by using Mann-Whitney U tests because of the abnormal data distribution of the Chinese group. They also compared the groups in reading and pen writing by running two independent t-tests since the data were all normally distributed. Cohen's d was used to determine the effect size for the two independent t-tests, and Grissom and Kim's probability of superior outcome $\hat{p}_{a>b}$ ($\hat{p}_{a>b} = \frac{U}{n_a n_b}$) (2012) was used to determine the effect size for the Mann-Whitney U test.

For the second research question, the relationships among the ideal L2 selves of the five language skills within each group were examined using either a Pearson Product-Moment correlation (for normal data distribution) or Spearman's ρ (for abnormal data distribution) tests. For the third question addressing the differences between digital and pen writing within each group, related-samples Wilcoxon Signed Rank test (for abnormal distribution) and paired-samples t-test (for normal distribution) were used. The researchers read the qualitative data carefully and coded it individually. Then, they compared their codes and made agreements for improvements, including removing the redundant data, merging the similar, splitting the different, adding the missing, and rephrasing the coding, which allowed a greater depth and breadth of understanding.

Results and discussion

Ideal L2 self and differences between Chinese and French/Spanish learners

The first research question sought to discover what ideal L2 self in speaking, listening, reading, pen writing, and digital writing that Chinese and French/Spanish learners desire to achieve, and if there are significant differences in ideal L2 self between the two groups.

The means (Table 2.1) showed that the Chinese language learners reported the ideal self between 4.27 and 4.71, indicating that, overall, students' answers ranged from *slightly agree* to *agree* regarding the statements about the ideal L2 self. The mean of each skill's ideal L2 self is 4.64 (speaking), 4.71 (listening), 4.24 (pen writing), 4.27 (digital writing), and 4.46 (reading). The French/Spanish participants reported the ideal self between 3.75 and 4.16, indicating that, overall, students' answers ranged from *slightly agree* to *agree* for the statements about the ideal L2 self. The mean of each skill's ideal L2 self is 3.96 (speaking), 4.16 (listening), 3.77 (pen writing), 3.75 (digital writing), and 4.04 (reading). Chinese language learners showed a higher ideal L2 in their oral communication skills (speaking and listening) than in their literacy competence (reading and writing). The result is reasonable since nonalphabetical Chinese characters present difficulty for English L1 speakers. French/Spanish learners displayed a higher ideal L2 self in their receptive ability (listening and reading) than in their productive ability (speaking and writing). The result is also reasonable because the vocabulary of English could help the students in reading French and Spanish given that the three languages have a common etymological origin (i.e., cognate languages).

In the open-ended questions, the participants provided verbal comments about their ideal L2 self to interpret the total scores. They also compared their needs for each of the skills. The participants' answers corroborated the results and provided insight into language learners' ideal self. The L2 Chinese learners' comments explained their higher ideal L2 self in speaking and listening by a perceived greater usefulness and lower difficulty level for these two skills. They claimed that speaking and listening are essential for daily life and workplace communication and commented that learning characters demanded a massive amount of memorization of images and sounds, which made pen writing most difficult with reading a close second. Respondents noted that writing and reading "are less similar

TABLE 2.1 Descriptive data of Chinese and French/Spanish skills

		Speaking of C/FS	Listening of C/FS	Pen Writing of C/FS	Digital Writing of C/FS	Reading of C/FS
Mean		4.64/3.96	4.71/4.16	4.24/3.77	4.27/3.75	4.46/4.04
Mode		6.00/3.83	4.17/4.67	3.17/3.50	6.00/3.50	4.67/5.00
S.D.		.963/1.10	.948/1.05	1.05/1.08	1.31/1.20	.975/1.06
Mean by Percentiles	25	3.8/3.16	4.13/3.33	3.33/3.00	3.17/2.83	3.67/3.17
	50	4.67/3.83	4.83/4.17	4.33/3.67	4.42/3.67	4.58/4.00
	75	5.50/4.83	5.50/5.00	5.17/4.83	5.33/4.67	5.21/5.00

Note: "C" – Chinese; "FS" – French/Spanish. C/FS – Chinese/French/Spanish.
N (Chinese) = 74; N (French/Spanish) = 83.

to" reading in English, and it is easy to "forget what the characters look like." Accurately remembering characters to handwrite from memory is the "biggest struggle." Briefly, L2 Chinese students' ideal L2 self was higher in the skills that were deemed more useful, which were also regarded as less difficult.

Comments of L2 French/Spanish participants revealed that they also believed speaking and listening were more useful. They felt challenged by writing and speaking commenting that the grammar is complex; rather than simply translating the language, they must "independently come up with the right vocabulary and grammar" and deal with conjugation, gender specificity, and tenses, especially imparfait and passé compose. Although speaking was viewed as more useful, the ideal L2 self in speaking did not surpass the one in reading, possibly because of its difficulty. Therefore, L2 French/Spanish learners' ideal L2 self was higher in the less difficult skills, but not necessarily in more useful ones.

Considering the reasons for choosing a particular language to study, the decision to learn Chinese as opposed to other available languages was often influenced by learners' beliefs about China's future as a growing economic world power and increased job opportunities. For example, students commented that they "plan on using Chinese in my future career path," "look forward in the future to doing business in China," "need speaking and listening for future job requirements," and have a need "for listening/speaking, especially if I aspire to live in China in the future." While students learning Chinese said the language would be helpful for their future careers, this particular opinion was valid if they were planning on living in or traveling to China, whereas the French/Spanish participants thought the knowledge of language to be beneficial for their future careers independent of their future living or travel plans: "I want to be a teacher. ... I need to be able to talk to and understand my students somewhat," and "I want to use Spanish but I don't think I will live in a Spanish-speaking country." Deemphasis of traveling abroad is understandable since there is a large Spanish-speaking population in the U.S.

Each language group stated that enjoyment is an important motivator, as seen from the following comments: "I would compare my needs for Spanish with that of flying a plane. I don't need to fly every day, nor do I need it in my job. But it would bring me satisfaction and be very useful"; "I have enjoyed it (the French class)"; "I love learning languages, and I believe that I am effectively learning Chinese."

In comparing the two groups, the Mann-Whitney U test showed that there was a significant difference between the Chinese and Spanish/French groups in the ideal L2 self of speaking ($p = .001$), and the effect size is 67% (1–0.33), indicating that for 67% of the time. A significant difference of ideal L2 self was also found in listening ($p = .001$) by 65% (1–0.35) of the time, and digital writing ($p = .007$) by 62% (1–0.38) of the time. An independent t-test showed that a disparity of ideal L2 self existed in pen writing ($p = .007$) with a medium effect size ($d = 0.44$). Briefly, the results unfolded a significant difference of ideal L2 self for all skills except for reading ($p = .01$) (Table 2.2).

TABLE 2.2 Comparison between Chinese and French/Spanish learners' scores

	Mann-Whitney U Results		
	U	z	$\hat{p}_{a>b}$
Speaking	2019	−3.70	0.33
Listening	2134	−03.30	0.35
Digital Writing	2308	−2.67	0.38
	Independent t-test		
	t		d
Reading	2.59*		0.41
Pen Writing	2.76*		0.44

$N = 157$; *$p < .01$;

The previous findings demonstrated that, although the Chinese and French/Spanish language learners held different motivational strengths regarding achieving an ideal L2 self in different skills, each group hoped to use the language in their future career and/or travel. To achieve their goal, Chinese learners anticipated living abroad, which probably led to their stronger motivational strength in most of the skills (Gonzales, 2010). Each group claimed they enjoyed learning because they perceived that language knowledge could be useful in the future.

In conclusion, the analysis of ideal L2 self showed that the French/Spanish group was more confident in their receptive skills and the Chinese group in productive skills of oral communication, while significant group differences existed, i.e., the Chinese group was stronger in ideal L2 self in all skills except for reading. Both groups planned to use the language in their future career or travel, and they enjoyed learning because of the language's perceived usefulness. China's economic strength and potential job opportunities mediate the vision of learners' ideal self as someone living abroad and using Chinese in the workplace, a vision believed to contribute to their stronger motivational strength (Gonzales, 2010), while French/Spanish learners thought that they would use the language independent of their travel plans. Both Chinese and French/Spanish learners' data displayed that their ideal L2 self was shaped by internal (enjoyment) and external (practicality in the future) factors.

Relationships among the ideal L2 selves of the five skills

The second research question aimed to measure the strength of relationships among the ideal L2 selves of the five skills in each group.

TABLE 2.3 Correlation of language skills

Chinese N = 74 *p < .01		Listening	Digital Writing	Reading		
	Speaking Listening	.950* (Spearman)	.712* (Spearman) .711* (Spearman)			
	Pen writing			.905* (Pearson)		
French/Spanish N = 83 *p < .01		Listening	Reading	Pen writing	Digital writing	
	Speaking Listening Reading Pen writing	.947* (Pearson)	.920* (Pearson) .911* (Pearson)	.906* (Pearson) .868* (Pearson) .931* (Pearson)	.669* (Pearson) .637* (Pearson) .708* (Pearson) .704* (Pearson)	

Note: Pearson correlation was run for normally distributed data while Spearman correlation was run for abnormally distributed data.

In the L2 Chinese group, the relationship between the ideal L2 self of speaking and listening was the strongest ($r = .950$) followed by another strong relationship between the ideal L2 self of reading and pen writing ($r = .905$), digital writing and speaking ($r = .712$), and digital writing and listening ($r = .711$) (Table 2.3). In the L2 French/Spanish group, the strongest relationship existed between the ideal L2 self of speaking and listening ($r = .947$). The ideal L2 self of reading correlated with that of speaking ($r = .920$) and listening ($r = .911$); the ideal L2 self of pen writing correlated with that of speaking ($r = .906$), listening ($r = .868$), and reading ($r = .931$); the ideal L2 self of digital writing correlated with that of speaking ($r = .669$), listening ($r = .637$), reading ($r = .708$) and pen writing ($r = .704$). The strongest relationship between the ideal L2 self of speaking and listening in each group is plausible since speaking and listening are often simultaneously engaged in oral communication. The results of multiple correlations showed that developing the ideal L2 self of one skill will increase the ideal L2 self of other skills. This result aligns with the perception that different language skills are interdependent, that is, each skill can impact the others (Dash & Dash, 2007; Nan, 2018). Therefore, an increase in overall motivation depends on the increase of the ideal L2 self in each skill.

Differences between pen and digital writing

The third research question focused on differences in ideal L2 self in pen and digital writing skills. The related-samples Wilcoxon Signed Rank test and paired-samples *t*-tests showed no difference for Chinese ($p = 0.870$) or for French/Spanish ($p = .905$). This result, while being consistent with the subtle mean difference between the two skills (Table 2.1) was not anticipated given the onerousness of pen writing as compared to digital writing. However, students' comments provided explanations for this result. Chinese students noted that although typing is less laborious, they lacked confidence in their knowledge of pinyin (a romanization system to transcribe the sound of Chinese characters), saying that "typing can be hard for me if I don't fully understand the pinyin of what I'm trying to say." The Chinese learners' comments also demonstrated their insufficient knowledge of cultural slang used in social media. "I feel weak in typewriting skills because informal language and slang are often used. I don't quite have a knowledge of this." The comments of the French/Spanish group suggested their lack of interest in the target language use on social media: "[T]ypewriting or using social media would be less common"; "I do not need to write Spanish fluently on social media," and "I probably won't use Spanish in social media." These comments revealed that the learners have limited use of L2 digital literacy in social media despite its important role in locating, interpreting, and applying information, as well as creating and sharing content (Loewus, 2016) in the target language.

To summarize, while a higher ideal self in digital writing was expected for the French/Spanish group whose use of a Latin keyboard required less effort than handwriting, the similar strength of ideal self in pen and digital writing for both groups was not anticipated. However, student comments explained their discomfort with digital writing based on their unfamiliarity with L2 social media, lack of knowledge of L2 social media vocabulary, lack of experience in L2 digital writing, and insufficient pinyin knowledge (Chinese learners).

Limitations of the study and suggestions for future research

Several limitations of the study warrant a cautious generalization of results to other contexts. One shortcoming stems from the use of the Mann-Whitney U test (nonparametric) and t-test (parametric) to analyze the group differences. MANOVA or ANOVA with Bonferroni corrections may perform a more optimal analysis since ANOVA is robust to normality distribution. Also, while the study ran Spearman correlation for the data of non-normal distribution, using Pearson is possible unless the level of non-normality is massive.

Additionally, the study participants were drawn from the same university. Surveying students of other languages in diverse educational contexts will provide a better understanding of the ideal L2 self. Future research should also investigate intermediate- and advanced-level learners since their longer L2 experience may lead to different perceptions about their future goals. Depending on the language, context, and level of proficiency, future career goals may or may not play a unique role in ideal L2 self, other aspects of ideal L2 self may become prominent, and the ideal L2 self may vary in speaking, listening, reading, and writing (pen and digital). Expanding the scope of ideal L2 self-research will improve our understanding of the motivation of foreign and second language learners.

Classroom implications

Ideal L2 self and learning experiences

Since the French/Spanish group was more confident in their receptive skills and the Chinese group in oral communication, exposing Chinese and French/Spanish learners to activities that stress the value of their less developed skills (reading/writing and speaking/writing, respectively) can add enjoyment to learning. Also, given the correlation among the ideal L2 selves of different skills, increasing the ideal L2 selves of the challenging skills will augment motivation in general. Additionally, constantly informing French/Spanish learners of the study or work abroad opportunities will enhance their desire for a stronger ideal L2 self.

In the L2 motivational self-system, learner experience is a motivational component referring to the motives "related to immediate learning environment and experience" (Dörnyei and Ushioda, 2009, p. 29). However, the study results showed that students projected their ideal L2 self into future application, so instructors should create an immediate learning environment that serves learners' plans. Since L2 French/Spanish learners are less confident in speaking and writing, these skills can be improved by cultural activities relevant to students' plans and interests. For example, reading a French/Spanish story of an appropriate difficulty level can be followed by speaking and writing activities, e.g., narrating, comparing (with another story), or connecting people, events, or perspective of the story with similar aspects of a French/Spanish community they are familiar with. Also, learners can celebrate French/Spanish festivals, play target language games, watch movies, and complete speaking/writing activities to demonstrate their understanding and reflect on cultural issues. These skills will contribute to language and cultural competence and promote future communication. Since L2 Chinese learners feel less confident in reading and writing but motivated to use the language for travel and visits, working with authentic materials about places, events, and people of China can advance their understanding of the country and people, and provide meaningful contexts for reading and writing activities. Thus, students can write a recommendation of a place, an introduction of a person, or a travel itinerary. Similarly, they can read about and compare places, people, or events, or express their opinions in writing. These activities can improve the ideal L2 of the skills in which learners feel less confident. Second, as both groups of students in the present study intend to use language in their careers, learners need to be informed about current career opportunities requiring L2 skills, such as business and management, government, diplomacy or national security, teaching, or translating, to name just a few. Awareness of how L2 skills can lead to a rewarding career can encourage students to develop a comprehensive ideal L2 self. Instructors should be familiar with the sources offering internship, study, or job opportunities at home and abroad and remember to inform their students in an effort to increase their ideal L2 self. While all the aforementioned activities are applicable to other languages, the choice of a specific one depends on the skills the students need to foster.

Pen and digital writing

Digital and pen writing can be combined in one course so that both modes match learners' needs and lesson objectives. For example, pen writing assignments are suitable for spelling exercises in an alphabetical language and can help memorize Chinese characters. Given the result of lower ideal L2 self in Chinese pen writing, instructors should teach character structure to help learners formulate orthographic knowledge-based learning strategies, making memorization more effective (Xie, 2019). Also, pinyin instructions should highlight the accuracy of pronunciation and spelling, particularly for easy-to-confuse syllables. Meanwhile, the omnipresence of digital writing necessitates mastery of digital modes. Engaging students in authentic social media writing experiences will engender the "wow" moments and increase their confidence. Instructors can familiarize learners with the appropriate platforms, explain the expected L2 cultural norms, teach commonly used slang and vocabulary, and encourage students to learn independently and share with their peers. Finally, the ubiquitous use of digital writing in the job market necessitates formal digital writing assignments. Composing a job application letter, writing an email to a boss, or creating a resume in the target language can prepare students for future formal writing situations.

Conclusion

This study investigated the ideal L2 self of postsecondary Chinese, French, and Spanish beginning learners in speaking, listening, reading, pen and digital writing skills. The results showed that the ideal L2 selves of the five skills are interdependent. In other words, improving the ideal L2 self in one skill will advance those in other skills. In this study, Chinese language learners felt more confident in oral communication than in literacy, while French/Spanish learners expressed more confidence in receptive than in productive skills. Thus, the study stressed the importance of developing the ideal self of the skills in which student confidence is low, i.e., reading and writing for Chinese learners and speaking and writing for French/Spanish learners. Also, a significant group difference in the strength of ideal L2 self existed in all skills except for reading. The students in each group projected their ideal L2 self into a future use of the language in the real world, such as in their career or travels, while Chinese learners specifically indicated the possibility of living abroad, which probably led to their stronger motivational strength in most skills. Both groups indicated that the practicality of the language made learning enjoyable. The results underscore the importance of improving learners' ideal L2 self by connecting immediate learning experiences to future situations of language use. It was also found that students' ideal L2 self of digital writing did not exceed that of handwriting because they lacked familiarity with the vocabulary, social media platforms, or skills in pinyin input (Chinese), which necessitates promoting these competencies in low-level courses. It is hoped that the study findings develop our understanding of beginner learners' motivation in terms of ideal L2 self and encourage the integration of the four language skills to prepare learners for higher-level courses and for future engagement in real-world communication.

Note

1 The survey instrument can be viewed at https://tinyurl.com/22n582v4.

References

Campbell, N., & Storch, E. (2011). The changing face of motivation: A study of second language learners' motivation over time. *Australian Review of Applied Linguistics, 34*, 166–192. https://doi.org/10.1075/aral.34.2.03cam

Cohen, V., & Cowen, J. (2007). *Literacy for children in an information age: Teaching reading, writing, and thinking.* Thompson Wadsworth.

Dahlström, H., & Boström, L. (2017). Pros and cons: Handwriting versus digital writing. *Nordic Journal of Digital Literacy, 12*(4), 143–161.

Dash, N., & Dash, M. (2007). *Teaching English as an additional language.* Atlantic Publishers & Distributors.

Dörnyei, Z. (2005). *The psychology of the language learner.* Lawrence Erlbaum.

Dörnyei, Z. (2014). Motivation in second language learning. In M. Celce-Murcia, D. M. Brinton, & M. A. Snow (Eds.), *Teaching English as a second or foreign language* (pp. 518–531). Cengage Learning.

Dörnyei, Z., & Ushioda, E. (Eds.) (2009). *Motivation, language identity and the L2 self.* Multilingual Matters.

Gardner, R. C. (1985). *Social psychology and second language learning: The role of attitudes and motivation.* Arnold.

Gonzales, R.. DLC (2010). Motivational orientation in foreign language learning: The case of Filipino foreign language learners. *TESOL, 3*, 3–28.

Grissom, R. J., & Kim, J. J. (2012). *Effect sizes for research: Univariate and multivariate applications* (2nd ed.). Taylor & Francis.

Hsu, L. (2013). English as a foreign language learners' perception of mobile assisted language learning: A cross-national study. *Computer Assisted Language Learning, 26*(3), 197–213.

Kong, J. H., Han, J. E., Kim, S., Park, H., Kim, Y. S., & Park, H. (2018). L2 motivational self system, international posture and competitiveness of Korean CTL and LCTL college learners: A structural equation modeling approach. *System*, *72*, 178–189. https://doi.org/10.1016/j.system.2017.11.005

Littlewood, W., & William, L. (1981). *Communicative language teaching: An introduction*. Cambridge University Press.

Loewus, L. (2016, November 8). What is digital literacy? *Education Week*. https://www.edweek.org/teaching-learning/what-is-digital-literacy/2016/11

Mendoza, A., & Phung, H. (2019). Motivation to learn languages other than English: A critical research synthesis. *Foreign Language Annals*, *52*, 121–140. https://doi.org/10.1111/flan.12380

Nan, C. (2018). Implications of interrelationship among four language skills for high school English teaching. *Journal of Language Teaching and Research*, *9*(2), 418–423. http://dx.doi.org/10.17507/jltr.0902.26

Noels, K. (2009). The internalization of language learning into the self and social identity. In Z. Dörnyei, & E. Ushioda (Eds.), *Motivation, language identity and the L2 self* (pp. 295–313). Multilingual Matters.

Oakes, L. (2013). Foreign language learning in a "monoglot culture": Motivational variables amongst students of French and Spanish at an English university. *System*, *41*, 178–191. https://doi.org/10.1016/j.system.2013.01.019

Rao, Parupalli. (2018). Developing speaking skills in ESL or EFL settings. *International Journal of English Language, Literature, and Translation Studies*, *52*(2), 286–293. https://doi.org/10.33329/ijelr.52.286

Richards, J. C. (2005). *Communicative language teaching today*. Cambridge University Press.

Taguchi, T., Magid, M., & Papi, M. (2009). The L2 motivational self-system among Japanese, Chinese, and Iranian learners of English: A comparative study. In Z. Dörnyei, & E. Ushioda (Eds.), *Motivation, language identity and the L2 self* (pp. 66–97). Multilingual Matters.

Xie, Y. (2014). L2 self of beginning-level heritage and non-heritage post-secondary learners of Chinese. *Foreign Language Annals*, *47*(1), 189–203.

Xie, Y. (2018). Motivation of ideal Chinese L2 self and global competence: A case study on postsecondary Chinese language learners. *Chinese as a Second Language | 漢語教學研究—美國中文教師學會學報*, *53*(2),163–186.

Xie, Y. (2019). Instructional interventions and character learning strategies: A study on orthographic study assignments In K. Sung (Ed.), *Teaching and learning Chinese as a second or foreign language: Emerging trends* (pp. 127–141). Rowman & Littlefield.

3
EXPERIENCE WITH APPLICATION OF USAGE-BASED MODEL OF LANGUAGE TO BEGINNING L2 INSTRUCTION

Serafima Gettys

Most foreign language (FL) instructors in higher education are keenly aware of students' high attrition rates from FL courses beyond novice levels of instruction. While millions of college and university students show up in beginning language courses, only a small fraction chooses to continue language study beyond the first semester or year.

One of the many reasons for students' giving up on language study might be a lack of resultative motivation described by Skehan (1989), as a consequence rather than a cause of prior learning experience. Past failures are particularly detrimental in FL learning contexts where second language (L2) learning failure is a frequent occurrence (Dörnyei, 1994) and leaves students with disbelief in their ability to master the language. As aptly noted by Richard Brecht and cited by Friedman (2015), "It isn't that people don't think language education is important. It's that they don't think it's possible." What is it in beginning FL courses that disenchants students and undermines their belief in themselves?

In his 2014 focus article in *Language Educator*, VanPatten lamented the fact that too frequently teachers' views on language are not psychologically real seeing it as "rules or paradigms traditionally found in textbooks" (p. 24). Underlying traditional treatment of language as it is reflected in most textbooks is a distorted vision of language teachers still uphold. This chapter holds the assumption that to be effective and emotionally rewarding, any pedagogy must be based on (a) what we know about how the mind learns languages and (b) how language is represented in the mind. The more psychologically real the instructors' view of language is, the more organic students' experience of learning the language is.

Psycholinguistic theories offer various, and often competing, perspectives on language. One of the most recent experimentally tested conceptions, largely unknown to language educators, is the usage-based model of language and

DOI: 10.4324/9781003058441-4

language learning (Barlow & Kemmer, 2000; Bybee, 2008, 2009, 2013; Ellis, 2006; Langacker, 2005, 2010; Tomasello, 2008, 2009). It has powerful pedagogical implications, some of which, while generally congruent with communicative methodology, challenge some mainstream teaching practices.

This chapter has two goals. Its first goal is to introduce several pedagogically relevant aspects of usage-based theory underlying the approach tentatively called usage-based instruction (UBI). The UBI was experimentally tested in our 2018 quantitative study (Gettys et al., 2018) which investigated its impact on the development of oral skills in learners of Spanish as an FL. The study showed that students exposed to UBI demonstrated faster response times, longer utterances, and were perceived as closer to native speakers when compared to the control group taught in a textbook-based course. One of the issues arising from the 2018 study was the psychological impact of UBI; specifically, it enhanced students' engagement, which was observed throughout the instructional process and reflected in positive course evaluations. This prompted a qualitative study to analyze how students exposed to UBI methodology interpreted their learning experiences in beginning courses. Therefore, the second goal of the chapter is to investigate the psychological impact of UBI on first-semester students of Russian in a small private Midwestern university.

The two goals dictated the structure of the chapter. After presenting the main tenets of usage-based theory that underlie UBI, it analyzes the results of a small-scale action research study that used qualitative measures to record students' personal judgments regarding their first-semester experience of Russian language study and discusses its pedagogical implications.

The nature of language learning in usage-based perspective

The term "usage-based" (Langacker, 1987) introduces an innovative approach to language and language acquisition shared by scholars of cognitive linguistics and cognitive grammar (Barlow & Kemmer, 2000; Langacker, 2005, 2008), construction grammar (Goldberg, 1995, 2003, 2006), corpus linguistics (Römer, 2009; Sinclair, 1991; Wray, 2005), usage-based linguistics (Bybee, 2008, 2009, 2013; Bybee & Hopper, 2001), and cognitive perspective in Second Language Acquisition (Ellis, 2006). The central premise of the usage-based approach is that language system in the mind of the speaker is shaped by specific instances of both understanding and producing the language and is emergent, i.e., arises gradually in the mind as a result rather than condition of language use (Gettys et al., 2018).

Integral to the usage-based theory is the idea that language is learned from lexically specific exemplars, i.e., words, phrases, and sentences acquired through the input from the environment. The exemplars are first imitated and memorized, and then retrieved from memory in communicative situations similar to the context of initial encounter of the exemplar. Gradually, as learners acquire a large number of exemplars through repeated use and analogical generalizations, abstract linguistic schemas develop. These are semantic, phonological, or symbolic structures that lack the specificity of concrete utterances (Langacker, 1987). Schematization underlies linguistic creativity- a human ability to express meaning by producing sentences one has never experienced before. Language grammar, therefore, is seen as "nothing more than schemas" (Tyler, 2012, p. 52) formed from concrete exemplars rather than a collection of rules (in usage-based perspective, rules are regarded as mere tools for describing language).

Usage-based theory underscores the sequential nature of language learning as strings of sounds in words and sequences of lexical units in phrases (Ellis, 1996). Underlying sequential learning is a psychological mechanism of chunking or grouping individual units of information (chunks). The mind processes chunks as individual wholes that are retrieved from memory as prefabricated pieces.

Psycholinguistic correlates of chunks are constructions, i.e., conventionalized form-meaning correspondences learned by means of associative learning and by mapping linguistic form into meaning, at the same time strengthening the associations between co-occurring elements of the language (Ellis, 2002). In usage-based perspective, language is an inventory of constructions present at morpheme, word, phrase, chunk, and sentence levels of linguistic structure. Learning a language, therefore, is essentially the learning of constructions. For L2 learners, it is also a process of reconstruction of already existing first language (L1) constructions in L2.

Construction learning is accomplished by general mechanisms of imitation, concept learning and categorization, analogy, chunking, associative learning, generalizations, recognition, recall and reliance on prior knowledge. Constructions are entrenched as patterns of neurological activity forming the linguistic knowledge in the speakers' mind (Ellis, 2006). Entrenchment, according to Langacker (2010), is a gradual process of cognitive routinization and development of cognitive routines or habits. Each occurrence causes the units' further entrenchment and increases ease of activation. The degree of entrenchment crucially depends on frequency of occurrence of a particular construction (Ellis, 2002; Goldberg, 2003, 2006; Larsen-Freeman, 2012). The more frequent the use of a particular unit, the deeper its entrenchment, the less effort is required to access and retrieve it from memory, and the faster and less error-prone the process becomes. With sufficient rehearsal, access, activation, and retrieval, processes become automatic and no longer require attention.

Related research

The applications of usage-based theory to L2 teaching are nascent and scarce. Prior attempts to do so focused almost exclusively on providing students with in-depth understanding of the constructions' meaning to raise students' linguistic awareness as part of explicit focus-on-form instruction *about* the language in the light of cognitive grammar (Cadierno, 2008; Maldonado, 2008; Manzanares &

López, 2008; Niemeier & Reif, 2008; Turewicz, 2000; Tyler, 2008; Tyler et al., 2010). For example, Cadierno (2008) views the teaching of motion constructions through the prism of cognitive linguistics and the focus-on-form approach. Her pedagogical proposal integrates grammar and communication while emphasizing the conventionalized form-meaning relations in the expressions of motion. However, as Langacker (2008) notes, form-focused approaches are better applicable to L1 or advanced L2 learners. Although the view of language as an array of constructions is fundamental, it constitutes only one aspect of usage-based theory of language learning that can be incorporated into L2 instruction. One reported attempt (Verspoor & Nguyen, 2015) to apply usage-based theory to teaching L2 communication was characterized by almost exclusive pedagogical focus on comprehensible input while ignoring other significant pedagogical dimensions of the usage-based model. Thus, such concepts as language as an array of constructions, psychological mechanism of chunking underlying their acquisition, entrenchment, the fact that language system in the speaker's mind is shaped not only by understanding but also by producing the language, and the pedagogical implications related to these concepts seem to be largely disregarded in the instructional sequence offered by Verspoor and Nguyen's (2015) study.

This chapter describes a usage-based approach to classroom instruction (UBI) that employs several implications of the usage-based theory, namely, (a) a departure from conventional componential treatment of language as a set of grammar rules and taxonomies and vocabulary lists, timing, and the role of explicit instruction; (b) a curriculum based on thematically organized specific exemplars of constructions; (c) constructions learned in chunks; (d) learning outcomes expressed by a set of specific constructions, and (e) instructional sequence that leads students from plentiful focused input, through multiple iterations in both input and output activities to their automatic use.

The study

The aim of this study was to discover students' psychological perspectives on UBI. A small-scale investigation of a qualitative nature was undertaken to gain an in-depth understanding of student experiences of UBI, as L2 learners' perceptions and perspectives of their own language learning, or learners' voice, are a crucial research need (Barkhuizen, 1998; Leki, 2001).

The study was conducted within action research framework, a type of inquiry led by practitioners in their own educational settings to improve instructional practice and use their findings to directly and immediately advance classroom practices in the hope to contribute to the improvement of education in their modest way. Research questions in action research arise from local events, problems, and needs, and are based on the researcher's own concerns and professional areas of interest. With over more than 40 years teaching experience in higher education in Russia and the USA, I observed how textbook explanations challenge and intimidate learners, often leading to frustration, thus discouraging students from further learning. The following research question guided the study:

> How do students experience UBI? What specific aspects of learning do students discern in the approach?

Setting

The study took place at a small Midwestern university FL program. Established in 2004, it has been offering students three-credit elective courses in Spanish, French, German, Italian, Arabic, Chinese, Japanese, Polish, and Russian. As stated in its mission statement, the program seeks to make FL study accessible to all students, providing them with quality instruction and leading to immediate practical learning outcomes with an emphasis on oral communication. Most of the undergraduates are the first generation of college students from local small-town high schools; virtually all of them work. These students enter the university with specific career goals and often feel that they cannot distract themselves from their major requirements by learning an FL, which is often perceived as a luxury few can afford. Therefore, to fulfill the program mandate, we focused on developing a user-friendly teaching approach tailored to our students' unique needs, which led to the development of UBI for beginning language courses.

The course

The course's main goal is developing oral communication skills and reaching Novice-Mid or Novice High proficiency levels within the context described by the American Council on the Teaching of Foreign Languages (ACTFL) guidelines (ACTFL, 2012).

The usage-based concept of language as an array of constructions suggested the possibility of circumventing the traditional way of presenting grammar as a set of rules, paradigms, and declension and conjugation taxonomies. Instead, we designed the course around specific thematically organized exemplars of L2 constructions; the course and individual units' objectives we also stated in terms of exemplars. Thus, the topic "Personal Information: Family" translates into a set of lexically concrete constructions (e.g., "I have a big/small family," "My family is small/big," "My mom's/her name is …," "My mom/she is … years old …") that serve as highly specified lesson objectives, with each lesson having a new objective reached at the end of the class. In developing such goals, grammar is not used as an organizing principle or a free-standing all-inclusive element such as, for example, "formation/declension of Genitive case of nouns and its use after numerals" or "formation/declension of nouns/pronouns in Dative case." Instead, grammar is incorporated into and limited to the acquisition of the aforementioned lexically specific constructions. It is expected that as the learners gain more experience in the target language, pattern generalization and development of abstract schemas will eventually happen through analogy, at which point students can take a broader view of the given grammatical phenomena. In sync with the usage-based postulate about the psychological mechanism of chunking and to ease students' short memory load, longer constructions are first chunked into smaller phrases. Chunks are automatized before they are integrated into and practiced in a longer construction. Thus, in preparing students to say, "There are two, three, four people in my family," the instructor begins with a chunk "two, three, four, … people" introduced through input activities. To do this, she may display images of two, three, four people on the board while saying the words out loud (one person, two people, three people, etc.), thus modeling the next input activity. To strengthen the initial form-meaning association, the instructor asks a student to point to the image matching the phrase they hear in Russian while others are watching. To ensure the fluent use of constructions, each chunk undergoes a complete cycle of highly structured activities progressing from modeling, input, and scaffolded production to communicative activities.

Method

The study relied on interpretive research paradigm (Denzin & Lincoln, 2005) for analysis of factors contributing to enhanced student engagement. Since success, sense of progress and efficiency, etc., are not tangible experiences but psychological conditions that result from subjective perception, the study adopted the interpretive phenomenological analysis (IPA) – a qualitative research method that examines how people perceive their life experiences and is particularly suitable for the analysis of complex unquantifiable topics. The IPA usually employs individual interviews, journals or diaries, and focus groups. These are transcribed verbatim, and the researcher generates codes from the data and looks for "themes" in the codes. Themes are recurring patterns of meaning throughout the data (e.g., ideas, thoughts, feelings) that allow the researcher to study the respondent's psychological world.

Data source

We chose a semi-structured learning journal as a data source for this study. The analysis of L2 written journal reflections provided a valuable insight into students' views of their own experiences as language learners (Allison, 1998; Tse, 2000). Students described their learning experience in online journals assigned for homework during the 5th, 10th, and 15th week of the course; each entry was required to be at least 350 words long. To offer some explicit writing suggestions, we encouraged students to write about the course pace, learning load, the extent to which the objectives of each class were achieved, course and language difficulty, the amount of mental effort required, their perceptions of learning and of themselves as language learners, changes in motivation, comparison with prior language learning experience, etc. Those, however, were only suggestions rather than specific questions participants had to respond to. Although journals were not graded, students could earn additional course credits for them.

Participants

A small sample of undergraduates (four female and six male) participated in the study. All were enrolled in Beginning Russian in spring 2021 while pursuing a variety of academic majors. The group comprised four sophomores, five juniors, and one senior. All students, except one, took FL courses in high school (French and Spanish). Only one student had a prior two-year experience of studying Russian at a charter school. Given the results of her placement exam, however, both she and the tester agreed that she should take Beginning Russian. Six students were taking the course as an elective, while four students intended to use the credits to fulfill the optional General Education Globalization requirement.

Findings

The analysis of students' journals revealed several major themes.

Students' perception of the course effectiveness: How successful the course was in producing a desired result

Comments about the course goals and objectives were found in almost all students' entries. Recall that each lesson objective was expressed in terms of highly specified construction, such as, "Saying if you have siblings and how many siblings you have" or "Saying what year student you are." In describing class objectives, students characterized them as "clear" and "concise." One student noticed that goals were achieved in every class. This student wrote, "I feel for every class we achieve the goal for that class. For example, we were able to say our full name and nationality at the end of our last class, which was the end goal." Another noted, "We learn something new every day." Still another felt the sense of accomplishment: "By the end of class, I can accomplish the goal."

Some students noted that the course exceeded their expectations: "When I registered for the course, I thought it would be kind of a 50/50. Meaning a 50% chance I would do well or a 50% chance that I would do poorly but so far that has not been the case." Several clearly indicated that they feel they are doing "way better" and that the course turned out to be easier than they expected:

"I thought I wasn't going to be any good at it," and "it was much easier to pick up than I thought I did better than what I thought I was going to do." These statements support an earlier claim that students expect language courses to be difficult and even overwhelming. Perhaps their earlier high school experience contributed to these expectations.

Students' perception of the course efficiency: The ratio of time and mental effort and the results achieved or ability to produce language with a minimum amount of effort

As the course progressed, some students felt that it became "a little more difficult" but described the extent of difficulty as "easy to keep up with" or "moderately difficult." Some students noted that although the course became more complex, this complexity was still manageable. Others commented that it was quite easy.

One student described the course difficulty with an upside-down bell curve, i.e., with symmetrical or "normal" distribution:

> If I were to graph the difficulty of the course, I would use an upside-down bell curve ... since at the beginning we were going over content that is completely new to somebody who has never attempted to learn Russian before, in the middle we were applying what we learned to talk about things like ourselves and the weather, and as we reached the end of the course more and more kept being added to remember.

Another student came up with a somewhat contradictory statement saying that the course was challenging because "it requires you to be actively engaged and practice the language."

At the same time, several students found that they "have learned a lot" or were "covering a lot." These statements point to a strong sense of progress, which more traditional courses often do not provide; despite their time and effort investment, students often do not experience growth in their proficiency. A couple of students, however, doubted their ability to retain the material. In their opinion, regular reviews were necessary: "We covered a lot, but will I remember?" These quotes indicate that students realize the importance of memorization but at times do not trust their memory.

The sense of course efficiency was best described by an older (26 years old) student: "I feel the course has a healthy balance of new content to be learned and time in which to learn and practice said content."

In describing the course, several students compared it with their previous language learning experience in favor of the university course. For example, a student noted, "I made a lot of mistakes in Spanish but in Russian I am doing just fine." Some attributed the relative ease and pace of the course to the university class size as compared to big Spanish classes in high school: "[B]ecause we're such a small class and we all must participate I feel like I am learning it faster." Others credited the change in educational settings: "Learning a language in college is much different, and a lot better, than learning one in high school." Also, students felt that they are "learning a lot faster with this class than any of my Spanish classes in the past," or "it is a lot less stressful. My high school's Spanish class was very fast-paced, and I found it hard to keep up with the class."

The dynamics of motivation

Some students made explicit statements about the increased motivation to study Russian, e.g.,

> My motivation to study Russian has increased since the beginning of the semester. As the course has progressed, I've discovered that I find Russian to be very enjoyable to learn. At times it can be frustrating to get it right but once you do it is very rewarding.

A student who eventually chose to minor in Russian wrote,

> I would say that I'm more motivated to learn Russian since it is now my minor, I thought the class was fun and it was much better than just taking another history class as an elective. It has increased since the beginning of the semester.

Another student noted, "I did not ever have the urge to stop."

The pace of the course and the sense of progress in language learning

Overall, students seemed to feel comfortable in the course. It was seen as "steady," i.e., "neither fast, nor slow." Students felt "a steady progress throughout" or even "like I just learned it so much faster that way." However, for several students, the course felt overwhelming and too fast: "There are times when it feels a little overwhelmed." It is important to note that students attribute the sense of progress to the amount of effort they invested. Thus, one student wrote, "I feel like I progressed throughout the duration of our course because I practiced in my free time." Some students, however, felt that they were reaching a plateau. The feeling of slower learning commonly occurs at the threshold between beginning and intermediate stages, and when the initial excitement of learning something new is gone: "During the first few weeks I felt that I was learning a lot but when I got to the end, I began to hit a plateau." Another student thought that "there wasn't a plateau but more so at the end there were more complex things that made the information that we were learning more complex."

Students' view of themselves as language learners

Much of students' journal writing reflected their perceptions of themselves as language learners: "I originally saw myself as someone who could learn another language but that it would be much harder than it actually was." Others noted that their confidence in speaking Russian "has gone up a bit." Some revealed that they share their success with family members, another indication of students' self-efficacy: "I have had some learning successes because after class or the next day I explain to my parents about what I have learned." Several statements directly indicated that students feel good about their success: "I'm very happy with myself and the skills I picked."

Many students reported growth in confidence in their language-learning ability, which is a crucial factor in the development of a "can do" attitude, and expressed hope to become fluent in the language at some point:

> I think my level of confidence in eventually becoming proficient grew by the end of the semester. I never really had low confidence but now ... I'm more capable of learning the language since I know the basics and can pronounce words somewhat correctly.

Two students' entries showed that language anxiety is still a problem for some learners and may be inherited from their prior learning experiences: "I get embarrassed easily and tend to forget everything I know. I think I just need to work on putting things into question form because I definitely knew how to answer the questions in Russian." "I am happy that I survived the presentations. I struggled hard with presentations when I was taking Spanish in high school."

Nonetheless, most students indicated how pleasantly surprised they were by their achievement: "Before I took the class, I thought that I might struggle but that was not the case most of the time." Here are other similar statements: "Before the class, I was under the impression that I was going to struggle a lot but I don't think I struggled too much." "I thought this was going to be a repeat of my bad experience of learning Spanish in high school. My experience was far from that." However, one student admitted: "I think I did worse than anticipated when I signed up for the course. At the time I expected it to be an easy A since I was interested and did well in other language classes."

Because of the COVID-19 pandemic, the course was conducted in a hybrid format: Each week the class had two synchronous meetings online and one face-to-face meeting on campus. Therefore, one of the minor journal themes concerned the course online format. Those who mentioned it were unanimous in their preference for face-to-face instruction because they feel more anxious in the online class. Some students commented on insufficient writing, reading, and cultural activities in an online class.

Results and discussion

We feel that the study confirmed the positive impact of the UBI in the beginning language class. Suffice it to say that by the end of the first semester, three students chose to minor in Russian although they had no intention to do it at the time when they enrolled in Beginning Russian course.

The findings highlight the features of the UBI that students found appealing. They include students' perception of the course's effectiveness and efficiency, its accessibility and ease, comparisons with prior language experience in favor of the UBI and exceeded expectations, reported increased motivation to continue language study, and an improved view of self as a language learner. Because of the qualitative nature of the study, we can only make inferences about the cause-effect relationship between students' judgments and some features of the UBI that set it apart from more conventional teaching approaches.

Thus, for example, one might attribute students' perception of the course effectiveness (the measure of success in achieving the desired results) to the way course, unit, and individual lessons goals were developed around lexically specific constructions. In describing course goals and the extent to which they were reached, students characterized them as "clear," noting that each class had a very specific objective that was successfully reached by its end thus providing a sense of accomplishment that drives learning. Highly specific goals with clear endpoints that are realistically achievable within a certain time frame are known to increase learning motivation (Conzemius & O'Neill, 2009).

The fact that students found the course more user-friendly, i.e., accessible and relatively easy, and the resulting sense of self-efficacy that even led some students to change their beliefs about language learning outcomes may be attributed to partial abandonment of traditional componential "grammar + vocabulary" treatment of language associated with UBI. From the perspective of usage-based and cognitive load theory (Sweller, 1988), wordy and abstract textbook explanations, rules and complex conjugation, and declension taxonomies may feel superfluous and overburden learners' fragile working memory. Simply put, one cannot think about what one wants to say and how to say it in the target language while simultaneously retrieving complex grammatical rules from memory; the mere scope of the information prevents language material from entering the long-term memory and often overwhelms learners, annihilating their initial excitement about learning a new language.

Students' comments confirm the accessibility of the UBI-based course. Their descriptions of the amount of mental effort required for the course as "manageable," "easy to keep up with," and "moderately difficult" indicate the user-friendliness of the course. At the same time, students deemed the course rigorous and effective; some respondents were reasonably surprised by the amount of learning and a palpable sense of progress they experienced during the one-semester course. Arguably, the course ease and accessibility had a positive impact on students' sense of self-efficacy and their self-view as language learners. Interestingly, this realization came to students through comparison with their previous, mostly high school, language learning experience. Thus, in describing the course, students used such phrases as "a lot faster, "better," and "less stressful," which, in turn, could not but positively affect their motivation and confidence in their ability to succeed in learning the language.

Another prominent feature of the UBI course that sets it apart from today's dominant teaching paradigm is the emphasis on frequency, i.e., repeated use of language constructions leading to their entrenchment, or automatization. Although "common sense tells us that for second language learners repeated exposure and practice are essential to the development of the cognitive structures that lead to fluent and grammatical speech" (Bybee, 2008, p. 216), frequency and persistent development of automaticity are usually associated with drills and rote memorization and receive low priority in current mainstream methodology. The restricted amount of classroom input and output and the predominance of real-world communicative activities with little attention to target language forms prevent purposeful development of automaticity sufficient for communication. The UBI's focus on multiple exposures, iterative practice, and continuous review of grammar and vocabulary enforces the form-meaning associations in the new language, which ensures their transfer into and easy retrieval from long-term memory and ultimately contributes to oral fluency.

Limitations and future research

The present study has several limitations. Some of them are inherent to the nature of qualitative research methods. The study of attitudes, values, and relationships, while producing detailed and descriptive information, is difficult to quantify making the data interpretation and analysis subjective, fluid, and uncertain. Future research using diverse qualitative techniques, such as focus groups and interviews, triangulation, or a more robust quantitative methodology could further investigate the model's advantages as compared to more traditional views of the language as well as yield more objective results.

Perhaps the most obvious limitation of the presented study is transferability. The small sample size makes the results ungeneralizable beyond this group. Also, because of the hybrid format of the course conducted during the COVID-19 pandemic, the data were not triangulated. An analysis of a large group of students in diverse settings could clarify the benefits of UBI and confirm the study's validity.

A number of ethical issues is embedded in the study. First, confidentiality was affected as journals were submitted online, and the researcher knew the comments' authors. Second, the dual role of the instructor-researcher and the power imbalance between the participants and the researcher could have generated certain pressures and affected the participants' responses to questions. The fact that the researcher herself provided instruction makes it easy to detect bias.

Finally, the semi-structured format of the journals, which prompted, and, therefore, urged students to comment on several specific aspects of the course, presents another serious limitation since other important facets of the course remain unknown.

Classroom implications

The study of student perceptions of the effectiveness of a UBI-based course offers a number of important implications for the language teaching practice.

First, the lexically filled constructions make course goals and lesson objectives "SMARTer," i.e. more specific, measurable, attainable, relevant, aligned with the ultimate communicative goals, and achieved within the bounds of an academic session. Highly specific goals expressed by form-and-meaning constructions make learning focused, finite, concrete, and dynamic. They give students a sense of direction and progress as they experience tangible results at every step of the way: Most students can effortlessly use the target construction in communicative activities by the end of the class period. In addition, SMART goals satisfy what is known as "completion bias," or the human tendency to want to complete a task once they have started it, thus contributing to the development of self-efficacy.

Second, in UBI, the target structure is practiced through multiple iterations both in input and output activities until and to the extent that it is produced with a certain degree of automaticity and ease, i.e., without hesitations, self-corrections, and stumbling. Automaticity can be built by engaging communicative and semi-communicative activities that would involve students in a recurrent meaningful use of the target construction. Iteration leads to the development of fluency, which is often perceived by learners as naturalness, ease, and effortless retrieval from memory (Magnan et al., 2014). The latter, as this study found, appears to be one of the major goals college students have as they embark on language study.

Perhaps the most powerful pedagogical implication behind the UBI, as claimed by usage-based theory, is that language is learned as any other skill and "is governed by general laws of human learning" (Ellis, 2006, p. 101). Language teaching, therefore, should follow the general principles of human learning. In a language class, the UBI principles underscore the importance of repeated intensive goal-directed practice, coupled with targeted feedback, acquisition of componential lower-level skills before more complex skills to the point of fluent and automatic use, memory and memory retrieval, pattern practice, associative learning, and the role of L1 that connects new L2 material with already existing L1 knowledge. These teaching strategies and techniques have been moved to the periphery of L2 education by the prominent concept of language modularity that claims that language ability exists separately and is significantly different from other cognitive faculties (Ellis, 1997), which led to several decades of isolation of the language education field from the general theories of human learning.

Conclusion

We started this chapter with a discussion of factors that may alienate students from language study in beginning language courses and undermine their desire to carry on. The main assumption underlying the chapter is that high attrition rates from FL courses beyond novice level may result from earlier experience in beginning language courses, which frequently weakens students' belief in their ability to attain success in the undertaken endeavor. The chapter argues that such undesirable sentiments are at least partially triggered by conventional, textbook-based, structural all-encompassing curriculum aptly called the "grammar + vocabulary" approach (Tyler, 2012,) which does not agree with psycholinguistic reality of language processing, i.e., the extent to which the constructs of linguistic theory are reflected in human cognitive structures. As a result, novice language students often feel overwhelmed with extraneous mental load, which inhibits efficient learning and results in students' disbelief in their ability to reach meaningful levels of FL proficiency. Not only does it affect students' desire to continue language study, but it also prevents them from enrolling in beginning university language courses: by the time students begin language study at the university, they have already internalized failure in high school language courses. This learning disappointment can serve as an explanation of low initial enrollments in university FL courses.

Our search for a psychologically real model of language led us to a pedagogical approach based on the premises of usage-based conception of language. This small-scale study points, in its modest way, to a yet unexplored allure of usage-based model of language, which, as we have tried to show, approaches language and language learning in a novel way. Its main premises still await close examination both at the experimental and the classroom levels. Perhaps the most important issue requiring a multi-year investigation is the potential impact of usage-based methodology on students' enrollment in upper-level courses. At a time of dwindling enrollments in foreign, and especially less commonly taught language courses, it is vitally important to carefully listen to students' opinions about the accessibility of language courses. The more user-friendly a language course is, the more confidence it will inspire in learners, and the more likely they will come back for more.

References

Allison, D. (1998). Investigating learners' course diaries as explorations of language. *Language Teaching Research*, 2(1), 24–47.

American Council on the Teaching of Foreign Languages (ACTFL). (2012). *ACTFL Proficiency Guidelines 2012*. http://www.actfl.org/publications/guidelines-and-manuals/actfl-proficiency-guidelines-2012

Barkhuizen, G. P. (1998). Discovering learners' perceptions of ESL classroom teaching/learning activities in a South African context. *TESOL Quarterly*, 32(1), 85–108.

Barlow, M., & Kemmer, S. (Eds.). (2000). *Usage-based models of language*. Center for the Study of Language and Information.

Bybee, J. L. (2008). Usage-based grammar and second language acquisition. In P. Robinson, & N. C. Ellis (Eds.), *Handbook of cognitive linguistics and second language acquisition* (pp. 226–246). Routledge.

Bybee, J. L. (2009). Language universals and usage-based theory. In M. Christiansen, C. Collins, & S. Edelman (Eds.), *Language universals* (pp. 17–39). Oxford Scholarship Online. https://doi.org/10.1093/acprof:oso/9780195305432.001.0001

Bybee, J. L. (2013). Usage-based theory and exemplar representations of constructions. In T. Hoffmann, & G. Trousdale (Eds.), *The Oxford handbook of construction grammar* (pp. 49–69). Oxford Handbooks Online. https://doi.org/10.1093/oxfordhb/9780195396683.013.0004

Bybee, J. L., & Hopper, P. J. (2001). Frequency and the emergence of linguistic structure. *Typological Studies in Language, 45*, 1–27.

Cadierno, T. (2008). Motion events in Danish and Spanish: A focus-on-form pedagogical approach. In S. De Knop, & T. De Rycker (Eds.), *Cognitive approaches to pedagogical grammar: A volume in honour of René Dirven* (pp. 259–294). De Gruyter Mouton. https://doi.org/10.1515/9783110205381.3.259

Conzemius, A., & O'Neill, J. (2009). *The power of SMART goals: Using goals to improve student learning*. Solution Tree Press.

Denzin, N. K., & Lincoln, Y. S. (2005). Introduction: The discipline and practice of qualitative research. In N. K. Denzin, & Y. S. Lincoln (Eds.), *The SAGE handbook of qualitative research* (pp. 1–32). SAGE.

Dörnyei, Z. (1994). Motivation and motivating in the foreign language classroom. *The Modern Language Journal, 78*(3), 273–284.

Ellis, N. C. (1996). Sequencing in SLA: Phonological memory, chunking, and points of order. *Studies in Second Language Acquisition, 18*(1), 91–126.

Ellis, N. C. (2002). Frequency effects in language processing: A review with implications for theories of implicit and explicit language acquisition. *Studies in Second Language Acquisition, 24*(2), 143–188.

Ellis, N. C. (2006). Language acquisition as rational contingency learning. *Applied Linguistics, 27*(1), 1–24.

Ellis, R. (1997). *Second language acquisition*. Oxford University Press.

Friedman, A. (2015, May 10). America's lacking language skills. *The Atlantic*. https://www.theatlantic.com/education/archive/2015/05/filling-americas-language-education-potholes/392876/

Gettys, S., Bayona, P., & Rodríguez, R. (2018). From a usage-based model to usage-based instruction: Testing the theory. *International Journal of Education and Human Developments, 4*(2), 50–71.

Goldberg, A. E. (1995). *Constructions: A construction grammar approach to argument structure*. University of Chicago Press.

Goldberg, A. E. (2003). Constructions: A new theoretical approach to language. *Trends in Cognitive Sciences, 7*(5), 219–224.

Goldberg, A. E. (2006). *Constructions at work: The nature of generalization in language*. Oxford University Press.

Langacker, R. W. (1987). *Foundations of cognitive grammar: Theoretical prerequisites* (Vol. 1). Stanford University Press.

Langacker, R. W. (2005). Constructing a language: A usage-based theory of language acquisition. *Language, 81*(3), 748–750.

Langacker, R. W. (2008). *Cognitive grammar: A basic introduction*. Oxford University Press.
Langacker, R. W. (2010). *Grammar and conceptualization*. De Gruyter Mouton.
Larsen-Freeman, D. (2012). On the roles of repetition in language teaching and learning. *Applied Linguistics Review*, 3(2), 195–210.
Leki, I. (2001). Hearing voices: L2 students' experiences in L2 writing courses. In T. Silva, & P. K. Matsuda (Eds.), *On second language writing* (pp. 17–28). Lawrence Erlbaum.
Magnan, S. S., Murphy, D., & Sahakyan, N. (2014). Goals of collegiate learners and the standards for foreign language learning. *Modern Language Journal*, 98, 12–251.
Maldonado, R. (2008). Spanish middle syntax: A usage-based proposal for grammar teaching. In S. De Knop, & T. De Rucker (Eds.), *Cognitive approaches to pedagogical grammar: A volume in honour of René Dirven* (pp. 155–196). De Gruyter Mouton.
Manzanares, J. V., & López, A. M. R. (2008). What can language learners tell us about constructions. In S. De Knop, & T. De Rucker (Eds.), *Cognitive approaches to pedagogical grammar: A volume in honour of René Dirven* (pp. 197–256). De Gruyter Mouton.
Niemeier, S., & Reif, M. (2008). Making progress simpler? Applying cognitive grammar to tense-aspect teaching in the German EFL classroom. In S. De Knop, & T. De Rucker (Eds.), *Cognitive approaches to pedagogical grammar: A volume in honour of René Dirven* (pp. 325–365). De Gruyter Mouton.
Römer, U. (2009). The inseparability of lexis and grammar: Corpus linguistic perspectives. *Annual Review of Cognitive Linguistics*, 7(1), 140–162.
Sinclair, J. (Ed.) (1991). *Corpus, concordance, collocation*. Oxford University Press.
Skehan, P. (1989). *Individual indifferences in second language learning*. Edward Arnold.
Sweller, J. (1988). Cognitive load during problem solving: Effects on learning. *Cognitive science*, 12(2), 257-285.
Tomasello, M. (2008). Usage-based linguistics. In D. Geeraerts (Ed.), *Cognitive linguistics: Basic readings* (pp. 439–458). De Gruyter Mouton.
Tomasello, M. (2009). The usage-based theory of language acquisition. In E. L. Bavin (Ed.), *The Cambridge handbook of child language* (pp. 69–87). Cambridge University Press.
Tse, L. (2000). Student perceptions of foreign language study: A qualitative analysis of foreign language autobiographies. *The Modern Language Journal*, 84(1), 69–84.
Turewicz, K. (2000). *Applicability of cognitive grammar as a foundation of pedagogical/reference grammar*. Univerwersytetu Łódzkiego.
Tyler, A. (2008). Cognitive linguistics and second language instruction. In P. Robinson, & N. Ellis (Eds.), *Handbook of cognitive linguistics and second language acquisition* (pp. 456–488). Routledge.
Tyler, A. (2012). *Cognitive linguistics and second language learning: Theoretical basics and experimental evidence*. Routledge.
Tyler, A., Mueller, C. M., & Ho, V. (2010). Applying cognitive linguistics to instructed L2 learning: The English modals. *AILA Review*, 23(1), 30–49.
VanPatten, B. (2014). Creating a comprehensible input and output. *Language Educator*, 7(4), 24–26.
Verspoor, M., & Nguyen, H. T. P. (2015). A dynamic usage-based approach to second language teaching. In T. Cadierno, & S. W. Eskildsen (Eds.), *Usage-based perspectives on second language learning* (pp. 305–352). De Gruyter Mouton.
Wray, A. (2005). *Formulaic language and the lexicon*. Cambridge University Press.

4
ENHANCING GRAMMAR ACQUISITION AMONG BEGINNER-LEVEL LEARNERS OF CHINESE USING THE FLIPPED LEARNING MODEL

Hongying Xu

The role of grammar instruction in world language education is the subject of some debate. With the rise of the communicative approach in the late 1970s, some arguments arose over whether teaching grammar should remain a part of language instruction. Then, during the 1990s, there was a resurgence in grammar teaching. Scholars argue that although grammar teaching may not change the route of how learners acquire grammar, it can change the rate of their acquisition and increase the ultimate level of their proficiency (Ellis, 1995, 2002) with one provision: the target forms must be noticed in the input before there can be any intake and integration into their interlanguage (Schmidt, 2001; VanPatten, 2002). Therefore, the question is now *how* to teach grammar, rather than *whether* to teach it. Traditional grammar teaching mainly uses explicit instruction and presents target forms in an isolated manner, followed by drill-like decontextualized practice, the benefits of which have not been supported by the literature. There seems to be a consensus that grammar teaching must be integrated with communication to effectively develop learners' communicative competence (Ellis, 2002; Robinson, 2001). Thus, the question becomes: how can we "maximize the opportunity for a focus on grammar without sacrificing the focus on meaning and communication" (Nassaji, 2004)? Due to limited class time, it is unlikely that students can complete communicative activities right after they are exposed to new grammar patterns for the first time when their instructors explicitly introduce those points. It takes time for them to comprehend the meaning of those patterns with examples before they can try to use them in new situations.

A possible way to address this challenge is to employ a so-called flipped learning (FL) model to maximize communicative activity time in class by moving the explicit instruction of grammar outside of the classroom so that students can

DOI: 10.4324/9781003058441-5

study the patterns on their own – albeit with some guidance – before they come to class and then in class, they can practice using those grammar patterns in communicative contexts in a learning community. In addition to saving class time, the FL model can also reduce the cognitive load for beginning-level foreign language learners when they are involved in communicative activities because they have already been exposed to the new grammar patterns needed in those activities. They are more likely to focus on the task itself instead. Reduced cognitive load is also likely to lower learners' anxiety levels.

FL, also known as "The Flipped Classroom", is named so because it reverses the practice of the traditional model. It is defined by the Flipped Learning Network (2014) as

> a pedagogical approach in which direct instruction moves from the group learning space to the individual learning space, and the resulting group space is transformed into a dynamic, interactive learning environment where the educator guides students as they apply concepts and engage creatively in the subject matter.

In the past few years, there has been an increase in the adoption of the FL model by different disciplines and across different education levels. A variety of journal articles and books that investigate FL in such subjects as math, chemistry, and social sciences are available (Mehring, 2018).

Compared with other disciplines, the implementation of this innovative instructional model in foreign language classes, including English as a foreign language (Mehring, 2018), is not yet widely observed, despite a general agreement that FL fits well into the communicative and interactive nature of contemporary language education (Wang & Qi, 2018). Among the limited number of studies that focus on the implementation of this model in foreign language classes, the majority examined English as a foreign language (Chen et al., 2016; Mehring, 2018; Moranski & Kim, 2016). In addition, most studies examined the holistic effects of the FL model as perceived by the learners based on data collected from questionnaires and short surveys. To broaden the research scope, the present study, therefore, examined the effectiveness of using the FL model to help learners acquire Chinese grammar as measured by their comprehension and production of targeted grammar patterns.

Literature review

Grammar instruction in language learning

The role of grammar instruction in language education has been a focus of research in language teaching and learning (Ellis, 2001). Long (1991) proposed the distinction between the focus on forms (presentation of discrete grammar items), focus on form (an occasional shift of attention to linguistic forms), and focus on meaning (solely focus on communication) approaches. Doughty and Williams (1998) argue that the focus on form approach is more beneficial, as its primary focus is on meaning and communication, with the flexibility to shift to linguistic forms when needed. As summarized by Ellis (2001), research has shown that some attention to form is necessary for effective language learning to take place. In other words, explicit grammar instruction, which directs students' attention to linguistic forms and promotes their explicit grammar knowledge, has been found to facilitate second language development (DeKeyser, 2003; Ellis, 2002). However, explicit instruction is not, by itself, a sufficient means of getting students to internalize linguistic forms; they need to practice these forms through contextualized communication activities. Limited class time poses a challenge to the instructor who wishes to incorporate both steps. Using the FL model, which employs instructional videos and other resources to move explicit instruction outside of the classroom, can free up some class time for communicative activities.

The FL model and its implementation

The FL model reverses the ways the traditional design model allocates time and activities in the learning process. In the traditional model, students usually first encounter new content in the classroom from the instructor's lecture and then complete assignments outside of class by applying what they have learned in class. However, this model does not conform to Bloom's taxonomy (Anderson & Krathwohl, 2001), which argues that understanding and remembering new content is less cognitively demanding than applying new content to new situations. In other words, in the traditional model, students get less support with more cognitively demanding tasks. The FL model addresses this twist by having students learn new material outside of and before class and then practice what they have learned with their peers and instructor in class. Students can learn at their own pace; for example, they can pause and replay the instructional videos, which might reduce the cognitive load of the task (Abeyskera & Dawson, 2015). Consequently, class time can be devoted to answering more targeted questions and conducting higher-level learning activities, such as applying new grammar patterns to communications, with instant guidance from the instructor.

The FL approach gained wider recognition after Bergmann and Sams published their book *Flip Your Classroom: Reach Every Student in Every Class Every Day* in 2012 in which they reported how they flipped their classroom by assigning lecture videos for outside-of-class viewing and having students complete assignments, lab reports, etc., in class with their teacher's help. This resulted in a better and deeper student understanding of the subject compared to traditional classroom practices. Since then, FL, as a model of design, has gained proponents among educators in different fields at both the secondary and postsecondary levels, though it has been more "enthusiastically adopted among primary and secondary instructors" (Talbert, 2017, p. 38).

Research on the FL model began to flourish in the mid-2010s. Some studies found improved learning outcomes after the model was adopted in STEM classes (Battaglia & Kaya, 2015; Eichler & Peeples, 2016), business classes (Balaban et al., 2016), and other professional training courses (Bösner et al., 2015). Other studies reported increased student satisfaction, engagement, motivation, and learner autonomy. However, some studies reported that students using the FL model felt more agitation and less satisfaction with the tasks (Strayer, 2012), and complained of an increased workload (Khanova et al., 2015; Smith, 2013).

FL model in foreign language classes

Research investigating the adoption of this innovative course design in the foreign language field remains scarce, especially with respect to beginning-level language courses (Hung, 2015; Lee & Wallace, 2018; Moranski & Kim, 2016; Wang et al., 2018; Wang & Qi, 2018). Many scholars argue that the FL model conforms well with the social-cultural framework of second language acquisition, which argues that learning "happens during mediation" (Moranski & Kim, 2016, p. 831). Most foreign language learners do not have much exposure to or interaction with the target language outside of class. It is therefore extremely important to give them as many opportunities as possible to practice the target language use in class with guidance from the instructors. The FL model can be instrumental in creating such opportunities by moving the explicit teaching of linguistic components outside of the classroom and freeing up more class time for language practice in a communicative context with an instructor and classmates. How effective is this new design model in helping students achieve their learning objectives and what is their learning experience like? These questions still must be addressed before this model can be implemented on a large scale.

However, previous research elicited data on students' perceived gains in such aspects as satisfaction, engagement, and performance strictly through questionnaires and interviews. And, among the limited number of studies that did use objective measurements to gauge gains in learners' performances, most (Chen et al., 2016; Hung, 2015; Lee & Wallace, 2018) focused only on experienced learners of English as a foreign language. Some studies found that after employing the FL model, learners' attitudes were energized (Hung, 2015; Nguyen et al., 2019), their motivation increased (Chuang et al., 2018), and they became more willing to communicate (Hung, 2017). Other studies found that, using this model, learners made progress in their tests, writing skills, and oral presentations (Chuang et al., 2018; Hung, 2017; Nguyen et al., 2019). The participants in these studies were mostly intermediate or advanced learners of English. It is not clear whether the effects and benefits found in these studies can be replicated among beginning-level learners of other target languages.

In recent years, a handful of studies have examined the use of the FL model in the teaching of Chinese as a foreign language. Wang et al. (2019) looked at the effectiveness of the model in a business Chinese class in the U.K. and found that not only did learners take more responsibility for their own learning but their attitudes toward learning also improved. Wang et al. (2018) compared the use of the FL model with face-to-face communicative instruction. They measured "learners' academic performance" (p. 492) and found that the FL group learned faster and achieved better fluency, but they provided no obvious advantage in either accuracy or mastery of linguistic complexity.

In addition, most studies, regardless of the target language, examined the holistic performance among language learners rather than looking at specific language competencies, including the grammar. Moranski and Kim's (2016) research is among the very few studies that investigated whether the FL model (they used the term "inverted classroom") would help intermediate-level Spanish students learn the Spanish pronoun *se* and discovered that the FL group outperformed the in-class presentation group in the grammaticality judgment task. These results are encouraging. Can similar findings be obtained with learners' production of the target forms? Will the results be different if more than one target form is included in the study? And will beginner-level learners benefit as much from the FL model?

The present study attempts to fill the aforementioned research gaps by investigating the effects of the FL model on enhancing the acquisition of grammar among college students at the beginner level of Chinese. Specifically, it addresses the following research questions:

1. Is the FL model more effective at helping learners comprehend target grammar forms than the traditional grammar instruction model?
2. Does the FL model help with learners' production of the target forms?
3. What are learners' experiences of and attitudes toward using this FL model?

The study

Participants

This study used a convenient sample. The participants were drawn from two intact beginner-level Chinese classes from two different campuses within a Midwest public university system. There were 31 participants in total: 17 females and 14 males. Their average age was 19.4 years. None of the participants had had any exposure to the target grammar forms prior to this study, even though they had completed six weeks of Chinese classes when the study began. All participants were native speakers of English. Due to the limited number of participants, both groups (A & B) experienced both the FL model and the traditional model. In Unit 1, Group A ($n = 18$) underwent the FL model and Group B

(n = 13) underwent the traditional model. In Unit 2, the two groups switched: Group B did the FL model and Group A did the traditional model. This setup helped to balance out the differences between the two groups. Since this study used intact classes, the participants in each group were not equal in number.

Training

The target grammar patterns in this study were taken from two units (four target patterns from each unit) in the textbook used by the classes.[1] When employing the traditional model, the instructor used slides to explicitly explain the target grammar patterns in class, which was followed by a question and answer (Q & A) session and a limited practice session using exercises from the textbook. After class, students completed worksheets and exercises from the workbook that accompanies the textbook. When using the FL model, the instructor posted prerecorded instructional videos. Two days before class, the videos were assigned via the Canvas learning management system. After they watched the videos, students submitted a study report one day before class, which included self-checking exercises and a brief reflection on their learning. Instructors addressed misunderstandings or errors at the beginning of the class before students started to practice using the grammar patterns by completing individual and group communicative tasks. The instructors circulated in class to answer questions and give feedback. Both models used comprehension and production tasks to evaluate students' mastery of the target grammar patterns.

The textbook and workbook exercises include such activities as replacement drills, using target patterns to answer questions, or translating a short dialogue from English into Chinese.

In a previous study, videos created by advanced learners of Chinese were perceived by participants as helpful and enjoyable (Xu, 2019). Encouraged by the enthusiasm among learners, the present study used similar videos created by two Chinese majors who had studied Chinese in China. First, they produced slides based on their own understanding and with the help of reference books on Chinese grammar. After the slides were reviewed by a Chinese instructor and revised, they were used in the videos. Each video focused on one target grammar pattern. After the videos were reviewed by the instructor, they were uploaded to their YouTube account and shared with the instructors involved in this study.

The time involved in both procedures were comparable: around 80 minutes or so for each method, including in class and outside of class. As for the training materials, the slide sets used by instructors or by the advanced learners in the videos were the same. Therefore, the instruction of the target patterns in the two methods was also similar. As for the materials used to help students practice using the target patterns, efforts were made to make them as comparable as possible: before-the-class exercises in the FL method followed the pattern of in-class practice used in the traditional method. The task completed by individuals in class in the FL method was assigned to the students after class in the traditional method. However, the group activity used in class in the FL method was not used in the traditional method, which was an advantage of the FL method.

Measurements

Participants' acquisition of the target grammar patterns was measured in two ways: their comprehension of the target patterns and their production of those patterns in context. Their comprehension was measured via a translation task: participants read a dialogue in Chinese that contained the target forms and then translated it into English. Their production was measured via a fill-in-the-blank task, in which they were asked to complete two short dialogues in Chinese, based on the context and a few cues in English. The following is an excerpt of a production task:

> 小李: -- 你好!小王,你今天怎么样? (Hello, Little Wang, how are you doing today?)
> 小王: -- 我很好。小李,你呢? (I'm doing well. How about you, Little Li?)
>
> 小李: -- 我也不错! (I'm doing well too.)
> _____. (Find out if 小王 (Little Wang) is busy or not this weekend: use A-not-A question)

Participants' opinions on using the FL model were collected via a semi-structured questionnaire which surveyed (a) their previous experience in learning grammar in a foreign language classroom, (b) their motivation for learning Chinese grammar, (c) their perceived gains in their grammar using the FL model, and (d) their thoughts on what could be done to improve their learning experience and help them learn more effectively.

Procedure

The study consisted of two units. In the first unit, Group A experienced the FL model and Group B experienced the traditional model. To ensure participants' understanding of the process, Group A, the first group to experience the FL model, spent approximately 30 minutes in class learning about it. The instructor explained the possible advantages of the model and showed videos of what a flipped classroom looked like. After class, Group A participants started the procedure explained in the previous section. Group B, which was following the traditional model, without any additional explanation about the present study, went through the procedure described in the Training section. After both groups had learned and practiced the target grammar patterns, they completed the comprehension and production tasks in class. In the second unit, the two groups switched learning models but followed the same procedure as the first unit. After two units, the two groups completed the online questionnaire using *Qualtrics* survey software. The whole procedure took five weeks to complete: the first two weeks were spent on the first unit, the following two weeks on the second unit, and the last week on the questionnaire.

Data coding and analysis

Participants' performances were graded based on accuracy using the following criteria: a target grammar received 2 points if translated or produced accurately, 1 point if translated or produced inaccurately but indicated understanding, and 0 points if translated or produced completely inaccurately. Each task consisted of four target patterns; the total possible points were 8. The points were then converted into percentage accuracy rates for an easy and straightforward comparison. The questionnaire data based on the number of responses given under each option was also converted into a percentage.

Results

The results of the present study are presented in three subsections: (a) results from the comprehension task, (b) results from the production task, and (c) results from the survey. Since the two groups went through different training in each unit, the results from each unit are presented separately. A summary of the accuracy rates (%) is presented in Figure 4.1.

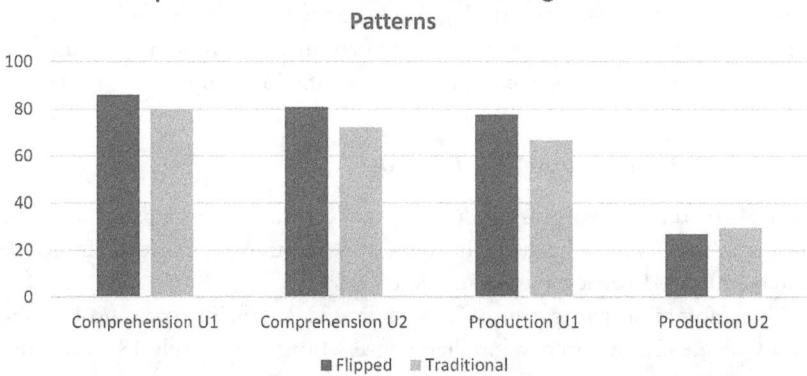

FIGURE 4.1 Accuracy rates from the comprehension and production tasks

Acquisition of target grammar patterns: Comprehension

For the comprehension task, only the translations of the target forms were graded. The accuracy rates of student comprehension of each target pattern in each unit were combined and averaged. The results indicated that the FL groups outperformed the traditional groups in their comprehension of the target grammar patterns in both units. In Units 1 and 2, the flipped group's average accuracy rate was higher than the traditional group by 6% and 8.5 %, respectively. Two two-tailed t-tests were conducted to determine whether these differences were significant. It was found that these differences were not significant: the Unit 1 t-test $t(29) = 1.21$, $p = .24$; the Unit 2 t-test $t(29) = 1.39$, $p = .18$.

Acquisition of target grammar patterns: Production

Similarly, in the production task, only the target grammar patterns were graded based on the criteria set beforehand. The accuracy rates of each participant's production of each target pattern from each unit were combined and averaged. The results from the production tasks were more complex than those from the comprehension task. In Unit 1, the FL group outperformed the traditional group in their production of the target grammar patterns by 10.9%. The t-test showed that the flipped group did significantly better than the traditional group ($t(29) = 2.35$, $p = .03$). However, in Unit 2, the flipped group's accuracy rate was lower than the traditional group's by 2.6%. The t-test showed that there was no significant difference between these two groups ($t(29) = 0.32$, $p = .75$). It is important to note that neither group did well on the production task. For this reason, an item analysis was conducted to determine if there was any difference in their performances across the target patterns. The results showed that the overall accuracy rates were below 50%, with the accuracy rates of one grammar pattern ("*-le*" to indicate the completion of an action) being extremely low in both groups (7.7% and 7.1%, respectively). Among all the participants, only three students attempted to use "*-le*" (one from the FL group and two from the traditional group), and one used it correctly (the one from the FL group).

Students' experience using the FL model

A semi-structured survey was conducted to collect data on participants' attitudes, perspectives as Chinese language learners, and experience using the FL model. Sixteen out of 31 participants submitted the survey.

First, most of the participants (62.5%) indicated that their primary goal in taking a Chinese class was to develop their conversational skills. Only 18.75% of the participants said that their primary goal was to learn Chinese grammar. However, most participants agreed on the importance of learning grammar and gave its importance a score of 8.5 ($SD = 1.33$) on a scale of 1–10. Interestingly, few

Enhancing grammar acquisition among beginner-level **51**

participants considered Chinese grammar difficult, rating it at 5.7 ($SD = 2.22$) on a scale of 1–10.

Participants were also asked to list other foreign languages they had taken and rate their experience learning the grammar of those languages. Of the respondents, 18.75% had never taken another foreign language, 56.25% had taken Spanish, 12.5% French, and 12.5% German. Among those who had taken another language before, almost half were taught grammar via class activities and drilling (46.7%), whereas the rest either completed assignments and worksheets (26.7%) or listened to instructors' repeated lecturing (26.7%).

The main part of this survey focused on participants' experience of and attitude toward the FL model. Participants were asked to respond to nine statements (Figure 4.2). The percentages for the options *strongly agree* and *agree* and the options *strongly disagree* and *disagree* were combined.

The majority of participants (81.25%) felt that they learned better through instructor lectures in class, whereas only around 1/3 (31.25%) of the participants felt that they learned better through the FL model. Similarly, more participants preferred the traditional instruction model over the FL model (88.24% vs. 52.94%) to help them learn grammar. However, they also overwhelmingly liked the group activities in class (87.5%) and checking their learning with a study report outside of class (76.47%), both of which were components of the FL model. In a follow-up question on participants' experience with the in-class activities in the FL model, students said they liked the group activities more than the individual work (87.5% vs. 43.8%).

Over half of the participants (52.94%) agreed that the videos were helpful. Almost half of the participants (43.8%) indicated that they watched all the instructional videos, and the rest of them admitted that they missed some of them. On the other hand, 37.5% of the participants stated that they watched the

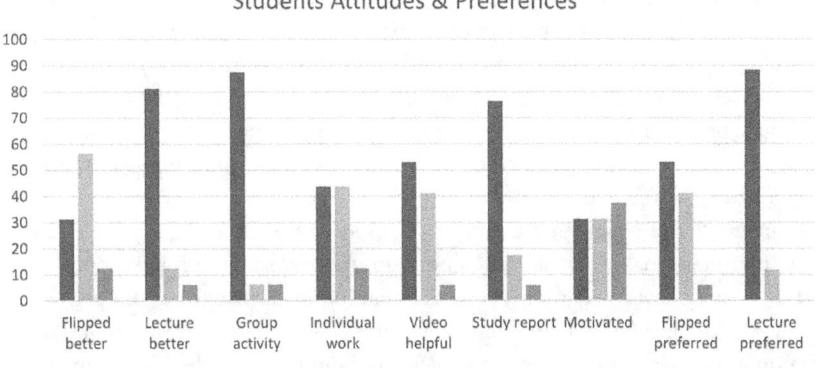

FIGURE 4.2 Participants' experience of and attitude toward the FL model

videos more than once. Some students (25%) paused the videos or rewound them while watching. Some students (25%) took notes when they watched the videos. 18.8% of the students preferred going through the questions in the study report first before they started the videos, while 12.5% of the students preferred to go to the questions after they watched the videos. The majority of students did not indicate a preference. As for the changes they hoped to see in the future, three students indicated that they would like the videos to give clearer explanations of how to use these patterns in different scenarios and explain them more slowly.

Discussion

The present study examined whether, compared to the traditional instruction model, the use of the FL model can better facilitate the learning of grammar patterns among beginner-level Chinese learners. Students from two beginner-level Chinese classes participating in this study experienced both the traditional instruction model and the FL model. Their comprehension and production of the target grammar patterns from two units were measured. In addition, they also completed a survey to share their attitudes, preferences, and experiences of the two different models.

The first research question explored the effect of the FL model on learners' comprehension of the target grammar patterns in communicative contexts. The results from the comprehension tasks showed that, in each unit, the group that used the FL model outperformed the traditional instruction group in their comprehension of the target patterns, although this advantage was not statistically significant. This finding conforms to the results of a meta-analysis study on the effects of flipped vs. non-flipped classes in achieving learning outcomes (Van Alten et al., 2019), which found a small effect of flipped classrooms in achieving learning outcomes. One explanation of these results could be the nature of the task: It was not very challenging for participants in either group to grasp the meaning of those target patterns in contexts after the training. The results might be different if more challenging comprehension tasks were employed.

The second research question explored whether the FL model could enhance learners' production of the target grammar patterns. The results were mixed. In producing the target patterns in communicative contexts, the flipped group did significantly better than the traditional group in the first unit. However, in the second unit, the group that used the FL model received a slightly lower score than the traditional group, although both groups performed this task poorly. The results suggest that the complexity of the grammar patterns should also play a role in the effectiveness of different design and instructional models. The second unit's grammar point was the notoriously tricky and difficult particle "-le", which had only recently been introduced for the first time. It is possible that those who had their instructor explain the challenging pattern in class in a traditional way benefited from getting immediate, on-the-spot answers to their questions.

The third research question examined learners' experience using the FL model, their attitudes toward it, and their preferences for learning grammar in the future. The survey results showed that although more than half of the participants liked the videos produced by advanced learners of Chinese and considered them helpful, they still preferred lectures by their instructors in class to videos outside of class. At the same time, they also liked the in-class group activities and the supplementary exercises in the study report designed for the videos to check their understanding of the target grammar patterns. It seems that learners prefer a mixture of both the traditional model and the FL model, which would be ideal if there were plenty of class time for both. Since the present study only flipped one unit for each group, it remains uncertain whether learners' attitudes and preferences would change if they had more experience with the FL model. Most students had been exposed to the traditional instruction of grammar for a long time and had become used to it. Perhaps they needed more time to adjust to this new model.

Limitations of the study

The present study had a small sampling and provided a somewhat limited experience with the FL model, so the conclusions are only tentative and should be generalized with caution. In addition, it was the two advanced learners of Chinese who produced the outside learning materials, instead of instructors. It is not clear if participants' attitudes and preferences would be different if instructor-produced videos, which might mimic in-class lecturing to a larger extent, were provided.

Another limitation lies in the design and methodology of this study. This study involved two instructors on two campuses within a state university system. Although the two instructors met multiple times to discuss the specific procedures of each teaching model, there still might be slight differences in the implementation. As part of regular instruction, the grammar patterns used in this study were selected from two units from the textbook. Some patterns (e.g., 了 (-le)) were harder than others (e.g., A-not-A as a Y-N question format). This factor was not controlled.

In the future, more research is needed on whether the nature of the outside learning materials will impact the efficacy of the FL model. If a larger number of learners could be recruited, there could be two FL groups: one using learner-produced videos and the other using instructor-produced videos.

Classroom implications

The study findings suggest several implications for flipped instruction. Firstly, the learning materials studied before class should include questions that allow students to show their understanding and to reflect on their learning. In this study, students were asked to submit a report after they watched the instruction videos. The report included questions to check their understanding of the grammar patterns. For example, for the pattern 一点儿 (yi dian er, a bit of), the questions was, "What does 一点儿 mean? What does 一点儿 modify? Where does it go? Can you give an example?" In addition, students were also asked to reflect on their study in the report. For example, they were asked,

> How long did you study the patterns? How did you complete the study report? Did you watch all the videos, and then start the report? Or did you answer questions to each pattern before you moved on to the next pattern? How well do you feel you are ready for activities to practice these patterns in class? Do you have any questions?

As was claimed in the meta-analysis study (Van Alten et al., 2019), students' performance was better in the flipped setting if quizzes were included. The instructional videos should include scenarios in which the target patterns occur in communicative contexts. Although it was not examined in this study, it might be worth a try to embed those checking questions into the videos to help students better understand the patterns during their processing stage. Low-stakes practice quizzes are an excellent tool for learning and can increase student motivation to watch the videos. Before-the-class learning tasks should be completed by the deadline because this step is a prerequisite for the in-class activities.

Secondly, the difficulty level of the grammar patterns seems to play a role in the effectiveness of the FL model. For challenging patterns, instructors may consider devoting some class time to more complicated aspects of those patterns in addition to the videos. For example, the results of this study showed that students were exceedingly challenged by using 了 ("-*le*") as an aspect marker to indicate the completion of an action. Instructors may need to give some explicit explanations in class to address any confusion or questions identified from students' study reports.

Thirdly, instructors should provide specific guidelines to ensure each student's participation and involvement in the group activities. From what the instructors observed in class, some students were not active in the group activities. They may have been more motivated if they were given more specific guidelines.

Finally, instructors should provide some metacognitive training to get students accustomed to this new teaching and learning model, including the rationale behind the FL model, the strategies behind using learning materials independently, reflection on their learning strategies, etc. The survey results showed that students' judgment of their learning with the different models was not consistent with the accuracy rate results of the tasks. This indicated that their judgment may have been influenced by their previous learning experiences. With years of foreign language learning in the traditional model, students may rate the traditional method higher due to its familiarity. Being accustomed to coming to class to learn new material in the traditional model, students need more support to embrace this new model.

Conclusion

The present study found that the FL model mostly enhanced beginner-level Chinese learners' acquisition of grammar patterns as measured by their comprehension and production of the target grammar patterns, although this advantage was not always significant. Moreover, students indicated positive experiences with the FL model. They liked the learning materials provided before class. They showed some variety in approaching the materials, such as pausing, replaying, or skimming through the instructional videos, which is not possible in the traditional instruction model. They also enjoyed the various group activities in class, which is unlikely to be included on a comparable scale in the traditional model due to the large amount of time spent on lecturing. It seems that the nature of the tasks and the difficulty level of the target patterns also played a role in determining the effectiveness of the FL model in facilitating students' grammar learning. Overall, participants accepted the FL model, which was completely new to them. Learners' accuracy rate in both comprehension and production, as well as the survey data, provide positive evidence to support the effectiveness of the FL model. As a large amount of language instruction has been transitioned to an online format under the COVID-19 circumstances, this study provides valuable input for those who consider redesigning their curricula for grammar instruction.

Note

1 The textbook used is *Integrated Chinese Book 1*. The target grammar patterns used in Unit 1 are (1) adverbial phrases (time, frequency); (2) to distinguish between 喜欢 (to like), 想 (would like to), 觉得 (to feel, to think); (3) to form a Y-N question in the affirmative-negative format (A-not-A Q). The target grammar patterns used in Unit 2 include (1) 吧 used as a sentence-final particle to soften the tone of a command; (2) to distinguish between 一下 (briefly), 一点儿 (a little bit of something), 有一点儿 (to some degree); (3) 在 to introduce the location of an activity; (4) 了 to indicate the occurrence and completion of an action or event.

References

Abeyskera, L., & Dawson, P. (2015). Motivation and cognitive load in the flipped classroom: Definition, rationale and a call for research. *Higher Education Research and Development, 34*(1), 1–14.

Anderson, L. W., & Krathwohl, D. R. (2001). *A taxonomy for learning, teaching, and assessing: A revision of Bloom's taxonomy of educational objectives*. Longman.

Balaban, R. A., Gilleskie, D. B., & Tran, U. (2016). A quantitative evaluation of the flipped classroom in a large lecture principles of economics course. *The Journal of Economic Education, 47*(4), 269–287.

Battaglia, D. M., & Kaya, T. (2015). How flipping your first-year digital circuits course positively affects student perceptions and learning. *International Journal of Engineering Education*, *31*(4), 1126–1138.

Bösner, S., Pickert, J., & Stibane, T. (2015). Exploring students' learning attitude and achievement in flipped learning supported computer aided design curriculum: A study in high school engineering education. *Computer Applications in Engineering Education*, *23*, 514–526.

Chen, H. J., Wu, W. C. V., & Marek, M. W. (2016). Using the flipped classroom to enhance EFL learning. *Computer Assisted Language Learning*, *30*(1–2), 1–21.

Chuang, H. H., Weng, C. Y., & Chen, C. H. (2018). Which students benefit most from a flipped classroom approach to language learning? *British Journal of Educational Technology*, *49*(1), 56–68.

DeKeyser, R. (2003). Implicit and explicit learning. In G. Doughty, & M. Long (Eds.), *The handbook of second language acquisition* (pp. 313–348). Blackwell Publishing.

Doughty, C., & Williams, J. (1998). Pedagogical choices in focus on form. In C. Doughty, & J. Williams (Eds.), *Focus on form in classroom second language acquisition* (pp. 114–138). Cambridge University Press.

Eichler, J. F., & Peeples, J. (2016). Flipped classroom modules for large enrollment general chemistry courses: A low barrier approach to increase active learning and improve student grades. *Chemistry Education: Research and Practice*, *17*(1), 197–208.

Ellis, N. (1995). Consciousness in second language acquisition: A review of field studies and laboratory experiments. *Language Awareness*, *4*, 121–146.

Ellis, R., (2001). Introduction: Investigating form-focused instruction. *Language Learning. Supplement 1: Form-Focused Instruction and Second Language Learning*, *51*, 1–46.

Ellis, R. (2002). The place of grammar instruction in the second/foreign curriculum. In E. Hinkel, & S. Fotos (Eds.), *New perspectives on grammar teaching in second language classrooms* (pp. 17–34). Erlbaum.

Flipped Learning Network. (2014, March 12). *Definition of flipped learning*. https://flippedlearning.org/definition-of-flipped-learning/

Hung, H. T. (2015). Flipping the classroom for English language learners to foster active learning. *Computer Assisted Language Learning*, *28*(1), 81–96.

Hung, H. T. (2017). Design-based research: Redesign of an English language course using a flipped classroom approach. *TESOL Quarterly*, *51*(1), 180–192.

Khanova, J., Roth, M. T., Rodgers, J. E., & McLaughlin, J. E. (2015). Student experiences across multiple flipped courses in a single curriculum. *Medical Education*, *49*(10), 1038–1048.

Lee, G., & Wallace, A. (2018). Flipped learning in the English as a foreign language classroom: Outcomes and perceptions. *TESOL Quarterly*, *52*(1), 62–84.

Long, M. H. (1991). Focus on form: A design feature in language teaching methodology. In K. de Bot, R. Ginsberg, & C. Kramsch (Eds.), *Foreign language research in cross-cultural perspective* (pp. 39–52). John Benjamins.

Mehring, J. (2018). The flipped classroom. In J. Mehring & A. Leis (Eds.), *Innovations in flipping the language classroom: Theories and practices* (pp. 1–9). Springer Nature.

Moranski, K., & Kim, F. (2016). 'Flipping' lessons in a multi-section Spanish course: Implications for assigning explicit grammar instruction outside of the classroom. *The Modern Language Journal*, *100*(4), 830–852.

Nassaji, H. (2004). Current developments in research on the teaching of grammar. *Annual Review of Applied Linguistics*, *24*, 126–145.

Nguyen, N. Q., Lee, K. W., Nguyen, D. N. P., & Naidu, S. (2019). An investigation into using Flipped Classroom Model in an academic writing class in Vietnam. *International Journal of Computer-Assisted Language Learning and Teaching, 9*(1), 32–57.

Robinson, P. (2001). Task complexity, cognitive resources and syllabus design: A triadic framework for examining task influence on SLA. In P. Robinson (Ed.), *Cognition and second language instruction* (pp. 287–318). Cambridge University Press.

Schmidt, R. W. (2001). Attention. In P. Robinson (Ed.), *Cognition and second language instruction* (pp. 3–32). Cambridge University Press.

Smith, J. D. (2013). Student attitudes toward flipping the general chemistry classroom. *Chemistry Education: Research and Practice, 14*(4), 607–614.

Strayer, J. F. (2012). How learning in an inverted classroom influences cooperation, innovation and task orientation. *Learning Environments Research, 15*, 171–193.

Talbert, R. (2017). *Flipped learning: A guide for higher education faculty*. Stylus.

Van Alten, D., Phielix, C., Janssen, J., & Kester, L. (2019). Effects of flipping the classroom on learning outcomes and satisfaction: A meta-analysis. *Educational Research Review, 28*, 1–18.

VanPatten, B. (2002). Processing instruction: An update. *Language Learning, 52*, 755–803.

Wang, J., An, N., & Wright, C. (2018). Enhancing beginner learners' oral proficiency in a flipped Chinese foreign language classroom. *Computer Assisted Language Learning, 31*(5-6), 490–521.

Wang, J., Wang, D., & Xing, M. (2019). Flipped class for practical skills to enhance employability: A case study of business Chinese. *International Journal of Computer-Assisted Language Learning and Teaching, 9*(1), 19–31.

Wang, Y., & Qi, G. Y. (2018). Mastery-based language learning outside class: Learning support in flipped classrooms. *Language Learning & Technology, 22*(2), 50–74.

Xu, H. (2019). The effectiveness of different modalities in facilitating grammar acquisition in the flipped classroom. *International Journal of Computer-Assisted Language Learning and Teaching, 9*(4), 37–50.

5
BUILDING BEGINNING SPANISH LANGUAGE LEARNERS' LINGUISTIC AND CULTURAL COMPETENCE THROUGH ONLINE TASK-BASED INSTRUCTION

Lina Lee

According to the World-Readiness Standards for Learning Languages (The National Standards Collaborative Board, 2015), building three modes of communication – interpretive, interpersonal, and presentational skills – is vital for learners to effectively use the target language in real-world contexts. Moreover, one of the goal areas of the Standards is to establish a strong connection between communication and culture because its relationship is deeply rooted and tightly interwoven. In the Cultures standards, the 3 Ps: (1) Products, (2) Practices, and (3) Perspectives are often used as a pedagogical framework by teachers to integrate cultures into their language instruction (see Cutshall, 2012 for details). To develop communicative competence, task-based instruction (TBI) is arguably one of the most effective pedagogical approaches because it promotes authentic language use and supports second language acquisition (SLA) principles, including exposure to input and opportunities for output (Ellis, 2003). More importantly, TBI follows a learner-centered approach that involves students in active knowledge construction, as opposed to passively receiving information from the instructor. With the advent of new technologies, a wide range of digital learning resources and tools has been incorporated into TBI to promote second and foreign language (L2) learning and development (e.g., González-Lloret, 2016; Lee, 2016). From a pedagogical perspective, technology interventions not only overcome the physical and temporal constraints of conventional classrooms but also empower teachers to create individual and social spaces for students to engage in meaningful communication using authentic tasks, and culturally relevant materials (Allen & Gamalinda, 2021; Lee, 2017; Luo & Yang, 2018).

Research studies have explored the potential of online TBI by addressing evolving topics, such as task design, language development, and focus on form (Chong & Reinders, 2020). For example, Fouz-González (2020) reported that

DOI: 10.4324/9781003058441-6

English as a foreign language (EFL) learners benefited from performing sound identification tasks with the *English File Pronunciation* software program. As a result, students improved their pronunciation. Other studies have shown positive effects of computer-mediated communication (CMC) tasks on the development of learners' cultural knowledge and awareness through virtual exchanges (e.g., Lee, 2018; O'Dowd & Lewis, 2016). Although researchers and practitioners have continued to explore the ways in which TBI is facilitated by digital technology and its impact on L2 development, there is a lack of research on the application of TBI for online beginner-level world language courses at the university level. Therefore, the study aims to address the gap by exploring the effectiveness of TBI mediated by synchronous and asynchronous CMC tools (e.g., *Zoom*, *Padlet*) on the development of adult novice learners' linguistic and cultural competencies.

Literature review

Using tasks in language teaching and learning

One of the effective ways for exploring the fundamental tenets of the communicative language approach is the emergence of TBI, which focuses on doing real-world tasks through meaningful interactions (Ellis, 2003; Samuda & Bygate, 2008). Unlike a traditional Presentation, Practice, and Production (PPP) approach to teaching grammatical structures and vocabulary with controlled practice activities (see Richards & Rodgers, 2001 for details), TBI underscores the importance of using tasks relevant to real-life situations that make students feel personally connected to learning materials. Rather than manipulating isolated linguistic forms used by PPP, authentic tasks provide ample opportunities for language learners to receive input, negotiate meaning, and produce output that contributes to SLA (Lee, 2002). While tasks should mainly involve learners in expressing meaning, focus-on-form instruction helps them develop a better understanding of the relationship between form and meaning (Ellis, 2016). A growing body of research drawing from various theoretical approaches (e.g., cognitive-interactionist,[1] sociocultural[2]) has shown the potential impact of tasks on L2 learning and development (Ahmadian & Mayo, 2018; Bygate et al., 2001; Long, 2015; Shehadeh & Coombe, 2012). For example, Erlam (2019) found that beginner-level French students were able to make form-meaning connections for target lexical and grammar items using input-based tasks. Another study by Fu and Nassaji (2016) revealed that EFL students were able to notice their errors and produce target language forms through task-based learning in conjunction with form-focused instruction. The study suggests that corrective feedback is critical to assist learners in noticing linguistic problems that may lead to error correction and improve language accuracy.

Challenges of TBI

Even though TBI has evolved into a potentially effective approach to language learning and development, a few drawbacks have been discussed in the literature. For example, Littlewood (2007) argues that TBI is not suitable for beginners because they have insufficient language knowledge to take part in a task. To address the concern, Ellis (2017a) suggests that TBI for beginner-level learners can be facilitated by pedagogic input-based activities to develop their receptive skills and prepare them to move to output-based tasks to build their writing and speaking skills. Another challenge is the progression of cognitive demands required for students to successfully carry out target tasks. Based on the cognitive hypothesis[3] of task-based language learning, Robinson (2011) proposes that a simple-to-complex task sequence should be developed to gradually increase learners' cognitive demands, the quantity of interaction and opportunities for the negotiation of meaning. Essentially, tasks should respond to learners' abilities and needs by activating their prior knowledge, allowing time for planning, and executing tasks (Nunan, 2010). Finally, Lee (2016) stresses that tasks need to be compelling to stimulate students' interest and motivation to empower them to become self-regulated learners.

Technology-mediated task-based language learning

Research studies on the application of digital technologies for TBI across different instructional contexts have shown promising affordances that derive from implementing CMC tasks for meaningful interaction in virtual language learning environments (Farr & Murray, 2016; Thomas & Reinders, 2010; Ziegler, 2016). For example, Lee (2016) found that TBI enabled students to use the target language to build interpretive, interpersonal, and presentational skills through various types of CMC tasks, including viewing short films, writing blogs, creating podcasts, and interacting with peers. Significantly, CMC tasks shifted the focus of instruction from the teacher to the students to promote active learning. Another study of Lee (2011) shows that pedagogical tasks enhanced learners' understanding of grammar points through focus on form. Learners benefited from receiving corrective feedback from expert speakers on the erroneous language forms. As a result, they improved the accuracy of their writing. Apart from the development of language proficiency, building cultural competence is a fundamental part of language learning. To this end, Lee and Markey (2014) employed culture blogs for students to explore the relationship among the products, practices, and perspectives of the target culture. Consequently, students demonstrated their awareness of cultural similarities and differences, and their attitudes of openness and appreciation for the target culture, which are the key components of effective communication among speakers of difficult cultural backgrounds (Byram, 1997). The study concludes that giving students the opportunity to reflect on their own perspectives is pivotal for a profound cultural learning that goes beyond the superficial "facts only" approach.

Despite the potential of online TBI for L2 learning, challenges of implementing communicative tasks have been identified as follows: digital literacies, learner readiness, and language proficiency levels (see Chong & Reinders, 2020; Lee, 2019; Reinhardt & Thorne, 2019 for more information). For example, Ellis (2017b) suggests that tasks should be carefully designed to allow students to work at their own level of readiness. Hampel (2010) maintains that the integration of digital literacies should be part of teaching pedagogies to help students develop critical skills and effective strategies to create digital content and communicate through multiple channels. To promote learner autonomy, teachers need to establish a stimulating learning environment for students to be fully involved and in charge of their own learning (Lee, 2016). Since TBI for online elementary language courses at the postsecondary level remains an underdeveloped area, this study examines how CMC tasks affect adult novice language learners' engagement and performance in a fully online summer course. In particular, the study focuses on learners' perceptions of design features and course practices, including task types, digital platforms, peer interaction, and instructional interventions through modeling and linguistic scaffolding.

Research questions

The three research questions that guided this study are as follows:

1. How do beginning students perceive the effectiveness of TBI in a fully online language course?
2. Do CMC tasks enhance the development of beginning students' linguistic and cultural competencies?
3. What impact does instructional scaffolding have on beginning students' engagement and performance?

Methodology

Context of the study

The study was set up using one fully online section of a second-semester Spanish course (Elementary II) over a five-week period. The course was designed to continue to develop language skills while expanding core vocabulary and cultural knowledge obtained in the Elementary I course. In addition to the commercial e-text version of *Experience Spanish* (Amores, Suárez-García & Wendel, 2014) and the learning management platform of *Connect*, four-skill-integrated learning tasks using real-world topics were created to foster active and interactive learning. Synchronous and asynchronous CMC tools were utilized to support TBI and encourage social engagement among students (see "Course Design, Tasks, and Digital Tools" section for details). Instructional scaffolding through task modeling and linguistic feedback was used to facilitate the learning process and enhance performance. It was hoped that the learner-centered approach to TBI would encourage beginning students to take an active role in their own learning. Additionally, self-access learning modules hosted by *Canvas*, the university's Learning Management System, would engage them in performing learning tasks independently and working with their peers collaboratively.

Participants

Twenty-four students enrolled in an Elementary Spanish II course participated in the study. All participants were native speakers of English. More than 90% of the students ($n = 22$) had successfully completed the first semester of elementary Spanish before enrolling in this course. Two students enrolled directly into Elementary Spanish II based on their scores on the placement exam. Thus, they had a basic knowledge of Spanish vocabulary and grammar structures. The participants were 58% female ($n = 14$), 42% male ($n = 10$), and between the ages of 19 and 23. None of them majored in Spanish, and only one student was a Spanish minor. Since more than 95% of the students ($n = 23$) enrolled in the course to fulfill the foreign language graduation requirement, they were not considered to be highly motivated language learners. In terms of computer knowledge and skills, students were competent users of digital technology, as they grew up in the digital age and were also familiar with *Canvas*.

Course design, tasks, and digital tools

CMC tasks were informed by Lee's (2016) four-skill-integrated approach for the development of the three modes of communication based on the World-Readiness Standards for Learning Languages (The National Standards Collaborative Board, 2015): (1) interpretive, (2) interpersonal, and (3) presentational. In addition, the Cultures Goal area of the Standards was adopted to design learning tasks to develop beginning students' cultural competence. From Cultural Products, Practices to Perspectives, students used the target language to engage in discussions about the cultures of different Spanish-speaking countries. While tangible culture (see Lee & Markey, 2014) enabled students to learn about physical artifacts, such as food and monuments, intangible culture provided them with the opportunity to explore immaterial manifestations of the target culture, including healing traditions and festive events. According to Deardorff (2006), students need to be open-minded to people from other cultures to understand cross-cultural perspectives with respect in a non-judgmental way. They are encouraged to critically reflect upon cultural similarities and differences. As learners develop their cultural awareness through personal discovery and social engagement, they may reduce their ethnocentrism and show their appreciation for other cultures. The more positive the attitude shown by the students, the more developed their knowledge and skills become. To this end, CMC tasks were created to allow students to interact and collaborate with their peers to share and exchange their cross-cultural viewpoints in ways that go beyond a superficial "facts only" approach and gain cultural awareness and sensitivity to shape their own cultural values, attitudes, and beliefs (Byram, 1997).

Authentic listening and reading materials (e.g., videos, songs, commercials, short stories) were used for the exposure to comprehensible input, one of the critical elements of SLA. Output-based tasks with an emphasis on certain grammar structures were created for students to express ideas (content) and practice linguistic form (grammar). Different types of CMC tasks were created to engage students in meaning-focused L2 use. Some tasks required students to use interpersonal skills to exchange ideas with their peers, whereas others allowed them to boost their presentational skills. Moreover, learning tasks focused on the development of students' cultural competency skills. For example, Spanish food allowed students to demonstrate their knowledge of cultural products, such as *paella* (rice dish) and *sangria* (mixed drink), discuss the practices of eating typical food on holidays, and share their perspectives about Spanish cuisine and mealtimes with their peers (see the section "Research Question 2: Effects of CMC Tasks on Language and Culture Learning" for details).

With respect to daily assignments, students were responsible for completing two learning tasks using various types of digital tools. For example, beginning students posted a blog entry to describe their childhoods. Other examples of tasks and tools included the use of asynchronous CMC tools, such as *Padlet* and *Flipgrid* for students to share and exchange information about their hobbies and travel plans to a Spanish-speaking country. Upon completion of the first blog assignment, the author collected the blog addresses and posted them in *Canvas*. The author divided the class into small groups of six students who were asked to read, comment on, and respond to each other's entries. The small group size enabled team members to become quickly acquainted with each other so that they felt comfortable making contributions. To facilitate scaffolding through peer feedback, and increase interaction and collaboration among students, the author assigned one linguistically strong student to each group. Individual contributions and collaborative effort are less likely to occur without proper guidance. Thus, the author provided guidelines to the students, explaining how to carry out assigned tasks. All assignments were graded based on the quality and quantity of students' work in three major areas: (1) content and organization, (2) language use, and (3) comments and responses.

Data collection and analysis

Quantitative and qualitative data were collected to provide multiple sources of information to address the three research questions: (1) post-surveys,

(2) self-reflective blogs, (3) focus-group interviews, and (4) learning tasks. The instructor obtained permission from the students to use the data for the study.

Post-survey

The online survey created by *Google Forms* consisted of ten statements. A 5-point Likert scale ranging from 1 (*strongly disagree*) to 5 (*strongly agree*) was used to evaluate the effectiveness of technology-mediated TBI. Students indicated their level of satisfaction by ranking each statement from 1–5 (5 being the highest score). The survey was voluntarily completed by 83% of the students ($n = 20$). Statements 1–5 were used to answer the first research question concerning students' reactions to the efficacy of TBI, whereas Statements 6–8 were employed to answer the second research question about the development of language skills and cultural knowledge. Statements 9–10 were utilized to answer the third research question regarding the impact of pedagogical interventions on student engagement and performance (see Table 5.1.). It should be noted that students did not respond to the survey in the target language due to their low language proficiency levels.

Student reflections

Students wrote a reflective blog in the target language as their final assignment to make observations on the effectiveness of online task-based language learning.

TABLE 5.1 Students' reactions to online TBI

Statements of the survey	Mean	SD
1. I had a positive experience with online task-based learning.	4.15	0.61
2. Learning tasks allowed me to use the target language in a meaningful way.	4.10	0.32
3. I benefited from using four-skill integrated learning activities.	4.09	0.43
4. I found topics and learning tasks interesting and stimulating.	4.22	0.55
5. I enjoyed working and interacting with my classmates throughout the course.	4.04	0.79
6. Creating video recordings in *Flipgrid* helped me build my speaking ability.	3.99	0.84
7. Blogging helped me improve my writing skills.	4.17	0.66
8. I gained cultural knowledge and awareness through online discussions.	4.30	0.47
9. The instructor provided clear guidance on how to carry out learning activities.	4.21	0.53
10. The instructor gave constructive feedback on my assignments.	4.11	0.59

$N = 20$.

Nearly 92% of the students (*n* = 22) wrote their reflective entries using the following questions as guidance:

1. Did you find learning tasks useful for the development of your language skills and cultural knowledge? Give a brief explanation.
2. Did you find topics and assignments appealing? Why or why not?
3. Did you find peer comments and teacher feedback beneficial? Briefly explain.
4. Do you have any additional comments you would like to share?

Focus-group interviews

At the end of the semester, the instructor conducted group interviews with students from *Zoom* to secure an in-depth understanding of how online TBI affected their overall performance. Each group consisted of five to six students. Each interview lasted approximately 30 minutes and was recorded digitally for data analysis. Beginning students had limited language proficiency to express their opinions about the course in the target language. Thus, all interviews were conducted in English.

Content analysis was applied to the reflective blogs and focus-group interviews to determine factors that affected their participation and performance throughout the course. The reflective blogs were read and analyzed using an open coding procedure to identify recurring themes that emerged in the entries (Saldaña, 2009). Responses on similar topics were grouped together and incorporated into the survey results to report the findings. Data from student-generated online postings on *Blogger* and *Padlet*, and video recordings on *Flipgrid* and *Zoom* provided additional evidence to illustrate and support the findings.

Findings and discussion

Research question 1: Students' reactions to online TBI

As shown in Table 5.1., the high rating (4.15 out of 5) indicates that most students had a gratifying experience with TBI mediated by digital tools (Statement 1).

They often used words such as "fun" and "worthwhile" to describe their fulfilling experiences with TBI because they were able to use the target language for authentic communication (Statement 2). The following comments exemplify students' positive responses to TBI:

> At the beginning, I was overwhelmed by the amount of coursework, but I ended up enjoying this online course. I really liked how the assignments allowed me to use Spanish to share my personal stories with the class. I think this made online learning less boring and more exciting.

> I liked the way the course was set up focusing on using Spanish for genuine communication with real audience, not just memorizing vocabulary lists and grammar rules. Although I made mistakes, I was able to express myself and share my own experience with others. What a practical way to learn Spanish!

The comments point to the importance of using the target language for real-world communication from the beginning of instruction. As a result, more than 80% of the students ($n = 17$) acknowledged that TBI helped them build the three modes of communication (Statement 3). For example, this student shared her view about the benefits of using input-based tasks:

> I can write but I always have trouble understanding Spanish. I found podcasts most helpful to improve my listening skills. Initially, I struggled to understand what native speakers said. But after using podcasts on a regular basis, my listening comprehension got better. I was able to understand most conversations without transcripts.

This comment reveals that listening to native-speaker podcasts exposed students to authentic input, which has been found to be imperative for expanding language learners' listening comprehension (Rosell-Aguilar, 2018).

Most students ($n = 18$) found topics and tasks intriguing and engaging (Statement 4). For example, one student shared her observations about learning the target culture by watching *YouTube* videos:

> I found cultural topics and activities most interesting. I learned so much about how Spaniards celebrate Christmas from watching the videos posted in Canvas. I didn't know anything about the Christmas lottery El Gordo and the important Three Kings Day for kids; a day of gifts for them. I found them fascinating! Watching videos with subtitles also helped me remember more vocabulary and understand words in context.

The results point to the value of using real-world authentic materials for learning the target language and culture. There was a clear consensus among the students ($n = 16$) that they took pleasure in working and interacting with their peers online (Statement 5). One student made the following comment on peer interaction via *Padlet* during the final interview:

> It was a lot of fun to use Padlet to discuss different cultural topics. I was eager to share my post about Argentina football and the video about the biggest stadium in Buenos Aires with my classmates. Most of us seemed excited about reading each other's posts and responding to them. For me, the cultural exchange was the best part of the course.

Nevertheless, a few students (*n* = 4) preferred the traditional approach. One student expressed disapproval of using TBI on his reflective blog:

> I had difficulties with writing and speaking assignments. I spent too much time on homework. To be honest, I would prefer to do online exercises and take chapter exams instead of writing posts and making video recordings.

Another student echoed this view:

> I had a hard time understanding some of the assigned readings, so I was not able to respond to the instructor's prompts and share my thoughts on my blog. I think assignments should focus more on doing exercises to practice new words and grammar points.

It is apparent that the students experienced challenges with TBI. The finding suggests that teachers need to introduce TBI to students and teach them effective strategies to perform real-world tasks (Nunan, 2010).

Research question 2: Effects of CMC tasks on language and cultural learning

Overall, students were satisfied with the learning outcomes. Eighty percent of them (*n* = 16) responded favorably to the use of video recordings that helped them build their presentational and interpersonal communication (Statement 6), whereas more than 80% of the students (*n* = 17) agreed that they benefited from creating blog posts (Statement 7). Although the beginning students produced simple sentences and made linguistic errors, CMC tasks allowed them to develop language fluency and accuracy, as illustrated in the following blog post:

> El verano pasado fui a Nueva York *visitar *mi tía y mis primos. Salí temprano y manejé *para 5 horas. Cuando llegué, vi *mi prima con el perro Chip afuera. Para el almuerzo, mi tía hizo hamburguesas con queso. Después de *comiendo, mis primos y yo caminamos en *la parque y jugamos el Frisbee con Chip. [* = error or missing word]
>
> (Last year I went to New York to visit my aunt and cousins. I left early and drove for 5 hours. When I arrived, I saw my cousin with the dog Chip outside. For lunch, my aunt made cheeseburgers. After eating, my cousins and I walked in the park and played the Frisbee with Chip.)

The quotation demonstrates the student's ability to convey ideas with grammatical accuracy in the past tense verbs and his understanding of the meaning-form relationship for effective communication (Ellis, 2016).

Remarkedly, more than 85% of the students ($n = 18$) found social engagement on *Padlet* and *Zoom* valuable to develop their cultural knowledge and awareness (Statement 8). The findings indicate that online discussions afforded students the opportunity to exchange cultural perspectives with their peers, as shown in the following real-time exchange about Spanish eating customs (translated to English):

S1: I like the Spanish Mediterranean diet shown in the video. Spaniards don't eat fast food. They have a healthy lifestyle. I think we eat too much fast food like pizza, burgers, and fries. The rice dish called "paella" with seafood looks delicious.

S2: I don't like seafood. I'm a vegetarian. I eat cheese and eggs. I don't understand why Spaniards eat dinner so late. I am usually hungry by 6:00 p.m. I eat a big dinner.

S3: Because lunch is the biggest meal of the day. In Spain, people eat lunch around 2:00. They spend a few hours eating and chatting with the family. The also take a nap called "siesta" after lunch. I found it interesting.

S1: In Spain, it's important to eat and spend time with the family. Do you eat lunch or dinner with your family?

S3: I'm from New Jersey. I don't see my family very often when I'm in school. I'm busy because I also work. I think we work too much and don't spend enough time with families.

S2: I agree. I only see my family on holidays like Christmas. We usually have dinner together. My mom makes the best pasta with alfredo sauce. I like how Spaniards take time from work to eat lunch with their families.

S3: I didn't know Spaniards take a nap during the day. It's strange to me. I think I'll get a headache if I take a nap, hahaha…

These beginning-level students' reflections indicate that they engaged in a meaningful conversation that required them to go beyond their traditional role as responder to the instructor's questions. The students shared their perspectives about Spanish food culture through social interaction, which enhanced their interpersonal skills, one of the American Council on the Teaching of Foreign Languages (ACTFL, 2011) three modes of communication. Additionally, unstructured tasks using open-ended questions gave students the freedom to explore both tangible (e.g., food, holidays) and intangible (lifestyles of everyday people) cultures. Students expressed their interest in the target culture by asking follow-up questions, such as "Do you eat lunch or dinner with your family?" Most importantly, the exchange raised students' awareness of cultural norms and practices and exhibited their skills to interpret and discover cultural differences; one of the objectives of intercultural competence defined by Byram (1997).

A closer look at the data reveals that students made use of visual communication by adding photos and videos to enhance content sharing and social engagement. It appears that students found multimodal elements of digital platforms useful for them to create and share content with their peers as this student observes:

> I enjoyed sharing photos of my family and friends on my blog. I think it added a personal touch when communicating with a broad audience. I remember that one of my classmates made a brief video about his neighborhood. It made the content more appealing to your viewers, and easier for them to join the conversation.

This echoes the finding from previous studies reporting that students benefited from using multimodal formats (e.g., text, audio, video) to express meaning and interact with others (Lee, 2019). The study implies that engaging students in multimodal learning takes into account different learning styles and preferences to meet their individual needs.

Research question 3: Impact of instructional interventions on student engagement and performance

As shown in Table 5.1., most students ($n = 17$) valued the instructor's intervention by monitoring their learning progress throughout the course (Statement 9). The comments gathered from the reflective blogs attest to the students' approval of the instructor's presence that kept them from falling behind with the coursework and created a supportive online learning environment. For example, the following student praised the guidance given by the instructor:

> The instructor often reminded us of upcoming assignments and encouraged us to post questions. I think using questions was a great way for us to engage in discussions and respond to each other's comments. In addition, the instructor always responded to my questions in a timely fashion and offered extra help.

Similarly, one student underscored the effective modeling strategy along with prompts provided by the instructor to guide him to complete learning tasks:

> The instructor's modeling helped me understand what was expected and gave me clear directions to undertake each assignment. I also liked how each assignment was guided by specific prompts. I used them to organize my thoughts before making posts and video recordings. I found them very helpful.

These comments are in line with the findings of Lee's (2016) study regarding the positive impact of the instructor's intervention on students' learning performance.

When students rated their views about the effect of linguistic scaffolding, most respondents (*n* = 17) found the instructor's feedback useful and beneficial to build their language accuracy (Statement 10). One student explained the following during the final interview:

> I don't think I was able to correct my own mistakes on the blog without the instructor's constructive feedback. I found the grammar explanations clear and easy to understand. I know I made less mistakes and improved my writing skills by the end of the course.

Through expert scaffolding, students gained a better understanding of certain grammar points, as exhibited in the following real-time discussion regarding the usage of the present subjunctive:

STUDENT: I noticed that I made quite a few mistakes with the subjunctive. Can we go over them? I can share my screen from my phone.
TEACHER: O.K. Let's take a quick look at your blog. The first verb "tienen" in the third sentence "No creo que las mujeres tienen derecho …" (I don't believe that the women have right …) should be in the subjunctive because it conveys a feeling of doubt.
STUDENT: Ah, yes. I remember now. Should I change it to "tengan"?
TEACHER: Correct. How about the last sentence "No quiero que los niños sufren …" (I don't want the children to suffer …)?
STUDENT: Is "quiero" one of the verbs that involve desire or need? If so, I need to change the verb from "sufren" to "sufran."
TEACHER: Excellent. You may want to review pp. 341–343 and watch the grammar tutorial video again. Keep in mind that the subjunctive is used when you want to express something you want someone else to do. For example, the sentence "Ojalá que vengas a verme esta noche" (I hope that you come to see me tonight) indicates one's wish.
STUDENT: I think I understand it better now. Thank you!

The example shows that the instructor's scaffolding through collaborative dialogue enhanced the student's knowledge of a complex grammar point. As Lee (2019) argues, novice learners with basic language proficiency are not equipped to make error corrections. Thus, expert intervention through the focus-on-form procedure plays a key role in drawing learners' attention to linguistic features while focusing on meaning making.

Limitations and future research

Many more studies are still needed to fully understand the role of TBI mediated by digital technology and its impact on the development of adult novice students' language skills and cultural knowledge. Course design and content chosen by one single instructor cannot be representative of the multitude of online TBI settings available. The study recognizes the small sample size and the short duration of a five-week summer session. Future research would need to look at increasing the size, as well as the course length to determine whether the technology-enhanced TBI affects how beginning language students individually and collaboratively work in virtual learning environments. The study included only post-surveys. A future study using the pre- and post-surveys together with a larger sample will contribute to a better understanding of the impact of TBI on fully online elementary language courses. Moreover, the population of this study only involved beginning learners whose primary goal was to complete the institution's foreign language requirement. Additional studies are needed to understand how TBI affects the performance of students from different language proficiency levels in a fully online learning setting. Finally, it would be worthwhile to explore how online peer feedback affects social interaction and collaborative engagement with a focus on form and error correction.

Classroom implications

Although limited due to the sample size and duration, this study addresses a gap in the existing research on fully online courses at the introductory level and points to important pedagogical implications. Firstly, learning tasks related to real-life scenarios enable beginning students to use L2 actively and meaningfully to engage in interactive and collaborative online learning. Both input and output-based tasks allow for exposure to the target language, negotiation of meaning, and production of L2 that are necessary for SLA. Secondly, the combined modes of synchronous (e.g., *Zoom*) and asynchronous (e.g., *Padlet*) digital platforms prove to be effective to facilitate TBI and enhance task performance in L2. Thirdly, tasks rely on the use of linguistic and metacognitive skills. Adult novice learners with limited language proficiency may experience difficulties expressing meaning. Thus, teacher intervention through modeling and prompting provides beginning students with clear directions to perform a task. Fourthly, the instructor's linguistic scaffolding through corrective feedback plays a facilitative role in bringing students' attention to focus on form, which enhances beginning learners' language development. Finally, topic-based tasks using authentic materials along with open-ended questions provide beginning students with an excellent avenue to explore cultural products, practices, and perspectives through interactive online discussions.

Conclusion

Lee (2016) observes that securing sufficient time for content creation and peer interaction and providing proper guidance to students throughout the learning process are essential for a fruitful experience with online TBI. As illustrated throughout this chapter, the four-skill-integrated tasks mediated by digital platforms were pedagogically effective and appropriate for beginning students to interact with their peers to engage with and share culturally meaningful content in order to develop three modes of communication and their cultural competence. Thus, L2 educators are strongly encouraged to take full advantage of and integrate widely available technologies into TBI to promote student-centered learning within a socially bounded learning environment. Although TBI for fully online language courses can be challenging for beginning postsecondary students who are used to the teacher-led approach to L2 learning, this study serves as a practical application of how language educators can create communicative learning tasks, choose appropriate digital tools, and design pedagogical interventions that engage students in the process of online language learning.

Notes

1 Cognitive-interactionist approach views language learning as an individual cognitive effort. Learning occurs when internal (cognitive capacity) and external (environmental elements) factors reciprocally interact. Ortega (2009) suggests that comprehensible input, negotiated meaning, pushed output and noticing as "environmental ingredients" contribute to optimal L2 learning.
2 Sociocultural approach stems from Vygotsky's ideas of the co-construction of knowledge through social interaction and collaboration with others. During the collaboration, the learner develops cognitive skills and advances their knowledge by the assistance of an expert or a more capable peer.
3 According to Robinson (2003), the cognitive hypothesis of task-based language learning proposes that increased task complexity influences the quality of language production. When tasks are cognitively and functionally demanding, learners are required to produce more complex and accurate language output.

References

Ahmadian, M. J., & Mayo, M. D. P. G. (Eds.). (2018). *Recent perspectives on task-based language learning and teaching*. De Gruyter Mouton.
Allen, H. W., & Gamalinda, S. (2021). Making podcasts in the collegiate French writing course. *CALICO Journal, 38*(1), 1–16.
American Council on the Teaching of Foreign Languages. (2011). *21st century skills map: World languages. Partnership for 21st century skills*. https://eric.ed.gov/?id=ED519498
Amores, M., Suárez-García, J. L., & Wendel, A. (2014). *Experience Spanish*. McGraw-Hill Education.
Bygate, M., Skehan, P., & Swain, M. (Eds). (2001). *Researching pedagogical tasks: Second language learning, teaching, and assessment*. Pearson.
Byram, M. (1997). *Teaching and assessing intercultural communicative competence*. Multilingual Matters.
Chong, S. W., & Reinders, H. (2020). Technology-mediated task-based language teaching: A qualitative research synthesis. *Language Learning & Technology, 24*(3), 70–86.

Cutshall, S. (2012). More than a decade of standards: Integrating "cultures" in your language instruction. *The Language Educator*, 7(2), 32–37. https://www.actfl.org/sites/default/files/publications/standards/Cultures.pdf

Deardorff, D. K. (2006). Identification and assessment of intercultural competence as a student outcome of internationalization. *Journal of Studies in International Education*, 10(3), 241–266.

Ellis, R. (2003). *Task-based language learning and teaching*. Oxford University Press.

Ellis, R. (2016). Focus on form: A critical review. *Language Teaching Research*, 20, 205–428.

Ellis, R. (2017a). Position paper: Moving task-based language teaching forward. *Language Teaching*, 50(4), 507–526.

Ellis, R. (2017b). Task-based language teaching. In S. Loewen, & M. Sato (Eds.), *The Routledge handbook of instructed second language acquisition* (pp. 108–125). Routledge.

Erlam, R. (2019). Input-based tasks in the French language classroom. In M. Zhisheng, & J. A. Mohammad (Eds.), *Research L2 task performance and pedagogy in honour of Peter Skehan* (pp. 229–251). John Benjamins.

Farr, F., & Murray, L. (Eds.). (2016). *Routledge handbook of language learning and technology*. Routledge.

Fouz-González, J. (2020). Using apps for pronunciation training: An empirical evaluation of the English file pronunciation app. *Language Learning & Technology*, 24(1), 62–85.

Fu, T., & Nassaji, H. (2016). Corrective feedback, learner uptake, and feedback perception in a Chinese as a foreign language classroom. *Studies in Second Language Learning and Teaching*, VI(1), 159–181.

González-Lloret, M. (2016). *A practical guide to integrating technology into task-based language teaching*. Georgetown University Press.

Hampel, R. (2010). Task design for a virtual learning environment in a distance language course. In M. Thomas, & H. Reinders (Eds.), *Task-based language learning and teaching with technology* (pp. 131–153). Continuum.

Lee, L. (2002). Enhancing learners' communication skills through synchronous electronic interaction and task-based instruction. *Foreign Language Annals*, 35(1), 16–23.

Lee, L. (2011). Focus on form through peer feedback in a Spanish–American telecollaborative exchange. *Language Awareness*, 20(4), 343–357.

Lee, L. (2016). Autonomous learning through task-based instruction in fully online language courses. *Language Learning & Technology*, 20(2), 81–97.

Lee, L. (2017). Learners' perceptions of the effectiveness of blogging for L2 writing in fully online language courses. *International Journal of Computer-Assisted Language Learning and Teaching*, 7(1), 20–34.

Lee, L. (2018). Using telecollaboration 2.0 to build intercultural communicative competence: A Spanish–American exchange. In D. Tafazoli, E. G. Parra, & C. A. H. Abril (Eds.), *Cross-cultural perspectives on technology-enhanced language learning* (pp. 303–321). IGI Global.

Lee, L. (2019). An exploratory study of using personal blogs for L2 writing in fully online language courses. In B. Zou, & M. Thomas (Eds.), *Recent developments in technology-enhanced and computer-assisted language learning* (pp. 145–163). IGI Global.

Lee, L., & Markey, A. (2014). A study of learners' perceptions of online intercultural exchange through Web 2.0 technologies. *ReCALL*, 26(3), 1–20.

Littlewood, W. (2007). Communicative and task-based language teaching in East Asian classrooms. *Language Teaching*, 40, 243–249.

Long, M. (2015). *Second language acquisition and task-based language teaching*. Wiley Blackwell.

Luo, H., & Yang, C. (2018). Twenty years of telecollaborative practice: Implications of teaching Chinese as a foreign language. *Computer Assisted Language Learning*, *31*(5–6), 546–571.

Nunan, D. (2010). A task-based approach to materials development. *Advances in Language and Literacy Studies*, *1*(2), 135–160.

O'Dowd, R., & Lewis, T. (2016). *Online intercultural exchange*. Routledge.

Ortega, L. (2009). *Understanding second language acquisition*. Hodder.

Reinhardt, J., & Thorne, S. (2019). Digital literacies as emergent multifarious repertoires. In N. Arnold, & L. Ducate (Eds.), *Engaging language learners in CALL: From theory and research to informed practice* (pp. 208–239). Equinox.

Richards, J. C., & Rodgers, T. S. (2001). *Approaches and methods in language teaching*. Cambridge University Press.

Robinson, P. (2003). The cognitive hypothesis, task design, and adult task-based language learning. *Second Language Studies*, *21*(2), 45–105.

Robinson, P. (2011). Task-based language learning: A review of issues. *Language Learning*, *61*(S1), 1–36.

Rosell-Aguilar, F. (2018). Autonomous language learning through a mobile application: A user evaluation of the *busuu* app. *Computer Assisted Language Learning*, *31*(8), 854–881.

Saldaña, J. (2009). *The coding manual for qualitative researchers*. SAGE.

Samuda, V., & Bygate, M. (2008). *Tasks in second language learning*. Palgrave Macmillan.

Shehadeh, A., & Coombe, C. A. (2012). *Task-based language teaching in foreign language context: Research and implementation*. John Benjamins.

The National Standards Collaborative Board. (2015). *World-readiness standards for learning languages* (4th ed.). Alexandria, Virginia: National Standards in Foreign Language Education Project.

Thomas, M., & Reinders, H. (Eds.). (2010). *Task-based language learning and teaching with technology*. Continuum.

Ziegler, N. (2016). Taking technology to task: Technology-mediated TBLT, performance, and production. *Annual Review of Applied Linguistics*, 36, 136–163.

PART II
Teaching intercultural competence

6
INTEGRATING CULTURE IN LANGUAGE CURRICULUM FROM BEGINNING TO INTERMEDIATE LEVEL IN A BLENDED LEARNING ENVIRONMENT

A design-based empirical study

Shenglan Zhang

Language, the expression, embodiment, and symbol of cultural reality (Kramsch, 1998) is inextricably bound to culture. People use words to express facts, ideas, or events against "a stock of knowledge about the world that other people share" (p. 3). Language conveys meanings through different words, tones of voice, accents, conversational styles, gestures, and facial expressions. Furthermore, an individual's social identity is developed through their language. The profound bond between language and culture dictates that target culture (TC) should be learned along with its language from the onset of instruction. (Byram, 2014; Byram et al., 1991; Chastain, 1988). Seelye (1974) pointed out as early as the 1970s that "culture must be taught during the first two years of foreign language study" (p. 3) and that "whatever can be taught in the target language should be taught in the target language. [...] When this is not realistic, do it in English" (p. 6).

Even though instructors realize the importance of incorporating culture into language instruction from the outset of language learning (Byram et al., 1991; Newton et al., 2010), culture is neglected in many classroom settings (Lázár, 2011). One reason may be that some teachers tend to follow the old "skill before content" approach (Lázár, 2011), in which a grammatical syllabus draws students' attention to linguistic accuracy and ignores the learners' cultural awareness or development of intercultural communicative competence. Furthermore, some teachers seem to lack time to incorporate cultural learning in the classroom or after class (Yang & Chen, 2016). Many novice teachers, even though they are culturally conscious and devoted, are "often too preoccupied by their own developing teacher personality to have the time and energy to incorporate the cultural dimension in language teaching" (Lázár, 2011, p. 125). In addition, there is a shortage of appropriate resources and techniques for teaching TC in the classroom setting (Arikan, 2011). Culture, as Vahdany (2005) says, "has always been touched but not hugged dearly enough: its relevance and contribution to language teaching has grown blurred and mystic" (p. 93). The issue is exacerbated by a lack of adequate materials for teaching culture and culturally appropriate interactional skills. While concrete vocabulary and grammar points can be easily explained and practiced, the fluidity and impalpability of culture present a challenge for classroom instruction.

Many models and approaches to culture learning and teaching – such as using authentic materials (e.g., Kozhevnikova, 2014), study abroad (Schwieter et al., 2018), field trips (Alcânatara, 2016), watching videos (e.g., Desai et al., 2018), etc. – have been proposed and tested (Fu, 2018; Jiang, 2011; Knouse & Abreu, 2016; Oakley et al., 2018; Sun, 2013; Wang & Crooks, 2015). However, empirical studies of culture learning in classroom settings at the curriculum level (Byram, 2014), that is, beyond a single language course, are scarce. The purpose of this two-year study is to investigate the effectiveness of an approach that integrates culture learning into a curriculum for beginner- to intermediate-level Chinese-as-a-foreign-language (CFL) classes in a blended learning environment. The approach, called Culture Learning in a Blended Classroom (CLBC), was designed to address the lack of time for culture teaching in the face-to-face (FTF) classroom while considering students' TC acceptance level and their learning environment, the available resources, and the social context.

Literature review

Different ways of teaching culture have been proposed, but no research has been done on integrating culture into the curriculum in a blended learning environment. Some popular methods for teaching culture focus on using computer-mediated communication technology (CMC) to facilitate exchanges between foreign language learners and native speakers to enhance cultural learning (e.g., Angelova & Zhao, 2014; Schenker, 2013; Zhang, 2016). Specifically, Angelova and Zhao (2014) used discussion boards and the email function in *Blackboard* to connect teacher education students in the United States with first-year English learners in China to provide grammar tutoring and culture learning. They found that the CMC project not only improved American students' teaching skills through tutoring non-native speakers of English but also developed their cross-cultural awareness.

Schenker (2013) studied a college-level third-year German class in the United States and an advanced English high school class in Germany that spent 12 weeks in electronic communication using emails, blogs, videoconferences, and class essays. Her results show students' high interest in learning about culture both before and after the project, confirming that telecollaboration can be an effective tool for cultural instruction. Zhang (2016) used *Skype* and *WeChat* to connect beginning-level CFL learners in the United States with advanced English learners in China. The CFL students chose a cultural topic, interviewed Chinese students about it, and presented their findings in class. This tandem project increased CFL learners' understanding of Chinese culture and their interest in learning the language. Similarly, Jiang (2011) shared trial results of using a web-based platform for intercultural dialogue called the "China-USA Business Café." The Café, which featured a series of online interactive tasks designed to teach culture to Chinese and American business students, proved to be highly effective. Oakley et al. (2018) explored the use of a digital story exchange between middle school students in Australia and China in support of language learning and intercultural understanding. Their study focused on the opinions of the participating instructors who reported that the cultural exchange activity improved their students' language skills and intercultural understanding.

Literature also describes the role of authentic materials, behavior culture, and ethnographic methods in teaching culture. For example, Brown (2010) studied the use of authentic target language (TL) films in a freshman English as a foreign language (EFL) classroom to teach cultural vocabulary and expressions. She found that sufficient time for information processing and repeated exposure to authentic cultural expressions solidify the culture learning. Fu (2018) introduced a lesson for a Chinese for Medical Professions language course that utilized real-life, doctor-patient conversations. Students developed cultural awareness by exploring the sociocultural significance of communicative behavior as well as various ways in which doctors obtain patient information. Qin (2013) taught behavior culture in a CFL classroom and found that when students spoke the TL, their behaviors were more culturally appropriate and in better accord with the rules and norms of the TC. Robinson-Stuart and Nocon (1996) examined the effects of an ethnographic approach on promoting positive attitudes toward TL speakers and found that the learners' attitudes toward the study of Spanish improved after using the approach. The ethnographic approach adopts ethnographic interviews in teaching TC; an interviewer asks the interviewee "deliberately open" questions and "continually listen[s] to and interact[s] with what the speaker has said" (p. 436). The ethnographic approach allows students to interact with representatives of the TC in a less formal setting, which increases students' awareness "of the process of culture in very real ways" (p. 436).

To solve the problem of insufficient time for cultural instruction in the classroom, Zhang (2019) designed and examined an approach to teaching culture to beginning-level foreign language learners in a blended learning environment. Using edited authentic materials and ethnographic interviews, her methodology effectively enabled learners to learn TC primarily through out-of-class work. As more empirically tested methods are needed to explore systematic ways of integrating culture teaching and learning in a blended learning environment, this chapter examines the effectiveness of a five-step approach on improving learners' TC acceptance level, interest in language learning, and their cultural awareness. Student perceptions of the approach regarding the in- and out-of-class time devoted to cultural learning are also surveyed.

Definition of culture and the CLBC conceptual framework

Starting from the 1970s, scholars began to pay attention to the importance of culture in language teaching (Nostrand, 1974). Culture, as defined by the National Center for Cultural Competence (2021), refers to an

> integrated pattern of human behavior that includes thoughts, communications, languages, practices, beliefs, values, customs, courtesies, rituals, manners of interacting and roles, relationships and expected behaviors of a racial, ethnic, religious or social group; and the ability to transmit the above to succeeding generations.
>
> *(Goode et al., 2000, p. 1)*

Culture is an integral part of language (Byram, 1997; Keesing, 1994; Kramsch, 1993); in fact, the realization of the importance of language produced a broader definition of culture because, as Keesing (1994) stated,

> it is not that "cultural studies" are preoccupied only with paintings, statues and symphonies: an increasing engagement with language and semiotic theory has led to a considerable broadening of the old concept of "culture" as high art, a broadening in an anthropological direction.
>
> *(p. 49)*

Culture is often categorized into a "Big C" culture and "little c" culture (Halverson, 1985). The former refers to the most overt cultural forms such as architecture, holidays, literature, and food (Brooks, 1968) that would be discovered first when learning about a new community and need minimal instruction to learn. The latter, in contrast, is less visible. It involves the patterns of living and everyday behavior of the TL community, such as cultural norms, communication styles, and verbal and nonverbal language symbols, which are challenging for beginning language students to notice and understand.

The integration of culture into language learning is closely tied to the nature of learning. The CLBC approach is grounded in the constructivist theory of learning, which recognizes that students actively construct new knowledge through their personal experience and through the interaction of prior knowledge and new events (Vygotsky, 1962, 1971). A constructivist classroom emphasizes student-centered learning with the instructor providing scaffolding, or systematic support, by incorporating students' prior experiences and knowledge into the development of new skills (Wood et al., 1976). As students master the skills, they enter the Zone of Proximal Development (ZPD), which describes the difference between what they can do with or without the teacher's support. The constructivist instructor leads her students through ZPD by modeling skills, providing clues, and developing learning activities appropriate for their proficiency level (Oliver, 2000). In developing the CLBC approach for the beginning- to intermediate-level learners, the author was guided by the belief that students' prior cultural knowledge should be considered, and that learning is primarily a social activity (Dewey, 1963) that includes social interactive opportunities. Interacting with other people, particularly the TC bearers, allows students to improve their communitive skills, develop the TL, and learn about its culture. Following Kramsch's (1993) proposal that foreign language teachers should consider crossing interdisciplinary boundaries to identify effective ways for students to learn culture, the CLBC approach adopted ethnographic interviews – a well-established research method in social and linguistic anthropology – as a cultural learning tool. Ethnographic interviews feature immersive observation and structured, one-on-one interviews, and complement the cultural learning process in the classroom (Byram, 1997).

CLBC considerations

The CLBC design considers the students' learning environment and their TC acceptance level. The adoption of the blended learning model allowed for the movement of most of the cultural instruction online, thus solving the problem of insufficient time for cultural instruction. While students engage in cultural activities outside of class, the regular class meetings are devoted to speaking and writing practice, which requires human interaction. Research shows that blended learning improves pedagogy while increasing access and flexibility of learning (Graham, 2006; Thomas & Brown, 2011; Zhang & Jaramillo, 2021). At the time the CLBC approach was implemented, the university strongly encouraged blended learning, so students were familiar with this instructional mode. In addition, the relatively large and diverse community of the college town made it easy to connect students with TC bearers for their cultural activities.

To implement CLBC, the instructor needs to recognize their learners' individual language and culture learning processes. The majority of students in this study were from the American Midwest. While they were curious and motivated to learn the Chinese language and culture, their linguistic knowledge was minimal, while cultural knowledge was derived mainly from mass media. As novice learners challenged by Chinese tones and characters, they were already fully loaded cognitively by a new language, so overwhelming them with a large amount of new cultural information during the FTF class meetings seemed counterproductive. Conveying certain cultural activities to an out-of-classroom mode provided the necessary balance of linguistic and cultural instruction.

CLBC principles

Based on the understanding of "Big C" and "little c" culture and striving to increase efficiency of learning, the CLBC approach follows three principles.

First, students should be familiarized with the more perceptible "Big C" culture elements before moving to the more subtle and abstract "little c" culture. Second, cultural learning should start within a small community (class and campus), subsequently extending to a larger and more authentic TC community (e.g., the Chinese community in the campus town or another city). The understanding of basic TC facts and fundamental social and cultural conventions should precede learners' full engagement in the community (Chapelle, 2016; Kinginger, 2008; Ware & Kramsch, 2005). Thus, after becoming familiar with and discussing and reflecting on some "Big C" cultural elements with the teacher and their peers, students are ready to experience a broader TC context to observe and to interact. Becoming acquainted with certain aspects of TC strengthens learners' confidence, supplies topics for interaction with TL native speakers on campus, and provides points of attention for future cultural learning through genuine social interaction in a larger, authentic TL community (Kramsch, 1993).

The third principle assumes that culture learning should develop from being receptive to being interactive – from receiving information through multimedia materials to interacting with people in real life. The learners who begin by primarily receiving information progress to conducting cultural research on their own move to examining peoples' behaviors through multimedia resources, then advance to interacting with TC bearers, and finally deepen their understanding of Chinese culture by observing an authentic community.

Five steps of the CLBC approach

Based on the aforementioned principles, the five-step approach was designed to provide students with a basic but solid mastery of both the "Big C" and "little c" culture. Within the approach, the teacher gradually changes their role from "sage on the stage" to "guide by the side" (King, 1993) to promote active and meaningful learning. The process of completing the five steps enables students to explore culture individually in the classroom, online in groups, on campus with TL native speakers, and in an authentic TC community. While it is important to follow the sequence of the steps, the amount of time devoted to each step is flexible.

Step 1: Learning from instructor-made videos

The first step is for beginning-level learners who have just started learning Chinese. Each week of the semester, students are required to closely watch one short (two to three minutes long) teacher-created video clip explaining critical cultural information. The videos are recorded in English, occasionally using familiar words and expressions in the TL, and incorporate text, animations, images, and graphs related to the themes of the learning units. The themes of the video clips were selected according to American Council on the Teaching of Foreign Languages (ACTFL) proficiency guidelines (ACTFL, 2012) for beginning-level students and include greetings, names, numbers, holidays, ages, calendar, birthdays, pastimes, privacy, calligraphy, colors, family, education, and religion. Each video contains information about the basic cultural facts. For example, the video about greetings shows how to greet others of different familiarity and seniority in various social contexts; the names clip explains how parents name their children and how people address each other in different social situations. Students should be prepared to answer true/false questions about the clips in quizzes and exams.

Step 2: Exploring culture in small groups

Step two continues cultural learning for beginning students. After they gain familiarity with the basic elements of TC from the instructor-made videos, they are required to research one of the topics of personal interest in a group. Throughout the semester, the group needs to agree on one cultural topic, research it outside of the classroom using on- and off-line resources, prepare a ten-minute presentation about the topic, and present it in class; students can choose from but are not restricted to the topics covered in the videos. The deliverables for this assignment include a group PowerPoint document and students' oral presentation on the cultural topic. Both can be in English or in the TL and must meet the following criteria: The PowerPoint document must have a title and at least four content slides, logically connected to one another and featuring texts and supporting images, animations, or graphs organized in a visually appealing way. The oral presentation should include a description of the cultural facts and phenomena and the critical analysis of the historical reasons for these norms and the current practices. The oral presentations take place in person.

Step 3: Watching instructor-edited movie clips, answering questions, and discussing online

Students who have accomplished the first two steps and progress to the second or third semester of learning (intermediate-low proficiency) complete the third step outside of class individually or in groups by watching three instructor-edited movie clips. The chosen movie scenes demonstrate the Chinese traditions of dinner etiquette, of being a guest, and the common theme of familial love in contexts (e.g., *Eat, Drink, Man, Woman* by Ang Lee). The total length of the three clips is less than six minutes. To help illustrate the culture presented in video clips, the instructor edited the scenes by adding notes providing a brief background of the story, the literal English translation of the main characters' Chinese speech, and an explanation of why they said it.

Throughout the semester, students need to watch the video clips, answer questions in writing, and participate in an online discussion and a brief large group question-and-answer (Q&A) session. The writing questions raise students' awareness of special cultural points, e.g., What is the setting for this micro-movie, rural China or a big city in China? How did the young mother and the daughter address the older woman? or What do people in your culture say when they need to interrupt the conversation and leave? After submitting their answers, students work in groups of five or six people of different genders and cultural backgrounds in an online forum in *Blackboard Learn*, the university learning management system. Using a new set of questions, students discuss the movie clips in English or in the TL, focusing on the similarities and differences between their own and the TL culture. While video watching, question answering, and group discussions happen outside of the classroom, a short final whole-class Q&A discussion of the movie clips occurs in person to clarify any confusion the students might have.

Step 4: Conducting an ethnographic interview with native speakers from the TC

This step can be accomplished in the third or fourth semester after the students finished step 3 but before step 5. The ethnographic interview involves interacting with TC bearers on an individual basis; it is an appropriate activity for intermediate-low proficiency learners who have gained familiarity with the TC in Steps 1 and 2 and observed and reflected on some daily life behaviors in step 3.

Before the ethnographic interview project was assigned, the instructor gave a ten-minute, in-person mini-lecture explaining the concept and the procedure of ethnographic interviews and provided an example of an interview as described in Robinson-Stuart and Nocon (1996). Students were given the time line, the instructions for completing the interview, and the requirements for the deliverables, which included an interview report and a reflection paper on the interview project in English or in Chinese. The entire step took place outside of the classroom.

Step 5: Reaching out and exploring the language and culture in community

The more open-ended final step is suitable for intermediate-level learners who have studied Chinese for at least two or three semesters. It includes the TC community experience similar – on a small scale – to being surrounded by the TC in a study abroad program.

Students are encouraged to explore the target language, culture, and people of their local communities by perusing a public library, local Chinese restaurants, and Chinese schools to find texts in the TL, as well as TC events, businesses, or social gatherings. For example, they can photograph a text that includes Chinese signs, characters, sentences and consider what the text means, how it is used in specific social and cultural settings, how this usage is different from or similar to their own culture, who the text audiences are, and how the intended audiences might react to the text. Students are also encouraged to observe the interactions of TC bearers with each other, their relationships, and other noticeable details of their behavior. The final deliverables are a two- to four-minute student-made video and a reflection paper in English or in Chinese.

Reflection, an important form of personal response to new information, situations, experiences, and events, is used in both steps 4 and 5 when the students receive an opportunity to interact with the real people and the community of the culture. The value of reflection for the "processing" phase of thinking and learning has been repeatedly highlighted by research (Bartimote-Afflick et al., 2016; Chen et al., 2017).

The study

This study intended to test the feasibility of the CLBC approach to integrating culture learning in the blended beginning and intermediate curriculum by answering the following questions:

1. What are students' perceptions of the approach and their views on the amount of time spent learning culture outside the classroom?
2. Does the approach increase students' cultural awareness and interest in learning the Chinese language and improve attitudes toward the Chinese-speaking community?

Methodology

This longitudinal study adopted a design-based research (DBR) method to investigate learners' perceptions of the CLBC approach during the two years of its implementation. Both quantitative and qualitative data were collected and analyzed to explore the impact of the approach on students' cultural awareness, their attitudes toward the TC community, and their interest in language learning. DBR has been described as systematic and flexible in improving teaching practice (Amiel & Reeves, 2008; Wang & Hannafin, 2005); it has the potential to (1) develop domain-specific learning; (2) discover the means intended to support that learning, and (3) bridge the gap between educational theory and practice (Bakker & Van Eerde, 2015; Wang & Hannafin, 2005). In DBR, reusable design principles are generated that others can use in practice in the future (Plomp, 2013).

Participants

A total of 43 students in four classes at a large Midwestern university in the US participated in the study over a period of two years. The first two steps were completed in their first year of study, steps 3 and 4 in the third, and step 5 in the fourth semester of the second year. Because the implementation of the entire approach took two years, seven students experienced the five steps consecutively in two years of their Chinese study. Four students experienced the last four steps without participating in the first step of the approach. Twenty-one students completed the first one, two, or three steps, and only 11 completed the last step. Sixty percent were male and 40% were female. They came from various majors, including engineering, mathematics, chemistry, linguistics, animal sciences, political science, global resources, and criminology. About 88% of the participants speak English as their native language, and 12% have a different native language including Khmer, Korean, Malay, Thai, and Vietnamese.

Data collection and analysis

After each step, the instructor administered a short survey asking for students' opinions about the step and their estimate of the amount of time they spent on the step activities outside the classroom. At the end of the two years, i.e., after the five steps were completed, a questionnaire was administered to a total of 22 students, some of whom completed all five steps, some who completed the last four steps, and some who experienced only the last step. The questionnaire consisted of yes/no, open-ended, and Likert-type questions that addressed: (1) the steps of the approach they had completed, (2) their opinion of the approach, (3) their views on the order of the steps if they had experienced more than one step, (4) the key points they learned, and (5) the impact of the approach on their cultural awareness, their attitudes, and their interest in learning the TL. In addition to the surveys and the questionnaire, students' reflection papers for the last two steps were also used as data.

The Likert-scale items in the questionnaire were analyzed using descriptive statistics. Drawing on grounded theory, the answers to the open-ended questions and the reflection papers were examined using the open-and-axial coding approach to label and categorize the data (Corbin & Strauss, 2015). The grounded theory research method focuses on forming a theory based on gathered data, which reduces the likelihood of researcher bias and assures that the theory is grounded in the data. After extracting the key points from the reflection papers, the data from the open-ended questions were sorted. Emerging thematic patterns in the survey and questionnaire were identified and categorized. The initial categorization was revisited and re-evaluated for a second time before the final data analysis.

Results and discussion

Time spent inside and outside the classroom

The activities involved in the five steps mostly happened outside of the classroom. The total reported amount of time spent FTF across the two years was two hours and 25 minutes, while the amount of time spent outside of class was about 20 hours and 36 minutes. The contrast of time spent in and outside of the classroom can be seen in each step: students spent 0.5 hour outside classroom and 5 minutes FTF watching videos (step 1), 4 hours outside classroom and 1.3 hours FTF on group research/presentation (step 2), 4.5 hours outside classroom and 30 minutes FTF watching and discussion edited movie clips and answering questions (step 3), 4.5 hours on ethnographic interview outside classroom only (step 4), and 7 hours outside classroom and 1.5 hours FTF reaching out to the community (step 5).

Eighty-six percent of the participants liked the fact that most of the culture learning activities happened outside of the classroom because it allowed them to study at their own pace, to "use class time for speaking", and gave them "more freedom to complete it." Another reason for students' appreciation of the out-of-class learning was that "each person can explore different things, and when we share it, we can learn stuff you didn't know." Some students liked it because "it allows you to be more independent," and "it makes it more personal." In short, studying culture outside of class appealed to learners because of the increased degree of control and personalization of their learning.

Students' perception of the CLBC approach

When asked what they learned through the culture learning activities, students reported that they explored a variety of topics far beyond those covered in step 1 and step 3 videos, e.g., Chinese medicine, the Lunar New Year, snacks Chinese people like, the phrase "wearing a green hat" (meaning that a woman cheats on her spouse), dining etiquette, traditional art, Chinatown in Chicago, Chinese restaurants in America and in China, Chinese censorship, campus life, parenting, education, dating, weddings and marriage, gift-giving etiquette, rural and urban life, the housing problem, hospitality toward guests, habits in praising people, unacceptable social customs. Students also reported that they discovered different ways of culture learning, such as interviewing TL speakers, going into the local TC community, and doing research online and indicated their increased awareness of the different cultures around them.

When asked to rate all the means of introducing them to Chinese culture in the steps they had experienced from 1 (least positive) to 10 (most positive), the average rating of 22 students who had completed only step 5 was 8.25. However, the average rating of the seven students who finished all five steps was 9.14 (Figure 6.1).

The high rankings for the CLBC approach could be explained by the following: (1) the topics were varied, new, interesting, and challenging; (2) the formats were diverse, engaging, and flexible; (3) in steps 4 and 5, some students enjoyed being "forced" to "leave the house on non-school days" to go to the library or the local TC community to explore Chinese culture; (4) the approach provided a "gradual warm-up to Chinese culture"; (5) there were opportunities to engage

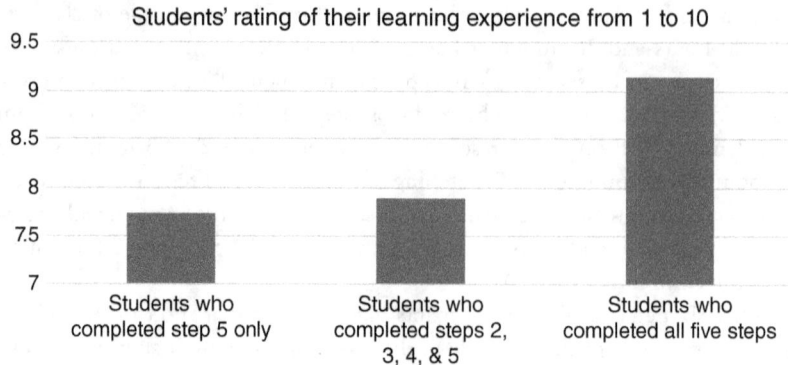

FIGURE 6.1 Students' average rating of their culture learning experience

in independent learning; (6) students could learn from classmates' presentations; (7) many cultural aspects were learned in detail.

The majority of students also enjoyed the order of the steps because "it was a natural flow that followed with the level of Chinese," "it did a good job at slowly introducing us into a new culture in multiple different formats," and "the gradual shifts from videos to community increased the engagement we have with Chinese culture." Students were aware of the gradual buildup and the progression from "easier to more involved," saying that they "got a broad view and then looked at how Chinese culture impacts life near me." One student reflected on the last step, "I learned more than I thought I was going to since I knew the basics and majority of Chinese culture." Some students would have preferred to reverse the order of steps 4 and 5 because they found the ethnographic interview more challenging than the authentic culture exploration.

Students suggested several improvements and additions to the sequence. First, an in-class culture day or a visit to "a restaurant or an Asian market during a class period" was proposed "to ensure that everyone is on the same page of cultural exposure." Second, the steps (except for step 1) should happen early in the semester so that all activities could be completed before the stressful time of final exams. Third, while some students needed constant reminders to complete the assignments because they are "very busy and online classes/assignments often get neglected", others wanted to be encouraged to step out of their comfort zones as "it can be uncomfortable to go out and experience culture."

Students' attitudes, interests, and cultural awareness

Those students who only experienced steps 1 and 2 of CLBC in their single year of language study reported that they acquired a substantial amount of cultural knowledge. They appreciated the chance to overview the different aspects of TC featured in the teacher-made videos and to collaboratively research one topic in depth. Those students who completed all five CLBC steps conveyed that the approach positively affected their attitudes to and respect for the people from the TL community, their cultural awareness, and their interests in learning the target language. Their scores (6.62, 6.86, and 6.85, respectively) on the improvements of all the three aspects on a 7-point Likert-type scale (with 7 as *strongly agree*) were slightly higher than those who completed the last four steps (6.08, 6.27, and 6.25, respectively) and much higher than those who only completed the last step (5.85, 6.09, and 5.06, respectively).

Classroom implications

This study adopted the DBR that stresses the improvement of instructional practices through iterative design, analysis, development, and application (Wang & Hannafin, 2005). It seeks to solve current real-world problems by designing and enacting instructional interventions. In this study, the problems of insufficient time and an added cognitive load of cultural instruction for beginning language students were solved by employing a blended learning format; moving most of the cultural activities online allowed students to learn at their own pace. DBR produces practical classroom interventions that can be confirmed and refined by other researchers and instructors; some of the study's implications are described next.

An important implication of this study is the feasibility of a combined online and FTF format for cultural activities, with most of the time allotted to virtual learning. The use of asynchronous online resources to teach students the TC in a blended learning setting offers important pedagogical advantages. Thus, CLBC instructors can help their students acquire cultural knowledge using a variety of online activities, preserving classroom time for practicing language skills. Online cultural learning can become more engaging through direct teaching using multimedia texts, encouraging students to independently research a topic of their interest, conducting ethnographic interviews, immersing in the TC community, and observing the target culture.

Second, it is essential to consider learners' TC acceptance level, their prior knowledge, and aspects of their immediate environment that could be used in teaching. While students may differ in the degree of their familiarity with the TL and culture, it is crucial to meet them where they are in terms of academic, cognitive, linguistic, and cultural development. To optimize cultural learning for low-level language students, cultural instruction should progress from more receptive to more interactive activities. Observing the TC first and actively engaging with it later eases language students into cultural interaction and provides for more effective learning. A possible cultural instructional sequence can begin with the most visible and basic (Big C) aspects of culture, transition to multimedia materials with added teacher explanations, add one-on-one interviewing of a native speaker, and, lastly, explore the culture and people in the local community. Finally, TC learning should not exclude beginning language learners. It is crucially important to start linguistic and cultural instruction at the same time, even though beginning students could seem overwhelmed by a new and challenging language. The results of the study show that novice learners benefit from the first-year introduction of TC in English, as it broadens their worldview and expands their knowledge no matter whether they continue or drop the TL after the first year.

Another implication of the study is the importance of peer collaboration in the process of cultural learning. As students share the results of their research and exploration during in-person meetings, they acquire new cultural knowledge and enhance their classmates' learning. They can relate to their peers' feelings and be more willing to interact with them than with the instructor, which can increase learner motivation and create a more personalized and engaging classroom. Sharing with classmates can also provide an authentic purpose for conducting the research, the interview, and the exploration in the community assignments. In addition, as was suggested by study participants, one class period could be devoted to a field trip to a restaurant or another TC establishment, or to a theme day (such as Chinese cooking day, Chinese clothes day). Including in-person cultural events in the curriculum not only underscores the importance of culture but also increases students' enthusiasm about learning the language and the culture.

Conclusion

This study analyzed students' perceptions of a five-step approach to integrating culture into the curriculum for beginning- through intermediate-level foreign language learners. The results showed that the CLBC approach could help improve students' attitudes toward the target cultural community, increase their interest in learning the language, and improve their cultural awareness. The study demonstrated the importance of imparting TC knowledge to beginning TL learners in their native English. The early introduction allows students to broaden their overview of TC culture and lays a foundation for a more interactive, personalized, and in-depth exploration of TC at later stages of language study. The order of the five steps facilitates a gradual introduction to the TC through a variety of formats and engaging activities. The CLBC approach places cultural learning mostly outside of the classroom, allowing the instructor to devote their in-person classroom meetings to language skill practice. The students in the study enjoyed the flexibility and the independent learning experience CLBC provided. They also felt that the blended learning format offered them more freedom and control of their own learning.

The exploration of the effectiveness of a five-step culture teaching approach in a blended environment and the study of beginning- and intermediate-level student perceptions is hoped to contribute to the body of knowledge about integrating cultural instruction into a world language curriculum. That said, the scope of the study is somewhat limited by its small sample size. In many world language programs, the enrollment numbers decrease from beginning to advanced courses as fewer students continue learning the language to an upper level. The participant group for this study followed the same pattern, and the number of students who experienced all five CLBC steps was small, which may reduce the applicability of its results.

This study describes an attempt to integrate language and culture instruction in a blended learning environment at a curriculum level, a much-needed development in foreign language instruction (Zhang, 2019). However, further research is necessary to examine such issues as whether reordering steps 4 and 5 and/or adding more steps will increase culture learning. Furthermore, the five steps were piloted in a two-year period, and they worked effectively. While the study findings suggest the benefit of completing all five steps, it is necessary to investigate whether the five steps of the CLBC approach, with some modification, can be implemented in one year, that is, in the first two semesters of language learning, so that students accomplish the first two steps in the first semester and steps 3 and 4 (and possibly a simplified version of step 5) in the second semester. If a modified one-year version of CLBC is found to benefit cultural learning, all students, including those who commit to a single year of language study to satisfy their university language requirement, will have an opportunity to learn TC in depth.

References

Alcânatara, L. (2016). Using English to learn while learning to use English: International field trips as a way to learn (through) language. *International Journal on Language, Literature, and Culture in Education*, *3*(2), 141–149.

American Council on the Teaching of Foreign Languages (ACTFL). (2012). ACTFL proficiency guidelines. https://www.actfl.org/resources/actfl-proficiency-guidelines-2012

Amiel, T., & Reeves, T. C. (2008). Design-based research and educational technology: Rethinking technology and the research agenda. *Educational Technology Society*, *11*(4), 29–40.

Angelova, M., & Zhao, Y. (2014). Using an online collaborative project between American and Chinese students to develop ESL teaching skills, cross-cultural awareness and language skills. *Computer Assisted Language Learning*, *29*(1), 167–185.

Arikan, A. (2011). Prospective English language teachers' perceptions of the target language and culture in relation to their socioeconomic status. *English Language Teaching*, *4*(3), 232–242.

Bakker, A., & Van Eerde, H. A. A. (2015). An introduction to design-based research with an example from statistics education. In A. Bikner-Ahsbahs, C. Knipping, & N. Presmeg (Eds.), *Doing qualitative research: Methodology and methods in mathematics education* (pp. 429–466). Springer.

Bartimote-Afflick, K., Bridgeman, A., Walker, R., Sharma, M., & Smith, L. (2016). The study, evaluation, and improvement of university student self-efficacy. *Studies in Higher Education*, *41*(11), 1918–1942.

Brooks, N. D. (1968). *Language and language learning: Theory and practice*. Harcourt Brace Jovanovich.

Brown, S. K. (2010). Popular films in the EFL classroom: Study of methodology. *Procedia – Social and Behavioral Sciences, 3*, 45–54.

Byram, M. (1997). *Teaching and assessing intercultural communicative competence*. Multilingual Matters.

Byram, M. (2014). Twenty-five years on – From cultural studies to intercultural citizenship. *Language, Culture and Curriculum, 27*(3), 209–225.

Byram, M., Esarte-Sarries, V., Taylor, S., & Allatt, P. (1991). Young people's perception of other cultures. In D. Buttjes, & M. Byram (Eds.), *Mediating languages and cultures* (pp. 103–119). Multilingual Matters.

Chapelle, C. A. (2016). *Teaching culture in introductory foreign language textbooks*. McMillan.

Chastain, K. (1988). *Developing second language skills: Theory and practice*. Harcourt Brace Janovich.

Chen, P., Chavez, O., Ong, D. C., & Gunderson, B. (2017). Strategic resource use for learning: A self-administered intervention that guides self-reflection on effective resource use enhances academic performance. *Psychology Science, 28*(6), 774–78.

Corbin, J., & Strauss, A. (2015). *Basics of qualitative research: Techniques and procedures for developing grounded theory* (4th ed.). SAGE.

Desai, S. V., Jabeen, S. S., Abdul, W. K., & Rao, S. A. (2018). Teaching cross-cultural management: A flipped classroom approach using films. *The International Journal of Management Education, 16*(3), 405–431.

Dewey, J. (1963). *Experience and education*. Collier.

Fu, L. (2018). Displaying recipiency in doctor-patient conversations. *Chinese as a Second Language Research, 7*(1), 79–110.

Goode, T., Sockalingam, S., Brown, M., & Jones, W. A. (2000). *A planners' guide, infusing principles, content and themes related to cultural and linguistic competence into meeting and conferences*. Georgetown University Centre for Child and Human Development, National Centre for Cultural Competence.

Graham, C. R. (2006). Blended learning systems: Definition, current trends, and future directions. In C. J. Bonk, & C. R. Graham (Eds.), *The handbook of global learning: Global perspectives, local designs* (pp. 3–21). Pfeiffer.

Halverson, R. J. (1985). Culture and vocabulary acquisition: A proposal. *Foreign Language Annals, 18*(4), 327–32.

Jiang, S. (2011). China-USA culture exchange Café: Practice and reflections on teaching culture on the web. *Journal of Technology and Chinese Language Teaching, 2*(2), 23–36.

Keesing, R. (1994). Theory of culture revisited. In R. Borofsky (Ed.), *Assessing cultural anthropology* (pp. 301–310). McGraw-Hill.

King, A. (1993). From sage on the stage to guide on the side. *College Teaching, 41*, 130–35.

Kinginger, C. (2008). Language learning in study abroad: Case studies of Americans in France. *The Modern Language Journal, 92*(1), 1—124.

Knouse, S., & Abreu, L. (2016). Using Pinterest to facilitate the learning of culture. *NECTFL Review, 77*, 15–51.

Kozhevnikova, E. (2014). Exposing students to authentic materials as a way to increase students' language proficiency and cultural awareness. *Procedia – Social and Behavioral Sciences, 116*, 4462–4466.

Kramsch, C. (1993). *Context and culture in language teaching*. Oxford University Press.

Kramsch, C. (1998). *Language and culture*. Oxford University Press.

Lázár, I. (2011). Teachers' beliefs about integrating the development of intercultural communicative competence in language teaching. *Forums PRACHE*, *5*(5), 113–127.

National Center for Culture Competence (NCCC). (2021). Curricula enhancement module series. https://nccc.georgetown.edu/curricula/glossary.html

Newton, J., Yates, E., Shearn, S., & Nowitzki, W. (2010). Intercultural communicative language teaching: Implications for effective teaching and learning. http://dx.doi.org/10.13140/RG.2.1.3118.1526

Nostrand, H. L. (1974). Empathy for a second culture: Motivations and techniques. In G. A. Jarvis (Ed.), *Responding to new realities. ACTFL foreign language education series* (vol. 5, pp. 263–367). National Textbook.

Oakley, G., Pegrum, M., Xiong, X., Lim, C., & Yan, H. (2018). An online Chinese-Australian language and cultural exchange through digital storytelling. *Language, Culture and Curriculum*, *31*(2), 128–149.

Oliver, K. M. (2000). Methods for developing constructivism learning on the web. *Educational Technology*, *40*(6), 5–18.

Plomp, T. (2013). Educational design research: An introduction. In T. Plomp, & N. Nieveen (Eds.), *Educational design research – Part A: An introduction* (pp. 10–51). eNSCHEDE: Netherlands Institute for Curriculum Development (SLO.)

Qin, X. (2013). Teaching behavioral culture in Chinese classroom. *Journal of the Chinese Language Teachers Association*, *48*(3), 1–24.

Robinson-Stuart, G., & Nocon, H. (1996). Second culture acquisition: Ethnography in the Foreign Language Classroom. *The Modern Language Journal*, *80*(4), 431–449.

Schenker, T. (2013). The effects of a virtual exchange on students' interest in learning about culture. *Foreign Language Annals*, *46*(3), 497–507.

Schwieter, J. W., Jackson, J., & Ferreira, A. (2018). When 'domestic' and 'international' students study abroad: Reflections on language learning, contact, and culture. *International Journal of Bilingual Education and Bilingualism*, *24*(1), 124–137.

Seelye, N. (1974). *Teaching culture: Strategies for foreign language educators*. National Textbook Company.

Sun, L. (2013). Culture teaching in foreign language teaching. *Theory and Practice in Language Studies*, *3*(2), 371–376.

Thomas, D., & Brown, J. S. (2011). *A new culture of learning: Cultivating the imagination for a world of constant change*. CreateSpace.

Vahdany, F. (2005). Culture and language teaching. *Peyke Noor Journal*, *3*(2), 93–98.

Vygotsky, L. S. (1962). *Thought and language*. MIT Press.

Vygotsky, L. S. (1971). *Mind in Society: The development of higher psychological processes*. Harvard University Press.

Wang, F., & Hannafin, M. (2005). Designed-based research and technology enhanced learning environments. *Educational Technology Research and Development*, *53*(4), 5–25.

Wang, Y., & Crooks, S. (2015). Does the personalization of multimedia instruction influence the effectiveness of decorative graphics during foreign language instruction? *Journal of Technology and Chinese language teaching*, *6*(2), 29–38.

Ware, P. D., & Kramsch, C. (2005). Toward an intercultural stance: Teaching German and English through telecollaboration. *The Modern Language Journal*, *89*, 190–205.

Wood, D., Bruner, J., & Ross, G. (1976). The role of tutoring in problem solving. *Journal of Child Psychology and Child Psychiatry*, *17*, 89–100.

Yang, X., & Chen, D. (2016). Two barriers to teaching culture in foreign language classroom. *Theory and Practice in Language Studies*, *6*(5), 1128–1135.

Zhang, S. (2016). Learning through a CMC-based tandem project with native speakers: A descriptive study of beginning CFL Learners. *Journal of Technology and Chinese Language Teaching*, 7(2), 58–81.

Zhang, S. (2019). Culture learning through multimedia authentic materials and ethnographic interview in a blended learning environment. *Journal of Technology and Chinese Language Teaching*, *10*(2), 125–149.

Zhang, S., & Jaramillo, N. (2021). Seamless integration between online and face-to-face: The design and perception of a flipped-blended language course. *International Journal of Computer-Assisted Language Learning and Teaching*, *11*(4), 19–39.

7
INTERCULTURAL COMPETENCE IN ELEMENTARY-LEVEL LANGUAGE CLASSES IN HIGHER EDUCATION

Islam Karkour

When it comes to reconciling cultural differences, the world continues to be in crisis. Failure to bridge cultural differences has frequently resulted in a cycle of violence that begins with individual disputes and ends in genocide, wars, and terrorism. In a time when "human history is increasingly a race between intercultural education and disaster" (Coulby, 2006, p. 245), education assumes a critical role in bridging the cultural gaps and encouraging the appreciation of cultural differences. "Building positive relations among cultures, breaking down walls of prejudice and racism, and fostering international goodwill are noble – and critical – goals for universities and K–12 schools in the 21st century" (Hammer, 2012, pp. 115–116). While all subject fields can integrate cultural education (Coulby, 2006), a foreign language curriculum should include intercultural competence (IC) as a major component and goal if instructors want their students to establish "effective, positive relationships across cultural boundaries, required in a global society" (Van Houten & Shelton, 2018, p. 38).

This chapter highlights the role of the university world language (WL) programs in bridging cultures and encouraging students to acknowledge and respect cultural differences, particularly at the elementary level. The chapter reports on a recent study conducted in five elementary-level WL classes to investigate instructional pedagogies for integrating culture in WL curriculum and the related impact on students' growth in intercultural sensitivity (IS). The time frame of the study was one semester. While 15 weeks may be considered insufficient for any IS development, and "longer experiences will have a greater effect" on IC, "short-term experiences ($\mu = 3.8$ weeks) may mildly increase" intercultural competence (Lough, 2011, p. 459). In fact, several studies found indicators of improvement in language learners' IC levels over one semester (Durocher Jr., 2007; Elola & Oskoz, 2008; Jin, 2015).

DOI: 10.4324/9781003058441-9

Literature review

The relationship between culture and language is so close that the study of language and culture became synonymous (Cutshall, 2012). The origins of teaching culture in WL education can be traced back to the *high culture* era that emphasized the analysis of literature and arts through written texts (Byram & Peiser, 2015; Kramsch, 1995). In the 1950s, the advance of the communicative approach shifted the instructional focus to *low culture* in everyday encounters such as ordering food or shopping. A related distinction is made between the formal "Big C" and the daily life "little c" cultures (National Standards in Foreign Language Education Project, 2006; see also Chapter 6 in this volume). Over time, "language education … has ranged in its various endeavors from the teaching of grammar to the teaching of peace" (Lo Bianco et al., 1999, p. 13). As the dominance of the communicative paradigm in WL education began to subside in the '90s, the scope of cultural instruction widened to include improving students' sensitivity toward and increasing their understanding of other cultures. IS development is becoming even more important in today's globalized world as foreign language programs prepare students to interact and collaborate in a multilingual society. Language education could become a powerful tool to promote peace (Wagner et al., 2019) when a WL classroom encourages an "openness, interest, sensitivity, and compassion in intercultural interactions" (Ishihara, 2017, p. 20).

Several recent attempts to conceptualize IS refer to "intercultural competence" and "intercultural sensitivity" as synonyms (e.g., Anand & Lahiri, 2009; Cushner & Mahon, 2009). However, Hammer et al. (2003) define IC as "the ability to think and act in interculturally appropriate ways," while IS is "the ability to discriminate and experience relevant cultural differences" (p. 422). The two notions are closely connected, as IS leads to IC (Bennett, 2004). An interculturally sensitive person examines native and target cultural values and conventions. As they experience the otherness of different social groups, they reflect on the relationship among these groups, analyze their intercultural experience, and act on this analysis (Alred et al., 2006).

The concept of IS is central to the influential framework of the Developmental Model of Intercultural Sensitivity (DMIS) (Bennet, 1986, 1993a, 2017; Bennett & Bennett, 2004). DMIS assumes that as people experience cultural differences, they progress through a continuum of cultural awareness and sensitivity, or from ethnocentrism to ethnorelativism (Bennett, 2004, 2017). The ethnocentric stage involves "the experience of one's own culture as 'central to reality'"; the new cultural behaviors and beliefs are not questioned but are viewed as "just the way things are" (Bennett, 2004, p. 62). The ethnocentric stage consists of denial (constructing physical or psychological barriers to separate or isolate oneself from other cultures), defense (denigrating other cultures and manifesting superiority toward them), and minimization (superficially accepting cultural differences while believing all cultures to be essentially similar) phases (Bennett, 2017).

As a person's intercultural understanding increases and they begin to recognize, accept, and appreciate other cultures, they progress to the ethnorelative stages of acceptance, adaptation, and integration. First, one accepts the difference in cultural values, beliefs, and behaviors. Then, one adapts to cultural differences by engaging in culturally appropriate perception, feelings, and behavior and feeling empathy and pluralism toward the new culture. Finally, one integrates the other worldviews with their own (Bennett, 1993b).

A closely related IC model is Intercultural Development Continuum (IDC). Grounded in DMIS, it represents a change in one's mentality from the monocultural outlook of denial and polarization to an intermediary phase of minimization to the global mindset of acceptance and adaptation. IDC expresses IC as a continuum rather than a linear construct with minimization as an intermediate stage between monocultural and intercultural phases rather than an absolute ethnocentric or ethnorelative category (Hammer, 2012).

An essential aspect of progressing through the IS stages in WL classes is reflection, critical analysis, and comparison. Simply providing students with an intercultural experience without opportunities to reflect on it will not increase their IS; rather, it will create what Bennett (1997) calls "fluent fools," or someone whose fluency in a language does not translate into an understanding and acceptance of social and cultural norms. The comparative and reflective aspects of cultural learning are highlighted by other interculturalists (Byram & Peiser, 2015; Liddicoat & Scarino, 2013).

In the process of familiarizing themselves with the new culture and inevitably comparing it with their own, students may become conflicted about the difference between cultural values. The ability to resolve this inner conflict is at the heart of intercultural exploration (Crozet & Liddicoat, 1999). Rather than an absolute rejection of the target culture, or a confinement within the bounds of one's own culture, the intercultural exploration involves finding a third place between the two cultures (Kramsch, 1993) where an individual is comfortable with their own and the target culture. The third place does not make one discard their own beliefs, nor reject the values they find to be different; it reconciles diversity and unity and embodies the ability to compromise and accept cultural differences. Finding one's third place is essential for IC development in a WL class (Lo Bianco et al., 1999) where instructors should guide students through finding their third place rather than telling them where to locate themselves (Kramsch, 1993).

How can the concept of the third place inform WL education? Lo Bianco et al. (1999) suggest that "teaching methods, curricula and materials can either promote or impede the development of the third place, by including or excluding opportunities to reflect on the cultures involved in language learning" (p. 185). Involving students in a conscious reflection of their own and the target cultural meanings and values will help them negotiate cultural differences as they learn to become successful communicators in the target language (TL).

While some educators may believe that developing knowledge of culture is more suitable for advanced levels of WL learning, cultural instruction should commence in beginning WL classes (Crozet & Liddicoat, 1999). Integrating culture into elementary-level curriculum not only promotes students' IC growth (Wagner et al., 2019) but also provides insights into issues of social justice (Meredith et al., 2018) and facilitates their proficiency and interest in learning the TL (Tsou, 2005). Byram (1997) indicates that simple topics, e.g., greetings or clothing, could be essential for enhancing IS in elementary-level WL classes as the stories and values behind TL practices may raise awareness about the culture more effectively than solely TL vocabulary items. Similarly, comparing native and TL cultures helps students think critically about their culture, understand how others' perspectives differ from their own, and "learn how to distance themselves from their native language/culture environment to see it for the first time as what it really is, as just one possible world view and not the only world view" (Crozet & Liddicoat, 1999, p. 117).

In summary, to promote students' IS from the beginning of the language study, WL classes should develop knowledge about the target culture as well as create opportunities for critical thinking, comparisons, and intercultural exploration and guide students to the discovery of their own third place through personal reflection.

The study

The study aimed to assess the level of intercultural sensitivity of beginning-level foreign languages students over one semester and to investigate the role of WL classes in promoting IS by addressing the following research questions:

RQ 1.   Does the students' IS level change over one semester of language study?
RQ 2 a).   How and to what extent do WL teachers incorporate the target culture into their instruction?
b).   Is the IS level difference across WL classrooms related to specific teaching practices?

Methodology

This observational study used a mixed method to investigate levels of intercultural sensitivity in five elementary-level WL classes in a U.S. university and analyze teaching practices for integrating culture in WL curriculum and the related impact on students' IS growth. The dependent variable was students' IS numeric score according to the Intercultural Development Inventory (IDI), the assessment tool used to obtain quantitative measurements of students' levels of IS.

To investigate the change in IS level over one semester of language study, the IDI data was collected at the beginning and end of the semester; the pretest and posttest IDI score difference was analyzed. After the posttest administration of the IDI, the instructors were interviewed about their approaches to cultural instruction and their views on their students' levels of IS. The analysis of course syllabi yielded data about the importance of cultural objectives in WL curriculum.

Instruments

Three instruments were used for data collection: the IDI, interviews, and course syllabi. IDI is commonly used to assess IC through a 50-item survey that evaluates individual attitude toward cultural differences (Hammer, 2012). The IDI results are tallied with the IDC categories of denial, polarization, minimization, acceptance, and adaptation to yield a measure of one's level of IS. The IDI is deemed "a statistically reliable and valid measure of intercultural sensitivity applicable to people from various cultural backgrounds" (Fantini, 2009, p. 471).

In addition to the IDI, the five WL instructors underwent a flexible semi-structured interview while their course syllabi were analyzed to establish whether the course objectives included intercultural learning outcomes and their assessment. Following DeMarrais's (2004) suggestions for including broad open-ended questions and encouraging a detailed recall of specific incidents and experiences, the interview included questions about the instructors' approaches, learning outcomes, and opinions on teaching language and culture in their classes. The interviews were transcribed and coded, and the interview data was extracted and organized into themes. While some themes were *prefigured* based on best practices to teach culture according to existing literature, other themes were *emergent* from the interviews and thus useful in the context of this study (Creswell, 2012). Codes were developed by building on prefigured themes, as well as modifying themes according to emergent data patterns.

Participants

This study involved American undergraduate students enrolled in elementary-level language classes at a University in New England. Since students' lingua-cultural background, ethnicity, and the length of study abroad experience could impact their IS (Rexeisen, 2013; Rexeisen et al., 2008), the study subjects were selected from middle-class, European-heritage background students from relatively homogenous New England suburban communities.

To collect the data, 137 students and 5 instructors of different world languages were recruited to participate in the study. To preserve anonymity, the languages are referred to as Language A, B, C, D, and F. After administering the IDI online at the beginning of the fall semester, 127 responses were analyzed.

Six demographic questions addressing the subjects' countries of citizenship, native language, study abroad experience, and current class standing were added to ensure the uniformity of study participants.

After selecting a homogeneous study population and later removing students who did not complete the posttest at the conclusion of the fall semester, the number of study participants decreased to 71 elementary-level WL students (nine were enrolled in Language A, 9 in Language B, 20 in Language C, 15 in Language D, and 18 in Language F). Thirty-one participants were male, 38 were female, and 2 students chose not to define their gender.

Procedure

The study was designed to investigate students' IS over one semester (15 weeks) of language study. A one-group pretest-posttest design was optimal for measuring changes in students' IS levels. The online version of the IDI was administered at the beginning and the end of the fall semester.

The overall scores of the two IDI assessments were used to address RQ 1. A paired t-test compared the mean scores of the pretest and posttest measurements to determine the overall IDI score at the beginning and end of the semester. Also, each pretest IDI phase was compared to the same posttest phase.

To explore the instructors' practices in teaching culture and to analyze the relationship between their actions and the development of IS as measured by IDI, the five WL instructors were interviewed and asked to share their syllabi for analysis. The three course syllabi provided data for the study.

Results

Quantitative data analysis

Using a pretest/posttest model, students from five different WL classes were administered the IDI at the beginning and end of the fall semester. The unexpected results indicated that the pretest average mean score ($M = 84.84$, $SD = 15.08$) was higher than the posttest average mean score ($M = 82.30$, $SD = 15.37$). To determine the statistical significance of the difference, a paired samples t-test compared the average pretest and posttest scores. The t-test revealed a significant difference between pretest scores ($M = 84.84$, $SD = 15.08$) and posttest scores ($M = 82.30$, $SD = 15.37$) for the 71-student analytic sample ($t(70) = -10.06$, $p<.001$). The effect size for this analysis ($d = -1.19$) was found to exceed Cohen's (1988) convention for a large effect ($d = 0.80$), which suggested a large difference in the negative direction. This surprising result shows a decrease in students' average IS levels throughout the semester. Table 7.1 summarizes the pretest-posttest differences between the overall score means for the IDC subcategories.

As Table 7.1 indicates, the IDI mean score decreased across a semester of the WL study. On average, the entire participant group exhibited a statistically significant decrease of 2.54 between the pretest (84.84) and the posttest (82.30).

An unexpected decline in the overall IDI score of the five classes necessitated a profound analysis of each class. A comparison of the mean differences indicated that the only class to show a positive change of 5.11 was Language A, while for every other class, the change in the IC development was negative (Table 7.2).

The notable disparity between the pretest/posttest mean differences for Language A and other WL classes invites a discussion of reasons behind dissimilar progress in student IS development over the semester. What instructional practices led to the IDI score increase in Language A class? This question was addressed by qualitative data analysis.

Qualitative data analysis

The five elementary-level WL instructors in the study were interviewed individually, and their syllabi were examined. After the interviews were transcribed and coded, a thematic presentation was developed. The main interview themes presented and discussed in the following sections are supported by syllabus analysis where appropriate.

TABLE 7.1 Pretest vs. posttest scores on the IDI scale

IDC subcategory	Pretest		Posttest	
	Mean score	Number of students	Mean score	Number of students
Denial	64.41	11	62.18	11
Polarization	78.08	29	75.43	26
Minimization	96.68	29	95.94	32
Acceptance	123.52	2	125.26	2
Overall Score Mean	84.84	71	82.30	71

TABLE 7.2 Pretest vs. posttest scores for each class

Language class	Number of students	Pretest	Posttest	Means difference
Language A	9	87.56	92.68	5.11
Language B	9	82.93	76.74	−6.19
Language C	20	82.33	79.65	−2.68
Language D	15	91.01	84.57	−6.43
Language F	18	82.08	80.92	−1.16
Total	71	84.84	82.29	−2.54

Course objectives

To identify the presence of cultural instruction in their teaching practices, instructors were asked about their course objectives and the communicative skills they emphasized during class. None of the five interviewees indicated IC among the course objectives or skills. One of the participants recounted "all" of the skills she routinely stressed in her courses ("I focus on all four [skills] – reading, writing, speaking, [and] listening") without mentioning culture. Other participants highlighted certain skills, e.g., speaking, as central in their classes, but any reference to culture was notably absent from their comments. When a question about integrating culture was asked, all instructors stated that culture is present in their courses, although again, none mentioned it among the skills they focused on. The observable absence of cultural objectives in instructional practices was supported by syllabus analysis: of the three syllabi available for review, only Language A syllabus specified cultural objectives ("becoming familiar with the cultural contexts of major [Language A] speaking countries and beginning to recognize and understand differences and similarities between these cultures and their own") along with linguistic goals ("development of basic Language A speaking, listening, reading, and writing skills").

Pedagogy of teaching culture

Responding to the interview question about developing IC in their elementary-level WL courses, the five study participants indicated that they mainly rely on course textbooks to deliver cultural content, although all five mentioned their textbooks' superficial treatment of target culture. While all instructors occasionally discuss cultural points when they surface during grammar or vocabulary practice, Language B, C, D, and F participants did not indicate any additional cultural activities, as they deemed their textbooks an adequate and sufficient means of integrating TL culture into their courses. The cultural exploration in these classes mainly consists of verbal explanations and/or watching video clips on a textbook cultural topic, or, as one participant stated, "I tell stories, explain ... sometimes I show videos." Some instructors avoid teaching culture altogether; they believe that cultural discussions would challenge beginning students' linguistic abilities and are reluctant to allow the use of their native language for reflections. According to the Language D instructor, "[B]eing able to use the language, the target language, and talk about cultural topics, they're just not at the level to be able to do that right."

At the same time, the Language A instructor, whose class scored higher on the IDI posttest, described how the textbook cultural content was augmented by a weekly cultural exploration assignment accompanied by a two-page reflective paper in English. According to the syllabus, the weekly reading, writing, or research assignments lead to the end-of-semester research project on a student-selected topic, which included a three-page essay in English and a one-page summary of the essay in Language A. Students were also expected to compile a list of the most important TL words in their reflective papers. The aim of the reflection, according to the instructor, was to encourage students to compare their native and target cultures and ponder any perceived differences. The instructor mentioned wanting to "shake students a little bit and expose them to things that are uncomfortable or something they wouldn't necessarily go out and search for themselves." The participant also indicated that the Language A program received a grant from the TL country government for cultural activities. All Language A instructors collaborated to organize various cultural events for their classes, following up with required reflective papers about student cultural experience.

Adequate preparation for teaching culture

All instructors in the study felt adequately prepared for and confident in their methods of teaching culture to elementary-level students. Thus, one instructor stated that the IC learning goals are met by providing students with cultural information. Another instructor believed that authentic videos were impactful for their students' intercultural growth. Generally, the interview participants deemed verbal explanation and cultural video clips as sufficient means of IS development and indicated they did not seek other opportunities for cultural study.

Insufficient time to develop IS

Two out of the four instructors whose students' IDI scores decreased throughout the semester indicated that one semester of language study was insufficient for any impact on an individual's IS development. They believed that for the IDI scores to increase and a positive transformation in students' cultural mindset to occur, WL study should continue beyond one semester-long course; a period of three to four years of language study was suggested as an adequate time for IS development.

Discussion

The study aimed to investigate the change in the IS level in elementary-level college WL classes over one semester. The quantitative data show that at the beginning of language study, students were at the cusp of the IDC minimization phase, which is described as a transitional mindset between monocultural orientation and a more global worldview that highlights basic commonalities between the two cultures. At the end of the semester, the drop in ID scores indicated a regression toward the polarization phase on the IDC, which views cultural differences as opposing one another and may consider the other culture as threatening or inferior. The posttest mean score was, on average, significantly lower than the pretest mean score. This is a stunning and worrisome result.

In theory, studying a language should impact students' IS development; even a short-term experience can have a positive effect (Durocher Jr., 2007; Elola & Oskoz, 2008; Jin, 2015; Lough, 2011). While the literature suggests that learning a WL is one of the most powerful methods for growing and increasing students' IS (Byram & Peiser, 2015), the findings of this study point to a potential disconnect between the ideal theoretical world and classroom reality, which could be suggestive of a larger problem. Thus, Martha Nussbaum (1998) discussed how current American higher education fails to prepare cosmopolitan 'world citizens.' More recently, former Harvard University president Derek Bok (2006) noted that higher education in the United States falls short in many areas including diversity education. Furthermore, the IDI score difference reveals that only one language class in the study showed a minor improvement in IC development over the course of one semester. The disparity between the WL classes in this study invites a discussion of the possible reasons for dissimilar levels of student IS development, which follows in the next section.

Prioritizing culture in language classes

The difference in priority assigned to IC goals and classroom activities could be one reason for the IDI score difference between Languages A, B, C, D, and F. The analysis of qualitative data suggests that most elementary-level WL classes in the study did not prioritize IC development as language instructors did not mention IC among the skills addressed in class, treating culture almost as an afterthought. Any discussion of cultural issues in these classes was spontaneous and inconsistent, suggesting a somewhat inferior status of cultural study in contrast to language skill work. The secondary place of culture in the language class was reflected in course syllabi where IC was not stated among the key learning objectives. The lack of attention to IC and IS development may be explained by a common concern expressed by instructors: the discrepancy between the linguistic complexity of any cultural discussion and low language proficiency of their students seems to prevent the integration of culture beyond the textbook. Only the Language A instructor systematically incorporated cultural learning into their curriculum: their syllabus included cultural learning objectives among the course goals and textbook cultural content was supported by weekly reading, writing, vocabulary, and reflective activities on relevant topics.

Lack of training to teach culture

Another reason for differences in IS improvement could be instructors' inadequate training in cultural instruction. While four out of five instructors believed their pedagogy to be sufficient for IS development, they may lack awareness of the multifaceted nature of IS, as well as effective practices for teaching culture in elementary-level WL courses. Thus, one instructor demonstrated their lack of expertise by pausing the interview to ask if IS was the same as "big C or little c culture." Another instructor mentioned that their master's program in WL teaching did not prepare them for cultural instruction; although the importance of culture was highlighted in the program courses, they did not provide training on effective teaching methods in a classroom setting. While cultural information and videos have long been used for imparting cultural knowledge, they (and any cultural input) need to be accompanied by explicit cultural objectives, opportunities for cultural discussion, comparison, reflection, and assessment measures. WL instructors could be reminded to make target culture explicit for their students and facilitate it with direct teaching activities, similar to other language skill work.

Level appropriateness and first language (L1) use

IS development could also be impeded by instructors' belief that the beginning language class is not suitable for IC development because of the complexity of concepts and teaching materials. Due to this perceived need to maintain what one participant called "level appropriateness," three instructors in the study chose to avoid serious cultural discussions, opting instead for a superficial explanation of cultural notes provided by their textbooks. In consonance with Crozet and Liddicoat (1999), cultural instruction can and should take place in beginning classes. Elementary-level students should be encouraged to engage in cultural activities in the context of level-appropriate topics, e.g., family, clothing, or food. A cultural exploration in students' native language or a mix of L1 and second language (L2) may be an effective means of comparison, reflection, and developing empathy for the target culture (Komer, 2013; Kraemer, 2006; Wagner et al., 2019).

Reflection

Closely connected to the problem of level appropriateness and L1 use is the issue of cultural reflection. Exploring, comparing, and reflecting on cultural topics is paramount for IS development (Irvine, 2003; Marx & Moss, 2011; Sleeter, 2001; Wagner et al., 2019). The issue of reflection was mentioned by two instructors, albeit differently. While the Language A instructor required students to write weekly cultural reflections in English, the Language D instructor avoided reflective assignments because his elementary students' TL proficiency was inadequate for the task. This instructor also did not favor reflection in English, as he strongly discouraged the students' L1 use in his WL classes.

A reluctance to let students use their L1 is typical for WL classes (Komer, 2013). As instructors feel pressured to discourage L1 use, they eschew cultural discussions and reflections with their elementary-level students, as is seen from this study. Encouraging beginners to reflect in their native language will add depth to their ideas and advance their IS. Another solution to the language problem is for students to engage in L1 reflection outside of class so that instructors can follow up using the TL in class (Wagner et al., 2019).

Providing additional opportunities for cultural study

A prefigured and emergent theme in the study was a somewhat superficial treatment of cultural topics in elementary-level course textbooks mentioned by all instructors. According to Young and Sachdev (2011), course materials often overlook the cultural aspect of language instruction; even those textbooks that claim to teach culture only refer to its superficial features. Furthermore, some major language standardized tests, such as International English Language Testing System or Test of English as a Foreign Language do not evaluate IS, which may cause teachers to emphasize language skills needed for the test over cultural instruction (Bickley et al., 2014; Young & Sachdev, 2011).

The results of this study indicate that the difference in IDI scores could be attributed to specific teaching practices. While four professors fully depended on the textbook for cultural instruction in their elementary-level language courses, the Language A instructor systematically augmented the textbook curriculum with additional content and opportunities for reflection to enhance their students' appreciation of the target culture. In fact, the entire Language A program collaborated to organize extracurricular activities for all levels of language study, which was made possible by a Language A government grant. Students would meet outside of class to discuss current events and community affairs (e.g., elections) and reflect on their experience in the TL or English depending on their proficiency level. When during the interview the Language A instructor became aware of the IDI score difference between languages, he attributed a positive change in his students' IS development to the program-wide effort to promote the culture. For him, the high level of collaboration and participation among Language A instructors contributed more significantly to IS development than even the weekly opportunity to reflect on extracurricular cultural experience, which he named as the second reason for IDI score increase.

> We spent a lot of time as a program. I think that the weekly individual projects were important, but we spent so much time as a program talking about the [Language A] elections that I think that since I've started teaching. … I've never had a semester where all of the [Language A] classes … were all working towards the same thing and at that level of coordination was something new.

Limitations of the study and suggestions for future research

The study surveyed 71 students and 5 instructors of elementary-level WL classes to investigate the change in the students' level of IS expressed in the IDI scores over a course of one semester. The low number of instructor participants may be an important limitation of the study, as it affects its credibility; it is not clear whether the results are representative of a more general attitude to cultural instruction. Further research is needed to survey more WL instructors in different colleges to establish the prevailing pedagogies for cultural instruction and their impact on student IS development. A longitudinal study tracking the changes in students' IS over an extended period would help to address the issue of teaching culture in a WL class.

The study results could also be biased by the fact that the Language A program received a grant to promote cultural instruction in their teaching. While comparing a language program that enjoys financial support for cultural activities to other languages without this support may impact the study results, the conclusion suggests itself that additional incentives in the form of awards or grants may encourage instructors to intentionally promote target culture in their language teaching. Monetary prizes or professional recognition of classroom efforts in IS development may increase the presence of cultural activities in the elementary WL curriculum.

Yet another limitation of the study could be the choice of the IDI testing instrument, as its theoretical model, DMIS, has been criticized for the lack of a clear definition of each developmental stage, its linear, one-dimensional view of IC, and unsuitability for language education (Liddicoat et al., 2003; Zafar et al., 2013). While IDI is an accepted means of measuring IS, an additional or alternative testing instrument could have improved reliability and validity of the study.

The study suggests that Language A's slight IS increase could be attributed to supplemental cultural activities such as regular reflective assignments in students' L1. Further experimental studies are needed to highlight the role of reflection in IS development, address the language of reflection, and suggest effective ways of integrating cultural comparison and reflection activities into the first-year curriculum.

Classroom implications

The study offers several practical implications that can increase the level of IS development in elementary WL classes.

First, teacher education programs may not pay enough attention to cultural instruction with the result that some WL teachers recognize the importance of IS development but lack the ability to teach it (Golub, 2014; Meyer, 2007). By consistently educating trainees about the significance of incorporating culture into the WL curricula and equipping them with explicit strategies and techniques for cultural instruction pre- and in-service teacher preparation programs could become a critical "first step" for the development of students' IS (Bickley et al., 2014). Other opportunities for professional growth in cultural instruction are offered by professional on- and offline communities, educational publications on IC development, and workshops.

Second, beginning at the elementary levels, WL instructors should engage students in meaningful reflection and comparison activities between native and target cultures. Low-level students could rely on their L1 or translanguaging (a linguistic expression involving L1 and L2). Wagner et al. (2018) and Wagner et al. (2019) provide many examples of cultural activities along with an inventory of topics (e.g., environmental issues, houses around the world, modes of transportation, exploring cities) suitable for beginning language classrooms.

Third, to grant IS development a more prominent place in WL curriculum, it should be included in course learning goals and supported by additional classroom and extracurricular activities that encourage critical thinking, reflection, and comparison of students' native and target cultures. Also, traditional textbook vocabulary and grammar materials could be supplemented with cultural exploration and analysis of language features. Stating cultural objectives, including opportunities for discussion and reflection, and augmenting them with formative assessment measures will give IS development a more prominent place in an elementary WL classroom.

Conclusion

As our multicultural globalized world calls for interculturally competent communicators, WL college classes could fulfill the need for an increased IS. However, a single semester of language study does little to improve students' IS unless culture is given a prominent place in language curriculum, is facilitated by instructors' intentional efforts, and supported by extracurricular activities and opportunities to understand, compare, and reflect on students' native and target culture. This study raises concerns about the state of intercultural instruction in university WL classes echoing some previous research conclusions (e.g., Golub, 2014) by drawing attention to the development of IS in five elementary-level college WL classes. The low level of IS was attributed to low priority and unstructured treatment of cultural instruction in the WL curriculum. Participants in this study avoided cultural discussions because of the "level appropriateness" issue for beginning students, spontaneously injected cultural teaching whenever a suitable topic appeared in the textbook, and demonstrated a lack of familiarity with the recent developments and techniques in cultural instruction. In contrast, a modest IS growth was witnessed in the class where textbook content was systematically supplemented with additional cultural activities that encouraged reflections, comparisons, and critical thinking. These cognitive processes are widely accepted as essential for IS development (Deardorff, 2011; Irvine, 2003; Marx & Moss, 2011; Sleeter, 2001; Wagner et al., 2019). To promote IS development from lower stages of minimization to higher phases of acceptance and adaptation, the spur-of-the-moment cultural activities should become deliberate instructional efforts facilitated by objectives and assessment measures. Collaboration with other language classes in the program, administrative support, and financial and professional incentives for cultural instruction can contribute to IS growth.

More than 20 years ago, Steele (2000) wrote,

> [W]hat has been traditionally called culture can no longer be an add-on at the end of the language lesson but has to be reconceptualized within the framework of intercultural communicative sensitivity and integrated into the organizing principle of the curriculum.
>
> (p. 193)

Studying world languages may not bring a noticeable increase in students' intercultural sensitivity, especially in one semester, if language instruction does not integrate IS as one of the major course objectives. To that end, language teacher education should extend its preparation to teaching culture in addition to listening, speaking, reading, and writing skills. Our world needs interculturally sensitive individuals who understand and appreciate other cultures, and WL classes can help meet that need. While a foreign language requirement in many universities does not extend beyond a semester or two, and one's proficiency may decrease or even disappear soon after graduation, students' respect for and appreciation of cultural differences they acquired in WL classes may last forever. Promoting IC through foreign language education can help achieve peace, mutual understanding, respect, and appreciation of those who are different locally and internationally.

Acknowledgment

The research presented in this chapter is based on the thesis submitted to the Graduate School at the University of New Hampshire as part of the requirements for completion of a doctoral degree in education.

References

Alred, G., Byram, M., & Fleming, M. (Eds.) (2006). *Education for intercultural citizenship: Concepts and comparisons*. Multilingual Matters.

Anand, R., & Lahiri, I. (2009). Intercultural competence in health care: Developing skills for interculturally competent care. In D. Deardorff (Ed.), *The SAGE handbook of intercultural competence* (pp. 387–402). SAGE.

Bennett, J. M. (1993a). Cultural marginality: Identity issues in intercultural training. In R. M. Paige (Ed.), *Education for the intercultural experience* (2nd ed., pp. 109–135). Intercultural Press.

Bennett, M. (1993b). Towards ethnorelativism: A developmental model of intercultural sensitivity. In M. Paige (Ed.), *Education for the intercultural experience* (pp. 21–71). Intercultural Press.

Bennett, J. M., & Bennett, M. J. (2004). Developing intercultural sensitivity: An integrative approach to global and domestic diversity. In D. Landis, J. Bennett, & M. Bennett (Eds.), *Handbook of intercultural training* (3rd ed, pp. 147–165). SAGE.

Bennett, J. M., Bennett, M. J., & Allen, W. (2003). Developing intercultural competence in the language classroom. In D. L. Lange, & R. M. Paige (Eds.), *Culture as the core: Perspectives on culture in second language learning* (pp. 237–270). Information Age Publishing.

Bennett, M. (1986). A developmental approach to training for intercultural sensitivity. *International Journal of Intercultural Relations, 10*(2), 179–95.

Bennett, M. (2004). Becoming interculturally competent. In J. Wurzel (Ed.), *Toward multiculturalism: A reader in multicultural education* (2nd ed., pp. 62–77).

Bennett, M. J. (1997). How not to be a fluent fool: Understanding the cultural dimension of language. In A. E. Fantini (Ed.), *New ways in teaching culture* (pp. 16–21). TESOL.

Bennett, M. J. (2017). Developmental model of intercultural sensitivity. In Y. Kim (Ed.), *The international encyclopedia of intercultural communication* (pp. 1–10). Wiley.

Bickley, C., Rossiter, M. J., & Abbott, M. L. (2014). Intercultural communicative competence: Beliefs and practices of adult English as a second language instructors. *Alberta Journal of Educational Research, 60*(1), 135–160.

Bok, D. (2006). *Our underachieving colleges: A candid look at how much students learn and why they should be learning more*: Princeton University Press.

Byram, M., & Peiser, G. (2015). Culture learning in the language classroom. In J. M. Bennett (Ed.), *The SAGE encyclopedia of intercultural competence* (pp. 205–208). SAGE.

Byram, M. (1997). *Teaching and assessing intercultural communicative competence*.

Coulby, D. (2006). Intercultural education: Theory and practice. *Intercultural Education, 17*(3), 245–257. https://doi.org/10.1080/14675980600840274

Creswell, J. (2012). *Qualitative inquiry and research design: Choosing among five approaches*. SAGE.

Crozet, C., & Liddicoat, A. J. (1999). The challenge of intercultural language teaching: Engaging with culture in the classroom. In J. Lo Bianco, A. J. Liddicoat, & C. Crozet (Eds.), *Striving for the third place: Intercultural competence through language education* (pp. 113–126). Language Australia.

Cushner, K., & Mahon, J. (2009). Intercultural competence in teacher education. In D. Deardorff (Ed.), *The SAGE handbook of intercultural competence* (pp. 304–320). SAGE.

Cutshall, S. (2012). More than a decade of standards: Integrating "communication" in your language instruction. *The Language Educator, 7*(2), 34–39.

Deardorff, D. K. (2011). Assessing intercultural competence. *New directions for institutional research, 149*. https://doi.org/10.1002/ir.381

DeMarrais, K. (2004). Qualitative interview studies: Learning through experience. In K. DeMarrais, & S. Lapan (Eds.), *Foundations for research: Methods of inquiry in education and the social sciences* (pp. 51–68). Lawrence Erlbaum.

Durocher Jr., D. O. (2007). Teaching sensitivity to cultural difference in the first-year foreign language classroom. *Foreign Language Annals, 40*(1), 143–160. https://doi.org/10.1111/j.1944-9720.2007.tb02858.x

Elola, I., & Oskoz, A. (2008). Blogging: Fostering intercultural competence development in foreign language and study abroad contexts. *Foreign Language Annals, 41*(3), 454–477.
Fantini, A. (2009). Assessing intercultural competence: Issues and tools. In D. Deardorff (Ed.), *The SAGE handbook of intercultural competence* (pp. 456–476). SAGE.
Golub, A. S. (2014). Effects of German language teacher professional development on pupils' learning outcomes in intercultural competence. *Center for Educational Policy Studies Journal, 4*(4), 75.
Hammer, M. (2012). The intercultural development inventory: A new frontier in assessment and development of intercultural competence. In M. Vande Berg, R. M. Paige, & K. H. Lou (Eds.), *Student learning abroad* (pp. 115–136). Stylus Publishing.
Hammer, M. R., Bennett, M. J., & Wiseman, R. (2003). Measuring intercultural sensitivity: The intercultural development inventory. *International Journal of Intercultural Relations, 27*(4), 421–443.
Irvine, J. J. (2003). *Educating teachers for diversity: Seeing with a cultural eye.* Teachers College Press.
Ishihara, N. (2017). Teaching pragmatics in support of learner subjectivity and global communicative needs: A peace linguistics perspective. *Official Journal of the National Association of Teacher Trainers and Supervisors, 6*(5), 17–32.
Jin, S. (2015). Using Facebook to promote Korean EFL learners' intercultural competence. *Language Learning & Technology, 19*(3), 38–51.
Komer, W. (2013). Thinking through teacher talk: Increasing target language use in the beginning Russian classroom. *Russian Language Journal, 63,* 91–112.
Kraemer, A. (2006). Teachers' use of English in communicative German language classrooms: A qualitative analysis. *Foreign Language Annals, 39,* 435–450.
Kramsch, C. (1993). *Context and culture in language teaching.* Oxford University Press.
Kramsch, C. (1995). The cultural component of language teaching. *Language, Culture and Curriculum, 8*(2), 83–92.
Liddicoat, A. J., Papademetre, L., Scarino, A., & Kohler, M. (2003). Report on intercultural language learning. *Department of Education, Science and Training,* Canberra. http://www.asiaeducation.edu.au/docs/default-source/professionallearning-pdfs/gettingstartedwithintercultural.pdf
Liddicoat, A. J., & Scarino, A. (2013). *Intercultural language teaching and learning.* Wiley-Blackwell.
Lo Bianco, J., Liddicoat, A. J., & Crozet, C. (1999). *Striving for the third place: Intercultural competence through language education.* The National Languages and Literacy Institute of Australia.
Lough, B. J. (2011). International volunteers' perceptions of intercultural competence. *International Journal of Intercultural Relations, 35*(4), 452–464.
Marx, H., & Moss, D. M. (2011). Please mind the culture gap: Intercultural development during a teacher education study abroad program. *Journal of Teacher Education, 62*(1), 35–47. https://doi.org/10.1177/0022487110381998
Meredith, B., Geyer, M., & Wagner, M. (2018). Social justice in beginning language instruction: Interpreting fairy tales. *Dimension, 90,* 112.
Meyer, B. (2007). The intercultural competences developed in compulsory foreign language education in the European Union. http://ec.europa.eu/education/404_en.htm
National Standards in Foreign Language Education Project. (2006). *Standards for foreign language learning in the 21st century.* Allen Press.

Nussbaum, M. C. (1998). *Cultivating humanity*. Harvard University Press.
Rexeisen, R. J., Anderson, P. H., Lawton, L., & Hubbard, A. C. (2008). Study abroad and intercultural development: A longitudinal study. *Frontiers: The Interdisciplinary Journal of Study Abroad, 17*(1), 1–20.
Rexeisen, R. J. (2013). The impact of study abroad on the development of pro-environmental attitudes. *The International Journal of Sustainability Education, 9*(1), 7–19. https://doi.org/10.18848/2325-1212/CGP/v09i01/55295
Sleeter, C. E. (2001). Preparing teachers for culturally diverse schools: Research and the overwhelming presence of Whiteness. *Journal of Teacher Education, 52*(2), 94–106.
Steele, R. (2000). Language learning and intercultural competence. In R. D. Lambert & E. Shohamy (Eds.), *Language policy and pedagogy: Essays in honor of A. Ronald Walton* (pp. 59–78). John Benjamins Publishing.
Tsou, W. (2005). The effects of cultural instruction on foreign language learning. *RELC Journal, 36*(1), 39–57.
Van Houten, J. B., & Shelton, K. (2018). Leading with culture. *The Language Educator, 13*(1), 34–39.
Wagner, M., Cardetti, F., & Byram, M. (2019). *Teaching intercultural citizenship across the curriculum: The role of language education*. American Council on the Teaching of Foreign Languages (ACTFL).
Wagner, M., Conlon Perugini, D., & Byram, M. (Eds.) (2018). *Teaching intercultural competence across the age range: Theory and practice*. Multilingual Matters.
Young, T. J., & Sachdev, I. (2011). Intercultural communicative competence: Exploring English language teachers' beliefs and practices. *Language Awareness, 20*(2), 81–98.
Zafar, S., Sandhu, S. Z., & Khan, Z. A. (2013). A critical analysis of 'developing intercultural competence in the language classroom' by Bennett, Bennett and Allen. *World Applied Sciences Journal, 21*(4), 565–571.

8
THE CULTURE PORTFOLIO
Assessing growth toward intercultural competence

Julianne Bryant

Culture learning in the language classroom has long been a recognized benefit to studying language (American Council of Trustees and Alumni [ACTA], 2017). The *National Standards in Foreign Language Education Project* (NSLEP) states that "only the study of world language empowers learners to engage successfully in meaningful interaction, both orally and in writing, with members of other cultures" (NSLEP, 2015, p. 79). This idea was challenged, however, when Wright (2000) completed a study showing that not only do language students not progress in intercultural competence (IC) when culture is presented as cultural facts but that students even regressed in their ability to be open-minded and flexible to culturally different others. However, when culture learning was approached as a reflective process of discovery, students, even at the beginning levels of language learning, made significant gains in IC. Since this study was conducted, much has changed in the field of foreign language instruction.

In 2004, the Modern Language Association (MLA) appointed an ad hoc committee to investigate the status of language instruction in higher education within a U.S. context and to make recommendations for the field. The report, published in 2007, identified the ability to understand not only other languages but also other cultures, among the five most critical needs, and called for a transformation of language programs and their structure "to produce a specific outcome: educated speakers who have deep translingual and transcultural competence" (Modern Language Association Ad Hoc Committee on Foreign Languages, 2007, p. 3) which enables students to not only interact between languages but to "reflect on the world and themselves through the lens of another language and culture" (p. 3). The publication of the report marked a shift in many language programs in colleges and universities around the nation.

At the time of Wright's (2000) study, the structure of many language programs did not allow much room for culture learning beyond cultural facts, especially in the beginner-level language courses that centered on learning linguistic forms to engage with the culture at a future point in time once the language was mastered sufficiently. The publication of the MLA report caused an increase in literature calling for a shift in focus in the language classroom (Barski & Wilkerson-Barker, 2019; Byram, 2012; Furstenberg, 2010; Rifkin, 2012a, 2012b; Wilkinson et al., 2015). Instructors have been charged to "teach language for cultural discovery rather than language and cultural discovery" (Wilkinson et al., 2015, p. 8), where culture learning drives the curriculum and grammar and vocabulary take on a supportive role (Furstenberg, 2010; Wilkinson et al., 2015). And, although the MLA report focused primarily on undergraduate majors, there was a growing awareness that development of translingual and transcultural competence needed to begin in the low-level classes (Barski & Wilkerson-Barker, 2019; Johnson & Mullins Nelson, 2010; Wilkinson et al., 2015), which not only required a shift in the curriculum, but also a new role for the instructor. In the new model, the teacher's role changes from the primary transmitter of information or the voice of authority to one that helps students recognize patterns, ask questions, and discover their new linguistic and cultural identities (Furstenberg, 2010; Wilkinson et al., 2015), which requires considerable planning on the part of the instructors and necessitates different materials.

Although culture learning in the language classroom is no longer reduced to tidbits of factual information but is considered a process of development over time, the change in instruction has occurred slowly and intermittently. The textbook industry largely continues to ignore the recommendations of the field (Bragger & Rice, 2000) primarily focusing on grammar, with culture presented as facts that can be easily excluded from teaching. Yet, there have also appeared several new language textbooks specifically aimed at centering culture in the beginning and intermediate language-learning process (Forester et al., 2007, 2017, 2018; Woolsey et al., 2019). Still, Wilkinson et al. (2015) argue that "while the treatment of culture in these instructional materials has become more intentional, more colorful, more interesting, more authentic, and more nuanced in recent years, the fact remains that it continues to be optional" (p. 2) and further state that "we cannot expect to lay the foundation for 'deep translingual and transcultural competence' if cultural learning remains superficial and optional" (p. 2). In a study (Barski & Wilkerson-Barker, 2019) conducted to better understand the extent to which a general education language course can support intercultural skill development, students' IC was measured before and after the course, demonstrating that little or no cultural learning took place. The investigators thus concluded that language courses with no explicit emphasis on IC development do not demonstrate growth in that area (p. 504). This chapter seeks to advance research on cultural instruction in a language classroom by means of a conceptual replication (as described in Porte & McManus, 2019) of Wright's (2000) study wherein the control group follows the prescribed curriculum, and the treatment group completes a culture portfolio project throughout the semester. The two-group design allowed us to determine whether the shift in materials and focus produces more growth toward IC compared to the original study, and whether increased growth is possible with the portfolio assignments added.

Motivation for the study

The theoretical motivation for the study is based on the transformative learning theory (Mezirow, 1997), which states that adult learners (as opposed to children whose learning processes are different) process new information by applying personal interpretation to the new experience to create meaning. As learners reconsider and critically reflect on their past ideas, experiences, and critical incidents, their perspective transforms. Rather than internalizing facts, transformative learning involves interpreting meaning, questioning the existing status quo, and developing a new mindset. Transformative learning informs the development of IC as critical, and reflective reading, writing, and discussion of cultural topics and issues can help students reconsider their previous beliefs, thus developing new and multiple perspectives. At the same time, engagement in cultural study, target culture encounters, and reflection can change one's thinking and behavior toward another culture, create a new worldview, and ultimately turn into a transformative experience.

Another motivation for the study is the state of world language education today. As colleges and universities face some unprecedented challenges (Parker, 2020; Schwalenberg, 2019), enrollments in the humanities are decreasing, and language programs are often considered the lowest-hanging fruit when budget cuts are implemented (Johnson, 2019). However, these institutions of higher learning continue to include IC in their mission statements and learning outcomes (Barrette & Paesani, 2017). As such, it is even more important to be able to quantify how the required language classes contribute to wider university efforts toward intercultural development. Although some recent studies have addressed assessing cultural learning objectives (Barrette & Paesani, 2017; Barski & Wilkerson-Barker, 2019), none have considered a guided cultural practice within a culture portfolio (as did Wright, 2000) or assessed cultural growth specifically with a curriculum that utilizes culture-centered textbooks. However, there is a growing body of work in the field of world language education that has moved toward bridging transformative learning theory and the work we do in the language classroom (Crane et al., 2018; Crane & Sosulski, 2020; Goulah, 2007; Ivers, 2007; Johnson, 2015; Johnson & Mullins Nelson, 2010; King, 2000; Sosulski, 2013). Also, few attempts have been made to assess cultural learning in the core curriculum since Wright's (2000) study. The current study investigates the hypothesis that placing culture at the core of language curriculum leads to noticeable IC growth among students as compared to instructional practices that ascribe to primarily teaching language (Barski & Wilkerson-Barker, 2019). Additionally, the question of whether a further adoption of the culture portfolio project implemented by Wright (2000) affects IC growth is addressed.

The study

Purpose

The purpose of this study was to examine whether the IC of Spanish language students who complete the culture portfolio exhibits a determinate and statistically significant growth compared with Spanish language students who do not complete these assignments. The following research question guided the study:

Is there a difference between the Cross-Cultural Adaptability Inventory (CCAI) gain scores of students in the treatment and the control group?[1]

Instrument and procedure

Replicating the original Wright (2000) study, this study utilized the CCAI as a pretest and posttest for both the treatment and control groups to measure IC growth (Kelley & Meyers, 1995a). The CCAI is a 50-item computer-generated or paper-and-pencil assessment instrument that was designed to measure four specific areas associated with IC: emotional resilience, flexibility and openness, perceptual acuity, and personal autonomy (Paige et al., 2003). Wright (2000) chose the CCAI for the original study specifically because "its design is based on factors that are consistently identified in the literature as being important for successful cross-cultural functioning" (p. 331). The use of CCAI also aligns with the MLA report's charge for language programs to prepare students to "function as informed and capable interlocutors with educated native speakers in the target language … [and] to reflect on the world and themselves through the lens of another language and culture" (p. 3). The measure was completed electronically by all study participants in the control and the treatment groups in the first week of class, and the posttest was administered as a pencil-and-paper assessment on the day of the final exam. In addition to the completion of the CCAI at the time of the pretest, students completed a Personal Data Sheet indicating their sex, age, year in school, major, and any previous experience abroad, as was done in the original study.

Research study design

Following the original study (Wright, 2000), this study used a quasi-experimental intact group design (two sections of the same class) to represent two groups that were evaluated with a pretest and posttest. All study participants in both the control and the treatment groups performed the CCAI in the first week of class. However, the original study was completed with first-semester

German students, while the present study was conducted with third-semester Spanish students following the original description of the study population in terms of number of semesters of language study rather than proficiency levels. Additionally, the original study was carried out with a total of 103 students in four sections, whereas this study was implemented with a total of 48 students in two sections, which constituted the total number of students enrolled in the class during the second semester of the spring of 2018–2019 academic year. After the 15-week treatment period in which one class followed the regular curriculum and the other completed the culture portfolio project, the posttest was administered. Four students who only fulfilled the pretest were not included in the study. The remaining 44 students were divided into a treatment group ($n = 19$) and a control group ($n = 25$). As with the original study, the difference between the pretest and posttest scores was used to compute gain scores that were analyzed to address the research question.

The culture-centered world language curriculum

The curriculum of the world languages program at Biola University is centered on culture. Thus, culture is approached not only as knowledge and information but as a process of learning necessary to interact effectively with others who might be different from ourselves. The implementation of a flipped curriculum allows us to focus on cultural topics in class, while grammar is practiced outside of class within homework assignments. Thus, in both control and treatment groups, classroom conversations and activities are centered around culture. An important part of the course work is out-of-class conversational practice on the *TalkAbroad* website where students engage in interactions with native speakers several times throughout the semester in each level of our core world language classes.[2] The course textbooks afford equal attention to language and culture; for example, the Spanish textbook, *Rostros*, used by both groups in the study, claims to have "two overarching goals: cultural proficiency and language proficiency" (Woolsey et al., 2019, p. 8). The four textbook units covered during the semester center around the following geographic regions: Unit One, Conquista y colonia (Conquest and Colony) includes the northern, central and southern areas of Mexico. Unit Two, El Caribe – Raza y mestizaje (The Caribbean – Race and Fusion), covers the countries of the Dominican Republic, Cuba and Puerto Rico. Unit Three, La gran Colombia – Independencia e identidad (The Great Colombia – Independence and identity), treats the areas of Venezuela, Panama, Colombia, and Ecuador. Finally, Unit Four, Centroamérica – Ecología y economía (Central America – Ecology and Economy), explores the regions of Guatemala, Honduras, Nicaragua, El Salvador, and Costa Rica.

An example of the way the cultural topics may be addressed in both groups is as follows. In the first unit, the class is exploring the region of Mexico. In class, students begin by identifying an influential person in their own lives and then describing someone who they consider to be a traitor (Woolsey et al., 2019, p. 29). The historical figure of "La Malinche" is then explored (Woolsey et al., 2019, p. 30). Next, students share what they admire about other cultures in relation to the idea of being "malinchista," followed by a discussion on when it is acceptable to admire other cultures (Woolsey et al., 2019, p. 31). Examination of the song "La maldición de la Malinche" by Amparo Ochoa (Woolsey et al., 2019, p. 32) is followed by an exploration of personal identity. Students share aspects of their own identity and discuss which identity traits can be changed. The classroom discussion topics are related to required out-of-class conversations with native speakers or heritage learners, in which participants consider personal stories of family, space, and identity. Spanish language is used to engage in cultural topics and to compare the content of authentic reading texts (be it historical texts or contemporary interview transcripts) and the live stories of their conversation partners (either Latin Americans living in other countries or heritage learners in the U.S.) and their own. Thus, in both groups, the study of language and culture in the context of a geographical region occurs on a deeper level than a mere presentation of facts and textbook themes to include additional issues as well as personal exploration.

The control group

Replicating the original study, the control group followed the university's prescribed language curriculum, while the treatment group completed a portfolio project. Every effort was made to keep all other elements congruent between the groups. The syllabus and textbook were identical in terms of content, assigned homework, quizzes, tests, exams, grading/attendance policies, and the amount of target language used by the instructor (85%–90%). Both sections covered the first four units of the course textbook. To maintain parity in both groups, the control group completed a different final project and writing assignments, which equaled 20% of the final grade, the same portion as the culture portfolio project with all its components.

The treatment group

Similarly to the original study, the treatment group had additional lessons in class regarding culture as a construct that can affect communication and understanding. Wright (2000) appended an example of one of his five lessons to the original research article (p. 340), which was adapted from Behal-Thomsen et al. (1993). His lesson was very similar in structure to how culture was treated in both the control and treatment groups of this study. However, the treatment group participated in two extra lessons on communication with other cultures. One lesson examined making cultural assumptions based on behaviors and implemented two activities from the book *A Handbook for Developing Multicultural Awareness* (Pedersen, 1988). Students were presented with the idea that we judge others' behavior based on our own cultural values (Pedersen, 1988, pp. 23–25), considered examples of some behaviors, and explored their own values behind them. The class then completed the "Draw a House Awareness" and the "Outside Expert Awareness" exercises as experiential activities (Pedersen, 1988, pp. 28–29). During another class, students focused on body language and nonverbal communication that can impede effective communication even when both parties share the same language (Pedersen, 1988) and completed a gesture quiz (Nine-Curt, 1976). The two lessons, along with other cultural discussions embedded in the curriculum, followed the approach outlined by Wright (2000, p. 335). However, because the original study was done in a first-semester class, the cultural lessons were conducted in English. The two lessons were conducted in the target language.

In addition to the culture lessons, the treatment group completed the culture portfolio assignments, which were grouped together as part of a semester-long process, culminating in a poster presentation at the university's Celebration of Research and Scholarship in the final weeks of the semester. In the original study, Wright (2000) included the instructions that were given to students for the portfolio, which was described as "engaging in a topic through a multistep process" (p. 341). His model was a four-step process that consisted of a plan/outline, culture questions, a draft, revision of the draft, and the poster presentation adapted from Moore (1994).

This perceptual replication study, however, utilized a modified version of the cultural objectives and performance tasks that were developed by Schulz (2007) as a means of organizing the portfolio into weekly assignments. Thus, students received weekly feedback from the instructor and could revise each performance task prior to the final portfolio presentation, which synthesized their learning within each objective. For the presentation, students chose a geographic region from the course content and completed in-depth research through the use of websites, research articles, and interviews with native speakers on the *TalkAbroad* platform or heritage learners studying at the same university. Students in the treatment group were assigned a conversation partner/heritage student for three 30-minute conversations/interviews outside of class; they also attended a cultural event and participated in a community service project with this partner. In addition to conversation sessions, they completed one *TalkAbroad* online interview with a native Spanish speaker living in a Spanish-speaking country from the area they were researching; in the original study the students did not interview heritage or native speakers as part of the project. The treatment group also completed three in-class writing assignments in which they reflected on the cultural topics discussed in class. They later revised their essays for inclusion in their portfolios.

The control group

The control and treatment groups maintained parity in most areas except for the culture portfolio assignments. As an out-of-class assignment, the control group students participated in three 30-minute discussions with native speakers from the *TalkAbroad* website; the conversation topics were identical to the ones covered in the conversation sessions of the treatment group with heritage learners, which also aligned with the cultural course curriculum. Instead of reflecting on the topics in the culture portfolio, the control group students wrote a 400-word reflection paper summarizing what they learned from their partners. During the semester, they also completed two in-class essays, but instead of the cultural reflections on the topics covered in class and in culture portfolio assignments, control group students (1) wrote a letter to a friend or a loved one and (2) described a family story or event to elicit writing in the present tense and the past tense, respectively. At the end of the semester, control group students partnered with classmates to choose a country and create an interactive PowerPoint as a final presentation of the country's history, typical food, music, geography, and an important public figure (author, actor, athlete, artist, etc.).

Data analysis and discussion

This replication study revealed significant differences between the treatment and the control groups' mean gain scores (see Table 8.1). The treatment group also experienced increased IC growth as compared to the original study, as seen from the statistical differences in gain scores for the subscales *flexibility/openness*, *perceptual acuity*, and the CCAI composite score. However, the gain scores in the subscales *personal autonomy* and *emotional resilience* were not significantly different.

TABLE 8.1 Results of *t*-tests on CCAI Composite and subscales for the original (Wright, 2000) and current studies

Scale	Group	Mean Gain Study 1	Mean Gain Study 2	p-value Study 1	p-value Study 2
Flexibility/openness	Control	−1.20	1.92		
	Treatment	2.40	3.74	0.004	0.007
Personal autonomy	Control	−0.36	1.12		
	Treatment	1.10	0.53	0.04	0.170
Emotional resilience	Control	−0.50	−0.28		
	Treatment	1.80	2.00	0.10	0.086
Perceptual acuity	Control	0.70	0.36		
	Treatment	1.70	1.84	0.36	0.06
CCAI Composite	Control	−1.29	3.12		
	Treatment	7.00	8.11	0.01	0.004

Note: Study 1 is Wright (2000); Study 2 is the current study.

Mean gain scores for the treatment group in the replication study exceeded the original study in the categories of *flexibility/openness, emotional resilience, perceptual acuity*, and the CCAI composite scores. Additionally, the control group's scores in the replication study surpassed the original study in the areas of *flexibility/ openness, personal autonomy, perceptual acuity*, and the CCAI composite scores.

Flexibility/openness

Of the three subscales displaying a statistically significant difference for the treatment group, the *flexibility/openness* subscale ($p = 0.007$) aligns most accurately with the learning outcomes of the core modern languages program at the university: someone who is flexible and open to others who are different is better able to interact in other cultures. Table 8.1 shows statistically significant differences occurring in this area, not only between the treatment and the control groups but between the gain scores in the treatment group of the original study (+2.40) and this replication study (+3.74). The control group in the replication study also made gain scores (+1.92) as opposed to the regressive scores of the control group in the original study (−1.20). The gain score difference suggests a marked benefit in the flexibility and openness skill area to the focus on culture in the materials and curriculum of the program.

Personal autonomy

According to Kelley and Meyers (1995a), "[P]eople with high personal autonomy feel empowered" and "have a strong sense of identity. Personal autonomy also includes the ability to maintain one's own personal values and beliefs, to take responsibility for one's actions, and to respect oneself and others" (p. 2). This is the one area in which the treatment group made the least amount of growth (0.53) as opposed to both the control group (1.12) and the treatment group from the original study (1.10). Because the focus of the culture lessons and the culture portfolio was on understanding the values of the other culture, the area of personal autonomy demonstrated minimal growth. It is noteworthy to emphasize that the control group in this study displayed similar growth to the treatment group of the original study, once again suggesting that the focus on culture in the curriculum and materials has created opportunity for growth along the spectrum of culture learning.

Perceptual acuity

According to Kelley and Meyers (1995a),

> Perceptual acuity is associated with attentiveness to interpersonal relations and to verbal and nonverbal behavior. It also involves paying attention to

the context of the communication, being able to read people's emotions, being sensitive to one's effect on others, and communicating accurately.

(p. 2)

Treatment group gain scores for this subscale significantly exceeded control group gain scores ($p = 0.006$). Gain scores for both the original study (1.70) and the replication study (1.84) were similar, although the replication study does demonstrate slightly higher growth. Perceptual acuity appears to be the one area that clearly benefited from the cultural lessons and the culture portfolio assignments, as the control group in the replication study made even less progress (0.36) than did the control group in the original study (0.70).

Emotional resilience

Kelley and Meyers (1995a) characterize emotional resilience (ER) as "one's ability to cope with the unfamiliar and to react positively to new experiences" (p. 2). The ER score is meant to predict a person's ability to "maintain emotional equilibrium in a new or changing environment" (Kelley & Meyers, 1995b, p. 14). Once again, since ER focuses more on self than others, it is not directly related to the goals of the class or the culture portfolio. For that reason, the lack of statistically significant ER growth seems understandable for the treatment group in both the original study and the replication study. It is worth noting that although the replication study displayed slightly more growth in ER (2.00), both treatment groups were similar (1.80). Also, both control groups displayed regressive scores in this area, indicating lower ER after taking the class than at the beginning. Since ER scale determines the degree of individual recovery from unpleasant or negative feelings associated with cross-cultural experiences (Kelley & Meyers, 1995b), one can assume that students who did not complete the reflective practice provided by the culture portfolio may have experienced some of the cultural content negatively.

CCAI composite

The combined mean gain scores for the four CCAI dimensions were significantly higher for the treatment group in both the original study (0.01) and the replication study (0.004), providing supporting evidence for the benefits of the culture portfolio for cultural learning and growth. As the most reliable indicator of cross-cultural adaptability, the composite score suggests that, even though the control group in the replication study did not demonstrate a regressive score (3.12) as did the control group in the original study (−1.29), the gain scores for both treatment groups (7.00/8.11) significantly outweigh the gain for the control group of the replication study. Consequently, a shift of curricular focus to culture allows world language programs to progress along the IC continuum. The composite score also provides further evidence for Wright's (2000) conclusion that "a desire to interact effectively with people of different cultural backgrounds does not necessarily develop on its own" (p. 337) and supports the integration of the culture portfolio into language teaching pedagogy.

Classroom implications

Based on the results of this replication study, I can make the following recommendations to enhance IC development in a world language classroom.

A curriculum with culture at the core

First, it is important that students experience a curriculum that centers on the development of IC at the core. Culture is a priority in the National Standards for World Readiness (2015) in both Cultures and Communities standards; to achieve these standards and a deeper level of understanding, culture learning must extend beyond the culture-specific knowledge (e.g., foods, greetings, customs) that is so often a part of language curriculum (Deardorff, 2009). It is essential that student portfolio learning is supported in the themes and discussions that occur in the classroom. Similarly, the beginner-level language courses that are conceived as a curriculum can include portfolio projects that span across various courses – allowing for the time and consistency necessary to grow in IC (Chávez et al., 2003; Rifkin, 2012b).

Experiential culture lessons

In addition to a culture-centered curriculum, evidence from Wright's (2000) study and this replication suggest that integrating culture lessons into specific class sessions can produce further IC growth. Other research in the field shows that additional cultural instruction can not only promote intercultural competency but also increase positive attitudes toward the language and culture (Acheson et al., 2015; Michelson, 2019). The lessons that are experiential in nature and regard culture as a social construct with value-based rules and behaviors allow students to begin experiencing culture on a personal level, first examining their own values and behaviors and then shifting this focus outward (Pedersen, 1988). Attention should also be given to nonverbal methods of communication that can be even more difficult to navigate than the language itself (Nine-Curt, 1976). Within the lessons, students should be encouraged and supported to engage in cultural interactions that occur outside of class, which helps them to develop "skills for interpreting cultural interactions" (Jacobson et al., 1999, p. 477).

Interactive assignments

Students can engage in interactive practice with native speakers and heritage language learners in the local community and in online platforms similar to *TalkAbroad*, which connects them with a native speaker in the target language country. These interactive assignments were completed by the control group in the replication study and may have contributed to the IC growth that occurred even without the added portfolio assignments, as opposed to the regressive scores that occurred among the students in the control group of the original study. The interactions help students become observers of culture, ask questions, and interpret findings based on evidence from authentic experiences developing ethnographic skills suggested by Abrams et al. (2006). Additionally, these intentional experiences can motivate students to learn more on their intercultural journey (Cubillos & Ilvento, 2018; Cranton, 2006; Furstenberg, 2010; Tecedor & Vasseur, 2020; Wilkinson et al., 2015). Designing interactive tasks requires extensive coordination and organization on the part of the instructor, but as one of the most essential elements to the students' engagement with the culture portfolio, they provide a transformative learning experience. Deep intercultural learning occurs when students can engage in interaction with another culture while they investigate, discuss, and reflect on this learning in the classroom and through connected assignments. Other scholars have argued that "without direct experience of the culture, culture learning is only *cognitive boundary crossing*, the acquisition of a *scholarly skill* which leaves unexamined and unchallenged the learners' previous beliefs and attitudes" (Paige et al., 2003, p. 187). The personal contact and dialogue made possible through interactive assignments can create a deeper level of understanding that has been documented through research (Abrams, 2002; Johnson & Mullins Nelson, 2010; Jurasek, 1995; Kramsch, 1993; Robinson-Stuart & Nocon, 1996). The treatment group in this replication study also engaged in several conversations with heritage learners and participated in a cultural event and a service project with this conversation partner. Cubillos and Ilvento (2018), in their summary of recent research, have stated,

> [M]eaningful personal interactions must be cultivated and developed over time, requiring the confluence of five essential factors: equality of status during contact, a social context that supports equality between groups, collaborative engagement towards a shared goal, opportunity to develop the level of intimacy necessary to contradict previously held stereotypes, and the support of applicable authority figures.
>
> *(pp. 261–262)*

The sustained interpersonal contact was achieved by pairing the students with heritage learners who studied at the same university, thus creating a relationship that may have stimulated the increased IC growth among students in the treatment group of the replication study (Cubillos & Ilvento, 2018). Although some communities might not have access to heritage learners within the same schools, these relationships can be formed through sister schools in different countries (Cubillos & Ilvento, 2018) or through service projects in the community (Rifkin, 2012b).

Community service

Students in the treatment group of this replication study participated in group community service projects. Although absent from the original study, a service project incorporated into the portfolio assignments allows students to apply their culture learning in a target language community, thus providing an opportunity for IC growth and allowing them to experience "language and culture learning for now, and not just for some future application in the so-called real world" (Byram, 2012, p. 10). The benefits of community service projects have been documented by other scholars (Clifford & Reisinger, 2019; Pak, 2020; Rifkin, 2012b; Wagner et al., 2018) who have noted positive gains in knowledge, attitudes, and behaviors due to intense interactions with target language communities.

Research and reflection

As students completed a series of research tasks for their chosen region, they needed to report and reflect on their findings. Regular reflection is recommended as an integral part of the portfolio process and student reflections can serve as data (part of a triangulated assessment process) that can "capture evidence of perspective transformation" (Crane & Sosulski, 2020, p. 76). Low-stakes reflective writing assignments "allow learners to confront their beliefs about cultural difference while directing their attention to specific aspects of the experience," pushing them to display IC (Tecedor & Vasseur, 2020, p. 780) and track their growth and development through each intercultural interaction (Crane & Sosulski, 2020; Cranton & Hoggan, 2012; Deardorff, 2009; Wilkinson et al., 2015).

Timely formative assessment

It is important that students submit their work on a regular basis, which provides opportunities for structured formative assessment through instructor feedback, or "targeted intervention" (Deardorff, 2009, p. 479). While submitted assignments allow the instructor to assess whether students are understanding the concepts, the feedback can guide them in their work (Furstenberg, 2010). Assignments can be included as part of the homework so that work that needs deeper reflection or further research can be marked for revision for the final project. Submitting their assignments affords students the opportunity to revisit their thinking and reassess their learning. Since these performance tasks are scheduled assignments that students complete throughout the semester, formative assessment becomes an integral part and a built-in function of the culture learning process (Fantini, 2009: Moore, 1994; Schulz, 2007; Wilkinson et al., 2015).

A place for summative assessment

Students should be given the opportunity to present their work in a public forum, e.g., a university or departmental event. A final presentation allows them to synthesize their learning and present examples for their audience. In addition to their portfolio, students in this study prepared a poster presentation for the university's Celebration of Scholarship and Research in both English and Spanish that they could adapt depending on their audience. The instructor can grade student presentations as part of the class project assignment while other forms of assessment can occur within the same venue. For example, teams of faculty can assess the university's core curriculum global citizenship goal or intercultural competency outcome. The culture portfolio is a collection of artifacts that can be assessed across a program to measure growth and determine how well students are achieving the learning outcomes. This evidence of learning can further inform a program's "curriculum development, assessment practices, and refinement of student learning outcomes" (Barrette & Paesani, 2017).

Conclusion

Whereas the benefits of centering a world language curriculum on culture learning have been documented in the literature, studies that measure growth in IC within courses are lacking. Classroom-based evidence has shown that without a directed effort to teach culture, students do not achieve progress in culture learning within language classes (Barski & Wilkerson-Barker, 2019; Wright, 2000). This replication study sought to measure IC learning growth within two types of classes that subscribe to a curriculum with culture at the core, one with a culture portfolio project and one without. Although the present study had additional elements in both control and treatment groups in comparison to the original study by Wright (2000), the results demonstrate a broad alignment of the findings suggesting the benefits of materials that focus on culture learning, interactive practice with native and heritage speakers, and community service. Evidence shows that utilizing textbooks that center culture and providing students with opportunities to interact with native speakers throughout the semester produces growth toward IC, as was seen in both the treatment and control groups. However, in both the original study and this replication study, those students who participated in experiential culture lessons and engaged in reflective practice through a culture portfolio project demonstrated more growth in intercultural learning as measured by the CCAI. Future research could further isolate these variables to determine which ones produce more growth and could measure students' progress across several beginner-level courses.

Notes

1 Wright's study also included a research question to see if other variables such as sex, age, or major influenced gain score differences. This study also examined the data for these variables, but no correlation was found, so the question and discussion of these elements was eliminated from the chapter.
2 Students in our program begin to converse with native Spanish speakers through the *TalkAbroad* website in their first semester of language study. Our flipped curriculum allows us to use the classroom as a laboratory for conversation practice, even at the beginner level, to prepare students for out-of-classrrom conversational experiences. The *TalkAbroad* conversation partners are trained to interact with basic language learners.

References

Abrams, Z. I. (2002). Surfing to cross-cultural awareness: Using internet mediated projects to explore cultural stereotypes. *Foreign Language Annals, 35*(2), 141–160.

Abrams, Z.I., Byrd, D. R., Boovy, B., & Möhring, A. (2006). Culture portfolios revisited: Feedback from students and instructors. *Die Unterrichtspraxis, 39*(1), 80–90.

Acheson, K., Nelson, M., & Luna, K. (2015). Measuring the impact of instruction in intercultural communication on secondary Spanish learners' attitudes and motivation. *Foreign Language Annals, 48*(2), 203–217.

American Council of Trustees and Alumni (ACTA). (2017). What will they learn? 2017–18. A survey of core requirements at our nation's colleges and universities. goacta.org/resource/what-will-they-learn-2017-18/

Barrette, C, & Paesani, K. (2017). Conceptualizing cultural literacy through student learning outcomes assessment. *Foreign Language Annals, 51*(2), 331–343.

Barski, E., & Wilkerson-Barker, D. (2019). Making the most of general education foreign language requirements. *Foreign Language Annals, 52*(3), 491–506.

Behal-Thomsen, H., Lunquist-Mog, A., & Mog, P. (1993). *Typisch Deutsch? Arbeitsbuch zu Aspekten Deutscher Mentalitat* [Typically German? A workbook for aspects of German mentality]. Langenscheidt.

Bragger, J. D., & Rice, D. B. (2000). Foreign language materials: Yesterday, today, and tomorrow. In R. M. Terry (Ed.), *Agents of change in a changing age* (pp. 107–140). National Textbook Company.

Byram, M. (2012). Language awareness and (critical) cultural awareness – relationships, comparisons and contrasts. *Language Awareness, 21*(1–2), 5–13.

Chávez, A. F., Guido-DiBrito, F., & Mallory, S. L. (2003). Learning to value the "other": A framework of individual diversity development. *Journal of College Student Development, 44*(4), 453–469. https://doi.org/10.1353/csd.2003.0038

Clifford, J., & Reisinger, D. S. (2019). *Community-based language learning: A framework for educators*. Georgetown University Press.

Crane, C., Fingerhuth, M., & Huenlich, D. (2018). "What makes this so complicated?" On the value of disorienting dilemmas in language instruction. In S. Dubreil, & S. L. Thorne (Eds.), *Engaging the world: Social pedagogies and language learning* (pp. 227–252). Heinle.

Crane, C., & Sosulski, M. J. (2020). Staging transformative learning across collegiate language curricula: Student perceptions of structured reflection for language learning. *Foreign Language Annals, 53*(1), 69–91.

Cranton, P. (2006). *Understanding and promoting transformative learning: A guide for educators of adults*. Jossey-Bass.

Cranton, P., & Hoggan, C. (2012). Evaluating transformative learning. In E. W. Taylor, & P. Cranton (Eds.), *The handbook of transformative learning* (pp. 520–535). Jossey-Bass.

Cubillos, J., & Ilvento, T. (2018). Intercultural contact in short-term study abroad programs. *Hispania, 101*(2), 249–266.

Deardorff, D. K. (2009). Implementing intercultural competence assessment. In D. K. Deardorff (Ed.), *The SAGE handbook of intercultural competence* (pp. 477–491). SAGE.

Fantini, A. E. (2009). Assessing intercultural competence: Issues and tools. In D. K. Deardorff (Ed.), *The SAGE handbook of intercultural competence* (pp. 456–476). SAGE.

Forester, L., Antoniuk, D., Dykstra-Prumi, P., & Antoniuk, O. (2007). *Weiter geht's! Intermediate German language and culture*. Live Oak Multimedia.

Forester, L., Antoniuk, D., Wegel, C., Budarz, S., & Douma, J. (2018). *Auf geht's! Beginning German language and culture* (4th ed.). Live Oak Multimedia.

Forester, L., Antoniuk, D., Woolsley, D., Casarez-Heyda, C., & Douma, J. (2017). *Ritmos: Beginning Spanish language and culture* (2nd ed., Vol. 1–2). Live Oak Multimedia.

Furstenberg, D. O. (2010). Making culture the core of the language class: Can it be done? *Modern Language Journal, 94*, 329–332.

Goulah, J. (2007). Village voices, global visions: Digital video as a transformative foreign language learning tool. *Foreign Language Annals, 40*(1), 62–78.

Ivers, J. J. (2007). Metacognition and foreign language cultural instruction. *Journal of Transformative Education, 5*(2), 152–162.

Jacobson, W., Sleicher, D., & Burke, M. (1999). Portfolio assessment of intercultural competence. *International Journal of Intercultural Relations, 23*(3), 467–492. https://doi.org/10.1016/S0147-1767(99)00006-1

Johnson, S. (2019, January 22) Colleges lose a 'stunning' 651 foreign language programs in 3 years. *The Chronicle of Higher Education*. https://www.chronicle.com/article/colleges-lose-a-stunning-651-foreign-language-programs-in-3-years/

Johnson, S. M. (2015). *Adult learning in the language classroom*. Multilingual Matters.

Johnson, S. M., & Mullins Nelson, B. (2010). Above and beyond the syllabus: Transformation in an adult, foreign language classroom. *Language Awareness, 19*(1), 35–50. https://doi.org/10.1080/09658410903079165

Jurasek, R. (1995). Using ethnography to bridge the gap between study abroad and the on-campus language and culture curriculum. In C. Kramsch (Ed.), *Redefining the boundaries of language study* (pp. 221–251). Heinle & Heinle.

Kelley, C., & Meyers, J. (1995a). *Cross-cultural adaptability inventory*. National Computer Systems.

Kelley, C., & Meyers, J. (1995b). *Cross-cultural adaptability inventory: Manual*. NCS Pearson.

King, K. P. (2000). The adult ESL experience: Facilitating perspective transformation in the classroom. *Adult Basic Education, 10*(2), 69–89.

Kramsch, C. (1993). Language study as border study: Experiencing difference. *European Journal of Education, 28*(3), 349–358.

Mezirow, J. (1997). Transformative learning: Theory to practice. *New Directions for Adult and Continuing Education, 74*, 5–12.

Michelson, K. (2019). Global simulation as a mediating tool for teaching and learning language and culture as discourse. *Foreign Language Annals, 52*(2), 284–313.

Modern Language Association Ad Hoc Committee on Foreign Languages. (2007). *Foreign languages and higher education: New structures for a changed world*. Modern Language Association.

Moore, Z. T. (1994). The portfolio and testing culture. In C. R. Hancock, & S. Brooks-Brown (Eds.), *Teaching, testing and assessment: Making the connection* (pp. 163–182). National Textbook Company.

National Standards in Foreign Language Education Project (NSLEP). (2015). *World-readiness standards for learning languages* (4th ed.).

Nine-Curt, C. J. (1976). *Teacher training pack for a course on cultural awareness*. National Assessment and Dissemination Center for Bilingual Education.

Paige, R. M., Jorstad, H. L., Siaya, L., Klein, F., & Colby, J. (2003). Culture learning in language education: A review of the literature. In D. L. Lange, & R. M. Paige (Eds.), *Culture as the core: Perspectives on culture in second language learning* (pp. 173–236). Information Age Publishing.

Pak, C. (2020). Exploring the long-term impact of service-learning: Former students of Spanish revisit their community engagement experiences. *Hispania, 103*(1), 67–85.

Parker, S. (2020). The future of higher education in a disruptive world. *KPMG International*. https://assets.kpmg/content/dam/kpmg/xx/pdf/2020/10/future-of-higher-education.pdf

Pedersen, P. (1988). *A handbook for developing multicultural awareness*. American Counseling Association.

Porte, G., & McManus, K. (2019). *Doing replication research in applied linguistics*. Routledge.

Rifkin, B. (2012a). Learners' goals and curricular designs: The field's response to the 2007 MLA report on foreign language education. *ADFL Bulletin, 42*(1), 68–75.

Rifkin, B. (2012b). The world languages curriculum at the center of postsecondary education. *Liberal Education, 98*, 54–57.

Robinson-Stuart, G., & Nocon, H. (1996). Second culture acquisition: Ethnography in the foreign language classroom. *The Modern Language Journal, 80*, 431–449.

Schulz, R. (2007). The challenge of assessing cultural understanding in the context of foreign language instruction. *Foreign Language Annals, 40*(1), 9–26.

Schwalenberg, L. (2019, January 29). Changes in attitudes toward higher education must prompt changes within institutions. *The Badger Herald*. https://badgerherald.com/opinion/2019/01/29/changes-in-attitudes-toward-higher-education-must-prompt-changes-within-institutions/

Sosulski, M. J. (2013). From Broadway to Berlin: Transformative learning through German hip-hop. *Die Unterrichtspraxis/Teaching German, 46*(1), 91–105.

Tecedor, M., & Vasseur, R. (2020). Videoconferencing and the development of intercultural competence: Insights from students' self-reflections. *Foreign Language Annals, 53*(4), 761–784.

Wagner, M., Conlon Perugini, D., & Byram, M. (Eds.). (2018). *Teaching intercultural competence across the age range*. Multilingual Matters.

Wilkinson, S., Calkins, P., & Dinesen, T. (2015). Creating a culture-driven classroom one activity at a time. *Central States Conference on the Teaching of Foreign Languages Report*, 1–16.

Woolsey, D., Casarez-Heyda, C., Forester, L., Antoniuk, D., & Douma, J. (2019). *Rostros. Intermediate Spanish language and culture* (Vol 1–2). Live Oak Multimedia.

Wright, D. A. (2000). Culture as information and culture as affective process: A comparative study. *Foreign Language Annals*, *33*(3), 330–341.

9
EMPLOYING CONCEPT MAPS IN TEACHING FOREIGN LANGUAGE CULTURE

Elmira Gerfanova

In recent years, much attention has been devoted to developing student intercultural competence (IC), which is defined as a multidimensional framework of knowledge, attitudes, skills, and beliefs that constantly evolves as new knowledge about target cultural concepts assimilates into the person's experience (Byram & Wagner, 2018; Deardorff, 2020). The diversity of modern local and global communities makes cultural understanding and communication a key competence of the third millennium (Griffith et al., 2016).

Kazakhstan's integration into the global economic community and the republic's international activity make the development of IC a high priority for its citizens. The significance of integrating the language and culture instruction in a foreign language (FL) classroom is documented in the Conception of Development of Kazakhstan Foreign Language Education (Kunanbayeva et al., 2004), the principal framework for FL education that aligns Kazakhstani FL instruction with national and international standards such as the Common European Framework of Reference for Languages (Council of Europe, 2001). The authors of the Conception note that learning a new language along with the new culture fosters one's intercultural communication abilities while helping avoid misunderstandings and conflicts that may be caused by historical, political, and religious differences across cultures (Kunanbayeva et al., 2004).

The components and principles of target language (TL) and culture integration in Kazakhstan FL education are thoroughly elaborated theoretically but turn into abstract notions when educators and students are faced with realities of classroom teaching. As instructors strive to achieve the program objectives, such as developing pronunciation, vocabulary, and grammar, as well as reading, writing, speaking, and listening skills, they are left with very little time to devote to intercultural goals. Even in a course specifically designed to integrate culture and

DOI: 10.4324/9781003058441-11

language skills, the main instructional focus remains on linguistic targets. Thus, while the title and the stated goal of a first-year "Basic Foreign Language in the Context of Intercultural Communication" course accentuate the development of intercultural communication skills by fostering students' intercultural understanding and awareness, only four hours out of the 45-hour course are allotted to learning about the target culture. Similarly, an analysis of leading English-language textbooks in Kazakhstan revealed that out of 2,400 learning activities, only 0.92% offered cultural information about history, holidays, food, places of interest, etc., never extending to such topics as gestures, communication style, or target cultural values or providing opportunities for comparison and reflection (Gerfanova, 2020). The prevalence of language over culture is common to many language programs in Kazakhstan where instructors struggle to cope with numerous tasks of teaching language relegating cultural learning activities to the background (Gerfanova, 2020); a similar disproportion of linguistic and cultural instruction is observed in other teaching contexts as well (Nemtchinova, 2020). Concept mapping can help bring cultural teaching to the forefront of language work as students use the TL to express and discuss the new and familiar concepts and relationships between them. Concept maps (CMs) allow learners to dive deeper into the intercultural aspect of communication, to understand similarities and differences between the two cultures, and to develop an appreciation of the target cultural perceptions and attitudes. They engage students in an active exploration of first language and target language cultural concepts, thus making students "more proficient at meaningful learning" (Novak & Cañas, 2007, p. 31). In this chapter, I will first discuss the importance of concepts for culture and the use of CMs for native and target cultural exploration and comparison, and then report the results of the study examining the effect of concept mapping on the development of cultural competence and beginning students' attitudes toward CMs in a first-year English-language and culture course at a Kazakhstani university.

Literature review

TL culture as a network of concepts

Researchers and educators worldwide agree that to communicate successfully with TL speakers students need to have a solid comprehension of the TL culture (Freitag-Hild, 2018). It has been emphasized that language skills cannot be taught in isolation since the linguistic code is linked to sociocultural context (Buttjes, 1990) and that language without culture turns into meaningless symbols which students can fill with erroneous meanings (Kramsch, 1995; Thanasoulas, 2001).

While it is difficult to provide a single definition of a complex and multifaceted phenomenon of culture, it is often seen as "the ideas, customs, skills, arts, and tools that characterize a given group of people in a given period of time" (Brown & Lee, 2015). Of particular importance to this study is the idea of culture as a network of interrelated concepts. Thus, Hong (2009) defines culture as "networks of knowledge consisting of learned routines of thinking, feeling, and interacting with other people, as well as a corpus of substantive assertions and ideas about aspects of the world" (p. 4). Another view suggests that culture is made of concepts and relationships between them; this conceptual system represents all the cultural information entering a person's mental world and enables understanding of culturally specific human interactions (Arutyunova, 1999; Karasik, 1996; Silversteine, 2004; Stepanov, 2004).

In their review of various interpretations of the notions of concepts and culture, Ojalehto and Medin (2015) stress that the two are deeply interconnected and interactive processes. They note that concepts form the building blocks of such cultural systems as artifacts, languages, practices, and values; they "permeate cultural behavior and are embedded in language and action" (Ojalehto & Medin, 2015, p. 251). In turn, culture can be regarded as the way of thinking about a particular concept or a series of related concepts that provides the members of the culture with a general orientation to the world, affects their cognitive processes, and shapes their attitudes and values.

As Ojalehto and Medin (2015) note, concepts can perform many functions and take on many forms, which results in multiple definitions of the notion of a cultural concept. One approach to concepts considers them as "units of thought" (Carey, 2009; Gelman, 2009). Expanding on this idea, culture may be viewed as the force determining "what we perceive, how we react to situations, and how we relate to other people" (Hofstede, 1984, p. 31).

Another approach regards concepts as nuclear units of a micromodel of culture that creates the picture of the world in the minds of members of a linguacultural community (Zusman, 2001). The concepts encompass universal (e.g., time, space), social (e.g., freedom, law), and culturally specific categories (e.g., national cuisine, colors, symbols) that have different connotations for members of a particular culture due to differences in sociocultural contexts and experiences in perceiving the surrounding reality (Kurganova, 2003, 2004, 2006). Given the interpretation of culture as a conceptual network, concept mapping presents an effective tool for cultural exploration that allows students to identify new and familiar concepts of the target culture, reflect on their significance, and verbalize their understanding of a cultural phenomenon.

CMs as a teaching and learning strategy

Concept mapping may be an effective means of teaching new cultural concepts. The strategy is based on Ausubel's (1968) assimilation learning theory and the idea of meaningful learning, according to which knowledge is structured as associations of concepts in one's memory with new meanings built on prior relevant concepts. Meaningful learning occurs when newly constructed concepts are incorporated into the appropriate existing ones and their relationships become more explicit. Ausubel's (1968) idea of interconnected old and new concepts brought forth CMs, a learning strategy developed by J. D. Novak in 1972, who described them as "graphical tools for organizing and representing relationships between concepts indicated by a connecting line linking two concepts" (Novak & Cañas, 2007, p. 29).

Since Novak's initial work, numerous studies described concept mapping as a highly efficient means of teaching and learning. Cliburn (1990) tested the effects of concept mapping in college science courses and concluded that mapping significantly improved student learning and memory retention. Chularut and DeBacker (2004), who investigated the effectiveness of CMs on student achievement when learning from English-language texts, observed the connection between concept mapping and self-efficacy and self-regulation strategies for language learning. The study revealed significantly higher gains in the students' achievement, self-efficacy, and the use of knowledge-acquisition strategies for the group that employed CMs than for the individual study group. Similarly, De Simone (2007) noted that maps facilitate thinking and learning in college courses by synthesizing and reorganizing information in a logical and visual manner. CMs have been proven to be effective in developing students' critical thinking and creativity (Bixler et al., 2015; Harris & Zha, 2013; Tseng, 2019) because building associative links stimulates cognitive processing, reduces information processing time, and improves the quality of concept assimilation.

In their meta-analysis of 55 studies involving constructing, modifying, or using node-link diagrams across an extensive variety of educational contexts, levels, and disciplines, Nesbit and Adesope (2006) found that the use of CMs resulted in better knowledge retention and transfer compared to other academic activities such as reading texts, attending lectures, and class discussions. Furthermore, CMs foster brainstorming allowing students to see the connection between the main and supportive ideas and activate their prior knowledge as they explore a new phenomenon. Zarei and Feizollahi (2018) in their study of 90 student writers learning English as an FL found that the combination of concept mapping and brainstorming is more effective than conventional teaching; those students who engaged in concept mapping managed to overcome their writing anxiety and achieve high scores on lexical and grammatical accuracy.

The use of CMs in an FL setting has been well documented in research literature. Studies examining the method's effectiveness in the development of speaking skills (Ghonsooly & Hosienpour, 2009; Kalanzadeh et al., 2014; Chen & Hwang, 2020; Kazemi & Moradi, 2019; etc.) indicate its positive effect on English as a foreign language (EFL) learners' oral performance and decreasing speaking anxiety. Research also shows that CMs can significantly improve students' reading and listening comprehension by organizing thought processes and building logical connections between ideas. For example, Sabbaghan and

Ansarian (2013) demonstrated that concept mapping enhanced the participants' listening comprehension skills and was viewed positively as a strategy for improving listening. Another study by Usman et al. (2017) found that concept mapping led to a significant improvement in EFL learners' reading comprehension skills, such as recognizing words and distinguishing main ideas and specific details.

CMs can facilitate vocabulary and grammar learning by allowing students to see relationships between words and their grammatical functions. Vakilifard et al. (2006) claim that concept mapping helped EFL learners understand the important concepts and existing relationships between them, which positively affected vocabulary learning. Their findings show that the experimental group that used CMs performed better in vocabulary comprehension tasks than the control group that used traditional instructional strategies. Similarly, Gopal (2002) reported the effective role of CMs in enhancing grammar knowledge, as EFL students who employed CMs in their learning demonstrated a better understanding of the concepts of English grammar than those taught through the traditional approach. Furthermore, many researchers note that CMs become even more effective when introduced at the beginner level of language proficiency before learning strategies have been firmly established (Mohamed et al., 2017; Romanko, 2016).

One area of research on concept mapping that seems to be lagging is its effectiveness for teaching culture. Few studies that analyzed the impact of CMs on learners' IC development view them as "a productive analytical tool to investigate intercultural dialogues, share concepts and knowledge, find shared solutions to problems and difficulties, make shareable decisions" (Indirli, 2010, p. 141, as cited in Navatiene et al., 2013). Schall (2010) described several mapping activities that engage schoolchildren in cultural explorations, noting that mapping strategies provide access to previously unknown aspects of culture, explore different perspectives on a cultural topic, and connect students' school experience and academic knowledge, which can increase motivation and the feeling of achievement. This chapter aims to add to the body of knowledge on the effectiveness of concept mapping for IC development as it investigates the effect of CMs on the development of cultural competence and explores beginning language students' attitudes toward concept mapping in a first-year English-language and culture course at a regional university in Kazakhstan.

The study

Given the potential of CMs for intercultural development in an FL classroom, this study was designed to explore the benefits of the method and students' attitudes toward it. The study was guided by two research questions:

RQ1. What is the effect of using CMs on students' learning about TL culture?
RQ2. What are EFL students' attitudes toward CMs as a TL culture learning tool?

Methodology

This mixed-method study is based on the collection and analysis of quantitative and qualitative data. Students' achievements on the pretest and posttest constituted the quantitative data, while a posttest questionnaire collected qualitative data. Prior to data collection, a *t*-test was conducted to ensure homogeneous sampling and compare learning gains in the experimental and control groups.

Participants

The participants of this study were forty 17- to 19-year-old students in their first year of study at a regional university in Kazakhstan. The students were registered for the "Basic Foreign Language in the Context of Intercultural Communication" course, which was conducted in English and met for four 50-minute classes a week for one academic semester (15 weeks). The subjects' level of TL proficiency was determined as A2 level according to the Common European Framework of Reference for Languages (Council of Europe, 2001). At this level, students can understand sentences and simple texts regarding family, work, school, or leisure-related topics, communicate in everyday situations on familiar matters, and use simple language to describe their experience and immediate environment and needs (Council of Europe, 2001). The participants never experienced learning through CMs prior to the study. The students were randomly assigned to the experimental and control groups to ensure internal validity of the study.

Instrument

The study used a pretest, a posttest, and a questionnaire. The draft test was pretested in a group of 50 students not participating in the study; the discrimination index of 0.1–0.3 and Kunder and Richardson Formula-20 value of 0.93 were used to determine its validity and reliability, respectively, indicating that the questions were effective for measuring the knowledge of the TL culture.

Both pre- and posttests consisted of 30 multiple-choice questions in English. The pretest was designed to check students' familiarity with basic TL cultural concepts such as symbols, heroes, traditions, and places prior to taking the course. The posttest targeted students' understanding of cultural concepts studied during the course, some of which were different from those in the pretest. The posttest scores of the control and experimental groups were compared to identify the progress each group made in learning the TL culture.

To explore students' attitudes toward the use of CMs for teaching culture, a questionnaire was administered to the experimental group immediately after the posttest. The questionnaire was adapted from Luchembe et al. (2014) and Trang (2017); the participants were asked to indicate their agreement or disagreement with ten close-ended statements about their interest and engagement with CMs on a 5-point Likert-type scale. In addition to ranking statements, the subjects were asked to answer one open-ended question, "What do you think about concept mapping? Please state your opinion in a couple of sentences," which encouraged them to articulate their experience of and attitudes to concept mapping immediately after the Likert-type questionnaire.

Procedure

Concept mapping was used in the experimental group, while the control group was exposed to traditional instructional methods of teaching TL culture such as discussions of course textbook readings and audio recordings, and videos on various cultural topics. Since the experimental group has never experienced concept mapping before, the process of familiarizing students with cultural CMs was organized in two stages. First, the instructor explained the essence of concept mapping, how to construct CMs, and how to employ them in learning. To practice creating a CM, students were asked to brainstorm about the concept of culture, e.g., what does "culture" mean? How can it be explained? What words come to their minds when they think about culture? Together with the instructor, students engaged in discussions and reflections and constructed a map of their associations linking related concepts together. Concept mapping continued at home as students were asked to expand their maps with more ideas and associations.

In the next stage of the CM activity, students continued mapping out the concept of culture. Then they exchanged maps with their classmates, which allowed them to see some conceptual associations they might have missed. After adding and prioritizing new associations and concepts and developing new links to organize them, students returned the maps to their owners. Map sharing and the subsequent class discussion allowed students to consider various perspectives and aspects of the concept of culture.

Data analysis and discussion

Both descriptive and inferential statistics were employed for pretest and posttest results. Before the t-test was conducted, the data was first checked for normal distribution to determine the reliability of the result interpretations (Luchembe et al., 2014). Following this purpose, the Shapiro-Wilk test was employed, which is valid for the small sample size. The significance level showing the p-value was checked. The significance level was set to 0.05, which is the most frequently used value in educational research. In both experimental and control groups, the normality test showed a Shapiro-Wilk value of more than 0.05, which implied that the data is normally distributed, and a t-test can be used.

A *t*-test, which was performed in both the experimental and control groups, indicated the homogeneity of the students' knowledge of the TL culture prior to the experiment. To answer RQ1 and investigate the effect of concept mapping on cultural instruction, a pretest and posttest were conducted to measure the level of TL knowledge before and after the treatment. The pretest mean scores for control and experimental groups were 59.15 and 62, respectively (Table 9.1). The main score difference of only 2.85 demonstrated relatively similar levels of TL cultural knowledge of both groups before the start of the experiment, which allowed for a reasonable comparison of the effect of CMs and traditional teaching approach on students' progress in TL culture learning. The relative similarity of the pretest mean scores would also confirm that if the treatment resulted in a significant mean score difference, the result would be attributed to the effect of concept mapping on student achievement rather than a chance occurrence.

The posttest data for the control and experimental groups are 62.65 and 72.5, respectively (Table 9.1). The posttest mean scores are significantly different at 12.5, which means that the experimental group who experienced concept mapping performed better on the test, showed progress in IC development, and generally became more culturally aware through the use of CMs than the control group. The statistically significant difference points to the effectiveness of CMs for teaching culture. Rather than simply consuming cultural facts presented by a teacher or textbook, constructing a CM requires students to understand the importance of each concept in the overall perspective as they prioritize new and familiar cultural information and link concepts with one another. This cognitive engagement improves the retention of learning material and promotes meaningful learning.

To answer RQ2 and explore EFL students' opinions of CMs as a TL culture learning tool, an attitude questionnaire was administered at the end of the treatment to the experimental group that employed CMs to learn about the TL. The quantitative analysis of the frequency of responses is supported by qualitative data from students' answers to the open-ended question asking them to write one to three sentences expressing their personal opinions on concept mapping as a learning tool in English.

Students' ratings of questions about their attitude toward concept mapping as a learning tool revealed that most learners understood how to construct CMs

TABLE 9.1 Pre- and posttest results for control and experimental groups

	Group	N	Mean	STD. deviation
Pretest	Control	20	59.15	4.3734
	Experimental	20	62	4.2895
Posttest	Control	20	62.6470	7.8060
	Experimental	20	75.2	3.4

and enjoyed both creating the maps and discussing them with their classmates as seen in 90% of *agree* and *strongly agree* responses. Eighty percent of students thought that concept mapping is a useful revision strategy and that they will use it in other classes. High response frequency (77% of *agree* and *strongly agree*) to questions targeting the use of CMs for language and culture learning demonstrated that students find the tool very effective and want to use it regularly as it helps them understand, perceive, and reflect on new cultural phenomena. Seventy percent of respondents indicated that they would continue using CMs to learn the TL and culture.

Students' favorable attitude toward CMs is also seen in their verbal responses, 60 % of which expressed satisfaction with the learning tool. Many respondents described the activity as "fun, especially when we discuss them with the groupmates" and said that they "liked to look for key concepts in the texts, it was like a game." Several comments addressed the effectiveness of CMs for learning: "If I want to remember some material, I always can look through the maps that we have." "We discussed, we shared our ideas, we learned to see information deeper, and it seems to me I understand better, and I remember what we learned better." "Concept maps help me see what we learn more clearly, I think I'll try to use them in other disciplines." Students shared that they "enjoyed concept maps. It was easy and interesting" and liked "that we worked in groups and discussed our maps." Many felt that "concept maps helped me to understand the material better, we compared cultures, and concept maps made things simple. It was a good idea to teach us how to use concept maps."

At the same time, the survey responses identified several challenges that students encountered in the process of concept mapping. One hundred percent of respondents agreed that CM was impeded by the lack of TL vocabulary. The problem of insufficient vocabulary became especially acute for beginning-level students, who spent an excessive amount of time identifying the lexical item they needed to express a cultural concept, retrieving it from the memory or, if they did not know it, consulting a dictionary and then recording it onto the map. Another challenge, demonstrated by 80% of *agree* and *strongly agree* responses, concerned organizing map concepts and ideas into a hierarchical structure. Again, the process of prioritizing and ordering the map elements and pondering the connections between them took a long time. The vocabulary and structural difficulties made 75% of respondents *agree* and *strongly agree* that CM was a time-consuming process; 15% of the students in the experimental group stated their negative attitude to concept mapping describing the maps as "useless," "a waste of time," and "difficult to understand." One student admitted that CMs were "very hard for me, I even felt angry when we had them, but it was our task and I had to do it. It was like a stress." Another was not interested in CMs "may be because I need more time and more words to do this task well. I just didn't like them, and always felt not comfortable even if we had this in groups." Students' confusion about and initial misunderstanding of CMs is reiterated in their comments with 25% of negative responses, for example:

> I remember it was difficult to work with concept maps and at first I could not understand how to cope with them. It took very much of my time, and very much of my effort. I think I will not often use them in my future study.

> I felt I was not confident when we had concept maps in our classes. I didn't understand what to do, how to draw them, what to write, I didn't understand how to link boxes. Now I feel a bit more confident, we practiced and practiced, and I think now I see how to make concept maps.

To summarize, the use of concept mapping improved student cultural knowledge in the experimental group as measured by pre- and posttests; questionnaire rankings and answers also demonstrate their largely positive attitude toward the CMs. While some students seemed to be confused and uncertain about CMs and disheartened by the amount of time it took to articulate and arrange their ideas into a map, the majority of the participants felt that the benefits of CMs significantly outweigh the perceived shortcomings of the activity. Also, students' comments seem to indicate that their initial discomfort diminished as their map construction skills improved and their confidence grew.

Limitations of the study and suggestions for future research

An important limitation of this study is the small number of participants and its narrow context since only one language course in one university was surveyed. While the study results are indicative of general CM benefits for teaching TL culture, an analysis of language and culture courses in other language programs and universities could shed more light on how concept mapping can contribute to the development of IC. Another notable limitation of the study is the participants' novice level of FL proficiency. While 100% of students expressed frustration with the lack of vocabulary and language skills necessary to complete the maps, it could be assumed that a survey of more linguistically advanced students could yield different results. More research is needed to assess the effectiveness of CMs in promoting IC development at an intermediate and advanced level of FL study.

Future research may also want to explore the role of CMs in developing higher-level cognitive skills (e.g., analysis, synthesis, reasoning, and judgment) associated with teaching FL culture. While the connection between concept mapping and critical thinking skills has been suggested for a long time (Novak & Cañas, 2007), there is very little actual research data on its effect on these skills, particularly in the context of TL culture teaching. In fact, Cañas et al. (2017) note that the CM research is disconnected from classroom practices; even when instructors are aware of the benefits of CMs for developing higher-level cognitive skills, they often do not know how to engage students in practicing them. An analysis of instructors' actions and experiences with CMs will allow educators to understand how to take full advantage of the tool.

Classroom implications

The study showed that students' understanding of new cultural concepts and enjoyment of learning increased with the use of CMs. Language instructors should take into consideration the effectiveness of concept mapping for teaching and comparing native and target cultures. Considering my classroom experience with CMs, as well as difficulties outlined by the study participants, I suggest the following steps in applying the method in a FL classroom based on Ragisha and Gafoor (2014).

1. Introduction stage, at which the instructor introduces the notion of concept mapping, explains its benefits, and models concept mapping by exploring a concept with students and creating a hierarchical structure based on their input. (This stage may be omitted if students are familiar with CMs).
2. Brainstorming phase, at which students, after having been presented with a cultural concept, discuss its meaning and generate as many associated sub-concepts as possible (orally or in writing, individually or in groups).
3. Organizing phase, at which students group their concepts into broader categories, adding more associations as they come to their mind.
4. Layout phase, at which students demonstrate their understanding of the given cultural concept by evaluating the importance of the various categories for the concept: they create a hierarchical structure with the most important categories at the top of the map and less significant concepts positioned below. The arrangement of concepts and categories may be different for different learners.
5. Linking phase, during which the students contemplate the connections between the main and subordinate concepts and categories and provide lines, arrows, and cohesive devices (e.g., *because of, first… then*), making meaningful associations within and between the elements of the map.
6. Finalizing stage, at which students reexamine their CMs to see whether the given cultural concept is represented to the best of their understanding and prepare for a class presentation. Student presentations of their CMs are naturally followed by a class discussion of cultural concepts depicted in the maps. As students deliberate together on their own and their classmates' maps, they are encouraged to further explore the cultural concept(s) under discussion and expand their maps with this new information.

The problems of lack of time and insufficient vocabulary reported by the study participants become critical for novice-level students who have little or no experience with CMs and may not have developed adequate linguistic skills to accomplish the activity in the TL. To alleviate these challenges, instructors need to encourage and support students' use of CMs by explaining the benefits of the learning strategy, stressing its process-oriented rather than one-time nature, and providing multiple practice opportunities to increase the level of comfort with CMs. Pre-teaching vocabulary pertinent to the cultural topic at hand can equip students with the lexical means necessary to complete the task. Collaborative concept mapping with pairs or groups engaging in brainstorming, discussing, and ordering ideas can also help save time and increase students' confidence as they produce a CM together with their classmates; novice-level students can use their native language for some of the discussion. Finally, partial CMs with some of the content provided by the instructor may decrease the time on task and make the CM process appear less overwhelming.

Concept mapping is a flexible tool that supports linguistic and cultural instruction. Multifaceted CMs can be created in a traditional pen-and-paper layout or online via software computer programs (e.g., *Mindmeister*, *MindMup*, *Lucidchart*; *Jamboard*); both formats can be easily adapted to individual or collaborative forms of learning. The software programs offer options for customizing colors, sizes, and fonts, as well as embedding images and Internet links, resulting in a visually appealing, well-organized, and easy-to-read map. Another common alternative is a hybrid CM (Mugnai, 2017), which combines digital and analog mapping, e.g., completing a software-produced outline or part of the map by hand.

Conclusion

Concept mapping is a flexible strategy that invites beginning-level students to consider TL cultural concepts from multiple perspectives by creating a visual representation of associated subcategories and conceptual meanings. It targets both linguistic and cultural knowledge and skills as students articulate conceptual relationships to include in their maps and share their maps with their classmates. The vast potential of concept mapping for fostering conceptual knowledge and reasoning, as well as promoting student collaboration and engagement, makes it an important tool in a language and culture classroom. It is hoped that after experiencing CMs, students will be more willing to explore the target culture independently, thus furthering their IC in the TL. The results of the study confirm earlier research citing the advantages of CMs in improving student engagement and learning (Chularut & DeBacker, 2004; Chen & Hwang, 2020; Gopal, 2002; Harris & Zha, 2017; Nesbit & Adesope, 2006). While many students in the experimental group expressed their confusion about the technique and described it as effort- and time-consuming, introducing and modeling the activity, providing ample in- and out-of-class time to develop the map, and equipping students with additional vocabulary related to the specific cultural topic being discussed can alleviate learners' concerns and help them realize the benefits of CMs.

References

Arutyunova, N. D. (1999). *Yazyk i mir cheloveka*. [Language and the world of a person]. Moscow: Yazyki russkoi kul'tury.
Ausubel, D. P. (1968). *Educational psychology: A cognitive view*. Holt, Rinehart and Winston.
Bixler, G. M., Brown, A., Way, D., Ledford, C., & Mahan, J. D. (2015). Collaborative concept mapping and critical thinking in fourth-year medical students. *Clinical Pediatrics, 54*(9), 833–839.
Brown, H. D., & Lee, H. (2015). *Teaching by principles: An interactive approach to language pedagogy*. Pearson Education.
Buttjes, D. (1990). Teaching foreign language and culture: Social impact and political significance. *Language Learning Journal, 2*, 53–57.
Byram, M., & Wagner, M. (2018). Making a difference: Language teaching for intercultural and international dialogue. *Foreign Language Annals, 51*(1), 140–151. https://doi.org/10.1111/flan.12319
Cañas, J., Reiska, P., & Michelson, A. (2017). Developing higher order thinking skills with concept mapping: A case of pedagogic frailty. *Knowledge Management and E-Learning, 9*(3), 348–365.
Carey, S. (2009). *The Origin of Concepts*. Oxford University Press.
Chen, M.-R. A. and Hwang, G.-J. (2020). Effects of a concept mapping-based flipped learning approach on EFL students' English-speaking performance, critical thinking awareness and speaking anxiety. l*British Journal of Educational Technology, 51*(3), 817–834. https://doi.org/10.1111/bjet.12887
Chularut, P., & DeBacker, T. (2004). The influence of concept mapping on achievement, self-regulation, and self-efficacy in students of English as a second language. *Contemporary Educational Psychology, 29*, 248–263.
Cliburn, J. W. (1990). Concepts to promote meaningful learning. *Journal of College Science Teaching, 19*(4), 212–217.
Council of Europe. (2001). *Common European framework of reference for languages: Learning, teaching, assessment*. Press Syndicate of the University of Cambridge.
De Simone, C. (2007). Applications of concept mapping. *College Teaching, 55*(1), 33–36.
Deardorff, D. (2020). *Manual for developing intercultural competencies: Story circles*. Routledge.
Freitag-Hild, B. (2018). Teaching culture – intercultural competence, transcultural learning, global education. In C. Surkamp, & B. Viebrock (Eds.), *Teaching English as a foreign language*. J. B. Metzler. https://doi.org/10.1007/978-3-476-04480-8_9
Gelman, S. A. (2009). Learning from others: Children's construction of concepts. *Annual Review of Psychology, 60*, 115–40.
Gerfanova, E. (2020). *Kognitivnyy i lingvokul'turologicheskiy podkhody v formirovanii vtorichnoy yazykovoy lichnosti v usloviyakh inoyazychnogo obrazovaniya* [Cognitive and linguocultural approaches to the formation of second language identity in the context of foreign language education] [Doctoral dissertation, Sh. Ualikhanov Kokshetau University].
Ghonsooly, B., & Hosienpour, A. (2009). The effect of concept mapping on EFL speaking fluency. *Iranian Journal of Applied Linguistics, 12*(1), 87–114.
Gopal, P. (2002). Concept mapping – A pedagogical tool for grammar lessons. https://www.academia.edu/905880/Concept_Mapping_A_Pedagogical_Tool_for_Grammar_Lessons
Griffith, R. L., Wolfeld, L., Armon, B. K., Rios, J., & Liu, O. L. (2016). Assessing intercultural competence in higher education: Existing research and future directions. *ETS Research Report Series, 2*, 1–44. https://doi.org/10.1002/ets2.12112

Harris, C., & Zha, S. (2013). Concept mapping: A critical thinking technique. *Education*, *134*(2), 207–211.

Harris, C. M., & Zha, S. (2017). Concept mapping for critical thinking: Efficacy, timing, & type. *Education*, *137*(3), 277–280.

Hofstede, G. (1984). *Culture's consequences: International differences in work-related values* (Vol. 5). SAGE.

Hong, Y. (2009). A dynamic constructivist approach to culture: Moving from describing culture to explaining culture. In R. S. Wyer, C.-Y. Chiu, & Y.-Y. Hong (Eds.), *Understanding culture: Theory, research and application* (pp. 3–23). Psychology Press.

Kalanzadeh, G. A., Maleki, Z., & Raz, A. (2014). Concept maps and reading comprehension among EFL learners. *International Journal of Innovation and Research in Educational Sciences*, *1*(2), 174–180.

Karasik, V. (1996). Kul'turnyye dominanty v yazyke [Cultural dominants in the language]. In V. Karasik (Ed.), *Yazykovaya lichnost': kul'turnyye kontsepty* (pp. 3–16). Peremena.

Kazemi, A., & Moradi, A. (2019). The influence of concept mapping and rehearsal on speaking accuracy and complexity. *Cogent Arts and Humanities*, *6*(1). https://doi.org/10.1080/23311983.2019.1597463

Kramsch, C. (1995). The cultural component of language teaching. *Language, Culture and Curriculum*, *8*(12), 83–92.

Kunanbayeva, S. S., Karmysova, M. K., Ivanova, A. M., Arenova, T. D., Zhumagulova, B. S., Kuznetsova, T. D., & Abdygapparova, S. K. (2004). *Kontseptsiya razvitiya inoyazychnogo obrazovaniya* [The concept of development of Kazakhstan foreign language education]. Kazakh Ablai Khan University of International Relations and World Languages.

Kurganova, N. I. (2003). *Obraz doma u russkikh i frantsuzov* [The concept of home in Russian and French cultures]. *Mezhkul'turnaya kommunikatsiya i sovremennyye lingvisticheskiye teorii*.

Kurganova, N. I. (2004). *Sem'ya glazami frantsuzov* [Family through the eyes of the French]. *Lingvistika i lingvisticheskoye obrazovaniye v sovremennom mire*.

Kurganova, N. I. (2006). *Kartina mira rossiyan i frantsuzov cherez prizmu kul'turnykh predstavleniy o yede* [The picture of the world of the Russians and the French through the prism of cultural ideas about food]. Materialy XXXV Mezhdunarodnoy Filologicheskoy konferentsii. Saint-Petersburg.

Luchembe, D., Chinyama, K., & Jumbe, J. (2014). The effect of using concept mapping on student's attitude and achievement when learning the physics topic of circular and rotational motion. *European Journal of Physics Education*, *5*(4), 10–29.

Mohamed, A. A., Garas, A. F., & Khairia, A. E. (2017). Effect of concept mapping on critical thinking skills of baccalaureate nursing students. *International Journal of Research in Applied, Natural and Social Sciences*, *5*(11), 59–76.

Mugnai, M. (2017). Mind Maps: New Perspectives. *NeMLA Italian Studies (The Italian Digital Classroom)*, *39*, 125–142.

Navatiene, J., Rimkeviciene, V., & Racelyte, D. (2013). Methodology for development of intercultural competence. http://farintercultura.ch/wp-content/uploads/2016/07/1_METHODOLOGY-FOR-DEVELOPMENT-OF-INTERCULTURAL-COMPETENCE.pdf

Nemtchinova, E. (2020). Intercultural competence in a Russian language class: Issues in teaching and assessment. In E. Dengub, I. Dubinina, & J. Merrill (Eds.), *The Art of Teaching Russian* (pp. 333–359). Georgetown University Press.

Nesbit, J. C., & Adesope, O. O. (2006). Learning with concept and knowledge maps: A meta-analysis. *Review of Educational Research*, *76*(3), 413–448.

Novak, J. D., & Cañas, A. J. (2007). Theoretical origins of concept maps, how to construct them, and uses in education. *Reflecting Education*, *3*(1), 29–42.

Ojalehto, B. L., & Medin, D. L. (2015). Perspectives on culture and concepts. *Annual Review of Psychology*, *66*, 249–275.

Ragisha, K. K., & Gafoor, K. (2014). Effect of concept mapping on pedagogic content knowledge of elementary student teachers. *Journal of Humanities and Social Science*, *19*, 31–35.

Romanko, L. (2016). The role of concept mapping in the development of critical thinking skills in student and novice nurses: A quantitative meta-analysis. https://open.library.ubc.ca/media/stream/pdf/24/1.0228162/4

Sabbaghan, S., & Ansarian, F. (2013). Do they know that they know? EFL learners' attitude towards concept mapping in listening comprehension. *International Journal of Research Studies in Educational Technology*, *2*(1), 57–70.

Schall, J.-M. (2010). Cultural exploration through mapping. *The Social Studies*, *101*, 166–173.

Silversteine, M. (2004). "Cultural" concepts and the language – Culture concepts. *Current Anthropology*, *45*(5), 621–652.

Stepanov, Yu. S. (2004). *Konstanty. Slovar' russkoj kul'tury* (Constants. Dictionary of Russian culture). Academic Project.

Thanasoulas, D. (2001). The importance of teaching culture in the foreign language classroom. *Radical Pedagogy*, *3*(3). https://radicalpedagogy.icaap.org/content/issue3_3/7-thanasoulas.html

Trang, P. (2017). The effects of concept mapping on EFL students' reading comprehension. *European Journal of English Language Teaching*, *2*(2),178–203.

Tseng, S. S. (2019). Using concept mapping activities to enhance students' critical thinking skills at a high school in Taiwan. *Asia-Pacific Education Researcher*, *29*, 249–256.

Usman, B., Maidatija, R., & Fitriani, S. S. (2017). Using concept mapping to improve reading comprehension. *English Education Journal*, *8*(3), 292–307.

Vakilifard, A., Armand, F., & Baron, A. (2006). The effects of 'concept mapping' on second language learners' comprehension of informative text. In A. J. Cañas, & J. D. Novak (Eds.), *Concept maps: Theory, methodology, technology. Proceedings of the Second International Conference on Concept Mapping*. Universidad de Costa Rica.

Zarei, A., & Feizollahi, K. (2018). Concept mapping and brainstorming affecting writing anxiety and accuracy. *Journal of Modern Research in English Language Studies*, *5*, 117–144.

Zusman, V. G. (2001). *Kontsept v kul'turologicheskom aspekte* [Concept in cultural aspect]. Dekom.

PART III
Teaching with technology

10
PATHWAYS TO DIGITAL L2 LITERACIES FOR TEXT-BASED TELECOLLABORATION AT THE BEGINNING LEVEL

Maria Bondarenko and Liudmila Klimanova

Over the past decades, there has been a growing interest in the use of social media, including social networking sites (SNSs), in second language (L2) learning and teaching (SLLT), particularly text-based telecollaboration. Telecollaboration is a computer-assisted intercultural exchange where participants in distant locations interact using online tools. While the first telecollaboration projects were conducted via email (e.g., Warschauer, 1996), in the Web 2.0 era, telecollaboration is tied to interactive, participatory tools, including teleconferencing and social media (cf. the notion of telecollaboration 2.0 in Guth & Helm, 2010). Although videoconferencing has been recognized as an increasingly popular tool of virtual exchange (Çiftçi & Savaş, 2018), telecollaboration via Web 2.0 platforms, such as SNSs, continues to be widely used in intercultural online exchanges (Schenker & Poorman, 2016). Lewis and O'Dowd (2016) argue that today virtual exchange (including text-based telecollaboration) "has begun to enter the mainstream of foreign language education" (p. 21). It has been found to increase student motivation (O'Dowd, 2007) and to develop language (Ritchie & Black, 2012), pragmatic (Zhang, 2014), intercultural (O'Dowd, 2007), and digital skills (Guth & Helm, 2010).

Against this backdrop, it becomes evident that the text-based telecollaborative activities at low L2 proficiency levels – Novice, according to the American Council on the Teaching of Foreign Languages (ACTFL) Proficiency Scale (ACTFL, 2012), or A.1, according to the Common European Framework of Reference for Languages (CEFR) (Council of Europe, 2001) – remain under-researched. Schenker (2017) explicitly states that most educators use telecollaboration primarily in intermediate or advanced-level language courses. Despite a vast body of research on telecollaboration and social media in SLLT (e.g., Belz & Thorne, 2006; Dooly & O'Dowd, 2012; Guth & Helm, 2010; O'Dowd, 2007;

O'Dowd & Lewis, 2016), few publications discuss text-based virtual exchange at the beginner level, and even fewer examine SNSs-mediated telecollaboration for beginners. Thus, Dunne (2014) shows that an asynchronous email exchange between first-year Japanese and Chilean English as a foreign language students who used English as a lingua franca to complete task-based activities minimized intercultural tension and unmanageable levels of incomprehensibility. Schenker (2012, 2015) reports on email exchange projects between second semester (A.1.2 level) American students of German and German native speakers. She explores different aspects of communication, including developing intercultural competence (Schenker, 2012) and negotiating strategies of meaning (Schenker, 2015). Zhang (2014) examines the benefits of telecollaboration for teaching L2 pragmatics (opening and closing dialogues) to first-semester learners of Chinese who communicated with native speakers via a chat platform in Adobe Acrobat Connect Pro. To explore the feasibility of text-based telecollaboration for beginners, Klimanova and Bondarenko (2018) conducted an experimental project with four groups of beginning learners of Russian in the first semester of instruction from three partner universities (three groups from two Canadian universities and a group of Russian native speakers in Russia). Their analysis showed that beginners were able to maintain multi-turn written conversations in the L2 and demonstrated linguistic complexity by using sentential and multi-sentential turn construction units above the beginner-level benchmark established by proficiency guidelines (ACTFL, 2012). Examining affective factors related to learner satisfaction and motivation within this telecollaborative project, Klimanova and Vinokurova (2020) concluded that text-based virtual exchange is generally perceived positively by beginners. These studies empirically demonstrated the feasibility and manifold benefits of text-based telecollaboration for L2 beginners. Why is text-based telecollaboration still unpopular in the beginning L2 classroom?

The lack of attention to telecollaboration at the beginner level may be rooted in interrelated conceptions of the L2 learner, the writing process, and digital technology. Previous research has shown that beginners have difficulty attending to form and meaning simultaneously while processing input and output within meaning-based L2 learning practices (Ellis, 1997; VanPatten, 1996), of which telecollaboration is one. One way to address this challenge is to allocate explicit form-based teaching to the initial stage of learning to lay linguistic foundations and postpone implicit meaning-based teaching to later stages (Ellis, 2005; Littlewood, 1981).

Skepticism about teaching communicative writing to novice learners is often mirrored in teaching methodology (e.g., Ferris & Hedgcock, 2013; Hinkel, 2015) and textbooks (see Klimanova and Bondarenko (2018) for an in-depth analysis of novice writers' typical descriptions in teaching methodology and proficiency standards). The sociocultural (Vygotskian) trend in SLLT (Lantolf & Appel, 1994; van Lier, 2004), which views language learning as a collaborative process, offers scaffolding as an effective way to overcome beginners' difficulties in meaning-based communication. Scaffolded instruction refers to various kinds of interaction with the environment, such as teacher-steered interpersonal dialogue, recasting errors, peer-peer collaborative dialogue, dialogical journaling, and other collaborative activities that guide, support, and encourage beginners' verbal output and self-expression (Donato, 1994; Peyton, 2000; Swain, 1985; Swain & Watanabe, 2012; van Lier, 1996).

We argue that specific features of digital social media environments can provide such scaffolding and pedagogical affordances for developing writing at the beginner level, while prior knowledge of SNSs can help students reap the benefits of this scaffolding. In this chapter, we aim to develop a comprehensive view of the semiotic mechanisms of digital technology, digital literacies, and their pedagogical potential and relationship to traditional literacies relevant for beginning L2 learners. We begin by drawing on the socio-semiotic educational paradigm to discuss three dimensions of digital literacies and propose a conceptual framework for beginning- level telecollaboration. We move on to explore features of the SNS digital environment to show how they can support beginners by capitalizing on their knowledge of digital artifacts. This conceptual exploration will be illustrated by published (Klimanova & Bondarenko, 2018; Klimanova & Vinokurova, 2020) and unpublished data from a large empirical study of communication practices during a telecollaboration project conducted in elementary Russian L2 classes. Last, we present a model that describes the complex interface between digital and traditional literacies in the L1 and L2, which is important for understanding the benefits of telecollaboration at beginning levels.

Toward a holistic understanding of digital literacies

Originally proposed by Gilster (1997), who studied the digital aspects of computer-mediated communication (CMC), the term "digital literacies," also referred to as new (media) literacies (Sulentic Dowell, 2018), is still evolving and open to multiple interpretations (Belshaw, 2014). We can distinguish several trends in understanding digital literacies in relation to traditional literacy.

According to one interpretation, digital literacies are "built on the foundation of traditional literacy, research skills, technical skills, and critical-analysis skills taught in the classroom" (Jenkins, 2009, p. 4). This approach barely supports the possibility of text-based telecollaboration at the beginner level since learners must acquire traditional L2 literacy skills before they can read and write in digital environments.

An opposite trend is tied to an emerging socio-semiotic paradigm in education and CMC studies. This paradigm encompasses a range of interrelated research fields, including multimodal studies of CMC (Jewitt, 2008; Kress, 2010), Internet writing studies (Barton, 2015), and digital genres studies (Giltrow & Stein, 2009; Heyd, 2016; Luzón et al., 2010), which consider any social and cultural phenomenon (including education) as a social practice based on human interaction mediated by verbal, visual and auditive signs. As any human social activity necessarily involves a meaning-making process, semiotic systems shape social relations and society itself. The tools (media) that people use, "appropriate and transform" for communication have an impact on meaning and "influence and/or create new practices" (Freire, 1994, para 2). The socio-semiotic approach theorizes digital literacies as an important factor in social practices and processes of meaning-making (Barton, 2015; Belshaw, 2014; Thorne, 2003) and assumes that new forms of digital media do not supplement but rather reshape the notion of literacy and communication (Baron, 2000; Pegrum, 2011). The socio-semiotic paradigm addresses digital literacies from three interrelated complementary perspectives: (1) as specific individual skills, (2) as affordances provided by structural features of the digital environment, and (3) as specific habits of mind that condition the usage of affordances. We will briefly present each dimension to evaluate how the benefits of SNSs for L2 learning have been explored in SLLT literature.

Digital literacies from the skillset perspective

Skillset-driven definitions of digital literacies refer to a set of individual skills necessary to practice multimodal CMC, such as finding, evaluating, and communicating information through various digital platforms and digital genres (ACTFL, 2011; Trilling & Fadel, 2009). The repertoire of skills ranges from the purely technological to the social and emotional and may include items from the three basic literacies – media literacy, information literacy, and ITC (information and communication technology) literacy (Trilling & Fadel, 2009) – or up to as many as six, such as socio-emotional, photo-visual, information, branching, reproduction, and real-time skills (Eshet, 2012; Eshet-Alkalai, 2004), or more (Janssen et al., 2013).

Digital literacies from the affordances-driven perspective

The affordances-based perspective centers on structural properties of digital media that provide opportunities for actions and shape human behavior, including learning. Affordances were conceived by Gibson (1979) as possibilities for action offered by environments. This concept initiated a new school in psychology, and later in education (including L2 education), called the ecological or environmental school because of its focus on dynamic interaction between the individual and the environment. The affordances provided by social environments are always mediational and semiotic since they mediate communication and serve as tools in the meaning-making process.

In the field of human-machine interaction, the concept of perceived (or technological) affordances (Norman, 1988) emphasizes the possibilities of digital environments (toolbars, hyperlinks, and other structural elements inviting action), and links them both to users' mindsets and to the objects' usability (i.e., ease of handling, access, and control). In addition to the technological affordances, Kirschner et al. (2004) distinguish two other kinds of affordances related to utility in the field of educational technology: social and educational. Social affordances are properties of a digital environment "that act as social-contextual facilitators relevant for the learner's social interaction" (Kirschner et al., 2004, p. 51). They can make the learner feel a sense of belonging to a community prompting them to become a member of a group, comment on posts by other community members, share information, or engage in synchronous or asynchronous conversation. Educational affordances indicate whether and how a particular learning behavior can unfold in a digital environment. They may be linked to the specific content of a website, the way in which information is presented, or how a specific learning task is introduced and guided in the digital setting, how feedback is provided, and how performance is monitored.

In multimodal studies of the digital environment (e.g., Kress, 2010), affordances define the potentialities and constraints of different modes (speech, image, spatial configuration) in relation to the material structure and cultural use of a mode. Governed by different kinds of logic, different modes complement each other – hence the concepts of intermodal (Painter & Martin, 2011) or intersemiotic complementarity (Royce, 2007) – and afford meaning-making processes within a multimodal ensemble. Intermodal complementarity is an important conceptual tool for studying multimodal affordances that has been used in multimodal discourse analysis (Kress & van Leeuwen, 2001) as applied, among other things, to L1 and L2 education (e.g., Painter & Martin, 2011; Unsworth & Thomas, 2014).

Finally, in the field of SLLT, the concept of affordances gave rise to so-called ecological or semiotic language learning (van Lier, 1996, 2000, 2004). From this approach, it follows that context – physical, social, and symbolic – is a central element in language learning and that issues such as spatiotemporal structures and the embodiment of language (i.e., making meanings through bodily interactions with one's environment) are instrumental in creating learning opportunities. Based on Vygotsky's (1986) cultural-historical theory of social environments as sources of human cognitive development, van Lier (2000) defines affordances as "relationships," which comprise action and interaction, and which belong to the linguistic world of the learner (p. 91). Applying an ecological approach to telecollaborative practices, Thorne (2003) extends Vygotsky's and van Lier's theoretical framework to conceptualize the mediational affordances of Internet communication tools in relation to the interpersonal component of SLLT. Analyzing three case studies of intercultural telecollaboration projects conducted through email at higher levels of L2 proficiency, Thorne argues that inherent features of CMC create an interpersonal dynamic promoting interaction with partners, and therefore learning from them. Using the terminology of

Kirschner et al. (2004), Thorne's understanding of the pedagogical benefits of digital environments in SLLT is built on social affordances rather than on educational or technological ones.

Digital media from the mindset perspective: cultures-of-use

The affordances- and the skillset-driven approaches both acknowledge that one must be familiar with affordances to use them. To emphasize this phenomenological perspective "focusing on our habitualized use of technological artifacts" (Aagaard, 2018, p. 7), researchers conceptualize digital literacies as a mindset, as "issues, norms, and habits of mind surrounding technologies used for a particular purpose" (Belshaw, 2014, p. 207; Jones & Hafner, 2012). When applied to telecollaborative SLLT, Thorne (2003) calls this mindset a "culture-of-use of (digital) artifacts: historically sedimented characteristics that accrue to a CMC tool from its everyday use" (p. 25) in the form of individual preferences for a particular digital medium for various practices (e.g., using a synchronous chat to build an interpersonal relationship with a peer). The participants in three email-assisted telecollaboration projects analyzed by Thorne (2003) were able to reap pedagogical benefits such as learning from partners from being involved in a hyperpersonal (i.e., phatic, in-depth, and trustful) relationship thanks to their culture-of-use of Internet technology. CMC communication thus entails the possibility of informal relationships between interlocutors. This usage of CMC tools gave rise to informal relationships between users and facilitated learning from peers, but only for those users who were already familiar with CMC and had developed a culture-of-use of digital artifacts.

We combined the three explored dimensions of digital literacies – skillset-driven, affordances-driven, and mindset-driven dimensions – into one holistic model to explore the way social media have been represented in SLLT literature and to develop a conceptual framework for text-based telecollaboration in the beginning L2 classroom.

Studies of SNS in SLLT examined through the holistic model of digital literacies

Using the holistic three-dimensional model of digital literacies to examine how social media have been represented in SLLT literature, we can note significantly more studies of social affordances using the typology of Kirschner et al. (2004). For instance, most studies have been focused on learners' autonomy, self-presentation (e.g., Luzón et al., 2010; Reinhardt, 2017, 2018), socialization, negotiation of community, agency, identity, and development of intercultural and sociopragmatic skills (e.g., Blattner & Fiori, 2009; Chen, 2013; Klimanova & Dembovskaya, 2013; Thorne, 2016). Although researchers agree that L2 teachers should capitalize on the fact that technology and CMC are "already an integral part of many students' e-routine" (Blattner & Fiori, 2009, p. 5), they do not explain how it may benefit beginners. Little attention has likewise been paid to technological and pedagogical affordances (in terms of Kirschner et al., 2004) related to structural properties of SNSs (e.g., architecture, genres, layouts, etc.) and to the ways of enacting a particular learning behavior appropriate for beginning language learners (e.g., how the digital environment can help beginners to cope with a lack of basic vocabulary, language anxiety, simultaneous processing of input and output, language control and fluency within a meaning-based communication). Moreover, the rare studies of semiotic structure of SNSs from a technological and pedagogical perspective have been applied mostly to social media designed specifically for language learning, such as *Busuu* (e.g., Álvarez Valencia, 2016), but not to social platforms, such as *Facebook* and *VKontakte* (VK), that were originally created for purposes other than formal learning.

We argue that a mere reference to enhanced social interaction and its positive impact on learner motivation and socialization within a target language community – which is important for L2 learning at any level of proficiency – does not suffice to explain the specific pedagogical benefits of social media for novice learners' developing L2 writing skills. An additional semiotic analysis of SNS environments originally created for purposes other than formal learning is needed to reveal these benefits as well as to identify structural properties of SMSs and relate them to the meaning-making process (affordances) relevant for L2 learning.

In the next two sections, we will examine the pedagogical potential of SNSs from both the pedagogical-affordance and mindset perspectives using published and unpublished data from our previous telecollaboration project for Russian L2 beginners (Klimanova & Bondarenko, 2018) as an example. In this study, four groups of students ($n = 70$) – three elementary Russian sections and a group of Russian native speakers – from three partner universities participated in a text-based telecollaboration project carried out in the first semester of instruction (Novice Mid/High or A.1.1 according to ACTFL or CEFR guidelines, respectively) in two partnership formats: international (between Russian and Canadian students) and cross-institutional (between two Canadian groups of Russian learners using Russian as lingua franca). Over the period of two weeks, learners completed individual and collaborative written tasks (e.g., self-introduction, a verbal reaction to partners' posts, interview) by using Russian social media site VK. Class time was optimized to provide learners with necessary linguistic scaffolding via pre-task activities. The collected data included (1) students' written interactions in L2 and (2) the data retrieved from the motivational entry and exit surveys and daily journals. In the surveys and journals, students were asked to name and evaluate challenging, useful, joyful, and frustrating aspects of the social media–based written communication and share their strategies to cope with linguistic difficulties and communication breakdowns.

Social media affordances for supporting writing at the beginning level

The SNS environment demonstrates increasing complexity of linguo-social actions and growing explicitness through a structured architecture that supplies models and imposes restrictions on these actions when compared to other writing formats (e.g., pen and paper, typewriter and paper, word-processor and keyboard, email system and keyboard). The following semiotic characteristics of SNSs have a pedagogical potential for beginners. The SNS environment is (1) highly structured; (2) dialogical and collaborative (question-answer- or action-reaction-based); (3) multimodal and intertextual (providing access to external resources); (4) endowed with a highly explicit and standardized architecture that makes it (5) universal (transcultural), i.e., independent of linguistic codes and transferable across cultures; it is also (6) oriented toward short messages and various textual genres (status line and profile form); (7) supports both synchronous and asynchronous (delayed) communication; and (8) allows stylistic variation across language registers, including casual speech-oriented and stylistically neutral language accessible to beginners (Biber & Egbert, 2016). We will now consider features of SNSs that are conducive to productive L2 use at the beginner level: SNSs' metalanguage, textual micro-genres, dialogical structure, and the multimodal complementarity of social media.

SNSs' metalanguage as a target language

Pragmatic engagement with the metalanguage of SNSs makes it both a language to learn and a tool of learning (Meurant, 2009). For example, a telecollaboration project involving a Russian social networking platform can provide learners with an opportunity to practice typing and spelling in Cyrillic (both arguably fundamental digital and traditional literacy skills) and encounter essential CMC vocabulary, such as the Russian equivalents for "message," "search," "audio/video recordings," "What's up?," "like," "updates," "download," or "subscribe." Prior to the recent shift to distance L2 education due to COVID-19, this vocabulary, while useful in modern everyday life, was rarely taught in beginners' courses because of its noncompliance with typical basic communicative topics and text-types as prescribed by existing proficiency guidelines (e.g., ACTFL, 2012) or because of instructors' lack of interest in CMC and Internet-based instructional activities.

The personal profile page as a written micro-genre

From the perspective of digital genres analysis (Giltrow & Stein, 2009; Heyd, 2016) and multimodal studies (Kress, 2010), a SNS constitutes a system of interrelated multimodal micro-genres suggesting different linguo-social actions.

Among these, we can identify the status line, profile template, and text-based personal interview, which are all personally involving and suitable for beginners. For example, a status line constitutes a simple, title-like statement of 140 characters usually in the present tense and reflecting location in space and time or the "I feel/I think" status of the user (Klimanova & Dembovskaya, 2013). A digital profile form, featuring personal profile information (date of birth, marital status, profession), requires a formal style, nominal (one-word) sentences or short phrases, and has an explicit question-answer structure. Finally, the personal interview/questionnaire, containing information about personal habits, hobbies, moral statements, friendship, etc., has an informal/neutral register, allows for different kinds of language complexity, and has an explicitly dialogical (question-answer) structure.

In addition to vocabulary acquisition, these micro-genres promote the development of stylistic and sociopragmatic differentiation skills as a part of general L2 literacy. Beginners can become aware of these differences by comparing the vocabulary of the profile form (e.g., place of residence, place of work, marital status) with stylistically neutral speech-oriented equivalents usually learned in first-semester Russian language courses (e.g., Where do you live? Where do you work? Do you have a family?).

The SNS dialogical structure as a scaffolding for developing writing complexity

Literature on CMC conceptualizes computer-mediated writing in the framework of the speech-writing continuum (e.g., Baron, 2000; Crystal, 2001) emphasizing the essential characteristic of any form of writing, and especially SNS-mediated writing – its dialogicality, i.e., orientation toward other speakers' utterances (Baron, 2000). Supporting the assumption that the structural properties of Internet communication tools influence exchange structures and turn-taking (Herring, 2001; Werry, 1996), we argue that the dialogicality of SNS-mediated discourse is determined, amplified, and visualized by the explicit question-answer structure in SNS environments. This dialogical environment, designed to facilitate conversations, can potentially enhance the development of writing skills at the beginner level.

In conceptualizing the role of natural interaction in CMC, researchers (e.g., Chapelle, 2003; Schenker, 2017) relate the benefits of digital interaction to core concepts of cognitive L2 pedagogy, such as comprehensible input (Krashen, 1981) complemented by the interaction hypothesis (Long, 1996); the output hypothesis (Swain, 1985); negotiation of meaning, repetition, output planning, environmental scaffolding (van Lier, 2004); and incidental learning (Loewen & Reinders, 2011). These benefits are relevant to text-based telecollaboration. The explicit dialogical architecture of SNSs provides a necessary scaffolding for collaborative writing. It enables the development of written conversation through a question-answer mechanism. In addition, as an asynchronous mode of communication, text-based collaboration allows students to read posts at their own pace and delay response till they are ready to reply. These affordances help reduce cognitive load for beginners as they simultaneously juggle multiple aspects of communication such as turn-taking, grammar, vocabulary, and language control.

The following example from Klimanova and Bondarenko's (2018) data shows a Russian L2 beginning learner developing a meaningful complex text while answering his partners' questions. The conversation is quoted in English because conversational complexity, as measured by the number of introduced topics and mechanism of turn-taking, is not tied to the specific language.

> Initial post: My name is T. I am studying international relations and international politics at the University X. I am Scottish and Canadian [New topic I: statement →] My mother tongues are French and English. I am learning Russian, but I do not speak Russian well [New topic II: statement →]. I like the political history of Russia [New topic III: statement →] and the book Animal Farm. It is an allegory of the 1917 Revolution by George Orwell. Do you know [it]? [New topic IV: statement + question? →]
>
> [Topic IV: answer + question? →] Hi, T. Yes, I have read Animal Farm. What other books do you like? [Topic II: comment + oppositional statement →] I think you underestimate your Russian, you write very well in Russian.
>
> [Topic I: comment + question? →] Hi, T. Do you have Scottish roots? How?
>
> [Topic III: comment + question? →] Hi T. What topics from Russian history do you like?
>
> [Topic II: comment to comment] I have a dictionary. [Topic II: answer + New Topic →] I like Dostoevsky. I have read The Dream of a Ridiculous Man by Dostoevsky. The Little Prince by Antoine de Saint-Exupéry is my favorite book.
>
> [Topic II: answer + New Topic →] My father was born in Scotland. His family emigrated to Canada. I do not wear a kilt.
>
> [Topic III: answer + New Topic →] Foreign policy during the Cold War is very interesting. I studied the policy of Central Asia in Australia.
>
> *(Klimanova & Bondarenko, 2018, p. 79)*

The contents of the initial post were motivated by an assignment requiring beginning Russian learners to introduce themselves on the group wall of the social media site VK. The learner then introduced several new topics and ended with a direct question, forming a turn-taking episode. While the interlocutors ignored the initial question, their attention turned to three other topics: "I am Scottish,"

"I do not speak Russian well," and "I like the political history of Russia." Three native Russian-speaking partners posted responses ending with new questions inviting the L2 learner to develop his "story" further (i.e., an invitation to take the next turn in the conversation). The partners' reactions scaffolded the L2 learner's written output. We may assume that their responses also increased his confidence and motivation if the latter can be measured in terms of willingness to engage in turn-taking and continue the conversation instead of staying within the boundaries of the course assignment (simple introduction).

Social media supporting intermodal complementarity

The intermodal and intertextual settings of SNS forums provide tools for intermodal (Painter & Martin, 2011) or intersemiotic complementarity (Royce, 2007). Complementarity describes the complementary use of several semiotic modes (verbal, visual, auditive, kinesthetic), which create new opportunities for communication. In L2 learning and teaching, intermodal complementarity can be considered a part of strategic competence that relies on verbal and nonverbal means of coping with a communication breakdown (Canale & Swain, 1980). Strategic competence is essential for beginners in that it aids communication despite the lack of language skills.

In the above example, the novice Russian learner complemented his verbal expression of appreciation of Orwell's novel *Animal Farm* with an image of the book's cover. This intermodal gesture has at least three functions. First, the learner was able to compensate for his uncertainty about the Cyrillic transliteration of the author's name and translation of the book's title. Second, the visual presentation emphasizes the emotive aspect of the message (I like it). Finally, this visual reference increases the visibility of the post and draws the interlocutors' attention to the message.

Cultures-of-use of SNS for telecollaboration at the beginner level

Examining unpublished data that we collected from Russian L2 beginners' reflection journals after a six-week-long SNS-based telecollaboration exchange (Klimanova & Bondarenko, 2018), we observed how digital cultures-of-use (Thorne, 2003, 2016) support engagement with SNS platforms and activate the educational and social affordances of the digital environment (see the taxonomy of affordances in Kirschner et al., 2004), which frame students' L2 learning behavior.

Social media metalanguage

Our data show that at the level of digital memory and cognitive schemata, students successfully applied previous knowledge of social networks to decode the metalanguage of L2 social media, which presented an opportunity for incidental vocabulary learning (Klimanova & Bondarenko, 2018). Many students found "discovering Russian social networks" "the most difficult" yet "the most fun/interesting" part of the SNS-based telecollaboration project, saying, "I've learned new words thanks to VK (with all the settings in Russian)," and "[The process of registering on VK went] quite well. I have a great facility with social media in general."

Understanding peers' messages

Understanding online forums as a digital genre also helped students to decode peers' messages. Students could assume that comments somehow addressed the topic(s) of the initial post and rely on this context to guess the meanings of new words, as evidenced in the following journal entries: "From our pen pals' responses, I was able to master unknown grammar topics, words, and expressions," and "Speaking about nationality: we had not learned this material in class yet, and I learned how to say 'French' by observing the student presentations!"

Intermodal complementarity

Students' reflections reveal a strong reliance on the intermodal complementarity of CMC when they attempt to decode new language or make their own contributions to the discussion: "[…] I realized that it was easy to use photos to overcome my lack of vocabulary"; "The fact that we can add photos to posts or comments really makes the group livelier and more enjoyable to read! One advantage of using VK is that the layout is conducive to this type of exchange!"

Developing general digital literacies

We also observed the development of new digital literacies or reshaping of students' digital cultures-of-use. Among other realizations, students discovered the unreliability of *Google Translate* and the strategic utility of the "like" function ("[i]nsofar as my language level was insufficient, this function filled in, to an extent, for body language, intonation, and emotion, which count so much in oral communication but are absent or hard to convey in writing"). One student mentioned that thanks to the project, she had learned to navigate a social network she did not use in daily life.

Building students' confidence

Finally, the digital affordances of SNS and activation of students' digital literacies contributed to building students' confidence. Students felt rewarded for the effort they put into the project. In general, CMC enhanced their sense of belonging and created a more intimate affiliation with the target language, as noted in the following journal entry: "I felt proud that I could understand the majority of the written words and knew how to formulate a question by myself." In cases of reduced confidence, the opportunity to regard their own linguistic identity and ability in relation to others helped students to evaluate their limits realistically and regain motivation to fill in gaps in their knowledge. One learner wrote, "Now I definitely have a better sense of my limits in Russian, so it's no longer frustrating, and I cannot wait to get better."

The model of L2/L1 digital literacies interface and its pedagogical implications

Successful use of telecollaboration in the beginning L2 classroom is directly related to understanding its pedagogical affordances, which depends, in turn, on perceiving the complex multidimensional socio-semiotic mechanism of the interaction between the human and the digital, i.e., the socio-semiotic mechanism of human behavior in a digital environment.

We conceptualize digital L2 literacies as a dynamic interaction between different affordances provided by SNS environments and learners' digital skills and mindsets formed through previous experiences of using digital environments for social interaction. The structural characteristics of SNSs can be perceived by beginners (and L2 teachers) as a "natural" scaffolding mechanism for written communication in the L2 in noninstitutional digital communicative settings. The most important characteristics are the explicit dialogical architecture, microgenres, complementary multimodality, and universal (transcultural) highly structured environment, which are independent of local linguistic codes and cultural habits. For L2 beginners, this scaffolding is vital, as it allows them to overcome language-related obstacles that arise from attending to meaning-based tasks.

Learning through interaction with an L2 digital environment at the beginning level is effective if students are familiar with the general cultures-of-use of digital artifacts. Digital culture-of-use helps beginning L2 learners capitalize on the educational affordances provided by the dialogical structure of SNS platforms. From the perspective of cognitive pedagogy, a familiar digital environment helps reduce extraneous cognitive load and increase the encoding process by referring to prior world knowledge (Sweller et al., 2011). The discussion around digital literacies can thus be considered an extension of the conversation about the role of learners' prior experiences in L2 education (e.g., Zion et al., 2019). It becomes a point where cognitive L2 pedagogy meets ecological L2 pedagogy in explaining the pedagogical potential of the digital environment for beginning L2 learners.

The conceptualization of digital literacies from the socio-semiotic perspective as a three-dimensional notion combining affordances, cultures-of-use, and skills also makes it possible to deepen our understanding of the relationship between digital and traditional literacies in L2 learning. The pedagogical benefits of text-based telecollaboration for beginners rely on a complex interface between different kinds of literacies underlying the use of L2 digital platforms by beginning L2 learners. A representation of digital literacies as mere skills built upon traditional literacy fails to explain how L2 digital environments scaffold writing for beginners who do not yet have sufficient traditional literacy in an L2. Similarly, the assumption that pragmatic engagement with the L2 digital environment helps L2 learners to develop their L2 digital literacy (e.g., Meurant, 2009) is only a partial reflection of this process. The relationship between digital and so-called traditional forms of literacy in the L2 learning process seems rather to be reversed. We propose a L2/L1 digital/general literacies interface model for telecollaboration at the beginner level, in which individual digital culture-of-use initially developed in L1, which is partly independent of the linguistic component and therefore transferable to new linguistic environments, constitutes an asset for developing both traditional and digital L2 literacies. At the same time, exploring a familiar digital environment configured in a new language enables learners to develop and reshape their overall *individual* digital cultures-of-use (i.e., students' general digital literacies).

Conclusion

This chapter draws the attention of L2 educators to elaborating a conceptual framework for text-based telecollaboration in the beginning L2 classroom. While it has not addressed questions of design, implementation, and assessment, recent research (Klimanova & Bondarenko, 2018; Zhang, 2014) demonstrates that text-based telecollaboration can be conducted successfully in the beginning L2 classroom in different formats, such as international, cross-institutional, and between classmates. Participants can use the L2 as a lingua franca and interact with native speakers. SNS-assisted virtual exchange can be integrated into classroom activities and students' homework, both assessed and unassessed. It can take the form of free communication between peers, assigned collaborative tasks, and teacher-initiated written conversations. Integration of task-based activities can provide beginners with measurable communication objectives (Dunne, 2014; O'Dowd & Waire, 2009). For example, participants in the text-based virtual exchange discussed in Klimanova and Bondarenko (2018) and Klimanova and Vinokurova (2020) collected data from their interlocutors to compare social portraits of foreign-language learners in Russia and Canada and to explore cultural stereotypes expressed through spontaneous verbal associations with such concepts as Russia, the Russian people, Canada, Quebec, etc. Indeed, further empirical studies are needed to develop a comprehensive repertoire of SNS-assisted telecollaborative activities for beginners, analyze factors affecting success in implementing them, and produce recommendations for design and assessment. Yet such empirical studies are impossible while instructors do not appreciate the pedagogical potential of the digital medium for beginning-level writing. We hope the proposed conceptual framework will encourage further research and discussions in this area.

References

Aagaard, J. (2018). Magnetic and multistable: Reinterpreting the affordances of educational technology. *International Journal of Educational Technology in Higher Education*, *15*(4), 3–10.

Álvarez Valencia, J. A. (2016). Social networking sites for language learning: Examining learning theories in nested semiotic spaces. *Signo y Pensamiento*, *35*(68), 66–84. https://doi.org/10.11144/javeriana.syp35-68.snsl

American Council on the Teaching of Foreign Languages. (2011). *21st century skills map: World languages. Partnership for 21st century skills*. https://eric.ed.gov/?id=ED519498

American Council on the Teaching of Foreign Languages. (2012). *The ACTFL Proficiency Guidelines 2012*. ACTFL. https://www.actfl.org/resources/actfl-proficiency-guidelines-2012

Baron, N. (2000). *Alphabet to email. How written English evolved and where it's heading*. Routledge.

Barton, D. (2015). Tagging on Flicker as social practice. In R. Jones, A. Chik, & C. Hafner (Eds.), *Discourse and digital practices: Doing discourse analysis in the digital age* (pp. 48–59). Routledge.

Belshaw, D. (2014). The essential elements of digital literacies. http://digitalliteraci.es/

Belz, J. A., & Thorne, S. L. (Eds.) (2006). *Internet-mediated intercultural foreign language education*. Thompson Heinle.

Biber, D., & Egbert, J. (2016). Register variation on the searchable web: A multi-dimensional analysis. *Journal of English Linguistics*, *44*(2), 95–137.

Blattner, G., & Fiori, M. (2009). Facebook in the language classroom: Promises and possibilities. *International Journal of Instructional Technology and Distance Learning*, *6*(1), 17–28.

Canale, M., & Swain, M. (1980). Theoretical bases of communicative approaches to second language teaching and testing. *Applied Linguistics*, *1*(1), 1–47.

Chapelle, C. (2003). *English language learning and technology*. John Benjamins.

Chen, H.-I. (2013). Identity practices of multilingual writers in social networking spaces. *Language Learning & Technology*, *17*(2), 143–170.

Çiftçi, E., & Savaş, P. (2018). The role of telecollaboration in language and intercultural learning: A synthesis of studies published between 2010 and 2015. *ReCALL*, *30*(3), 278–298.

Council of Europe. (2001). *Common European framework of reference for languages (CEFR): Learning, teaching, assessment*. Cambridge University Press. https://rm.coe.int/1680459f97

Crystal, D. (2001). *Language and the internet*. Cambridge University Press.

Donato, R. (1994). Collective scaffolding in second language learning. In J. P. Lantolf, & G. Appel (Eds.), *Vygotskian approaches to second language research* (pp. 33–56). Ablex.

Dooly, M., & O'Dowd, R. (Eds.) (2012). *Researching online foreign language interaction and exchange: Theories, methods and challenges*. Peter Lang.

Dunne, G. (2014). Reflecting on the Japan–Chile task-based telecollaboration project for beginner-level learners. *TESL Canada Journal/Revue TESL du Canada*, *175*(31), 175–186.

Ellis, N. (2005). At the interface: Dynamic interactions of explicit and implicit language knowledge. *Studies in Second Language Acquisition*, *27*, 305–352.

Ellis, R. (1997). Task-based language teaching: Sorting out the misunderstandings. *International Journal of Applied Linguistics*, *19*(3), 221–246.

Eshet, Y. (2012). Thinking in the digital era: A revised model for digital literacy issues. *Informing Science and Information Technology*, *9*, 267–276.

Eshet-Alkalai, Y. (2004). Digital literacy: A conceptual framework for survival skills in the digital era. *Journal of Educational Multimedia and Hypermedia, 13*(1), 93–106.
Ferris, D. R., & Hedgcock, J. (2013). *Teaching L2 composition: Purpose, process, and practice.* Routledge.
Freire, M. M. (1994, September). A socio-cultural/semiotic interpretation of intercommunication mediated by computers [Conference presentation]. *L.S. Vygotsky and the Contemporary Human Sciences International Conference*, Moscow, Russia. https://psychology.hanover.edu/vygotsky/freire.html
Gibson, J. (1979). *The ecological approach to visual perception.* Psychology Press.
Gilster, P. (1997). *Digital literacy.* John Wiley & Sons.
Giltrow, J., & Stein, D. (2009). *Genres in the internet: Issues in the theory of genre.* John Benjamins.
Guth, S., & Helm, F. (Eds.) (2010). *Telecollaboration 2.0: Language, literacies and intercultural learning in the 21st century.* Peter Lang.
Herring, S. (2001). Computer-mediated discourse. In D. Schiffrin, D. Tannen, & H. E. Hamilton (Eds.), *The handbook of discourse analysis* (pp. 612–634). Blackwell Publishers.
Heyd, T. (2016). Digital genres and processes of remediation. In A. Georgakopoulou, & T. Spilioti (Eds.), *The Routledge handbook of language and digital communication* (pp. 87–102). Routledge.
Hinkel, E. (2015). *Effective curriculum for teaching L2 writing: Principles and techniques.* Routledge.
Janssen, J., Stoyanov, S., Ferrari, A., Punie, Y., Pannekeet, K., & Sloep, P. (2013). 'Experts' views on digital competence: Commonalities and differences. *Computers & Education, 68*, 473–481.
Jenkins, H. (2009). *Confronting the challenges of participatory culture: Media education for the 21st century.* The MIT Press.
Jewitt, C. (2008). *Technology, literacy and learning: A multimodal approach.* Routledge.
Jones, R. H., & Hafner, C. A. (2012). *Understanding digital literacies.* Routledge.
Kirschner, P., Strijbos, J.W., Kreijns, K., & Beers, P. J. (2004). Designing electronic collaborative learning environments. *Educational Technology Research & Development, 52*(3), 47–66.
Klimanova, L., & Bondarenko, M. (2018). Problematizing the notion of the beginning L2 writer: The case of text-based telecollaboration. In J. Demperio, M. Deraîche, R. Dewart, & B. Zuercher (Eds.), *Current trends in the teaching and learning of written proficiency* (pp. 64–91). UQAM Press.
Klimanova, L., & Dembovskaya, S. (2013). L2 identity, investment, and social networking in a Russian class. *Language Learning & Technology, 17*(1), 69–88.
Klimanova, L., & Vinokurova, V. (2020). Intercultural virtual communication and novice learners: Attitudes, perception and beliefs. In A. Oskoz, & M. Vinagre (Eds.), *Understanding attitude in intercultural virtual communication* (pp. 30–63). Equinox eBooks Publishing.
Krashen, S. (1981). *Second language acquisition and second language learning.* Pergamon.
Kress, G. (2010). *Multimodality: A social semiotic approach to contemporary communication.* Routledge.
Kress, G., & Van Leeuwen, T. (2001). *Multimodal discourse: The modes and media of contemporary communication.* Arnold Publishers.
Lantolf, J., & Appel, G. (1994). *Vygotskian approaches to second language research.* Ablex.
Lewis, T., & O'Dowd, R. (2016). Online intercultural exchange and foreign language learning: A systematic review. In R. O'Dowd & T. Lewis (Eds.), *Online intercultural exchange: Policy, pedagogy, practice* (pp. 21–68). Routledge.

Littlewood, W. (1981). *Communicative language teaching: An introduction.* Cambridge University Press.

Loewen, S., & Reinders, H. (2011). *Key concepts in second language acquisition.* Palgrave Macmillan.

Long, M. H. (1996). The role of the linguistic environment in second language acquisition. In W. C. Ritchie, & T. K. Bahtia (Eds.), *Handbook of second language acquisition* (pp. 413–468). Academic Press.

Luzón, M. H., Ruiz-Madrid, M. N., & Villanueva, M. Z. (2010). *Digital genres, new literacies and autonomy in language learning.* Cambridge Scholars Publishing.

Meurant, R. (2009). Developing critical L2 digital literacy through the use of computer-based Internet-hosted learning management systems such as Moodle. In D. Ślęzak, W. Grosky, N. Pissinou, T. Shih, T. Kim, & B. Kang (Eds.), *Multimedia, computer graphics and broadcasting* (pp. 76–83). Springer.

Norman, D. (1988). *The design of everyday things.* Basic Books.

O'Dowd, R. (Ed.) (2007). *Online intercultural exchange: An introduction for foreign language teachers.* Multilingual Matters.

O'Dowd, R., & Lewis, T. (Eds.) (2016). *Online intercultural exchange: Policy, pedagogy, practice.* Routledge.

O'Dowd, R., & Waire, P. (2009). Critical issues in telecollaborative task design. *CALL Journal, 22*(2), 173–188.

Painter, C., & Martin, J. (2011). Intermodal complementarity: Modelling affordances across image and verbiage in children's picture books. In H. G. Wen (Ed.), *Studies in functional linguistics and discourse analysis* (pp. 132–158). Higher Education Press.

Pegrum, M. (2011). Modified, multiplied and (re-)mixed: Social media and digital literacies. In M. Thomas (Ed.), *Digital education: Opportunities for social collaboration* (pp. 9–35). Palgrave Macmillan.

Peyton, J. K. (2000). *Dialogue journals: Interactive writing to develop language and literacy.* National Center for ESL Literacy Education.

Reinhardt, J. (2017). Social networking sites and language education. In S. Thorne & S. May (Eds), *Language, education and technology. Encyclopedia of language and education* (3rd ed., pp. 1–12). Springer.

Reinhardt, J. (2018). Social media in the L2 classroom: Everyday agency, awareness, and autonomy. In H. Castañeda-Peña (Ed.), *Technology in ELT: Achievements and challenges for ELT development* (pp. 17–34). Publicaciones DIE.

Ritchie, M., & Black, C. (2012). Public internet forums: Can they enhance argumentative writing skills of second language learners? *Foreign Language Annals, 45*(3), 349–361.

Royce, T. (2007). Intersemiotic complementarity: A framework for multimodal discourse analysis. In T. Royce, & W. Bowcher (Eds.), *New directions in the analysis of multimodal discourse.* Lawrence Erlbaum Associates.

Schenker, T. (2012). Intercultural competence and cultural learning through telecollaboration. *CALICO Journal, 29*(3), 449–470.

Schenker, T. (2015). Telecollaboration for novice language learners: Negotiation of meaning in text chats between non-native and native speakers. In E. Dixon, & M. Thomas (Eds.), *Researching language learner interactions online: From social media to MOOCs* (pp. 237–259). CALICO.

Schenker, T. (2017). Synchronous telecollaboration for novice language learners: Effects on speaking skills and language learning interests. *ALSIC, 20*(2), 1–18. https://doi.org/10.4000/alsic.3068

Schenker, T., & Poorman, F. (2016). Students' perceptions of telecollaborative communication tools. In C. Ludwig, & K. van de Poel (Eds.), *Collaborative language learning and new media: Insights into an evolving field* (pp. 55–71). Peter Lang.

Sulentic Dowell, M.-M. (2018). Toward a working definition of digital literacy. In M. Khosrow-Pour (Ed.), *Encyclopedia of information science and technology* (4th ed., pp. 2326–2335). IGI Global. https://doi.org/10.4018/978-1-5225-2255-3

Swain, M. (1985). Communicative competence: Some roles of comprehensible input and output in its development. In S. Gass, & C. Madden (Eds.), *Input in second language acquisition* (pp. 235–253). Newbury House.

Swain, M., & Watanabe, Y. (2012). Languaging: Collaborative dialogue as a source of second language learning. In C. A. Chapell (Ed.), *The encyclopedia of applied linguistics* (pp. 1–8). John Wiley & Sons.

Sweller, J., Ayres, P., & Kalyuga, S. (2011). *Cognitive load theory*. Springer.

Thorne, S. (2003). Artifacts and cultures-of-use in intercultural communication. *Language Learning and Technology, 7*(2), 38–67.

Thorne, S. (2016). Cultures-of-use and morphologies of communicative action, *Language Learning & Technology, 20*(2), 185–191.

Trilling, B., & Fadel, C. (2009). *21st century skills: Learning for life in our times*. John Wiley & Sons.

Unsworth, L., & Thomas, A. (Eds.) (2014). *English teaching and new literacies pedagogy. Interpreting and authoring digital multimedia narratives*. Peter Lang.

van Lier, L. (1996). *Interaction in the language curriculum: Awareness, autonomy and authenticity*. Pearson Education.

van Lier, L. (2000). From input to affordance: Social-interactive learning from an ecological perspective. In J. Lantolf (Ed.), *Sociocultural theory and second language learning*. Oxford University Press.

van Lier, L. (2004). *The ecology and semiotics of language learning: A sociocultural perspective*. Kluwer Academic.

VanPatten, B. (1996). *Input processing and grammar instruction in second language acquisition*. Ablex.

Vygotsky, L. (1986). *Thought and language*. The MIT Press.

Warschauer, M. (Ed.) (1996). *Telecollaboration in foreign language learning*. University of Hawai'i Second Language Teaching and Curriculum Center.

Werry, C. (1996). Linguistic and interactional features of Internet Relay Chat. In S. Herring (Ed.), *Computer-mediated communication: Linguistic, social and cross-cultural perspectives* (pp. 47–63). John Benjamins.

Zhang, D. (2014). More than "hello" and "bye-bye": Opening and closing the online chats in Mandarin Chinese. *Computer Assisted Language Learning, 27*(6), 528–544.

Zion, D., Nevat, M., Prior, A., & Titan, T. (2019). Prior knowledge predicts early consolidation in second language learning, *Frontiers in Psychology, 10*, 1–15.

11
STUDENT SATISFACTION AND ENGAGEMENT IN A BEGINNING UKRAINIAN BLENDED-LEARNING COURSE

Debunking fears of blending and lessons learned

Alla Nedashkivska

The implementation of technology in education has been described as one of the most pervasive pedagogical trends that continue to inspire the adoption of technology-assisted blended curricula (Mizza & Rubio, 2020). Blended learning (BL), the focus of this chapter, is understood broadly as involving the combination of face-to-face (F2F) and technology-mediated instruction (Graham, 2013). The adoption of new and unfamiliar practices such as BL is invariably accompanied by certain apprehensions and fears. Although interest in BL in general, and blended-language learning (BLL) in particular, is prominent in academia, instructors and students continue to exhibit noticeable anxiety, hesitancy, and skepticism (Mizza & Rubio, 2020).

The field of language learning and teaching still regards the F2F mode as "the gold standard" (Mizza & Rubio, 2020, p. 16) and remains skeptical of the effectiveness of technology. Online learning is judged as less optimal, limited, and limiting, particularly due to its lack of an in-depth interaction that only F2F settings are believed to foster effectively (Stickler & Hampel, 2019). In instructors' opinion, technology decreases student interaction, resulting in greater social isolation and disengagement (Heaton-Shrestha et al., 2009) and may be distractive (Ogunduyile, 2013). In BLL, instructors positively acknowledge learner autonomy but view decreased guidance as problematic (Bijeikiene et al., 2011) and question the effects of BLL on learners' development of language competence, primarily in speaking (Mizza & Rubio, 2020). In fact, our new reality imposed by the COVID-19 pandemic places the notions of online and technology-assisted learning at a new height and calls for more questioning and testing (Egbert, 2020; Guillén et al., 2020; Sivachenko & Nedashkivska, 2021).

When modern technology is introduced into language classrooms, students and instructors alike may experience anxiety, apprehension, skepticism, and fear of the unknown (Mizza & Rubio, 2020). Underlying these fears are assumptions that a reduction of instructional time in physical space may cause a decrease or loss of peer contact among students and between students and instructors. Additionally, students who are not self-regulated learners may potentially fail to engage independently with course materials, experience a decrease in focus on course tasks due to distractions caused by technology, and enjoy fewer language proficiency gains (Gleason, 2013; Yu-Fen, 2014).

At the University of Alberta, the first language courses to adopt BL in 2015 were in the Ukrainian language. Since then, we continuously monitored and improved BLL delivery, primarily based on studying students' feedback and perceptions, with encouraging results (Nedashkivska, 2019). In 2019–2020, we began to gradually introduce BL into other languages such as Arabic, French, German, Italian, Norwegian, Spanish, and Swedish. During the transition, instructors voiced various predispositions, apprehensions, and anxieties that echoed the concerns noted earlier and inspired this study.

This chapter explores student perceptions of their BLL experiences in one course. By studying language learners' views, I intend to address the fears of loss of peer and instructor contact, low student engagement, distractions, etc., commonly felt by those who have not yet adopted or are new to BLL. By discussing crucial BLL issues, I hope to continue the inquiry into the role of technology in second or foreign (L2) teaching and learning, online instruction, and BLL. The chapter concludes with the implications of the findings for other contexts of technologically assisted L2 learning and instruction.

BLL: A brief overview

The concept of BL and its various definitions has been widely discussed in the literature.[1] One description presents BL as a "thoughtful integration of classroom face-to-face learning with on-line learning experiences" (Garrison & Kanuka, 2004, p. 96) with the intent "to create a learning environment that functions as a seamless whole" (Mizza & Rubio, 2020, p. 11). For Mizza and Rubio (2020), BL constitutes "a formal teaching and learning experience that includes a multiaccess, balanced, guided, and monitored instructional environment" (p. 24) in which, although F2F meetings are reduced, the in-person and online components complement one another and enable student-instructor, student-student, and student-content collaboration and interaction. The BL model integrates "the online and traditional F2F class activities in a planned and pedagogically sound manner" (Mizza & Rubio, 2020, p. 24) where F2F and online learning complement, build on, and strengthen each other.

Scholarly literature on BLL continues to grow, with quantitative research dominating the field. Both small- and large-scale studies compare blended instruction with F2F to demonstrate that there are no significant differences in desired learning outcomes (Chenoweth et al., 2006; Young, 2008). Some studies show enhanced student learning outcomes in writing (Chenoweth & Murday, 2003) and speaking, particularly at lower proficiency levels (Rubio, 2014). In addition to 24-hour flexible access to resources and their reduced costs, advantages of BLL include its positive effect on students' performance (Scida & Saury, 2006), students' control over learning (Gimeno Sanz, 2009), and support of different learning styles (Bueno-Alastuey & López Pérez, 2013). Conversely, disadvantages of BLL include a lack of connection between in- and out-of-class learning spaces (Chenoweth et al., 2006), decreased student control over learning (Bijeikiene et al., 2011), heavier workloads for students, and students' inadequate computer skills (Bueno-Alastuey, 2009a, 2009b).

Qualitative research, particularly studies of instructors' and learners' preferences and attitudes, continues to be sparse, and scholars desire further exploration of how and why BLL may enhance the learning experience (Mizza & Rubio, 2020). Previous studies have addressed instructors' attitudes toward the effectiveness of technology, pedagogical considerations of adapting to BLL, and transformations of the instructor's roles in the new model (Anderson, 2018; Mizza & Rubio, 2020). Both instructors' and students' overall positive perceptions of BLL have also been noted (Isabelli, 2015). With regard to students' perceptions, the importance of individual learner characteristics and learning styles as key considerations in the design and implementation of BLL, particularly concerning learner self-discipline (Carr, 2014; Isabelli, 2015) and learners' level of language study (Cubillos, 2007) have been examined, along with students' appreciation of specific course-tools that enable a learning community online, promoting students' engagement and reducing anxiety (Enkin & Mejías-Bikandi, 2017).

Satisfaction and engagement

The present study is designed around two concepts: satisfaction and engagement. Satisfaction encompasses students' responses to and preferences for BLL. Therefore, questions framing the study of satisfaction include whether BLL offers benefits of temporal and spatial flexibility, the BLL resources are easy to access, and the online and F2F components complement and enhance each other so that students and instructors perceive technology-assisted self-study as helpful and contributing to learning (Owston et al., 2013).

Student engagement has been noted as crucial for success in BLL as it necessitates self-regulated learning and assists in overcoming a sense of isolation or motivational setbacks in an environment of reduced F2F connectivity. Engaged learners are "more efficient and effective, more focused and proactively committed to their learning" (Mizza & Rubio, 2020, p. 62). Through being engaged, students acquire new knowledge and skills and, importantly, also grow academically and personally (Kahu & Nelson, 2018). In this study, the concept of engagement is investigated at four levels: behavioral, emotional, cognitive (Fredricks et al., 2005), and agentic (Reeve, 2013; Reeve & Tseng, 2011). Behavioral engagement encompasses various aspects of course participation, including academic, social, and extracurricular activities. Emotional engagement refers to the various attitudes and reactions toward instructors, classmates, or institutions, which contribute to students' willingness to complete the course activities. These include reactions to the quantity and quality of interaction with an instructor and among classmates, perceptions of the quality of these interactions, and overall liking or disliking of the course. The cognitive dimension relates to students' preparedness and investment of effort toward mastering course content and the skills taught. Variables include students' willingness to consult the course material or ask questions to facilitate understanding and gain additional knowledge relevant to the course, and their perceptions of the course's effectiveness in improving their knowledge and understanding of major concepts and skills. Agentic engagement is tied to students' productive efforts in the process of instruction, including a conscious effort to make the lesson personally relevant, asking for clarification, requesting assistance, and communicating the level of self-interest, among other features (Reeve, 2013; Reeve & Tseng, 2011).

This chapter aims to contribute to this existing body of literature by focusing on a case of BLL in a beginners' Ukrainian language-learning class, the context that has not been previously explored, from the perspective of student satisfaction and engagement in a technology-assisted environment. The study was guided by the following questions:

1. What are students' experiences in a beginners' Ukrainian BLL classroom?
2. How do these experiences correlate with measures of student engagement and satisfaction with the proposed BLL model?

The study

Context

The BLL model explored in this chapter was first introduced in 2015. The primary aim was to revise the learning process by incorporating technology into an L2 classroom in an organized and pedagogically sound manner, responding to students' desires and needs for a technologically enhanced learning environment relevant to real-life situations (Sivachenko & Nedashkivska, 2017). We also wanted to offer students increased flexibility in their access to learning and instruction. By placing certain instructional elements online to be completed at learners' convenience, we freed up students' busy schedules. Overall, with our other languages shifting to BLL, we see BL as enabling pedagogical innovation, flexibility, and accessibility for students.

Our pedagogical design is based on the principles of Communicative Language Teaching (CLT) (Canale & Swain, 1980), a learner-centered approach that emphasizes the development of communicative competence through task-based activities. In BLL, reading, listening, and writing activities, as well as presentation of new vocabulary and grammar, occur mostly online, thus freeing class time for activities that resemble real-world communication in which functional language is practiced in an interactive and collaborative environment. This shift promotes learner-centered activities, supports meaningful communication in L2, and enables the implementation of CLT.

Our BLL model constitutes a transition from the traditional five 50-minute instructional hours per week plus homework to three F2F 50-minute classes plus three 30–60-minute technology-assisted online lessons, though completion time of these may vary. The model uses the online textbook *PodorozhiUA.com* (*TravelsUA*), which is designed to resemble a train trip, common in Ukraine, with in-class activities described as "meetings" and online lessons labeled "stations" and "transfers." This BLL e-textbook consists of 26 modules, each composed of three F2F and three online learning sessions (in our case, one module is intended to be completed over one week period). Importantly, each module represents a scaffolding continuum of carefully planned and interconnected F2F and online components. A typical F2F meeting, building on a preceding online lesson, resembles a regular language class but with greater emphasis on communication, practice, and application than on presentation and explanation of language forms and structures. A typical online "station" represents an instructional self-study connected to a preceding F2F class and introduces new forms and structures, thus making connections to the next F2F meeting. An online "transfer" reviews what students learned during the module and prepares them for the first F2F class of the next module. The online lessons are concurrent venues for practicing material introduced during F2F sessions, homework, introduction of new material, i.e., instructional input, and independent learning of new forms and structures in preparation for the subsequent F2F class.

The resources for both F2F and online lessons focus on communicative and collaborative activities. Their primary goal is the development of speaking, pronunciation, and communication skills; listening and reading comprehension skills are also targeted, while writing plays a less prominent role. The activities are sequentially organized and are available in a digital format, allowing for 24/7 access via computers, phones, and tablets. The F2F resources and audio recordings[2] are available online or can be printed, including audio scripts. In F2F classes, grammatical points are not introduced overtly but are presented and practiced in context, often following their initial introduction online. Students are encouraged to review the F2F resources following each class.

Self-study lessons in the "stations" incorporate online activities developed with such technological tools as *WP Courseware*, *H5P quizzes*, *Quizlet*, and *Audacity*. In these lessons, students receive instructional input (for example, vocabulary and grammar presentations on flip cards, videos, and podcasts) and then practice and produce output in mostly written (typed or handwritten on paper) and oral (repetition) formats. A series of training gamified exercises consist of "cards" that present new vocabulary or grammatical forms by demonstrating their spelling and pronunciation; "scatter," in which students match these new forms with respective images or grammatical forms; "learn," in which students are asked to type the new forms; "speller," in which students listen to an audio recording and type what they hear; and "handwriting," enabled by video technology, in which students watch a text slowly being handwritten and copy the technique by practicing handwriting on paper. These exercises allow students to practice and improve pronunciation, and develop listening, reading, and writing skills at their own pace, with as much practice as they wish. While online lessons have limited options for the development of oral communication, written communication skills are practiced in the online forums, at least once per module, starting with module three. The forums allow students to practice L2 writing by responding to prompts on a topic of an online lesson following simple language patterns provided in the module. Students also read each other's posts and react in writing to other students' posts in the later units. The forums encourage a group feeling and extend the social learning community to the virtual space. Online "transfers" also ask students to complete a writing task, which is handwritten and submitted, along with a speaking task that could be used as a warm-up activity during F2F class. Most online lessons also include at least one self-assessment quiz following either a review or an introduction of new material segment and culminate with a brief lesson assessment (the online "final stop"), which is graded to ensure completion. All self-assessment tools allow for multiple attempts to promote self-directed learning. To alleviate the need to consult with additional sources, the textbook includes reference resources for students, such as a glossary, grammar reference, verb conjugations, index, and a virtual Ukrainian keyboard. Instructor's resources include a manual with lesson plans and other class materials and a dashboard with a gradebook for tracking completion of online lessons.

The designed model of beginning-level Ukrainian instruction is intended to enable students to capitalize on the benefits of the F2F and online environments, which Mizza and Rubio (2020) have stressed as crucial in BLL. The online lessons not only enhance in-person teaching and learning but add activities that are well suited for self-paced learning, such as introduction of new vocabulary and grammatical forms and structures, listening and reading comprehension exercises, and, importantly, writing and typing activities. The F2F classes, supported by the online instructional units, are freed for more collaborative activities that focus on the development of learners' communicative competence in speaking and interaction.

Methodology

Data, participants, and procedures

Using the case study approach, this investigation is confined to a specific beginners' L2 course, focusing on learners' experiences within the BLL model. The study uncovers learners' lived experiences with respect to satisfaction and engagement, discussing them in light of existing students' and instructors' apprehensions reported in the literature.

The data were collected in 2018–2019 at the end of the fall semester with 17 undergraduate students participating (out of 23 enrolled). All participants were native speakers of English with no previous knowledge of L2 prior to enrolling in beginners' Ukrainian. The participants were 88% women; 71% reported having an average GPA ranging 2.7–3.3; 47% were taking five courses at the same time.

The primary data set comes from responses to a survey developed by the Centre of Teaching and Learning (CTL) at the University of Alberta to assess university courses that switched to BL. This online survey, not tailored specifically to BLL, included 59 questions to gather data about students, student satisfaction with the course, and behavioral, emotional, cognitive, and agentic student engagement (Fredricks et al., 2005; Owston et al., 2013). All but the last question were close-ended, asking for a ranking on a 5-point Likert scale (*strongly disagree/disagree/neutral/agree/strongly agree*).[3] The survey-based data allowed us to address the research questions quantitatively. Following the survey, students were invited to participate in a semi-structured interview, enabling qualitative analysis. Unfortunately for the purposes of this study, only one student volunteered. Both research instruments were administered by a researcher from the CTL, rather than the instructor, to avoid influencing responses.

The survey and interview data were analyzed separately, first identifying the emerging themes, and then comparing and relating these themes before interpreting them from the perspective of student satisfaction and engagement. Instructor's observations (notes on interactions and relationships in the course, discussions with students about their self-regulated learning, etc.) and data from web-generated gradebook and student online progress cards were used to verify student self-reports. Although limited in scope, the analysis provides empirical input on technologically enhanced BLL, its capacities, and its reception by students.

Results and analysis

This section provides a summary of results relevant to the two research questions, with additional details available in supporting documents.[4]

Satisfaction

General results with respect to student satisfaction are largely positive, supporting the conclusions of previous research on BLL (Isabelli, 2015).

The overall student scores are numeric values that describe the participants' ratings of the different dimensions of the BLL. The course had an overall student satisfaction score of 75% (Figure 11.1A) consisting of a student satisfaction with

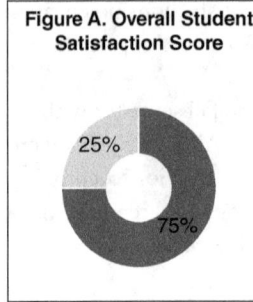 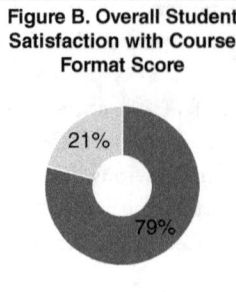 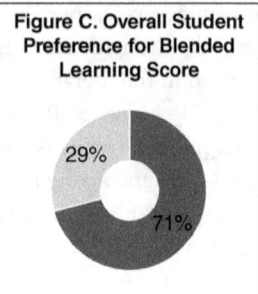

FIGURE 11.1 Student satisfaction

the course format (79%; Figure 11.1B), and a student preference for BLL (71%; Figure 11.1C).

The results are summarized to reflect the respondents' general agreement or disagreement with the survey questions on a 5-point Likert scale. The percentages reflect combined scores for *strongly agree* and *agree* or *strongly disagree* and *disagree* answers; *neutral* rankings are noted separately. More specific results demonstrated that 88% of students were satisfied and thought the BLL resources were well organized and easy to navigate. Eighty-two percent of participants indicated that the online resources in this course were helpful and believed that the online and F2F components enhanced each other. The student interview corroborated the survey results, but, most importantly, emphasized satisfaction with their process of learning, or "how they learn":

1. I really appreciate the BL just from how I learn… being able to go online, and the back and forth between the online and in-class really allowed me to apply what I learned, go over it a little bit more, and break it down. I find with lectures [in other classes], it's hard for me to really understand the material because there's just one way to look at it. But with the BL, there's multiple ways to approach and absorb the material.

In (1), the interviewee draws attention to the flexibility of access to the learning materials and the ability to use those materials at their own pace. The emphasis is on the learning process, which is multidirectional and adaptable to an individual learning style.

In addition, 59% of students believed that the course offered the convenience of not coming to campus as often. Fifty-three percent found the amount of course information and resources adequate, but 12% felt that the amount was overwhelming, with 35% voicing a neutral position. Students also expressed the willingness to continue with BLL (82%). The interviewee corroborated:

2. Yeah … I liked doing the online and in-class. It was kinda nice just to review what you learned a little bit more … after taking this class, I'm kind of wanting to take more language classes. … If they're all structured similar that would be a big plus.

In brief, student satisfaction has generated positive and reassuring results. Most respondents view the BLL model as helpful and flexible, and the resources as well organized, balanced, and complementary. Some respondents identify the benefits of time and place convenience. Many students praised BLL for allowing them to approach the learning process from multiple entry points rather than in a linear fashion.

Engagement

The engagement category of the survey yielded largely positive results (Figure 11.2).

The overall student engagement score is 83% (Figure 11.2A, consisting of four levels of engagement: emotional (84%; Figure 11.2B), cognitive (83%; Figure 11.2C), behavioral (81%; Figure 11.2D), and agentic (85%; Figure 11.2E).

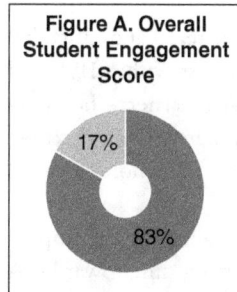
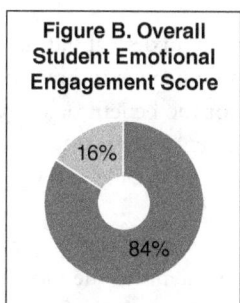
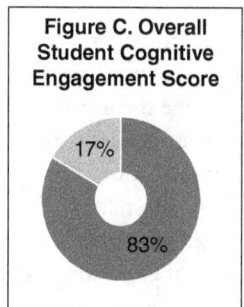
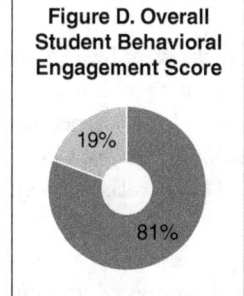
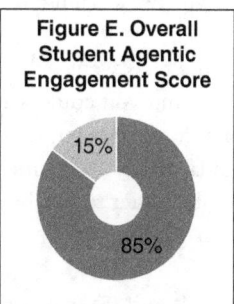

FIGURE 11.2 Student engagement

The more detailed results presented in the following sections provide additional insights into our understanding of student perspectives.

Behavioral engagement

Student behavioral engagement data indicate that 95% of students were able to follow the course schedule successfully, with 94% managing the assigned activities on time. These results suggest that a clearly organized, easy-to-follow course structure enables successful progress in the BLL. Ninety-four percent of students were able to consistently pay attention, and 76% were likely to ask questions in class, corroborated by the instructor's observations. Forty-one percent of the respondents felt that the BL model involved a more substantial time and effort investment than traditional courses, suggesting that students need to be provided with strategies to use the model effectively. The interviewee stated:

3. I was enjoying the class, learning the language, and didn't want to fall behind. That was one of the main motivators to keep up with all the work. ... Sometimes I'd be a little nervous, or ... anxious of, if it was a new subject that we were starting to learn, and I'd be a little overwhelmed with starting that, but once I got into it, I was more at ease and more comfortable.

In (3), the interviewee notes their anxiety about the new material and hints that they may not have had enough guidance in how to work best within BLL and organize the learning process for the benefit of an individual learner. The interviewee highlights that upon their "getting into it" and understanding the flow of information, they felt more comfortable and at ease, and thus more engaged and successful.

These results, supported by the instructor's observations, allude to the importance of explicitly introducing students to the model, investing time toward students "getting into it," building learners' comfort with the routine, and assisting them with self-regulated learning:

4. I felt like as the class went on and the weeks went by, everything started to kinda connect and you could kind of use what you learned.
5. I'm a bit of a slower learner. ... But ... once I just learned how to learn the material kinda on my own time, figured out how I was going to absorb it, it was a little bit easier to just breathe and kinda relax and enjoy the class ... it was all manageable.

It is evident from (4) and (5) that as the course progressed, the student gradually became more comfortable with the BLL, and they felt as though they were active and more a part of the learning process.

Emotional engagement

In the realm of emotional engagement, 88% of respondents liked taking the course. The students viewed the quality (100%) and amount (94%) of interaction with the instructor as appropriate, with similar results for the quality (88%) and amount (94%) of interaction with other students. 88% of respondents felt connected with peers and perceived the quality of their interaction as appropriate, including the interviewee:

6. Everyone got to know our names ... so we all kinda got to know each other ... we were all like best friends. ... I never felt like if I have to go work with that person it's going to be hard. We're all kinda on the same level, it was pretty easy to work with everyone there.

In addition, 71% valued relationships they built with peers in the course, and 82% of students did not feel isolated.

These results are significant for addressing the concerns about BLL noted in the introduction. In fact, the results of this study do not support claims that BLL reduces connectivity between students and an instructor and among students, instead pointing to students' perceptions of appropriate and quality connections that the model establishes. In this case, the learning community is present and positively constructed.

Anxiety levels were somewhat split: 35% of respondents felt anxious, 24% expressed neutral feelings, and 41% were not anxious in the course overall. In (3), the interviewee also mentions feeling anxiety but stresses that once they got used to the routine and grasped what was expected, their comfort level rose, and they felt at ease with the learning model. The emotional engagement factor is another reminder that students need time and guidance with respect to the learning process.

Cognitive engagement

One hundred percent of the surveyed students felt engaged in the course and were willing to review the course materials if they were not understanding what they were learning. Seventy-one percent used self-questioning to check their understanding of course materials. Ninety-four percent indicated that their grasp of key concepts and skills improved because of the effort they put into the course. As to additional reading to master the course concepts, however, the lower engagement scores (53% *neutral*, 29% *agree/strongly agree*) may not be surprising. From the students' perspective, a combination of F2F and online resources, including a variety of media texts and supplementary reference resources, was perceived as sufficient, with no need to consult additional external sources (perhaps also preventing technology-related distractions). Overall, the results of the cognitive engagement point to students' active learning, their willingness to take charge and responsibility of their learning, and their curiosity toward the learning material, even as they stayed within the learning resources provided to them.

Agentic engagement

Results that address agentic engagement particularly reinforce the learner-centered approach and students' active learning. Eighty-eight percent of students participated, or anticipated to participate, actively in the class overall, not giving activities minimal effort, with 76% feeling free to express their opinions. Seventy-one percent indicated that the instructor took their or other students' perspectives into consideration. Forty-seven percent felt they had some input in deciding how to learn in this class, which may be expected considering the routine and the predetermined structure of the BLL model, which does not require students to go beyond the resources at hand. The results, supported also by class observations, foreground active learning, and demonstrate students' willingness to participate in both in-class and online interactions. Freedom of expressing opinions and being heard further point toward connections and quality relationships, fostering a positive learning community. In addition, 71% felt that they did not rush through the activities, having freedom to navigate their learning at an individualized pace. When asked, "Do you think that BL allowed you to be more independent as a student?" the interviewee replied:

7. Yeah, I think it did … gave me the choice of whether or not I wanted to keep up with. …. The BL really kinda motivated you or gave you the choice of whether or not you were going to keep up and do the work.

In (7), the interviewee admits that the BLL provided more independence and motivation toward achieving success. Albeit indirectly, the student makes the point that the model motivates learners to sustain the language work and progress through the learning process, often independently.

The survey results are validated by the interview data cited in (1), underscoring active learning, flexibility in the learning process, and the changes BLL made to "how students learn." Namely, the interviewee appreciated the opportunity for multiple ways of "approach[ing] and absorb[ing] the material," juxtaposing and comparing this multidirectional approach with that of linear lecturing in other courses.

Regarding agentic engagement, respondents also indicated that they were not diverted by the internet or social media while studying online; 94% of respondents stayed on the assigned activities with no distractions. The results demonstrate that BLL facilitates learners' involvement with the task, whether F2F or online, increasing their investment in the learning process. These results are also supported by the web-generated gradebook data for all 23 students in this course, which showed a 90% average for student completion of all online lessons and their 87.4% cumulative grade average in the technology-assisted lessons.

Implications of the study and lessons learned

The results of this study should be of interest to those considering a transition to a technology-assisted BLL model, particularly at the beginners' level. The study of student perceptions of their satisfaction with BLL and their behavioral, emotional, cognitive, and agentic engagement in the model allows us to address some currently existing fears surrounding the transition of L2 learning to BLL.

The fear about the weakening or loss of the community of learners and relationships between students and instructor was not supported by the present findings. The results point out that in the examined BLL model, the learning community is established and present, and the group is perceived as strong and positive. Similarly, the fear about students being unprepared for the amount of independent and self-regulated learning required by blended courses was also deflated. The results suggested that respondents appreciate self-paced and individualized navigation through the course components. Moreover, students do not want to passively receive the online material; they are willing to take charge of and responsibility for their learning, as evidenced by their progress and completion, particularly of the online lessons. In fact, instructors may underestimate students' desire for independence and flexibility, especially regarding student satisfaction. Today's learners value options, including individualized pace of learning. The study respondents welcome new ways of learning and appreciate the "how they learn" aspect of the model, which provides diverse approaches to course materials rather than a traditional linear procedure. That said, instructors need to prepare students for independent learning, monitor their progress, and foster autonomy by constantly reminding students how best to keep themselves on track, as discussed further in the following section. Yet another fear of distractions offered by technology when substantial course elements are placed online for independent learning should not cause any stress for instructors, especially now that we have lived through challenges posed by COVID-19. Students reported that the BLL model facilitates their staying focused and "always on task" rather than causing distraction like the outside-of-class environment or other online media. However, these results are self-reported by students and should be interpreted with caution.

The discussion of instructors' fears in the context of student reactions to BLL and student reports of their satisfaction and engagement also point to several important lifelong learning skills. As part of a learning community, students gain a sense of responsibility while also taking charge of their own learning. Allowing students to personalize their learning space and assigning them responsibility for content and time management fosters development of their personal learning styles and routines. Remaining focused and staying on task are two other important skills that were enthusiastically noted by the study respondents.

Lessons learned 1

The design and structure of a BLL course should be simple and straightforward. Students should be able to navigate through the course components, both F2F and online, with an easy, consistent, and predictable organizational pattern. Clarity, coherent structure, and ease of use have been noted to affect student satisfaction with technology-assisted learning (Paechter & Maier, 2010). The study results also emphasize the importance of explicitly introducing students to the course model. Investing sufficient time toward familiarizing students with the routine and building their comfort with the learning process are vital for student success and retention in the course; confusion about course structure and organization causes students to miss course components and fail to complete the online lessons, which leads to poor preparation for F2F interaction. As a result, they gradually fall behind their classmates and subsequently withdraw from the course (as witnessed from class observations and online gradebook).

Students' clear understanding of course organization and assessment, as discussed in the following section, and their need to gradually ease into the learning process can lower student anxiety, enhance their comfort in the learning community, and improve their learning outcomes. These results may be relevant for any learning context, but particularly when technology-assisted self-regulated learning is crucial.

Lessons learned 2

Assessment is a critical part of any language course. While the survey did not include any overt questions about the assessment component of the course, the issues of assessment were addressed in the interview. It should be noted that in the model discussed in this chapter, assessments are integrated into the course syllabus. In fact, frequent and constant assessments are crucial in BLL, not simply for the sake of testing students but also for keeping them on track and on task. Small, frequent, and transparent assessment measures ensure students' independent studying and learning as they engage with the course material in a consistent and continuous manner. The following points were noted by the interviewee:

8. Yeah, it probably took like after the first week or so once we had done a quiz or two, once we had done a couple of the online assignments, you kinda got the flow of it like what she was expecting. After each week there was usually a written assignment. ... I did not want to fall behind [therefore I completed the online activities on my own]. ... [And the tests, midterm and

final] I really liked, so we did the practice online, so there was a practice test and told you what to prepare ... you weren't stressing so much about what to prepare, ... definitely ... no surprises ... really nice.

Based on lessons learned, the following graded course components may be suggested as assessment measures:

- preparation for and participation in F2F class, the latter depending on completion of online lessons
- online class participation or completion mark for online lessons – in our case, if students complete the online lesson, they receive 100% for that lesson; each online lesson ends with a brief online quiz, which is recorded in the online gradebook as completed or not
- weekly brief three- to four-minute in-class or online quizzes to ensure that students complete all of the online lessons and also review what was done in class
- weekly written homework assignments presented in the last online lesson of the module to encourage students to complete the "transfer" online
- brief three- to five-minute oral exams – e.g., in the middle and at the end of the semester; and
- written in-class or online tests – e.g., in the middle and at the end of the semester.

Conclusion

This study analyzed students' perceptions of their experiences in a beginners' level language classroom offered in a BL format. Concentrating on the respondents' satisfaction and engagement in this technology-assisted model, the results of the study disprove such commonly held fears of online and blended-learning instruction as loss of feeling of community and deterioration of peer and instructor relationships and students' inability to cope with self-regulated learning and distractions presented by technology. In fact, the results of this study clearly point to students' perceptions of appropriate and quality connections, manageable coursework, and their ability to remain focused throughout the course. The BLL model in the study promotes a robust learning community and offers practical suggestions to instructors considering this technology-assisted model. Although the limited number of participants in this study may have affected the quality and quantity of the data collected, it nevertheless offers a springboard for further inquiry. Future research should assess similar concepts in other BLL models. Additionally, studying the effects of BLL on student proficiency deserves attention. The studies of instructors' perspectives on and experiences with BLL teaching as well and their views of student learning and of their own practices remain limited (Anderson, 2018). As most studies of student satisfaction, including this one, focus on a single course, the research agenda needs to contrast different approaches to BLL in various courses. The results of this study may also inspire our present and future thinking amid a global pandemic. The massive transition to remote and online delivery of language courses around the globe provides a timely angle for research and practice.

Notes

1 See Mizza and Rubio (2020) for a detailed discussion of varying definitions of BL and inconsistencies in the use of terminology, e.g., blended, hybrid, flipped, and mixed.
2 All audio recordings are by native speakers of varying backgrounds, geographic locations, genders, and age groups to diversify student exposure to speech variants.
3 The survey is available at https://tinyurl.com/22n582v4.
4 I am grateful to Luis Francisco Vargas-Madriz from CTL for conducting the statistical analysis, providing charts, and an initial data interpretation.

References

Anderson, H. M. (2018). *Blended basic language courses: Design, pedagogy, and implementation*. Routledge.

Bijeikiene, V., Rasinskiene, S., & Zutkiene, L. (2011). Teachers' attitudes towards the use of blended learning in general English classroom. *Studies about Languages, 18*, 122–127. https://doi.org/10.5755/j01.sal.0.18.420

Bueno-Alastuey, M. C. (2009a). Using WebCT in a course of English for academic/specific purposes: The case of English for agriculture. In I. Gonzalez-Pueyo, C. Foz, M. Jaime, & M. J. Luzon(Eds.), *Teaching academic and professional English online* (pp. 127–152). Peter Lang.

Bueno-Alastuey, M. C. (2009b). WebCT design and users' perceptions in English for agriculture. In R. V. Marriott, & P. L. Torres (Eds.), *Handbook of research on e-learning methodologies for language acquisition* (pp. 480–496). Information Science Reference.

Bueno-Alastuey, M. C., & López Pérez, M. V. (2013). Evaluation of a blended learning language course: Students' perceptions of appropriateness for the development of skills and language areas. *Computer Assisted Language Learning*. https://doi.org/10.1080/09588221.2013.770037

Canale, M., & Swain, M. (1980). Theoretical bases of communicative approach to second language teaching and testing. *Applied Linguistics, 1*, 1–47. https://doi.org/10.1093/applin/I.1.1

Carr, M. (2014). The online university classroom: One perspective for effective student engagement and teaching in an online environment. *Journal of Effective Teaching, 14*(1), 99–110. Retrieved September 14, 2021, from https://www.learntechlib.org/p/161213/

Chenoweth, N. A., & Murday, K. (2003). Measuring student learning in an online French course. *CALICO Journal, 20*(2), 285–314. https://doi.org/10.1558/cj.v20i2.285-314

Chenoweth, N. A., Ushida, E., & Murday, K. (2006). Student learning in hybrid French and Spanish courses: An overview of language online. *CALICO Journal, 24*, 115–145. https://doi.org/10.1558/cj.v24i1.115-146

Cubillos, J. (2007). A comparative study of hybrid versus traditional instruction in foreign languages. *News from Northeast, 60*, 20–60.

Egbert, J. (2020). The new normal? A pandemic of task engagement in language learning. *Foreign Language Annals, 53*(2), 314–319. https://doi.org/10.1111/flan.12452

Enkin, E., & Mejías-Bikandi, E. (2017). The effectiveness of online teaching in an advanced Spanish language course. *International Journal of Applied Linguistics, 27*(1), 176–197. https://doi.org/10.1111/ijal.12112

Fredricks, J. A., Blumenfeld, P., Friedel, J., & Paris, A. (2005). School engagement. In K. Moore & L. Lippman (Eds.), *What do children need to flourish?* (Vol. 3, pp. 305–321). Springer US.

Garrison, D. R., & Kanuka, H. (2004). Blended learning: Uncovering its transformative potential in higher education. *The Internet and Higher Education, 7*(2), 95–105. https://doi.org/10.1111/ijal.1211210.1016/j.iheduc.2004.02.001

Gimeno Sanz, A. (2009). Online course design and delivery: The Ingenio authoring system. In I. Gonzalez-Pueyo, C. Foz, M. Jaime, & M. J. Luzon (Eds.), *Teaching academic and professional English online* (pp. 83–105). Peter Lang.

Gleason, J. (2013). Dilemmas of blended language learning: Learner and teacher experiences. *CALICO Journal, 30*(3), 323–341. https://doi.org/10.11139/cj.30.3.323-341

Graham, C. R. (2013). Emerging practice and research in blended learning. In M. G. Moor (Ed.), *Handbook of distance education* (3rd ed., pp. 333–350). Routledge.

Guillén, G., Sawin, T., & Avineri, N. (2020). Zooming out of the crisis: Language and human collaboration. *Foreign Language Annals, 53*(2), 320–328. https://doi.org/10.1111/flan.12459

Heaton-Shrestha, C., May, S., & Burke, L. (2009). Student retention in higher education: What role for virtual learning environments? *Journal of Further & Higher Education, 33*(1), 83–92. https://doi.org/10.1080/03098770802645189

Isabelli, C. A. (2015) Student learning outcomes in hybrid and face-to-face beginning Spanish language courses. In Pixel (Ed.), *Conference Proceedings: The Future of Education* (pp. 649–654). Edizioni Webster.

Kahu, E. R., & Nelson, K. (2018). Student engagement in the educational interface: Understanding the mechanisms of student success. *Higher Education Research & Development, 37*(1), 58–71. https://doi.org/10.1080/07294360.2017.1344197

Mizza, D., & Rubio, F. (2020). *Creating effective blended language learning courses: A research-based guide from planning to evaluation.* Cambridge University Press.

Nedashkivska, A. (2019). Student perceptions of progress and engagement in language learning: The blended-learning model (the case of Ukrainian). *Journal of the National Council of LCTL, 25,* 21–66. https://doaj.org/article/9ef79471d9cc4a54963195c4b7d7724a

Ogunduyile, A. O. (2013). Toward the integration of mobile phones in the teaching of English language in secondary schools in Akure, Nigeria. *Theory and Practice in Language Studies, 3*(7), 1149–1153. https://doi.org/10.4304/tpls.3.7.1149-1153

Owston, R., York, D., & Murtha, S. (2013). Student perceptions and achievement in a university blended learning strategic initiative. *The Internet and Higher Education, 18,* 38–46. https://doi.org/10.1016/j.iheduc.2012.12.003

Paechter, M., & Maier, B. (2010). Online or face-to-face? Students' experiences and preferences in e-learning. *Internet and Higher Education, 13,* 292–297. https://doi.org/10.1016/j.iheduc.2010.09.004

Reeve, J. (2013). How students create motivationally supportive learning environments for themselves: The concept of agentic engagement. *Journal of Educational Psychology, 105*(3), 579–595. https://doi.org/10.1037/a0032690

Reeve, J., & Tseng, C. M. (2011). Agency as a fourth aspect of students' engagement during learning activities. *Contemporary Educational Psychology, 36*, 257–267. https://doi.org/10.1016/j.cedpsych.2011.05.002

Rubio, F. (2014). Blended learning and L2 proficiency. In F. Rubio, & J. J. Thoms (Eds.), *Hybrid language teaching and learning: Exploring theoretical, pedagogical and curricular issues* (pp. 137–159). Heinle Cengage Learning.

Scida, E. E., & Saury, R. E. (2006). Hybrid courses and their impact on student and classroom performance: A case study at the University of Virginia. *CALICO Journal, 23*(3), 517–531. https://journals.equinoxpub.com/CALICO/article/view/23156/19161

Sivachenko, O., & Nedashkivska, A. (2017). Technologically enhanced language learning and instruction: Подорожі.UA: Beginners' Ukrainian. *East/West: Journal of Ukrainian Studies, 4*(1), 119–127. https://doi.org/10.21226/T2KG6Q

Sivachenko, O., & Nedashkivska, A. (2021). Student engagement in a remote language learning environment: The case of Ukrainian. *Russian Language Journal, 71*(2). https://scholarsarchive.byu.edu/rlj/vol71/iss2/4

Stickler, U., & Hampel, R. (2019). Qualitative research in online language learning: What can it do? *International Journal of Computer-Assisted Language Learning and Teaching 9*(3), 14–28. https://doi.org/10.4018/IJCALLT.2019070102

Young, D. J. (2008). An empirical investigation of the effects of blended learning on student outcomes in a redesigned intensive Spanish course. *CALICO Journal, 26*(1), 160–181. http://www.jstor.org/stable/calicojournal.26.1.160

12
DATA-DRIVEN LEARNING IN A LOW-LEVEL LANGUAGE CLASSROOM

Katya Goussakova

Corpora are electronic collections of written and spoken texts which are used for research and teaching. Primarily, they differ in size (e.g., mega, large, small), language (i.e., monolingual, multilingual), field (e.g., science, engineering, nursing), genre (e.g., newspaper, fiction, web, academic lectures), input (e.g., learner, native speaker), and access (e.g., free, downloadable, accessible online, commercial). Leech (1997) highlighted three avenues to the use of corpora data and corpus analysis. The first is the direct approach, when students are given an opportunity to interact with corpus data on- or offline in the form of teacher-created worksheets to explore language patterns and most frequently and naturally occurring lexicogrammatical structures. This approach is multifaceted as it includes "teaching about, teaching to exploit, and exploiting to teach" (Leech, 1997, p. 5). The second is the indirect approach, which addresses the writing of reference and instructional materials and creation of tests and other assessment tools, while the third approach includes the construction of teaching-oriented corpora, which concentrate on practical language use in the classroom. The focus of this chapter is on the direct approach, which has been gaining momentum in language classrooms since the late 1980s and is known as data-driven learning (DDL) (Johns, 1991). The term DDL is rather broad, but when it is defined, the hands-on application of corpora data and authenticity of texts and materials are usually mentioned. Moreover, inductive and self-directed aspects of language learning are invaluable DDL components. In this chapter, DDL is viewed as a student-centered language exploration method with access to authentic language through corpora (Boulton, 2011; Chen & Flowerdew, 2018; Friginal, 2018; Reppen, 2010).

Drawbacks and benefits of DDL

Even though positive and negative aspects of DDL application remain present, there is no doubt that the approach has earned itself a permanent place in a second language learning classroom.

For students

Independent corpus work may seem overwhelming for low-level and intermediate learners due to the complex nature of concordance (i.e., naturally occurring strings of words) searches (Johns, 2001). Gilquin and Granger (2010) noted that DDL "may be suitable for certain learners only," referring to various learning styles and multiple intelligences (p. 367). At the same time, some students have perceived DDL assignments as "tedious and off-putting" (Yoon & Hirvela, 2004), favoring direct instruction (Hadley & Charles, 2017). Lastly, from the implementation point of view, digital natives would have an upper hand over older students when technology is being used.

Limitations aside, through DDL, learners are exposed to the most frequently used vocabulary in naturally occurring forms and combinations. "Linguistic and situational co-occurrence patterns" (Reppen, 2010, p. 4), field-specific learning, and the discovery of irregularities are additional irrefutable advantages of DDL, especially for beginners. An adult language learner inductively engages in comparative linguistic analysis when working with corpus data comparing and contrasting language features (Johns, 1991). DDL may also help fossilized students by focusing their attention on specific lexicogrammatical patterns that resist traditional instruction (Vyatkina, 2016). Vyatkina and Boulton (2017) mentioned learner autonomy, perhaps the most pivotal DDL benefit, which allows the students to actively engage in language learning through critical thinking and exploration.

For teachers

From the instructors' perspective, inadequate access to computers, corpus software, or the Internet (Gilquin & Granger, 2010) may discourage DDL, and depending on the teaching context, some of those struggles may be more prominent. Thankfully, research has shown that printed DDL worksheets containing a limited number of language items are as effective as the online materials (Boulton, 2010; Vyatkina, 2016; Yoon & Hirvela, 2004). Since DDL is not part of the standard language teacher training, some educators are not familiar with corpus linguistics methods, tools, or benefits. Consequently, they may perceive DDL application as a daunting task as the translation of corpus findings into teaching materials that match student learning outcomes is a laborious and time-consuming process (Boulton, 2010; Granger et al., 2015). Even for English, the most used and researched language in DDL, ready-made materials are scarce (see Friginal, 2018; Karpenko-Seccombe, 2020; Poole, 2018), and when accessed, they may still require modification, which circles the responsibility of creating and implementing DDL back to the instructor. Furthermore, Vyatkina and Boulton (2017) argued that many corpora interfaces are designed by linguists for linguists rather than for students and teachers, who may find complex search syntax and highly technical outputs incomprehensible.

Encouragingly, the benefits of corpus-informed instruction outweigh the constraints. It has been suggested that Carter and McCarthy's (1995) "three Is" approach may be best suited for the DDL's overall integration into the language classroom when coupled with *intervention* – teacher's guidance (Flowerdew, 2009). In the original model, the first step was *illustration* when a target lexicogrammatical structure was retrieved from the corpus and examined by the students. Next, students engaged in sharing their corpus findings with peers during *interaction*. The third *I, induction*, happened when learners discovered a particular language pattern. Over time, the instructor's guidance in focusing students' attention on certain language features was found beneficial when employed after interaction, and the whole sequence became known as a guided-induction model.

Corpora may also serve as an invaluable language resource for both native and non-native speaking faculty, seeking to accurately respond to students' inquiries or refine their own language use (O'Keeffe et al., 2007). With DDL, instructors who teach beginning language classes may focus on the level-appropriate authentic language rather than rely on the sometimes randomly picked examples provided in the textbooks (Biber & Reppen, 2002). This approach respects students' time, individual learning goals, and effort while stimulating their interest in language learning.

DDL research in a low language proficiency classroom

Special journal issues such as *ReCALL* (Boulton & Pérez-Paredes, 2014; Chambers, 2007), the *Journal of English for Academic Purposes* (Thompson, 2007), *Language Learning & Technology* (Tribble & Barlow, 2001; Vyatkina & Boulton, 2017), and the *English Language Research Journal* (Johns & King, 1991) have been dedicated to the most nuanced applications of corpora in the classroom. Concurrently, corpus linguistics and language learning have been the focus of various seminal works (Biber & Reppen, 2015; Frankenberg-Garcia, Flowerdew & Aston, 2011; Granger et al., 2015; O'Keeffe et al., 2007; Reppen, 2010; Sinclair, 2004; Wichmann et al., 1997), not to mention numerous peer-reviewed articles published in top-tier journals. In this abundance of literature, experts often describe the direct access to language data in the context of higher levels of student language proficiency. Publications on the use of DDL in a low-proficiency classroom remain scarce. The following few articles with such focus have informed the study and practical applications described later in this chapter (Boulton, 2010; Johns, 2001; Vyatkina, 2016).

Johns (2001) equipped an English speaker learning beginner German with a concordance and a parallel (i.e., dual language) corpus to explore potentially confusing grammar and lexical chunks such as particles and conjunctions. Even though Johns (2001) concluded that beginners might make successful use of parallel concordance, it is difficult to overlook the fact that the student's educational background was in linguistics, thus making him an atypical learner, possibly more aware of various language patterns due to prior exposure to comparative linguistics. As any beginner language learner, nonetheless, the participant reportedly adopted the strategy of analyzing shorter and more manageable sentences from the corpus output due to his limited German proficiency. One significant practical takeaway from this study is the task completion flexibility allowed to the student. The participant could skip any of the 17 tasks if the corpus search produced too many hits.

Another attempt to further focus the students' language explorations through DDL was made by Vyatkina (2016). In her study, the experimental group of low-intermediate learners (A2 Common European Framework of Reference for Languages (CEFR) level (Council of Europe, 2001) had access to printed DDL materials (i.e., five to seven concordance lines) on 11 verb-preposition collocations in German as the instructors guided the students and provided feedback during a 40-minute guided induction (Carter & McCarthy, 1995; Flowerdew, 2009), while the control group was completing traditional textbook exercises after some practice. Considerable language gains resulted from interactions with corpus data even without computer access, and Vyatkina (2016) suggested "integrating brief paper-based DDL interventions into non-DDL syllabi" (p. 221).

Working with paper-based DDL materials, Boulton (2010) achieved similar results with the second-year learners of English at a French architectural school (A2 or B1 CEFR levels). The study included an experimental and a control group, pre- and posttests with 30 questions, and a survey, completed by 71 participants. Fifteen typically problematic and frequent grammar and usage items were chosen from students' writings, and the list was reviewed by English faculty. Instructional materials included two short booklets, in which five items were presented in DDL methods (i.e., lines of concordance from the British National Corpus), five with dictionary entries, and the remaining five without any reliance on online resources. The posttest was administered three weeks after the one-hour-long experiment to ensure medium-term recall. The researcher reported higher item accuracy with DDL and significant increase in scores for the DDL approach. Seventy-two percent of the students surveyed in the study expressed interest in completing more of the DDL activities. The fact that teacher-curated and specific language skill-focused DDL activities are effective even in print form should be excellent news to anyone teaching in contexts where individual computer access is not an option.

The study

To add to the body of DDL literature focusing on low-proficiency students, a DDL activity was devised for an English as a second language (ESL) classroom with a non-DDL syllabus (Vyatkina, 2016). The use of parallel corpus (Johns, 2001) in an ESL environment was not possible due to the heterogeneous first language population. Students' written language production was the focus of the activity; however, guided induction (Carter & McCarthy, 1995; Flowerdew, 2009) and the experimental design used by Boulton (2010) and Vyatkina (2016) were deemed inappropriate for the activity and the study as there was no instruction of a particular lexicogrammatical pattern, and students were not presented with pre-selected lines of concordance targeting a particular item. Instead, they conducted exploratory analysis of their own writing, which was later used to measure individual changes in vocabulary frequency over a period of six weeks. The activity had two objectives: (1) to raise the students' awareness of frequency of their written vocabulary and (2) to identify the words repeated more than three times and replace them with synonyms. This DDL activity focused on raising students' awareness of high-frequency vocabulary and how vocabulary frequency in English is directly linked to proficiency (Nation, 2001, 2011; Schmitt & Schmitt, 2014).

Writing topics varied, which provided for a relative participant autonomy (Johns, 2001; Vyatkina & Boulton, 2017) as students were to respond to at least one of the two questions and write about daily activities (e.g., shopping, eating out, dealing with stress, studying). Subsequently, the students were to analyze their own sentences by accessing the Corpus of Contemporary American English (COCA) using the integrated text analysis and the built-in monolingual dictionary features. Such work was meant to empower the students, encourage language exploration, and make the vocabulary analysis experience individualized and meaningful. Even though Chen and Flowerdew (2018) rightfully noted that "when too many computers from the same IP address use the website [COCA] at the same time, it results in halted/delated searches" (p. 344), COCA was chosen because students were going to access it at their own convenience rather than all together during class time. Every student accessed COCA directly through a personal computer, which was considered the new normal rather than a hindrance during the worldwide COVID-19 pandemic. COCA was referred to as "the most widely used corpus of English" by its creator, Mark Davies (2008–) and utilized in recent DDL studies (Brunson, 2019; Harb, 2018; Lee & Lin, 2019; Yaemtui, 2018). Moreover, as of December 2020, COCA contains one billion words from eight genres, making it an extremely robust resource for language exploration.

A three-page assignment administered to students included detailed step-by-step instructions, examples, screenshots of COCA output with explanations, and a grading rubric. Furthermore, the instructor created a screen-casting video to guide the students through the necessary steps of using COCA. The video was embedded in the learning management system (LMS) to provide the scaffolding and a form of asynchronous guided assistance for students. The assignment was first completed as a practice, followed by three submitted papers that were graded by the instructor and used for the current study.

This mixed-method, nonexperimental classroom research project was guided by the following research questions:

1. Is there statistically significant difference in vocabulary frequency between three writings produced by each student when the DDL approach is used?
2. Is there a relationship between the course grade and the low-, mid-, and high-frequency vocabulary usage when the DDL approach is applied?
3. How do students perceive their interaction with the COCA assignment?

Setting

The study was conducted in a large suburban state college in North America within the ESL nonintensive instructional context in spring and fall 2020 semesters. All students were enrolled in the class taught by the same instructor. It is necessary to mention that in spring 2020, the class was taught as a hybrid and met face-to-face once a week for 75 minutes until March when the remote instruction commenced via *Zoom* due to the COVID-19 pandemic. In fall 2020, the class met via *Zoom* for 75 minutes once a week for 16 weeks, and most of the students were participating in class using audio rather than cameras. In both semesters, the courses did not have DDL syllabi, and the students were completing classwork in the LMS and an online component of the course textbook.

Methods and instruments

Writing samples and students' DDL assignment submissions were retrieved from the LMS and rerun through COCA to ensure that the activity was completed as assigned. Students employed the COCA text analysis tool (former Word and Phrase), which produced vocabulary frequency ranges 1–500 (high), 501–3,000 (mid), and over 3,000 (low) for each writing sample. These statistics were checked twice for accuracy and used as dependent variables. The quantitative analysis included three writing samples produced two weeks apart from the middle to the final portion of the 16-week semester. From the 38 students on the rosters, three were excluded from the analysis, as they submitted only some or none of the required assignments. The learner corpus of writing samples in this study contained 33,264 words.

In the fall of 2020, a qualitative component was added to this classroom research project to gauge students' perceptions of the DDL work they completed (Boulton, 2010; Yoon & Hirvela, 2004). Students provided their initial independent oral and written (via *Zoom* chat) feedback about the experience with

COCA during a recorded class in late October. The *Zoom* session recording and chat were transcribed. At the end of the term, students filled out a ten-question survey created in Google forms, which contained open-ended, multiple choice, and yes/no questions.

Participants

In the final sample ($n = 35$), female ($n = 26$, 74.3%) and male ($n = 9$, 25.7%) students ranged in age from 17 to 60 ($M = 27.71$, $SD = 10.97$). For the majority, 22 (62.9%), Spanish was the preferred language, whereas three (8.6%) selected Haitian Creole, 2 (5.7%) Vietnamese, and 2 (5.7%) Mandarin. Each remaining student (2.85%) spoke Guajarati, Indonesian, Persian, Russian, Tagalog, and Turkish. The students received the following course grades in their writing class: A (20 = 57.1%), B (11 = 31.4%), and C (4 = 11.4%). The papers were graded by the instructor, as the use of raters was beyond the scope of this small-scale classroom research study; thus, there is no inter-rater reliability to report. Points were taken off for format, development, grammar and vocabulary use, and mechanics.

Results

The difference in vocabulary frequency

When testing the dependent variables for normality, the skewness was within range of $-.782$ to $+.962$ ($SE = .409$). The kurtosis improved after two outliers were excluded and was within range of -1.139 to $+.861$ ($SE = .798$). The Shapiro-Wilk's statistics ($W = .918$, $df = 33$, $p = .017$) confirmed that one of the variables (second writing low-frequency score) may not have been normally distributed, but the histogram and Q-Q plot analyses indicated that normality was a reasonable assumption. The means and standard deviations for the dependent variables are provided in Table 12.1.

Several dependent samples t-tests were conducted to determine whether there was a statistically significant difference in the means between low-, mid-, and high-frequency vocabulary usage in each writing sample as identified by the text analysis feature in COCA. The results were not statistically significant (from $p = .122$ to $p = .709$), which indicated that no changes in terms of vocabulary

TABLE 12.1 Means and standard deviations for the dependent variables

Frequency Range	Writing 1		Writing 2		Writing 3	
	M	SD	M	SD	M	SD
High	66.09	5.33	65.66	5.77	66.70	4.56
Mid	12.51	3.92	12.66	3.34	13.17	3.40
Low	9.12	3.23	9.86	3.17	8.86	3.25

usage occurred in the span of two weeks between each writing sample production. In other words, students continued to produce roughly the same number of low-, mid-, and high-frequency words in their writing.

The relationship between the course grade and vocabulary usage

Correlation coefficients were computed to determine whether there were relationships between low-, mid-, or high-frequency vocabulary usage and students' course grades. Scatterplots were reviewed before the analyses were conducted. There was a moderate positive relationship (Salkind, 2017) between midrange vocabulary in the first writing and the course percentage grade ($r = .449$, $n = 35$, $p = .007$). No other variables indicated the same result. Using Cohen's (1988) standards, the computed $r^2 = 0.2$ suggested a weak effect.

Students' perception of the DDL assignment

Sixty-seven percent of the students responded that each writing analysis assignment took them under an hour to complete, while 25% reported having taken between one and two hours, and one person stated that it took her between two and three hours. This information may serve as an indicator that the COCA text analysis feature was relatively user-friendly and not extremely time-consuming after the step-by-step instructions with screenshots and further guidance provided by the instructor. All students found the instructions for the assignment easy to understand and follow. When asked if COCA analyses improved their writing, 83.3% of the surveyed ($n = 12$) responded affirmatively.

The open-ended portion of the survey invited the students to share which parts of the COCA analysis they found most helpful and their overall opinion of the process. Parts of speech, vocabulary frequency, replacement of repeated words with synonyms, and the ability to learn new words were repeatedly mentioned by the students in the survey as the most useful features of this corpus activity. Students' overall opinion of the COCA analysis was mostly positive. Some students reported feeling that their writing improved as a result and indicated that COCA was a useful and user-friendly tool for vocabulary exploration. One student enjoyed compiling the lists of replaced words and their synonyms. In positive responses, referring to their writing and the assignment, students used the words "improved," "helped a lot," and "useful." Several students stated that changing the repeated words in the writing for the synonyms was an "annoying" process, while one student perceived the whole process as "a loss of time." In addition, the negative comments included the following phrases: "kinda boring"; "adding nothing to my knowledge"; "not helpful to me." Hadley and Charles (2017) and Yoon and Hirvela (2004) reported similar student emotions. Students' opinions diverged on whether providing screenshots of the original analysis, a list of repeated words and replacements with synonyms, and post-analysis were helpful features of the assignment.

Discussion

In short, the findings of this study could be summed up as follows. While the qualitative portion of this study suggested that most of the students enjoyed completing corpus work in COCA and participating in the DDL activity, there were no statistically significant changes in the students' usage of low-, mid-, and high-frequency words between the analyzed three writing samples in the span of six weeks. However, the high practical value of this project for the instructor and most students is very promising. Students were introduced to COCA and might refer to it in their future language studies, while the instructor obtained quantitative and qualitative data necessary to reflect on how to improve this DLL activity for future students. Vyatkina and Boulton (2017) called for publishing all studies in order "to avoid the *file-drawer problem*, a serious issue not just in the DDL field but in applied linguistics more broadly and, indeed, in scientific research as a whole" (p. 6), and this publication is a humble response to that request. Lack of frequency change between writing samples may be attributed to the naturally slow language development (Cummins, 2008) and a short span of about two weeks between writing samples. Hadley and Charles (2017) suggested that lack of social interaction and the feeling of isolation may contribute to the negative perception and not-significant findings in DDL, which may have been experienced by both faculty and students during the global pandemic. The results of this study corroborate the tenet that the active role of the instructor and "the appropriate level of teacher guidance or pedagogical mediation" (McEnery & Xiao, 2011, p. 371) are fundamental to DDL success. Perhaps, breaking the assignment into pieces and modeling its completion as well as thinking about additional ways of providing hands-on assistance could benefit the learners.

The only positive correlation of the midrange vocabulary in the first sample with the course grade calls for further investigation and possible shift of the focus to the parsed 501–3,000 frequency band. Means for this dependent variable were the only ones that continued to increase from the first ($M = 12.51$; $SD = 3.92$) to the last ($M = 13.17$; $SD = 3.40$) writing. This might be a modest indication that as students acquire more vocabulary words that are less frequent, the quality of their writing improves, positively affecting their course grades.

Limitations

No research project is without limitations. When writing samples were run through COCA, misspelled words and proper nouns were not recognized by the corpus and potentially skewed the frequency band count. A few writing assignments submitted for a grade included consistently inaccurate word choice, indicative of the synonym selection without consideration for genre or collocations. Post data collection, during individual consultations with the students who replaced the repeated words at random, targeted guidance and explanations were provided. Repeated words, the primary focus of the students' assignment, increased the percentage within their frequency band. Another significant factor is that the 501–3,000 frequency band is rather broad, and perhaps should be narrowed in future studies for significant changes to be observed. It is also highly likely that the choice of a topic and the task type affected vocabulary frequency distribution. Another limitation is a relatively small sample size. A priori power analysis for matched pairs means indicated the total sample size of 45, which was unachievable due to the course enrollment. Even though no statistically significant results were found in the quantitative portion of the study, students' positive responses to DDL are highly encouraging. Future research may be directed toward amassing writing samples even as small as several sentences regularly from the beginning of the semester, narrowing the mid-frequency band to no more than 2,000 most frequent words, and collecting frequency data after the removal of excessively repeated or misspelled words.

Practical application

Corpora-based activities may instill a love of language learning in beginner-level foreign language students. Nonetheless, language instructors who are eager to incorporate DDL can easily become perplexed by the volume of literature, complexity of tools, variety of corpora, and necessity to learn how the chosen corpora operate before creating their first level-appropriate task. It is beyond the scope of this chapter to list and describe the astounding quantity of corpus linguistics instruments; however, the following are several resources and tools for those beginner-level language instructors who are interested in exploring the DDL methods.

Resources and tools

For novice DDL faculty, creation of their own corpora is perhaps an unnecessary first step, but the selection of the appropriate corpus is essential.

1. The search for an adequate corpus in English could start at english-corpora.org, developed by Mark Davies, who also created El Corpus del Español (corpusdelespanol.org), funded by the U.S. National Endowment for the Humanities.
2. There are some other publicly available English corpora such as MICUSP, MICASE, BAWE, COCA, and HKCSE.
3. For teachers of English, one of the most comprehensive and up-to-date resources is "Corpus Tools, Online Resources, and an Annotated Bibliography of Recent Studies" chapter (Friginal, 2018, pp. 148–183). It provides detailed descriptions of at least 40 relevant tools and software before annotating over 60 recent articles on general use of corpus linguistics in

language teaching and learning as well as in writing and speech contexts. The book also contains a highly informative section on corpus-based lessons and activities for vocabulary, grammar, and speaking skills and suggests various types of corpora.
4. An impressive collection of corpus-related sites in languages other than English is maintained by Martin Weisser, offering parallel and multilingual corpora (http://martinweisser.org/corpora_site/corpora2.html).
5. To get a fuller picture of corpora availability, it should be cross-referenced with Learner Corpora around the World webpage (https://uclouvain.be/en/research-institutes/ilc/cecl/learner-corpora-around-the-world.html), created by the Centre for English Corpus Linguistics of the Université Catholique de Louvain, Belgium.

Even though beginner language learners are likely to be overwhelmed and intimidated by the direct access to a concordance, even with the native language support (Johns, 2001), concordancers and part of speech (POS) taggers are essential for any instructor venturing into DDL. The following examples are free and multilingual, available online, or downloadable.

1. The Compleat Lexical Tutor (v.8.3) (www.lextutor.ca), developed by Thomas Cobb, is filled with resources (e.g., flashcards, tests, cloze exercises, frequency searches) in English and French and allows for concordance searches in English, French, German, and Spanish. Karpenko-Seccombe (2020) described the application of Lextutor concordancer in the context of an English for Academic Purposes (EAP) writing instruction.
2. Thanks to Sheldon Smith, developer of the EAP Foundation (https://www.eapfoundation.com/vocab/highlighters/) site, English instructors may find practical resources for all language skills and over a dozen of general, academic, and subject-specific highlighters in one place (e.g., Academic Collocation List, Academic Formulas List, Academic Word List, Economics Academic Word List, Medical Academic Word List, New Academic Word List, New General Service Lists [NGSL]).
3. On his website, Laurence Antony (http://www.laurenceanthony.net/software.html) houses a powerful free concordancer and text analysis software AntConc (3.5.8) as well as other freeware corpus analysis tools.
4. Another invaluable DDL tool for a beginner language learner classroom is a free SKELL site (https://skell.sketchengine.eu/#home?lang=en), where learners of Czech, English, Estonian, German, Italian, or Russian, having entered the target word or phrase, are supplied with 40 sentences, collocations (i.e., word sketch), or similar words available as a list and a word-web infographic. Once registered in the Sketch Engine (https://www.sketchengine.eu/skell/), launched by the late Adam Kilgariff in 2004, users gain access to 537 corpora in over 14 languages.

5. Created by Toutanova and released in 2004, Stanford Log-linear POS (4.2.0) tagger (https://nlp.stanford.edu/software/tagger.shtml) can be downloaded with models for Arabic, Chinese, English, French, and German. Stanford Tagger powers a free online highlighting POS tool (part-of-speech.info) for English, German, French, or Spanish that can be used with writing and reading texts.
6. Helmut Schmid developed the TreeTagger (http://www.cis.uni-muenchen.de/~schmid/tools/TreeTagger/) at the Institute for Computational Linguistics of the University of Stuttgart, and it is freely available for noncommercial use with parameter files in over 25 languages.

Task ideas

Taking the needs of beginner language learners into account, DDL activities should contain clear objectives for the learner and offer native language support (whenever possible). DDL tasks should come with simple and concise instructions, employ free and user-friendly corpora (if accessed directly) or comparable handouts with targeted discrete tasks, and include meaningful faculty feedback.

For students starting to learn English, instructors may rely on the already published lists such as the NGSL (http://www.newgeneralservicelist.org/) or may choose to access corpora of their choice, which may be the only route for teachers of other languages. Limiting what is shared with the students to a few most frequent items seems appropriate for beginners of any language (Boulton, 2010; Vyatkina, 2016). An instructor may choose the five most frequent verbs (adjectives, adverbs, nouns, or any other parts of speech) depending on the instructional objective or ask students to choose the five most frequently used words in their daily lives and use them in affirmative or negative statements or questions. Lists combined with technology such as *Quizlet* or *Kahoot* permit for review and assessment opportunities that may be created by either students or faculty and shared with the class. Instructors may expand the task by adding collocations while limiting them in length and number.

Moreover, the students or the instructor may use corpus data to create error correction or cloze exercises using specific collocations or grammatical patterns (e.g., prepositions, phrasal verbs). Students may exchange those exercises and complete the assignments created by their classmates after the instructor's review, as well as run their sentences or assigned reading passages through POS taggers and compare their output to word order formulas (e.g., *be* + adjective) supplied by the instructors. Ideally, a distinction between spoken and written language should be made early and illustrated with corpora examples.

A few written sentences or a selected reading passage may also be run through a highlighter to identify the words on a particular list or through a text analysis tool of a corpus (if available) for frequency. The replacement of overused vocabulary words may be another writing task (as described earlier in this chapter). Many corpus tools provide clusters of related words, antonyms, and synonyms to the key word in addition to all its forms (i.e., a word family, lemmas), which could be particularly useful for novice language learners. For example, a SKELL search for a Russian verb "есть" (to eat) generated lists of the most frequently used nouns in four cases plus adverb, infinitive, and prepositional collocations. Such data may be used to create review sheets for noun forms and be viewed as an opportunity to learn the new words that can be practiced in short dialogs, recorded 30-second speeches, vocabulary scavenger hunts, bingo and Jeopardy games, or puzzles. There are plenty of online sites that can assist with the creation of such games and an infinite number of tasks that can be created using DDL.

Conclusion

Even though the DDL classroom research project described in this chapter did not yield significant quantitative results, students' responses to the described activity were mostly favorable. To make a DDL activity successful in the beginning and low-level classrooms, the following takeaways from this study could be considered. Students might do better when they:

1. Receive clear and concise visual and verbal DDL activity instructions
2. Are provided with a parallel corpus whenever possible
3. Are given an opportunity to practice any given DDL task before the work is graded
4. Analyze a limited number of sentences at a time
5. Are introduced to the DDL work early in the semester and are encouraged to complete it regularly
6. Are offered instructor guidance along the way

The digital age has allowed both learners and teachers to have continuous access to corpus-based resources, and incremental language exposure to varied contexts may motivate novice adult language learners to commit themselves to learning another language. Once adults enter beginner language classrooms, be it online, face-to-face, or blended learning environment, they are confronted with a myriad of challenges, some of which are limited exposure to the target language, lack of intrinsic and instrumental motivation, lack of cultural realia and authentic language, and absence of the communities of practice, all alongside multiple identities in their lives outside of the classroom. While DDL is hardly a panacea, and it does require time, corpus-related activities empower students who enjoy completing them and could also be engaged in creating them. Those activities provide students with meaningful and personally relevant foreign language explorations, as well as ignite lifelong interest in language learning, and there is no better time to start than from the beginning of that journey.

References

Biber, D., & Reppen, R. (2002). What does frequency have to do with grammar teaching? *Studies in Second Language Acquisition, 24*(2), 199–208.

Biber, D., & Reppen, R. (Eds.). (2015). *The Cambridge handbook of English corpus linguistics*. Cambridge University Press.

Boulton, A. (2010). Data-driven learning: Taking the computer out of the equation. *Language Learning, 60*(3), 534–572.

Boulton, A. (2011). Data-driven learning: The perpetual enigma. In S. Goźdź-Roszkowski (Ed.), *Explorations across languages and corpora* (pp. 563–580). Peter Lang.

Boulton, A., & Pérez-Paredes, P. (Eds.). (2014). Researching new uses of corpora for language teaching and learning. *ReCALL, 26*(2), 121–127.

Brunson, H. (2019). *Developing intermediate-level ESL grammar lessons for community college students using guided data-driven induction*. [Unpublished Master's thesis]. California State University.

Carter, R., & McCarthy, M. (1995). Grammar and the spoken language. *Applied Linguistics, 16*(2), 141–158.

Chambers, A. (Ed.). (2007). Integrating corpora in language learning and teaching. *ReCALL, 19*(3), 249–251.

Chen, M., & Flowerdew, J. (2018). A critical review of research and practice in data-driven learning (DDL) in the academic writing classroom. *International Journal of Corpus Linguistics, 23*(3), 335–369.

Cohen, J. (1988). *Statistical power analysis for the behavioral sciences*. Routledge.

Council of Europe. (2001). *Common European framework of reference for languages: Learning, teaching, assessment*. Press Syndicate of the University of Cambridge.

Cummins, J. (2008). BICS and CALP: Empirical and theoretical status of the distinction. In N. H. Hornberger (Ed.), *Encyclopedia of language and education*. Springer.

Davies, M. (2008). *The Corpus of Contemporary American English (COCA)*. https://www.english-corpora.org/coca/

Flowerdew, L. (2009). Applying corpus linguistics to pedagogy: A critical evaluation. *International Journal of Corpus Linguistics, 14*(3), 393–417.

Frankenberg-Garcia, A., Flowerdew, L., & Aston, G. (Eds.). (2011). *New trends in corpora and language learning*. A&C Black.

Friginal, E. (2018). *Corpus linguistics for English teachers: New tools, online resources, and classroom activities*. Routledge.

Gilquin, G., & Granger, S. (2010). How can data-driven learning be used in language teaching? In A. O'Keeffe, & M. McCarthy (Eds.), *The Routledge handbook of corpus linguistics* (pp. 359–370). Routledge.

Granger, S., Gilquin, G., & Meunier, F. (2015). *The Cambridge handbook of learner corpus research*. Cambridge University Press.

Hadley, G., & Charles, M. (2017). Enhancing extensive reading with data-driven learning. *Language Learning & Technology, 21*(3), 131–152.

Harb, G. (2018, March). *The application of COCA corpus for a more sophisticated word choice and better EFL writing quality* [Conference presentation]. *Proceedings of INTED 2018 Conference* (pp. 5530–5537). Valencia, Spain. doi: 10.21125/inted.2018.1306.

Johns, T. (1991). Should you be persuaded: Two examples of data-driven learning materials. *English Language Research Journal, 4*, 1–16.

Johns, T. (2001). A case for using a parallel corpus and concordance for beginners of a foreign language. *Language, Learning, & Technology, 5*(3), 185–203.

Johns, T., & King, P. (Eds.). (1991). Classroom concordancing. *English Language Research Journal, 4*, 1–31.

Karpenko-Seccombe, T. (2020). *Academic writing with corpora: A resource book for data-driven learning.* Routledge.

Lee, P., & Lin, H. (2019). The effect of the inductive and deductive data-driven learning (DDL) on vocabulary acquisition and retention. *System, 81*, 14–25.

Leech, G. (1997). Teaching and language corpora: A convergence. In A. Wichmann, S. Fligelstone, T. McEnery, & G. Knowles (Eds.), *Teaching and language corpora* (pp. 1–23). Longman.

McEnery, T., & Xiao, R. (2011). What corpora can offer in language teaching and learning. In E. Hinkel (Ed.), *Handbook of research in second language teaching and learning* (Vol. II, pp. 364–380). Routledge/Taylor & Francis.

Nation, I. S. P. (2001). *Learning vocabulary in another language.* Cambridge University Press.

Nation, I. S. P. (2011). Research in practice: Vocabulary. *Language Teaching, 44*(4), 529–539.

O'Keeffe, A., McCarthy, M., & Carter, R. (2007). *From corpus to classroom.* Cambridge University Press.

Poole, R. (2018). *A guide to using corpora for English language learners.* Edinburgh University Press.

Reppen, R. (2010). *Using corpora in the language classroom.* Cambridge University Press.

Salkind, N. (2017). *Tests and measurement for people who (think they) hate tests and measurement.* SAGE Publications.

Schmitt, N., & Schmitt, D. (2014). A reassessment of frequency and vocabulary size in L2 vocabulary teaching. *Language Teaching, 47*(4), 484–503.

Sinclair, J. (2004). *How to use corpora in language teaching.* John Benjamins.

Thompson, P. (Ed.). (2007). Corpus-based EAP pedagogy. *Journal of English for Academic Purposes, 6*(4). https://doi.org/10.1016/j.jeap.2007.09.010

Tribble, C., & Barlow, M. (Eds.). (2001). Using corpora in language teaching and learning. *Language Learning & Technology, 5*(3), 91–105.

Vyatkina, N. (2016). Data-driven learning for beginners: The case of German verb-preposition collocations. *ReCALL, 28*(2), 207–226.

Vyatkina, N., & Boulton, A. (Eds.). (2017). Corpora in language learning and teaching. *Language Learning & Technology, 21*(3), 66–89.

Wichmann, A., Fligelstone, S., McEnery, T., & Knowles, G. (Eds.). (1997). *Teaching and language corpora.* Routledge.

Yaemtui, W. (2018). *The effectiveness of data-driven learning (DDL) on teaching English collocations to Thai EFL students.* [Unpublished doctoral dissertation]. Thammasat University.

Yoon, H., & Hirvela, A. (2004). ESL student attitudes towards corpus use in L2 writing. *Journal of Second Language Writing, 13*(4), 257–283.

13

ПОЕХАЛИ! TRAINING RUSSIAN PREFIXED VERBS OF MOTION IN VIRTUAL REALITY

Kristin Bidoshi and Ekaterina Nemtchinova

Conceptualization of motion events in a second language (L2) is extremely difficult for L2 learners. Russian verbs of motion are especially challenging for students to learn, instructors to teach, and, as Hasko (2009) asserts, "notorious among Slavic linguistics for their idiosyncratic behavior in their lexical, syntactic, semantic, and aspectual characteristics" (Forsyth, 1970; Isachenko, 2003; Stilman, 1951; Vinogradov & Istrina, 1960) (p. 3). A deeper understanding of verbs of motion occurs only after concentrated in-country experience where students are exposed to numerous authentic contextual examples of the verbs in real time and in real places (Skripnikova, 2012). Hasko (2009) explains the need for increased and varied type of practice of verbs of motion; she writes, "[T]ime allotted to the presentation and practice of Russian motion talk in the ... curriculum is insufficient" and calls for "the creation of innovative teaching materials in the area of verbs of motion acquisition focused on unrehearsed spoken language, fostering learner self-expression, and close analysis of learner language" (p. 382).

Recent research highlights the positive effect of augmented and virtual reality (AR/VR) technology on the process of learning and training in all fields of education, including world language instruction. AR/VR tools expand the boundaries of a language classroom by providing access to locations and opportunities that would otherwise be unattainable. They create situated learning experiences immersing language students into cultural and situational contexts and increasing their sense of presence and involvement, which is particularly valuable for foreign (as opposed to second) language learners who lack the advantage of being surrounded by the target language (Wang et al., 2017). Immersion, involvement, and presence in the augmented or virtual reality (VR) gives students "active control and more authentic experiences, thus helping them learn more effectively and increase their retention" (Scrivner et al., 2019, p. 55).

DOI: 10.4324/9781003058441-16

The immersive experience also appeals to auditory, visual, kinesthetic, and symbolic learning styles and positively affects such aspects of learning as collaboration, problem-solving, critical thinking, and performance (Dunleavy et al., 2009; Jerry & Aaron, 2010; Scrivner et al., 2019; Wasko, 2013). AR/VR technology is believed to enhance students' perceptions and understanding of learning material (Lan et al., 2015) and increase learner autonomy (Hamilton, 2013). Although the exact degree of immersion depends on the specific technology utilized (VR is most immersive while mobile or desk-top applications such as *Second Life* is the least), all immersive experiences are associated with higher motivation and student acceptance when compared to traditional language teaching activities (Hein et al., 2021).

This chapter discusses a VR program, *Поехали!* [Let's go!], that allows students to train on the concept of verbal aspect in Russian prefixed verbs of motion in a visually realistic virtual environment. The chapter also outlines the results of a small-scale attitudinal study and provides a qualitative analysis of the data. We began with the following two goals in mind: (a) to develop a VR game to train students on the concept of verbal aspect in Russian prefixed verbs of motion in a visually realistic virtual environment and (b) to better understand our beginning language students' perceptions of the use of VR to train on prefixed verbs of motion. Specifically, we seek to understand how VR training affects student motivation and the likelihood of students using supplemental VR resources outside of the classroom, on their own time. Our program fulfills a significant need in existing materials. To our knowledge, no other existing application allows for this specific type of visually reinforced training in a virtual environment enhanced by motion, auditory, and visual cues.

Literature review

This chapter refers to several types of immersive technology. Augmented reality (AR), mixed reality (MR) and VR are immersive extended reality (XR) applications that combine physical and virtual experiences to digitally simulate or enhance the real world. While VR creates an autonomous artificial world completely obstructing one's physical reality, AR blends elements of the virtual and the real worlds as it enhances or augments what we hear, see, and feel, or, in the words of John Hanke, co-creator of *Ingress*, *Pokémon Go*, and *Google Earth*, "If virtual reality replaces the real world with fantasy, augmented reality seeks to add to the real world" (Peckham, 2016). In AR, users experience their existing natural physical environment (real-world locations), along with overlays of virtual information; the virtual and real worlds co-exist and are visible to the user at the same time. MR, which blends one's physical and digital experiences to create a hybrid world where the real and the virtual interact in real time, is sometimes confused with AR (Johnson-Glenberg et al., 2014).

Immersive virtual environments provide unique features impossible to achieve in in-person or traditional e-learning. A three-dimensional interface enables learners to interact with virtual objects in a physical space, making the learning experience come to life. The degree of immersion depends on the technology; from full immersion into a virtual environment and real-time interaction with objects and people afforded by VR to virtual interaction with objects in one's physical environment provided by AR or MR to less immersive experiences of viewing static objects and/or virtual information in a physical setting, these technologies allow learners to experience digital content in both physical and virtual spaces.

The unique features of AR/VR technology support the constructivist perspective of learning associated with Vygotsky's sociocultural theory and Piaget's cognitive development theory, which views learning as an active construction of knowledge through cognitive and sociocultural interaction with the environment (Kaufman, 2004). In a language classroom, constructivism emphasizes the importance of relevant linguistic, social, and cultural contexts and realistic settings for language learning, creation of meaning through experience, conceptual understanding rather than rote learning, and learner autonomy. Immersion into augmented or VR puts learners in contact with real-life experiences and situations where they interact with the context, environment, teachers, task, and each other and thus construct new knowledge. Rather than memorizing linguistic information, they actively participate in the process of learning by "engaging in hands-on minds-on manipulation of raw data in quest of identifying new and increasingly complex patterns, acquisition of novel concepts and construction of new understandings" (Kaufman, 2004, p. 305). As students immerse in realistic social and cultural contexts recreated by AR/VR, they actively engage in and gain more control, autonomy, and responsibility over their learning (Hamilton, 2013; Lee, 2011). The implications of constructivist principles provide AR/VR technologies with the advantages of contextualized language learning, active knowledge construction, and interaction in multidimensional environments that lead to improved student achievement.

Another theoretical underpinning of AR/VR learning is supplied by cognitive theory of multimedia learning (CTML) (Mayer, 2005) and its central premise that "people learn more deeply from words and pictures than from words alone" (Mayer, 2009, p. 47). As learners process information, they rely on verbal and visual channels to create mental representations from spoken or written words and images (e.g., pictures, photos, video). While each channel has a restricted capacity for information processing at any given time, learning involves a coordinated action of many cognitive processes (Mayer, 2005). Rather than processing auditory and visual information separately, our brain actively filters, selects, and organizes verbal and visual input, builds meaningful connections between words and images, and integrates new information with prior knowledge. Following CTML principles, AR/VR applications provide a multimedia presentation of auditory, written, and graphic input that appeals to both verbal and visual information processing channels, thus reducing the cognitive load for any single channel.

Motivation to learn a world language is a strong benefit offered by AR/VR. Researchers report an increased enthusiasm for learning generated by the new contextual and cultural content, imagery, interactivity, and collaboration inherent to many technology-based tasks, and the sense of novelty and enjoyment associated with advanced technology (Chen & Hwang, 2020; Chen, Smith, et al., 2020; Godwin-Jones, 2016). Hein et al. (2021), in their review of 54 studies of immersive technologies in foreign language learning, observe that both instructors and students generally find the AR/VR environments motivating and enjoyable. While learners are highly receptive to the new technology because of a perceived improvement in learning, reduced speaking anxiety, and increased attention, instructors appreciate its potential to motivate students to learn vocabulary, develop intercultural competence, and collaborate on tasks.

As researchers describe and analyze the use of AR/VR technologies in education, they also note certain shortcomings. A commonly cited drawback is the time and cost investment as well as logistical difficulties associated with the new technology (Chen & Hwang, 2020; Kozlova & Priven, 2015). Many instructors find that the immersive virtual features of the new technology distract their students from the learning task at hand (Hein et al., 2021; Huang et al., 2021). Another challenge is selecting the appropriate AR/VR application, integrating it into the curriculum, and aligning its affordances with the course syllabus and language competencies to be developed (Kozlova & Priven, 2015; Scrivner et al., 2019). Finally, several studies question the effectiveness of AR/VR tools in their classrooms as they failed to discover any significant change in learning outcomes. Thus, Tan et al. (2016) did not find improvement in student learning with *Second Life* as compared to traditional language-learning activities, as certain features of the 3D format made virtual communication problematic. Similarly, Dolgunsöz et al. (2018) note that VR videos did not have a significant effect on their English as a foreign language students' writing performance, although they find the technology promising in the long term. Yet another study (Chen & Chan, 2019) reported teachers' and parents' concerns about the effectiveness of AR vocabulary flashcards for young learners who tend to favor animation and sound effects over content. Technology shortcomings notwithstanding, researchers unanimously agree that AR/VR technology offers multiple benefits that allow for its successful integration into a variety of educational contexts.

Several recent surveys of existing research on immersive technologies in language classrooms (Hein et al., 2021; Huang et al., 2021; Parmaxi, 2020; Parmaxi & Demetriou, 2020) delineate linguistic skills supported by various AR/VR applications, each of which has its own scope of use and lends itself to different skill practice. One of the most frequently investigated skills is vocabulary. Researchers agree that immersive environments support vocabulary learning (Godwin-Jones, 2016; Lan et al., 2018; Scrivner et al., 2019; Vázquez et al., 2018). AR/VR technology creates authentic meaningful contexts for lexical learning while the combination of physical manipulation of 3D objects and audio and video input facilitates vocabulary retention and reinforcement. Lan et al. (2015) compared the effectiveness of traditional and virtual environments for learning Mandarin Chinese and concluded that the latter improves second language processing by offering "a rich learning experience comparable to, if not better than, that provided by the real natural learning environment" (p. 673).

Another common application of AR/VR technology is for teaching intercultural competence. Findings from various studies (e.g., Cheng et al., 2017; Shih, 2015; Yeh et al., 2020) suggest that contextualized intercultural encounters in a virtual environment benefit the development of cultural skills. The immersive environment provides students with a sense of being physically present in a target culture location, enabling them to "envision, experience, and understand diverse facets of [the target] culture and more vividly imagine their future role as participants in [target] communities" (Mills et al., 2020, p. 733).

Other linguistic skills researched in the literature on AR/VR are listening, speaking, and pronunciation (J.C. Chen, 2016; Melchor-Couto, 2017; Lan et al., 2016; Lan et al., 2018); basic target language communication (Yamazaki, 2018); reading, writing, and literacy (Dolgunsöz et al., 2018; Huang et al., 2020; Paquette et al., 2020; Pilgrim & Pilgrim, 2016); and pragmatics (Holden & Sykes, 2013; Taguchi, 2021). As to the target languages explored, the most popular is English as a second or foreign language, followed by Spanish, Chinese, Japanese, and French (Geng & Yamada, 2020; Parmaxi, 2020). This chapter seeks to add to the growing body of research on AR/VR by focusing on the development of grammar skills in a beginning Russian language classroom as both the linguistic skill and the target language have been underrepresented in the academic literature. By describing a VR program *Поехали!* that allows students to train on the concept of verbal aspect in Russian prefixed verbs of motion in a visually realistic virtual environment and discussing the results of a small-scale attitudinal study, we hope to highlight the benefit of immersive technology for beginning language learners.

Unlike the very popular online worlds of *Second Life* or *SimCity*, our program does not rely on heavily pixelated computer-simulated versions of the actual physical locations, but rather utilizes 3D digital representations of real places. Where *Second Life* recreates Moscow's Red Square in pixel form, for example, the *Поехали!* locations (around our campus and in a Russian grocery store in Albany, New York) appear to the user as they do to the person standing in them today. Moreover, the user is able to move from one location to another, behind, inside, and back outside of buildings, for example, as if they truly were immersed in the real environment.

The study

History of the Russian VR project

Unlike *Google Street View*, *CyArk*, or *YouVisit* technology (which employ 3D photographs that are stitched together and therefore do not simulate seamless movement), our program allows users to visually walk through and around in their environments, offering them rich interactive experiences with the physical spaces. The current project is the direct result of a pilot program, *A Stroll through Brighton*, created over the period of four weeks in the summer of 2016. That program models an authentic 3D environment that allows students to train on verbs of motion while being immersed in New York's Brighton Beach area. With the help of an undergraduate summer research student and the College's maker space director, we scanned locations in Brighton Beach with a Faro laser scanner, recorded voice-overs and video tutorials, and created a prototype game in the VR open-source game development software *Unity*.

The next stage of the project involved locating a more user-friendly video camera and a software package for rendering the 3D program. In the summer of 2019, we began work on the second stage of the project. We scanned specific locations on our campus (both inside and outside) and a Russian/East European grocery store in Albany, New York, with the Ricoh Theta S 360 camera. These visually realistic representations of real places were incorporated into the *3D Vista* software package as the backdrop for our VR game to train students on the verbs.

Small-scale attitudinal study

In spring term 2021, we conducted a small-scale attitudinal study using our most recent version of *Поехали!* to better understand students' perceptions of the use of VR in training prefixed verbs of motion. Specifically, we sought to learn from students more about their motivation, perceived improvement (or not) in their mastery of verbs of motion and the likelihood of their using VR resources to train on verbs of motion.

The *Поехали!* VR program is described in detail in the following section as it was the focus of the study. In our program, students navigate the Union College campus and an East European grocery store in Albany to find specific items, i.e., Tolstoy's *War and Peace* in the library and Russian food in the café and at the store. Students look around their surroundings as they listen to prerecorded oral instructions in Russian that direct their movement. The program opens with the student in the middle of Union's campus (Image 1.1).[1] In the next scene, the student finds herself inside a classroom. The whiteboards are filled with all of the different verbs of motion prefixes; when the student clicks on a prefix, a video appears to offer a visual and oral explanation of the meaning of that prefix

(Images 1.2–1.4). These instructional videos are meant as a review. Students who are already familiar with the prefixes or who don't need the review, may skip the videos and proceed directly to the game by clicking on the play button on the door. Once the student has exited the classroom, she will hear instructions about how to proceed. If the student chooses the correct route, her choice will trigger the next instruction. If she chooses the wrong path, she will receive immediate feedback, indicating that she's going the wrong way and directing her to the correct path. The story line has three segments; students are asked to go to Union College's Schaffer library to find Lev Tolstoy's *War and Peace*, to the College's student café to buy Russian food, and finally to take the College's shuttle to Dnipro, the East European grocery store in Albany. When the student has located the necessary item, she is instructed to "pick it up"; if the student selects Alexei Tolstoy's *Don Juan*, for example, instead of *War and Peace*, she will hear "That's not the correct book. Keep looking." Each of the three segments are separate and can stand alone or they can be linked together so that the student goes directly from the library to the café, to the store, for example.[2] There is a short comprehension quiz that focuses on the prefixed verbs of motion that were used in the program at the end of the Dnipro segment.

Methods and materials

Поехали! is accessible on PC, Mac, VR headsets, and *Google Cardboard*. The program is intended to be used outside of class to reinforce what students have learned in the classroom. Twelve novice-level Union College Russian language students participated in our study; six students were randomly assigned to the VR group and six to the control group. VR students used the pilot program outside of class to review the verbs while control group students completed *Golosa* Book 2 Student Activities Manual (SAM) homework exercises on the topic (Robin et al., 2014). All students received in-class instruction from their instructor on prefixed verbs of motion for a total of three days over the period of one week. In between meetings, students were expected to review what they had learned in class and to complete homework assignments. On teaching day one, all students participated in an introductory lesson on prefixed verbs of motion, which included a discussion of the meanings of the various prefixes and formation of the perfective and imperfective verbs; students completed in-class handouts on this material and a pre-survey questionnaire. For homework, the VR group was assigned the VR game, which they accessed online through their computers. They were provided with an English translation of the directions for the game. The control group was assigned workbook exercises from SAM. On teaching day two, the instructor reviewed with the students the meanings of the prefixes and the present tense of prefixed verbs of motion. All students also used an AR booklet created by the undergraduate summer research student that demonstrates each of the prefixed verbs of motion in video form to enhance students' understanding of the verbs; the videos were the same ones the VR students had as review in the VR program. Day two homework had the VR group engaging with the VR game while the control group did additional SAM exercises and an Imperative Activity worksheet created specifically for this study. In these exercises, students chose the correct prefixed imperative. For example, they had to select a Russian equivalent of "cross the street" from the following options (the incorrect forms are marked with an asterisk): *Обойдите через улицу [Go around across the street]; *Зайдите через улицу [Go into across the street]; Перейдите через улицу [Cross the street]. On teaching day three, all students reviewed the past tense of walking and driving verbs with prefixes, as well as prefixed imperatives and completed in-class exercises on these topics. They also completed a post-survey on this final day of instruction.

Data collection and analysis

Data was collected in the form of a pre-survey in *Google Forms* that all students completed on the first day of instruction; the pre-survey asked, among other things, for information about students' prior experience with VR, their preferred learning style, and their prior knowledge (if any) of Russian verbs of motion with prefixes. Following the final day of instruction, all students completed a *Google Forms* post-survey of their experiences. The post-survey form varied depending on the student's group placement; the control group answered questions about their experiences with standard textbook homework exercises on verbs of motion, their motivation to do those exercises, their perceived improvement, and the likelihood of their using resources like online reviews and textbook exercises on their own time. The VR group also answered questions on motivation, ease of use of the technology, and their perceived improved understanding of verbs of motion based on their experiences with the VR pilot program; they were also asked about their likelihood of using VR resources on their own time. Survey responses were reviewed in *Google Forms* at the following levels: summary, question, and individual. Summary-level data in the form of pie charts of percentages of students (who, for example, rated their experience with the VR program as either very positive, positive, neutral, negative, or very negative), was provided in *Google Forms*. The data was also exported to an Excel file for closer examination.

Students' perceptions

Students' experiences with VR technology were quite positive. While most students indicated either *limited* or *no prior experience* with using this kind of technology for either educational or recreational purposes, the vast majority described their experience with VR as either *very positive* (80%) or *positive* (20%). VR students overall also reported an increase in motivation when doing these exercises compared to doing textbook-based homework exercises. Sixty percent of the VR students said that VR motivated them *somewhat more* than regular homework exercises, with 20% indicating that they were *much more motivated*. A majority of the VR students also indicated that they would be likely to use VR resources on their own time; 80% indicated they would be *very likely* to do so, while 20% indicated that they would be *somewhat likely* to use such resources on their own.

In contrast, 50% of the control group rated their overall experience with their non-VR practice exercises as *positive*, while 37.5% rated it as *very positive* and 12.5% as *neutral*. Fifty percent of the control group reported that they would be *somewhat likely* to use textbook exercises and online reviews on their own time, while 25% said that that would be *unlikely* for them; another 25% declared they would *very likely* do the reviews on their own. In terms of motivation, 37.5% of the control group said they experienced *no change in motivation* (compared to a typical language class), while another 37.5% indicated they were *somewhat more motivated* than during a typical class. Twenty-five percent were *more motivated* than during a typical class (this might be due to the use of AR in the in-class review exercises).

In addition, a number of students remarked that the visual focus of VR was highly beneficial to their learning. One student wrote, "VR tech makes it possible to visualize situations instead of just reading. VR made studying more entertaining. [It is] excellent for visual learners!" Another commented, "VR felt like I was having a closer real-life experience with a professor. Loved it." The outcomes of this initial survey suggest that integrating VR technology for training on Russian prefixed verbs of motion is a promising strategy and that it has the potential to be more successful than traditional workbook exercises for grammar acquisition.

Limitations of the study

An important limitation of the present study is the number of students who participated; based on the small study sample, we are reluctant to draw detailed conclusions. The relatively low number of participants is a direct result of our small class sizes in Russian, probably a result of COVID-19. We hope to replicate the study to include pre- and posttests focusing on prefixed verbs of motion in a year when our enrollments are higher and/or pilot the program with other institutions.

Classroom implications

Поехали! could easily be incorporated into the beginning-level Russian language classroom to train students on verbs of motion; it could also be used in the intermediate-level classroom as a review of prefixed verbs of motion. Students working with any of the beginning- or intermediate-level Russian textbooks could use the program to reinforce their understanding of this difficult grammatical concept.

In our curriculum, introduction of verbs of motion occurs toward the end of the first year; *Golosa* Book 1, chapter 8 "In the Store" introduces un-prefixed verbs of motion while chapter 9 "What Will We Eat?" goes into more depth on verbal aspect. We suggest introducing prefixed verbs of motion with VR practice outside of the classroom following chapter 9 but before the final chapter 10 "Biography." In the second-year classroom, *Golosa* Book 2 chapter 5 "Hotel" covers prefixed verbs of motion; VR practice with a game such as *Поехали!* in the form of assigned homework could provide students with much-needed contextual practice on prefixed verbs of motion. One could also create supplemental written exercises on the prefixed verbs covered in *Поехали!* to test comprehension.

Overall, our study's findings are very encouraging with respect to the use of VR technology in the Russian language classroom. While the sample of this study was rather small, the almost exclusively positive nature of the feedback from students who used VR technology is quite convincing. Not only did students appreciate the variety offered by learning from these sources, but they also enjoyed the flexibility offered by being able to work remotely.

There are wide applications for a VR program that affords the student a realistic immersive experience to train on a grammatical concept within a cultural space. Consider, for example, a student preparing for a study abroad program in Russia. This student could use our program for training verbs of motion at the most basic level as she follows imperative verbal commands to traverse the Union College campus to find Tolstoy's *War and Peace* in our library and Russian food in our student café and in the local East European grocery store. In the near future, we will expand upon the program to include environments in Russia so that students will be able to walk around Red Square, to see the Kremlin, to navigate to Lenin's Tomb, for example, from their U.S. dorm rooms. Moreover, in our expanded program, students will be training on verbs of motion (reinforcing their grammatical knowledge of the language) and their knowledge of Russian culture.

While our prototype aims to train students on one specific complicated aspect of Russian grammar, the concept for this program is readily transferable to other languages and has broad applications in foreign language pedagogy. Russian verbal prefixes carry meanings that are generally associated with prepositions in other languages ("around," "up," "under," etc.); colleagues in French and German could adapt the model to train students on prepositions. Many French verbs require particular prepositions in order to complete their meaning; a similar program could help students visualize movement around a building, or up to a door, reinforcing the use of the correct verb and preposition. Two-way German prepositions, such as "in," "auf," "unter," or "neben," are especially problematic for students, as they require the accusative case to indicate motion, but dative case to indicate location. Consider the following two sentences: "Das Kind springt auf das Bett" (accusative case) and "Das Kind springt auf dem Bett" (dative). In the first sentence, the child is jumping onto the bed; in the second sentence, the child is jumping up and down on the bed. A VR program similar to *Поехали!* could significantly advance student comprehension of German prepositions as it provides an immediate visualization of actions associated with specific prepositions; the visual cues facilitate students' understanding of grammar and help them to decipher meaning. A student of Japanese could use a program similar to *Поехали!* to train on the proper use of target particles in Japanese verbs of motion. In this case, because the concept of a target in Japanese is extremely broad and extends to non-motion verbs (e.g., some common verb targets are time or the object location), in VR, students could immediately see and understand the difference between the sentences "Neko ga heya ni iru" (The cat is in the room) and "Neko ga heya ni aruiteitta" (The cat walked into the room.) A Spanish student could master the use of the 23 prepositions with practice in VR; the training could be later expanded upon to include compound prepositions, i.e., groups of words that function as prepositions. A beginning-level student could, for example, quickly visualize the difference between the prepositions *a* and *en*, in the following statements: "Voy a una casa" (I am going to a house) and "Estoy en una casa" (I am in a house).

VR has immense potential in language learning due to its capacity to engage students in complex grammar in meaningful ways, provide students with intrinsic motivation, and offer them a sense of independence in their learning. Simply put, VR can be used to empower and inspire students.

There are, naturally, limitations inherent in using VR in the classroom. The most obvious is the cost of access to VR technology. Although the *Oculus Go* provides a more enhanced experience to the user, the price tag is currently $200; *Google Cardboard* is more affordable at $8. Other limitations include difficulty establishing stable and fast Internet connections at home or at school and the problem of technical literacy for teachers. Because this study was conducted during COVID, some of our students were remote learners studying and learning from home. In order to allow for universal access to the program, we shifted to an online platform and did not utilize the *Google Cardboard* devices that had been donated to us for the study. Ideally, the students would have been completely immersed in VR with the use of *Google Cardboard*. Another pedagogical issue that should be taken into consideration is although many powerful tools such as *3D Vista* can be used to create stories for educational purposes, the software is primarily designed for use in professional situations that require live guided tours, e.g., virtual home showings for real estate. However, the challenges of mastering a new software product and adapting it to one's needs, as well as its substantial cost are balanced by the excellent technical support associated with the professional service.

Conclusion

This chapter outlined a VR program for teaching beginning-level adult learners of Russian in a university setting. It also discussed a small-scale attitudinal study that was conducted with 12 novice-level students. The objective of the study was to analyze the impact of VR-augmented instruction on student motivation. The findings show that our VR system could be an effective teaching tool for Russian language learners. Specifically, we found that students who engaged with the VR were more motivated to practice the verbs and were more likely to use the VR resource on their own time as compared to the non-VR students who were less motivated to do their textbook homework exercises and less inclined to do additional written exercises on their own.

Further development of the project includes the filming of locations of cultural significance in Moscow and St. Petersburg to expand this project to include 3D renderings of physical locations in Russia and designing a nonlinear story line based on the student's own choice of path and action. A detailed workflow "how-to guide" blueprint of the project will be developed so that language educators can follow to create their own interactive immersive environments for language training, at minimal cost to them. An experimental pretest/post-study will be conducted to focus on the acquisition of prefixed verbs of motion in the VR environment.

Acknowledgments

Kristin Bidoshi would like to thank Union College for its financial support of this project through Intellectual Enrichment grants and Undergraduate Student Summer Research grants. Specifically, she is thankful for the collaborative work of Amanda Ervin, former Union College maker space director, and each of the Union College undergraduate research students who have been involved in this project, including Natalia Brill, Ziyi Hu, Sean Miller, and Charles Deakin.

Notes

1 For program images, VR English translation instructions for students, teaching day handouts, student questionnaires, and a sample page of the AR booklet, please see https://tinyurl.com/22n582v4.
2 Instructors and learners can access a free open-source, web-based version of the first task on Union College Schaffer Library's Digital Collections website at vr. schafferlibrarycollections.org/game/tour/; the student assessment short comprehension quiz is located here: https://tinyurl.com/22n582v4.

Reference

Brandl, K. (2008). *Communicative language teaching in action: Putting principles to work.* Pearson Prentice Hall.

Chen, J. C. (2016). The crossroads of English language learners, task-based instruction, and 3D multi-user virtual learning in second life. *Computers & Education, 102*, 152–171.

Chen, R., & Chan, K. (2019). Using augmented reality flashcards to learn vocabulary in early childhood education. *Journal of Educational Computer Resources, 57*, 1812–1831.

Chen, M. R. A., & Hwang, G. (2020). Effects of experiencing authentic contexts on English speaking performances, anxiety and motivation of EFL students with different cognitive styles. *Interactive Learning Environments.* https://doi.org/10.1080/10494820.2020.1734626

Chen, Y., Smith, T., York, C., & Mayall, H. (2020). Google Earth virtual reality and expository writing for young English learners from a funds of knowledge perspective. *Computer Assisted Language Learning, 33*, 1–25. https://doi.org/10.1080/09588221.2018.1544151

Cheng, A., Yang, L., & Andersen, E. (2017, May). Teaching language and culture with a virtual reality game. *Proceedings of the 2017 CHI Conference on Human Factors in Computing Systems* (pp. 541–549). http://dx.doi.org/10.1145/3025453.3025857

Dolgunsöz, E., Yıldırım, G., & Yıldırım, S. (2018). The effect of virtual reality on EFL writing performance. *Journal of Language and Linguistic Studies, 14*(1), 278–292.

Dunleavy, M., Dede, C., & Mitchell, R. (2009). Affordances and limitations of immersive participatory augmented reality simulations for teaching and learning. *Journal of Science Education and Technology, 18*(1), 7–22.

Forsyth, J. (1970). *A grammar of aspect: Usage and meaning in the Russian verb.* Cambridge University Press.

Geng, X., & Yamada, M. (2020). An augmented reality learning system for Japanese compound verbs: Study of learning performance and cognitive load. *Smart Learning Environments, 7*(1). https://doi.org/10.1186/s40561-020-00137-4

Godwin-Jones, R. (2016). Augmented reality and language learning: From annotated vocabulary to place-based mobile games. *Language Learning & Technology, 20*(3), 9–19. http://dx.doi.org/10125/44475

Hamilton, M. (2013). *Autonomy and foreign language learning in a virtual learning environment.* Bloomsbury.

Hasko, V. (2009). The locus of difficulties in the acquisition of Russian verbs of motion by highly proficient learners. *Slavic and East European Journal, 53*(3), 360–384. http://www.jstor.org/stable/40651162

Hein, R. M., Wienrich, C., & Latoschik, M. (2021). A systematic review of foreign language learning with immersive technologies. *AIMS Electronics and Electrical Engineering, 5*(2), 117–145. http://dx.doi.org/10.3934/electreng.2021007

Holden, C., & Sykes, J. M. (2013). Complex L2 pragmatic feedback via place-based mobile games. In N. Taguchi, & J. M. Sykes (Eds.), *Technology in interlanguage pragmatics research and teaching* (pp. 155–184). John Benjamins.

Huang, H., Hwang, G., & Chang, C. (2020). Learning to be a writer: A spherical video-based virtual reality approach to supporting descriptive article writing in high school Chinese courses. *British Journal of Educational technology, 51*(4), 1386–1405. https://doi.org/10.1111/bjet.12893

Huang, X., Zou, D., Cheng, G., & Xie, H. (2021). A systematic review of AR and VR enhanced language learning. *Sustainability*, *13*(9), 4639. https://doi.org/10.3390/su13094639

Isachenko, A. V. (2003). *Grammaticheskii stroi russkogo iazyka v sopostavlenii s slovatskim: Morfologiia I–II* [Grammatical structure of the Russian language as compared to Slovak: Morphology I–II]. Iazyki slavianskoi kul′tury.

Jerry, T., & Aaron, C. (2010). The impact of augmented reality software with inquiry-based learning on students' learning of kinematics graph. *2010 2nd International Conference on Education Technology and Computer* (Vol. 2), IEEE, V2-1–V2-5. https://doi.org/10.1109/ICETC.2010.5529447

Johnson-Glenberg, M. C., Birchfield, D. A., Tolentino, L., & Koziupa, T. (2014). Collaborative embodied learning in mixed reality motion-capture environments: Two science studies. *Journal of Educational Psychology*, *106*(1), 86–104.

Kaufman, D. (2004). Constructivist issues in language learning and teaching. *Annual Review of Applied Linguistics*, *24*, 303–319.

Kozlova, I., & Priven, D. (2015). ESL teacher training in 3D virtual worlds. *Language Learning & Technology*, *19*(1), 83–101.

Lan, Y. J., Fang, S. Y., Legault, J., & Li, P. (2015). Second language acquisition of Mandarin Chinese vocabulary: Context of learning effects. *Educational Technology Research and Development*, *63*(5), 671–690.

Lan, Y. J., Fang, W. C., Hsiao, I. Y., & Chen, N. S. (2018). Real body versus 3D avatar: The effects of different embodied learning types on EFL listening comprehension. *Educational Technology Research and Development*, *66*(3), 709–731.

Lan, Y. J., Kan, Y. H., Sung, Y. T., & Chung, K. E. (2016). Oral performance language tasks for CSL beginners in second life. *Language Learning & Technology*, *20*(3), 60–79. http://dx.doi.org/10125/44482

Lee, L. (2011). Blogging: Promoting learner autonomy and intercultural competence through study abroad. *Language Learning and Technology*, *15*(3), 87–109. http://dx.doi.org/10125/44264

Mayer, R. E. (2005). *The Cambridge handbook of multimedia learning*. Cambridge University Press.

Mayer, R. E. (2009). *Multimedia learning* (2nd ed.). Cambridge University Press.

Melchor-Couto, S. (2017). Foreign language anxiety levels in second life oral interaction. *ReCALL*, *29*(1), 99–119.

Mills, N., Courtney, M., Dede, C., Dressen, A., & Gant, R. (2020). Culture and vision in virtual reality narratives. *Foreign Language Annals*, *53*(4), 733–760. https://doi.org/10.1111/flan.12494

Paquette, K., Laverick, D., & Sibert, S. (2020). Virtual reality experiences as an instructional strategy for promoting comprehension. *Reading Improvement*, *57*(4), 173–179.

Parmaxi, A. (2020). Virtual reality in language learning: A systematic review and implications for research and practice. *Interactive Learning Environments*. https://doi.org/10.1080/10494820.2020.1765392

Parmaxi, A., & Demetriou, A. (2020). Augmented reality in language learning: A state-of-the-art review of 2014–2019. *Journal of Computer Assisted Learning*, *36*, 861–875. https://doi.org/10.1111/jcal.12486

Peckham, M. (2016, July 13). Meet the mastermind behind this summer's Pokémon craze. *Time*. https://time.com/4404282/pokemon-go-john-hanke

Pilgrim, J. M., & Pilgrim, J. (2016). The use of virtual reality tools in the reading-language arts classroom. *Texas Journal of Literacy Education*, *4*(2), 90–97.

Robin, R., Evans-Romaine, K., & Shatalina, G. (2014). *Student activities manual for Golosa, a basic course in Russian* (Book Two, 5th ed.). Pearson.

Scrivner, O., Madewell, J., Buckley, C., & Perez, N. (2019). Best practices in the use of augmented and virtual reality technologies for SLA: Design, implementation, and feedback. In M.L. Carrió-Pastor (Ed.), *Teaching language and teaching literature in virtual environments* (pp. 55–72). Springer.

Shih, Y. (2015). A virtual walk through London: Culture learning through a cultural immersion experience. *Computer Assisted Language Learning*, *28*, 407–428. https://doi.org/10.1080/09588221.2013.851703

Skripnikova, I. (2012). The main difficulties when studying Russian verbs of motion in a figurative meaning. *Open Journal of Modern Linguistics*, *2*(4), 147–150. https://doi.org/10.4236/ojml.2012.24019

Stilman, L. (1951). *Russian verbs of motion: Going, carrying, leading*. King's Crown Press.

Taguchi, N. (2021). Immersive virtual reality for pragmatics task development. *TESOL Quarterly*. https://doi.org/10.1002/tesq.3070

Tan, S., O'Halloran, K. L., & Wignell, P. (2016). Multimodal research: Addressing the complexity of multimodal environments and the challenges for CALL. *ReCALL*, *28*(3), 253–273.

Vázquez, C., Xia, L., Aikawa, T., & Maes, P. (2018). Words in motion: Kinesthetic language learning in virtual reality. *2018 IEEE 18th International Conference on Advanced Learning Technologies (ICALT)*. https://doi.org/10.1109/icalt.2018.00069

Vinogradov, V. V., & Istrina, E. (Eds.) (1960). *Grammatika russkogo iazyka* [Grammar of the Russian Language]. Izdatelstvo Akademii Nauk.

Wang, Y. F., Petrina, S., & Feng, F. (2017). VILLAGE—Virtual Immersive Language Learning and Gaming Environment: Immersion and presence. *British Journal of Educational Technology*, *48*(2), 431–450. https://doi.org/10.1111/bjet.12388

Wasko, C. (2013). What teachers need to know about augmented reality enhanced learning environments. *TechTrends*, *57*(4), 17–21. https://doi.org/10.1007/s11528-013-0672-y

Yamazaki, K. (2018). Computer-assisted learning of communication (CALC): A case study of Japanese learning in a 3D virtual world. *ReCALL*, *30*(2), 214–231.

Yeh, H., Tseng, S., & Heng, L. (2020). Enhancing EFL students' intracultural learning through virtual reality. *Interactive Learning Environments*. https://doi.org/10.1080/10494820.2020.1734625

PART IV
Assessment and evaluation

14
AN EXPLORATION OF BEGINNER-LEVEL KOREAN LEARNERS' PERCEPTIONS AND PARTICIPATION IN COLLABORATIVE WRITING TASKS FOR LEARNING-ORIENTED ASSESSMENT

Yunjung Nam and Hakyoon Lee

Teaching and assessing writing in beginner-level foreign language (FL) classes is considered challenging because the learning options and task types are limited by a low level of language proficiency. For this reason, writing often does not receive due attention from the beginner-level FL/L2 (second language) educators, and, as Williams (2005) argues, "is often the last skill to be taught in L2 instruction" (p. 25). However, research has shown that writing can help initiate speaking activities (Cook, 2014) and provide meaningful opportunities for linguistic output, which is critical for L2 development (VanPatten, 2003). Despite the importance and benefits, teaching and assessing beginner learners' writing skills can be even more challenging if the target language does not share the same alphabet system with the learners' L1, such as Korean for English L1 speakers (Goodman et al., 2012), who need to master the alphabet and develop handwriting or keyboarding skills to be able to complete written assignments. Moreover, according to the Foreign Service Institute's (FSI) four-level categorization (n.d.), Korean is a category IV language,[1] which is among the most difficult FLs for the English L1 speakers. The Korean writing system may cause excessive anxiety because of very few cognates between English and Korean (Jee, 2014; Joo & Damron, 2015). One way to reduce the possible anxiety is to provide numerous opportunities for learners to practice writing utilizing their linguistic knowledge. For that purpose, this chapter explores the use of collaborative writing (CW) tasks for learning-oriented assessment (LOA). CW is defined as "the joint production or the co-authoring of a text by two or more writers" (Storch, 2011, p. 275) and is considered a socio-cognitive process of meaning making in that it involves multiple writers who negotiate, coordinate, and communicate to complete one single written product (Lowry et al., 2004). CW tasks were chosen to help beginner-level learners develop a comfort zone to articulate and externalize their linguistic knowledge to complete writing assessment tasks in collaboration with peers while enhancing L2 processing and learner engagement.

Theoretical framework

LOA in FL classrooms

With acknowledgment of the importance of classroom-based assessment (Leung, 2004; Rea-Dickins, 2006), there has been a growing awareness and efforts to establish assessment activities as a bridge between teaching and learning (Colby-Kelly & Turner, 2007). In this emerging paradigm, LOA has been theorized as a potential framework that integrates instruction, learning, and assessment in language classrooms (Purpura, 2004; Purpura & Turner, 2013). Whether the predominant purpose of assessment is formative or summative (see Chapter 15 in this volume), the key aim of LOA is to promote productive learning (Carless, 2007). In LOA, assessment tasks are considered learning activities that should align with the curriculum objectives and content to maximize learning opportunities (Carless, 2007). Tasks should be collaborative rather than competitive since LOA is expected to facilitate student involvement through self-monitoring and peer critique.

In the LOA framework, teachers are expected to interpret learner performance by drawing inferences from both learning processes and outcomes to facilitate and extend learning. More specifically to FL/L2 classrooms, Turner and Purpura (2016) present a working framework for LOA, with seven interrelated dimensions, including contextual, elicitation, proficiency, learning, instructional, interactional, and affective dimensions, arguing for more empirical research to expand upon the framework:

1) The contextual dimension concerns the social, cultural, and political context of learning on the macro-level (e.g., sociocultural norms) and micro-level (e.g., teachers' experiences)
2) The dimension of elicitation involves the situations where language is elicited for assessment purposes in diverse ways (e.g., planned, or spontaneous) inside and outside of classrooms
3) The proficiency dimension is crucial in that a model of L2 proficiency would inform what learners are expected to learn, what should be targeted, and what should be assessed
4) The learning dimension includes several subfeatures: (a) theories of learning and cognition (how L2 learners process information), (b) feedback plays an important role (closing learning gaps), (c) learners need to be responsible for their learning process through self-regulation

5) The instructional dimension relates to teachers' knowledge about language, subject matter, or pedagogical content knowledge, which is essential for effective LOA design and implementation
6) The interactional dimension involves the organization of LOAs in terms of teacher-learner interaction for scaffolding or interventions
7) The affective dimension is concerned with affective factors such as engagement level, learners' emotions, their attitudes toward learning and performance, or their motivation

Among these seven dimensions, the learning and the affective dimensions, which are more closely related to learners, are crucial constructs for this study to examine learners' perceptions, learning processes, and assessments. While previous studies have investigated teachers' strategies, knowledge, or perspectives for LOA (e.g., Gebril, 2021), little is known at present about how L2 learners process information for the actual learning and what roles assessment plays in enhancing learning, which is related to the learning dimension of the LOA framework. Although affective factors have a substantial influence on successful learning, few researchers have examined the affective dimension of learning and assessment (Turner & Purpura, 2016). Thus, it seems necessary to investigate how learners engage in the assessment process and how they perceive the assessment tasks as part of the affective dimension in the LOA framework. To fill this gap, this study explored the learners' affective and learning dimensions of the LOA framework using CW tasks. In this study, the affective dimension was analyzed by examining learners' perceptions, which include affective responses, such as general attitudes, interests, and preferences that may affect learning success. As for the learning dimension, this study focused on the meaning-making process with a peer during CW assessment tasks using the linguistic information learned in classes.

CW in FL classrooms

From a theoretical perspective, the use of collaborative work in L2 classrooms is supported by Vygotsky's (1980) sociocultural theory, which views human development as a socially situated activity. With this perspective, the role of teachers or peers in the learning process is critical, because their assistance can facilitate learners' development (Vygotsky, 1980). While participating in CW tasks, learners in pairs or groups can engage in meaningful negotiation and develop cognitively and linguistically with assistance from their peers. Given the potential benefits of collaborative work in L2 learning, CW has received increasing attention from FL/L2 researchers (e.g., Shehadeh, 2011; Storch, 2005). CW is defined as an instructional activity requiring learners to negotiate meaning and make collaborative decisions throughout the writing process to accomplish a writing task while sharing responsibility and co-ownership (Li, 2018; Storch, 2013).

Previous studies identified such benefits of using CW in L2 classrooms as an increase in target language use (Storch & Aldosari, 2010), noticeable advancement in vocabulary, content, and organization of L2 writing (Shehadeh, 2011), and improved grammatical accuracy of the output (Nassaji & Tian, 2010). However, for meaningful interactions to occur during collaboration, it is vital to know how learners – the key players in such interactions – perceive CW and how their perceptions influence their learning. Perceptions of CW can be defined as learners' views or interpretations of collaborative writing (Chen & Yu, 2019), which influence their positive or negative attitudes. Perceptions toward CW have been explored in terms of effectiveness, helpfulness, and preference (e.g., Shehadeh, 2011). In this chapter, perceptions are operationalized as learners' general attitudes, interests, and preferences.

While many previous studies found that learners overall have favorable attitudes to CW (Shehadeh, 2011), some reported negative student perceptions (Vorobel & Kim, 2017) due to their lack of confidence or concerns over their partner's emotions. Another important factor that affects the learner's attitudes and interactions is the channel or mode of CW. With the advancement of online technologies and tools, a growing body of research has recognized online CW tasks as opportunities for writing strategy development and improvement in content and organization (Elola & Oskoz, 2010; Kessler & Bikowski, 2010).

Regarding the CW processes, the learner interaction has been studied extensively both in face-to-face and online environments (Neumann & McDonough, 2015). Previous studies have explored the occurrence of language-related episodes (LREs) and other elements such as content or organization of discussion during the collaboration (e.g., Storch, 2005). Other studies examined the revision behaviors during the collaborators' mutual scaffolding, including multiple writing changes such as adding, deleting, or reorganizing (e.g., Li & Zhu, 2013). Some researchers investigated interaction styles, using categories such as collaborative vs. cooperative (e.g., Arnold et al., 2012) or collectively contributing vs. mutually supportive (e.g., Li & Zhu, 2013). Overall, the previous studies call for more research on the co-construction of meaning or negotiation to capture a fuller picture of learner interaction during the CW process.

Recently, L2 researchers have begun to focus on the use of CW in Korean as a foreign language (KFL) courses. Kim et al. (2018) investigated how heritage language learners and FL learners learn Korean honorifics through CW tasks. They discovered that heritage language learners might contribute more linguistic and cultural resources during the collaboration process due to their extensive exposure to the target language and culture and deem collaboration helpful and preferable to individual assignments. This positive perception was also found in Cho and Kim's (2019) study, where the collaborative task group perceived the tasks as easier, more enjoyable, and felt more confident than the individual task group.

Previous studies, however, mainly investigated intermediate- or advanced-level learners with little attention paid to beginner-level learners (Alwaleedi, 2017; Cho & Kim, 2019). Additionally, the studies on CW tasks among KFL learners focused on a face-to-face mode only. This study aims to explore the population of beginner-level KFL learners focusing on their perceptions toward CW assessment tasks and their interactions during the collaboration processes both in face-to-face and online modes.

The study

This chapter is a part of a larger research project that the first author conducted to investigate the professional self-development process of a novice KFL teacher who, after ten years of English-language teaching experience, started teaching Korean. The project was instigated by the novice KFL teacher's motivation and the need to know more about the effective implementation of CW tasks for LOA with a primary focus on the evidence that supports the use of CW tasks to enhance learning in terms of learners' affective dimension (i.e., perceptions) and learning dimension (i.e., participation operationalized as interactional episodes during CW tasks). Here, an interactional episode refers to segments of dialogues in which students talk about a certain topic or try to achieve a certain communicative purpose. Due to the COVID-19 pandemic, the instruction format unexpectedly changed from face-to-face to asynchronous online delivery after week 12. As a result, it was imperative to analyze the CW tasks in two different modalities (face-to-face and online) to better understand learners' perceptions and interactions.

This study attempts to investigate the following research questions (RQs):

1) What are beginner-level Korean learners' perceptions of CW assessment?
2) How do the interactional episodes during the CW process differ depending on the different modalities (face-to-face vs. online) between two focal pairs?

Method

Instructional context

This study was conducted in an elementary Korean course at a southeastern university in the U.S. The course was developed for undergraduate students with no prior or very limited knowledge of Korean. The course met three times a week for a 50-minute lesson over a 15-week semester. The course objective was to enable students to carry out basic communicative tasks with Korean native speakers.

Participants

A convenience sampling method was used in this study as the students in the first author's class were asked to participate. 19 students (eight pairs and a group of three) completed the data collection sessions with partially missing data. These students were mostly freshmen or sophomores with 14 female and five male adult learners at an average age of 19.24. Three of them self-identified as heritage Korean speakers, who were placed into this beginner-level class through a placement test. All the participants reported their L1 as English. To analyze the interactional episodes more in-depth, four focal participants were selected. Two male and two female students were selected to form male-female pairs (Pair 1 and Pair 2). Although learner characteristics were not measured through research instruments, the first author's observation notes showed that the focal participants had similar levels of motivation and participation in class activities while representing distinct levels of performance in other assignments and assessments (grammar and vocabulary quizzes). Pair 1 (S1 and S2) always achieved more than 90% on each quiz, while Pair 2 (S3 and S4) displayed some fluctuations in their performances but in the end, all four students passed the course.

Research instruments

Pre- and post-assessment perception survey

The pre- and post-assessment surveys were adapted from Chen and Yu (2019) to investigate learner perceptions of CW assessment activities. The pre-assessment survey included a question about general attitudes toward CW (Q1) and a question about their interests in CW (Q2). For the post-assessment survey questions, the same two questions were repeated with an additional question about their preferences for more CW tasks for assessment (Q3). For each question, students responded on a five-point Likert scale (1-*very unfavorable*, 2-*unfavorable*; 3-*neutral*; 4-*favorable*; 5-*very favorable*). Both pre- and post-assessment surveys also included open-ended questions about learners' attitudes toward CW activities and their perceived helpfulness for learning (see Appendix A for survey questions).[2]

Course materials and assessment tasks

During the data collection, the class covered three units in the textbook, *Integrated Korean: Beginning 1* (Cho et al., 2010). Each CW assessment task was assigned at the end of each unit as part of the summative assessment. Students were instructed to complete each task within ten minutes. As the LOA framework suggests, three assessment tasks were designed in line with the content of each unit (e.g., grammatical and lexical features in the context of the unit topic) (Appendix B).[2] To better align learning and assessment, different genres of assessment tasks were assigned for each unit: (1) descriptive writing with the visual cue of a campus map, (2) opinion-based writing about the Korean class and teacher, and (3) creative writing about a main character and his/her family in a children's book. To ensure validity, the assessment tasks were shared and reviewed by three elementary-level course instructors. They agreed that the assessment tasks were designed to measure learners' achievement in each unit. As for reliability of the assessment, two instructors scored the entire writing outcomes using the grading rubrics developed by the researchers (Appendix C).[2] Using exact agreement percentage, the inter-rater reliability was in the acceptable range for all three assessment tasks (assessment task #1 = .86, assessment task #2 = .90, assessment task #3 = .95).

Data collection procedure

Students participated in three CW (one face-to-face and two online) assessment tasks. Students were trained for both handwriting and typing in Korean through workbook exercises and assignments in the first three weeks of the course. They completed a pre-assessment survey before task implementations and a post-assessment survey after participating in each of the three CW assessment tasks. The interactions between pairs were audio-recorded for each of the three tasks. Assessment Task 1 was a face-to-face task; students completed the task in pairs in the classroom and were asked to handwrite on an assessment handout (Appendix B)[2] and audio-record their interaction using their cell phones. Assessment Tasks 2 and 3 were online; students met synchronously using video conferencing applications such as *Zoom* or *Webex* and typed their answers into a shared online document on *Google Docs* or *One Drive* depending on their preferences. Their interactions were also audio-recorded using tools available on their computers. After each CW assessment task, the students' final writing outcomes, audio recordings, and survey responses were collected.

Data analysis

To answer RQ1 about beginner-level Korean learners' perceptions of CW assessment, the responses ($n = 19$) to the pre-assessment survey in the beginning of the semester and three post-assessment perception surveys for face-to-face and online CW assessment tasks were analyzed descriptively. Cronbach's alpha reliability was checked for the responses to the pre-assessment and three post-assessment surveys. The results show that the reliability of responses to all surveys was in an acceptable range (0.92 for pre-assessment survey and 0.90, 0.79, 0.86 for the first, second, and third post-assessment surveys, respectively). Their responses were also compared by running a nonparametric repeated measures ANOVA (Friedman) test to examine any differences between pre- and post-assessment perceptions and between face-to-face and online modalities. The open-ended responses were manually analyzed for emerging topics (e.g., excitedness about the CW assessment, helpfulness of having a partner to write together).

To answer RQ2, how the interactional episodes differed during the CW process depending on the modalities (face-to-face vs. online), the data was coded by the authors through the iterative process using the coding scheme adapted from Storch (2005). The authors coded 10% of the data together using the initial coding scheme and resolved any discrepancies by adding more themes or subcategories and removing unnecessary or irrelevant codes. Then, the authors coded the rest of the data separately. The intercoder reliability was calculated using an exact agreement percentage, reaching 0.80, which was not as high as expected. The authors met again to resolve all the discrepancies and finalized the coding scheme, as described in the following, with exemplary episodes from the data. The Korean lexical items were transcribed using Yale romanization (Sohn, 1999); translations are provided in the brackets for sentence-level Korean. The following themes were discovered during the data analysis.

Task management: Discussing all the aspects related to task completion, including technology tools they need for online writing tasks

S2: Like how long does it have to be?
S1: So it seems like for describing the location we only need about one sentence. For describing her we need one sentence and then....

Interpreting the prompt: Reading the writing prompts, including any visual cues such as a map to follow the instructions

S1: Based on the campus map, follow the instructions below to write a short paragraph in collaboration with your buddy...

Generating ideas: Suggesting new ideas or deciding on certain ideas through negotiation to complete the task

S2: And her birthday. I just think of something. ... Ummmm
S1: Okay, and birthday...
S2: He's probably born in 2000 and then which month would you like?

Rereading: Reading or rereading the text they had composed

S1: Let's read it through and make sure everything is grammatically correct and spelled correctly.
S2: Okay.
S1: Alright ...
S2: 유미가 대학생이에요. 그리고 ... 생물학 ... 생물학을 배워요.
(Yumi is a college student. And ... biology ... she studies biology.)

Enrichment: Adding new words, replacing a word with a new one, or changing/modifying organization and structure of writing

S3: I am gonna ... I am gonna write ... Korean class is interesting. "However," there are a lot of homework ... because that's how we can fit the conjunction in...

LREs: Following Swain and Lapkin's (1998)'s definition, LREs refer to "dialogues in which students talk about language they are producing, question their language use, or correct themselves or others" (p. 326). The subcategories of LREs include grammar-based, lexis-based, and mechanics-based LREs.

LRE – Grammar

S2: 그런데 수업이 [*i*: a subject marker] (However, the class is...)
S1: 수업은 [*un*: a topic marker] (As for class)
S2: Yeah ... we can use either one, but it doesn't matter.
S1: Well, actually, you have to use 수업은 (as for class) ... because we're changing the topic ... we were talking about the ... We have a lot of homework, but the class is... Well, I guess I don't know we're talking about the class overall, so I don't know.

LRE –Lexical items

S2: 도서관 "앞에" (**aph**-ey), not "안에" (**an**-ey) (in front of library, not inside of library)

Reflection: Both positive and negative emotional expressions about the process and appreciation of the writing products

S3: Okay. Do you see any spelling errors?
S4: Hmm. I ... do not believe so.
S3: Okay.
S4: Everything seems right. Sino numbers...
S3: Yup.
S4: I think we are good.
S3: Cool.

Information Search: Searching for necessary information on the Internet or in the textbook

S3: I know. You know, the counter noun ... we have to have after the number ... I don't think it's new ... I think ... hold on ... let me

look up ... I remember ... translating the age ... let me get my textbook ... I remember numbers ... we had to do recently ... so ...
S4: Uh-hmm.
S3: "살 (sal)" [a counter noun for age]... okay... yup...

After the data coding, interactional episodes for the focal participants were visually displayed using Timescapes, an analytic tool that can display the writing processes and interactional episodes and show how much time the pairs spent in different types of episodes (Smith et al., 2017).

Results

Student perceptions

The descriptive statistics for the pre- and post-assessment surveys of the CW assessment tasks are displayed in Table 14.1. A nonparametric Friedman test of differences among repeated measures rendered a χ^2 value of 22.1, which was significant ($p < .001$) for Q1(general attitudes toward CW). However, the pairwise comparisons, using a series of Durbin-Concover tests, found only significant differences between the pre-assessment perception and each of the post-assessment perceptions ($p < .001$ for each pairwise comparison). In other words, the differences among the post-assessment surveys #1, #2, and #3 were not statistically significant. For Q2 (interests in CW), the result from a nonparametric Friedman test indicated significant differences ($\chi^2 = 13.4, p = .004$) among the repeated measures. The pairwise comparison found significant differences only between the pre-survey responses and each of all post-assessment responses ($p = .010$ for pre-assessment and post-assessment #1, $p < .001$ for pre-assessment and post-assessment #2, and $p = .004$ for pre-assessment and post-assessment #3).

TABLE 14.1 Student perceptions of CW assessment tasks

	Q1. How much do you like to write with others?		Q2. Would you be interested in writing with others?		Q3. Would you like to do more CW in the future?	
	M (SD)	Range	M (SD)	Range	M (SD)	Range
Pre-assessment	3.00 (0.82)	1–4	3.26 (0.81)	1–4	N/A	N/A
Post-assessment #1 (face-to-face)	3.68 (0.75)	3–5	3.74 (0.73)	3–5	3.74 (0.81)	2–5
Post-assessment #2 (online)	4.05 (0.91)	2–5	3.84 (0.96)	2–5	4.16 (0.83)	3–5
Post-assessment #3 (online)	3.95 (0.91)	2–5	3.74 (0.93)	2–5	3.95 (0.85)	3–5

There were no statistically significant differences among post-assessment survey responses. As for Q3 (preferences for more CW tasks for assessment), a nonparametric Friedman test showed nonsignificant results ($\chi^2 = 3.89$, $p = .143$), with no statistically significant differences across the three post-assessment surveys. Based on the statistical test results, this study found no differences in student perceptions between face-to-face and online CW assessment tasks.

Although there were no significant differences in the students' perceptions in the post-assessment surveys between the two formats (face-to-face vs. online), the open-ended questions produced interesting results. Open-ended question responses in the post-assessment surveys were found to be mostly positive for both online and face-to-face CW assessments. The most frequent responses to the CW experience included "enjoyable," "successful," and "helpful." When asked how they liked the online environment for CW, students' opinions varied slightly. While most of the respondents said the online CW process was not much different from face-to-face CW process, three participants reported frustration about experiencing technical issues and having conflicting schedules with their partners. Nevertheless, the students perceived online CW experiences as a new learning opportunity. The other four students reported that although it was "laggy," "slow," or "tedious" to do CW online, the online environment helped improve their Korean keyboarding skills and facilitated the collaboration process.

Interactional episodes

Besides the students' perceptions, their interactions were also analyzed. Table 14.2 displays the frequencies of codes for Pair 1 and Pair 2 in all three assessment tasks (Timescapes can be found in Appendix D).[2]

TABLE 14.2 Participation in assessment tasks for the focal participants

Assessment Task	Pair 1				Pair 2			
	1	2	3		1	2	3	
Formats	F2F	Online	Online	Total	F2F	Online	Online	Total
Task management	2	8	1	22	2	0	5	9
Interpreting prompts	6	2	2	10	1	3	2	6
Generating ideas	4	7	13	24	1	6	8	15
Rereading	1	7	13	21	0	0	0	0
Enrichment	2	2	3	7	0	3	0	3
LREs	3	6	7	16	3	1	5	7
Reflection	1	1	1	3	1	1	2	4
Information search	0	0	0	0	0	0	2	2
	4.24	11.49	15.56		3.07	3.20	7.40	

For both pairs, the interaction time increased over the assessment occasions, even though the CW assessment tasks were transitioned online. When calculated for total frequencies, both pairs engaged in generating ideas most frequently (24 for Pair 1 and 15 for Pair 2) in face-to-face and online formats. However, the results showed more differences between Pair 1 and Pair 2 than between the two formats. For example, Pair 1 did not accomplish any information search during the CW process even in an online format where they could easily access information through digital search tools. On the other hand, Pair 2 performed an information search in the second online CW (Assessment 3). Another noticeable difference was that Pair 1 read and reread their texts while composing or after the completion of their answer for all the face-to-face and online CW tasks, but Pair 2 never read or reread their writing in either face-to-face or online formats. While rereading the drafts, Pair 1 corrected lexical items (e.g., 스물 ➔ 스무살, adding a counter noun and changing the final consonant) or grammatical markers (e.g., 여동생가 ➔ 여동생이, replacing a wrong subject marker with a correct one), which certainly seems to have contributed to the accuracy of their final outcomes. Based on ad hoc analysis of grammatical accuracy of writing outcomes, Pair 1 did not have any lexical or grammatical errors in Assessment 1 and Assessment 2 but made only one minor error in Assessment 3. In contrast, Pair 2 had more than ten errors in Assessment 1, three errors in Assessment 2, and four errors in Assessment 3. Some of the errors were just typos that could have been corrected if they reread their writing.

For both face-to-face and online formats as shown in the timescapes (Appendix D), Pair 1 started with *task management* and then spent most of their time *interpreting prompts* and *generating ideas*. From the middle of the interaction and toward the end of the interaction, they engaged in *rereading*, *enrichment* and *reflection*. Regardless of the mode (face-to-face or online), Pair 1 always made sure that they reread and reviewed their texts, which might have resulted in longer interactions for all tasks compared to Pair 2. Pair 2 started their interaction with *LREs* in the face-to-face writing task because they were involved in silent individual writing without discussing tasks in the beginning. In online writing tasks, however, they began with *task management* and spent time on *interpreting prompts* and *generating ideas*. Particularly, for Assessment 3, they used their textbook and online tools in the *information search*. Pair 2 concluded their interaction with *reflection* as Pair 1 did.

Discussion

According to the pre-assessment survey, the students' initial perceptions were mostly neutral before participating in CW assessment (see Q1 and Q2 in Table 14.1). However, it seems that once they experienced the CW assessment, their perception of CW became positive. The positive perceptions were maintained over time, and no significant differences were found between face-to-face and online assessment tasks. Participants reported that their partner's assistance helped them successfully complete the assessment task or improved grammar and vocabulary accuracy in writing outcomes whether the tasks were face-to-face or online. This perception of value in peer assistance was found to critically affect attitudes toward CW experiences in previous research findings (Chen & Yu, 2019; Vorobel & Kim, 2017). Along with the favorable opinions, previous research also noted a few negative perceptions either because of lack of confidence in writing skills (Storch, 2005), or concerns about peers' feelings (Vorobel & Kim, 2017). However, such negative perceptions were not observed in the current data. The absence of the negative perceptions may be explained by the participants' use of their L1, English, for collaboration, which may have reduced anxiety and facilitated the negotiation process. Unlike advanced-level students who are expected to communicate in the target language, beginners do not experience the additional challenge of expressing disagreement in a socially appropriate way so as not to offend their partners. This outcome is supported by previous findings that learners generally demonstrate favorable attitudes toward CW (Dobao & Blum, 2013; Shehadeh, 2011). Additionally, the students' positive perceptions mostly persisted over time. The learners' positive perceptions toward CW assessment could be interpreted as a good sign, as affective factors play an important role in the learning and assessment process (Turner & Purpura, 2016).

Overall, there was no clear difference between two modes (face-to-face vs. online). Instead, differences were observed between Pair 1 and Pair 2 in interactional patterns. For example, for both face-to-face and online CW assessment occasions, Pair 2 never reviewed their writing together. However, Pair 1 always engaged in rigorous rereading and review processes, which increased the accuracy of their final outcomes: their Assessment 1 and Assessment 2 writing were free of errors, and they only had one minor error in Assessment 3. Contrastingly, Pair 2 had major errors and possibly avoidable typos or mistakes in their final writing outcomes. Compared to the face-to-face setting where they had to provide their hand-written response, Pair 2 had fewer errors when they typed their responses for online CW assessment tasks. Nevertheless, there were major errors in the use of target grammar points (e.g., counting numbers and using honorifics). It seems that mode (face-to-face vs. online) did not influence the participants' choices to reread and correct errors.

The study revealed several advantages of the online environment over the face-to-face format, as the online platform provided both pairs with more personal space and time for collaboration. The online environment is more likely to facilitate the quick start of collaboration and help the learners maintain their concentration on assessment tasks. For example, Pair 2 started the collaboration process right away in an online environment whereas their collaboration followed several minutes of individual writing in a physical classroom setting. Possibly, they were used to individual writing tasks in the classroom setting and disinclined to plunge into the actual CW assessment task straightaway. However, when they met online, their interaction was one-on-one and personal; the direct online contact might have prompted an immediate start of the collaboration process because silence would have created awkwardness. Also, Pair 2 seemed to be more focused on the assessment task and spent more time on collaboration in the absence of distractions typical of a face-to-face classroom space. This higher level of engagement and participation in online CW assessment seems to potentially contribute to more productive learning as it has been suggested that "learning transpires" in mutual attempts of interlocutors to make meaning (Turner & Purpura, 2016) in the LOA framework. The online environment seems to offer more opportunities to discuss and review tasks either synchronously or asynchronously.

Limitations and future research directions

The findings of a small-scale, classroom-based study are difficult to generalize as they are only representative of the samples in the current analysis. Besides the scope of research, there are several other limitations in this study. First, two different environments, face-to-face and online, were not properly controlled. That is, the ten-minute time limit for assignment completion was quite strictly enforced in the face-to-face setting. On the other hand, for the online assessment, although a ten-minute time frame was recommended to complete the assessment, the teacher did not enforce the time limit to accommodate the learners' different learning situations while quarantining at home due to COVID. Also, the class was delivered in an asynchronous format, following the institutional policy. As the lack of standardized time restriction raises serious issues in the assessment, future studies should explore both online and face-to-face environments with more rigorous research designs to ensure fairness and reliability of the assessment. Second, the study only utilized audio recordings. More synchronously captured data such as video recording of the learners' interaction during the CW processes will help enhance our understanding of student engagement in assessment. Lastly, regarding the LOA framework, this study focused only on the affective and learning dimensions. Other dimensions, for example, contextual or instructional ones, should be explored to broaden our perspective of using CW tasks for LOA in beginner-level FL courses. Overall, this study underscores the importance of flexibility in implementing assessment in a language classroom. More empirical studies are necessary to substantiate the benefits of online environments for CW assessment.

Pedagogical implications

The study presents a possible implementation of CW tasks for assessment to promote productive learning in a beginning-level college FL class. The in-depth analysis of the learners' interactions shows that beginning students could actively engage in and successfully accomplish the CW assessment tasks. The CW tasks are learning-oriented because the learners positively perceived the assessments (affective dimension) while the meaning-making process during peer collaboration created the social context for spontaneous elicitation of linguistic knowledge among beginner learners (learning dimension).

Another pedagogical implication draws on the finding that each pair maintained a similar organization of interactional episodes throughout multiple assessment occasions both face-to-face and online. To avoid a situation where learners repeat the same ineffective collaboration pattern, instructors need to carefully plan CW assessment and facilitate the process. For example, students can be presented with assessment rubrics that emphasize the collaborative aspects of the task. Modeling the achievement of the task and demonstrating when and how to collaborate may influence learners' collaborative behaviors during the assessment.

The findings also suggest potential benefits of online settings for CW assessment. The online environment provided more personal and private space for learner collaboration allowing them to focus on tasks without distractions thus maximizing their writing ability. The online setting can diversify the format of students' written responses. In the current study, students responded to visual and textual prompts by writing a text. However, other CW tasks may encourage students to respond through multiple modalities including text, images, and audio recordings, which might help further their writing abilities as previous studies have found (e.g., Vandommele et al., 2017).

Conclusion

This study explored the potential benefits of using CW for LOA in a beginner-level FL course. The student participants maintained positive perceptions toward CW experiences in both face-to-face and online formats. The analysis of interactions of two different pairs in the two modalities suggested that CW assessment tasks engage learners in social interaction with their peers where further learning opportunities are likely to transpire through spontaneous elicitation and meaning-making practices, central elements of the LOA framework. Although the current study did not find significant differences between face-to-face and online modes, it is hoped that this investigation of online CW assessment may offer new potential for beginner-level FL learners, especially in the era of the growing importance of online language education.

Notes

1 The four categories are based on the time lines of what the U.S. State Department's FSI has observed as the *average* length of time for an English-speaking student to learn a foreign language. Category IV Languages denotes languages "which are exceptionally difficult for native English speakers. It normally takes 88 weeks (2,200 class hours) to achieve proficiency." For more details, visit https://www.state.gov/foreign-language-training/.
2 The ancillary materials are available at https://tinyurl.com/22n582v4.

References

Alwaleedi, M. A. (2017). Examining language related episodes (LREs) of Arabic as a second language (ASL) learners during collaborative writing activities. *Theory and Practice in Language Studies*, 7(4), 256–263. http://dx.doi.org/10.17507/tpls.0704.03

Arnold, N., Ducate, L., & Kost, C. (2012). Collaboration or cooperation? Analyzing group dynamics and revision process in wikis. *CALICO Journal*, 29(3), 431–448. https://www.jstor.org/stable/10.2307/calicojournal.29.3.431

Carless, D. (2007). Learning-oriented assessment: Conceptual basis and practical implications. *Innovations in Education and Teaching International*, 44(1), 57–66. https://doi.org/10.1080/14703290601081332

Chen, W., & Yu, S. (2019). A longitudinal case study of changes in students' attitudes, participation, and learning in collaborative writing. *System*, 82, 83–96. https://doi.org/10.1016/j.system.2019.03.005

Cho, H., & Kim, Y. (2019). Learning Korean honorifics through individual and collaborative writing tasks and written corrective feedback. *Applied Linguistics Review*, 13(1), 19–47. https://doi.org/10.1515/applirev-2018-0075

Cho, Y., Lee, H. S., Schulz, C., Shon, H., & Shon, S. (2010). *Integrated Korean: beginning 1: KLEAR textbooks in Korean language* (2nd ed.). University of Hawai'i Press.

Colby-Kelly, C., & Turner, C. E. (2007). AFL research in the L2 classroom and evidence of usefulness: Taking formative assessment to the next level. *Canadian Modern Language Review*, 64(1), 9–37. https://doi.org/10.3138/cmlr.64.1.009

Cook, V. J. (2014). *The English writing system*. Routledge.

Dobao, A. F., & Blum, A. (2013). Collaborative writing in pairs and small groups: Learners' attitudes and perceptions. *System*, 41(2), 365–378. https://doi.org/10.1016/j.system.2013.02.002

Elola, I., & Oskoz, A. (2010). Collaborative writing: Fostering foreign language and writing conventions development. *Language Learning & Technology*, 14(3), 51–71. http://llt.msu.edu/vol14num3/elolaoskoz.pdf

Foreign Service Institute. (n.d.) https://www.state.gov/foreign-language-training/

Gebril, A. (Ed.) (2021). *Learning-oriented language assessment: Putting theory into practice*. Routledge. https://doi.org/10.4324/9781003014102

Goodman, K., Wang, S., Iventosch, M., & Goodman, Y. (2012). *Reading in Asian languages: Making sense of written texts in Chinese, Japanese, and Korean*. Routledge.

Jee, M. J. (2014). Affective factors in Korean as a foreign language: Anxiety and beliefs. *Language, Culture and Curriculum*, 27(2), 182–195. https://doi.org/10.1080/07908318.2014.918626

Joo, K. Y., & Damron, J. (2015). Foreign language reading anxiety: Korean as a foreign language in the United States. *Journal of the National Council of Less Commonly Taught Languages*, 17, 23–55. http://www.ncolctl.org/files/Foreign-Language.pdf

Kessler, G., & Bikowski, D. (2010). Developing collaborative autonomous learning abilities in computer mediated language learning: Attention to meaning among students in wiki space. *Computer Assisted Language Learning, 23*(1), 41–58. http://dx.doi.org/10.1080/09588220903467335

Kim, M., Lee, H., & Kim, Y. (2018). Learning of Korean honorifics through collaborative tasks: Comparing heritage and foreign language learners. In N. Taguchi, & Y. Kim (Eds.), *Task-based approaches to teaching and assessing pragmatics* (pp. 28–54). John Benjamins. https://doi.org/10.1075/tblt.10.02kim

Leung, C. (2004). Developing formative teacher assessment: Knowledge, practice, and change. *Language Assessment Quarterly, 1*(1), 19–41.

Li, M. (2018). Computer-mediated collaborative writing in L2 contexts: An analysis of empirical research. *Computer Assisted Language Learning, 31*(8), 882–904. https://doi.org/10.1080/09588221.2018.1465981

Li, M., & Zhu, W. (2013). Patterns of computer-mediated interaction in small writing groups using wikis. *Computer Assisted Language Learning, 26*(1), 62–81. https://doi.org/10.1080/09588221.2011.631142

Lowry, P. B., Curtis, A., & Lowry, M. R. (2004). Building a taxonomy and nomenclature of collaborative writing to improve interdisciplinary research and practice. *International Journal of Business Communication (1973), 41*(1), 66–99. https://doi.org/10.1177%2F0021943603259363

Nassaji, H., & Tian, J. (2010). Collaborative and individual output tasks and their effects on learning English phrasal verbs. *Language Teaching Research, 14*(4), 397–419. http://dx.doi.org/10.1177/1362168810375364

Neumann, H., & McDonough, K. (2015). Exploring student interaction during collaborative prewriting discussions and its relationship to L2 writing. *Journal of Second Language Writing, 27,* 84–104. https://doi.org/10.1016/j.jslw.2014.09.009

Purpura, J. E. (2004). *Assessing grammar.* Cambridge University Press.

Purpura, J. E., & Turner, C. E. (2013, March 16–19). Learning-oriented assessment in classrooms: A place where SLA, interaction, and language assessment interface. *ILTA/AAAL Joint Symposium on "LOA in classrooms,"* Dallas, TX, United States.

Rea-Dickins, P. (2006). Currents and eddies in the discourse of assessment: A learning-focused interpretation. *International Journal of Applied Linguistics, 16*(2), 163–188. https://doi.org/10.1111/j.1473-4192.2006.00112.x

Shehadeh, L. (2011). Effects and student perceptions of collaborative writing in L2. *Journal of Second Language Writing, 20*(4), 286–305. https://doi.org/10.1016/j.jslw.2011.05.010

Smith, B. E., Pacheco, M. B., & de Almeida, C. R. (2017). Multimodal codemeshing: Bilingual adolescents' processes composing across modes and languages. *Journal of Second Language Writing, 36,* 6–22. https://doi.org/10.1016/j.jslw.2017.04.001

Sohn, H. (1999). *The Korean language.* Cambridge University Press.

Storch, N. (2005). Collaborative writing: Product, process, and students' reflections. *Journal of Second Language Writing, 14*(3), 153–173. https://doi.org/10.1016/j.jslw.2005.05.002

Storch, N. (2011). Collaborative writing in L2 contexts: Processes, outcomes, and future directions. *Annual Review of Applied Linguistics, 31,* 275–288. http://dx.doi.org/10.1017/S0267190511000079

Storch, N. (2013). *Collaborative writing in L2 classrooms.* Multilingual Matters.

Storch, N., & Aldosari, A. (2010). Learners' use of first language (Arabic) in pair work in an EFL class. *Language Teaching Research, 14*(4), 355–375. http://dx.doi.org/10.1177/1362168810375362

Swain, M., & Lapkin, S. (1998). Interaction and second language learning: Two adolescent French immersion students working together. *Modern Language Journal*, *82*, 320–37.

Turner, C. E., & Purpura, J. E. (2016). Learning-oriented assessment in second and foreign language classrooms. In D. Tsagari & J. Baneerjee (Eds.), *Handbook of second language assessment* (pp. 255–272). De Gruyter.

Vandommele, G., Van den Branden, K., Van Gorp, K., & De Maeyer, S. (2017). In-school and out-of-school multimodal writing as an L2 writing resource for beginner learners of Dutch. *Journal of Second Language Writing*, *36*, 23–36. https://doi.org/10.1016/j.jslw.2017.05.010

VanPatten, B. (2003). *From input to output: A teachers guide to second language acquisition*. McGraw-Hill.

Vorobel, O., & Kim, D. (2017). Adolescent ELLs' collaborative writing practices in face-to-face and online contexts: From perceptions to action. *System*, *65*(4), 78–89. https://doi.org/10.1016/j.system.2017.01.008

Vygotsky, L. S. (1980). *Mind in society: The development of higher psychological processes*. Harvard University Press.

Williams, J. (2005). *Teaching writing in second and foreign language classrooms*. McGraw-Hill.

15
FEMINIST ASSESSMENT IN ELEMENTARY WORLD LANGUAGE COURSES

Veta Chitnev

Assessment, the process of collecting information about students' knowledge and skills and using it for various evaluation purposes such as assigning a grade to estimate learners' progress (Astin & Antonio, 2012), is an intrinsic aspect of educational practice. To evaluate their learners' knowledge and achievement, foreign language (FL) programs employ grade-based assessment during and at the end of a foreign language course, as well as holistic proficiency-based assessment of the four components of linguistic skill (listening comprehension, writing, speaking, and reading) that rates students' performance against a multi-level scale, e.g., the American Council on the Teaching of Foreign Languages (ACTFL) proficiency guidelines (ACTFL, 2012) and the Common European Framework of Reference (Cephe & Toprak, 2014; Council of Europe, 2001). Yet, while some schools are attempting to reconsider their grading and reporting practices by implementing alternative assessment policies (Brown University, n.d.), many higher education language programs still rely on grade-based testing as the evaluative tool in FL learning (Schinske & Tanner, 2014).

This chapter views assessment through a feminist lens. Feminist assessment practices comply with critical feminist pedagogy, a philosophy of education grounded in critical and feminist theories (Crabtree et al., 2009; Shackelford, 1992). Critical feminist pedagogy is student-centered; it fosters a positive classroom climate where the instructor expresses interest in students, provides rules for discussions, nurtures student-to-student relationships, establishes high and explicit expectations for all students, and gathers student feedback on teaching praxis (Wong & Saunders, 2020). Notably, these features of a feminist classroom are considered the best practices in education as numerous empirical studies in adult education demonstrate that active student-centered learning practices, a supportive classroom climate, and encouragement of student questions and

DOI: 10.4324/9781003058441-19

participation in content-rich discussions facilitate learning (Hoidn & Klemenčič, 2020). This chapter attempts to address the discrepancy between critical feminist pedagogy and typical measurements of student FL abilities. A consideration of feminist pedagogy principles in the context of assessment will not only make the latter more student-friendly and fair but will ultimately improve learning outcomes in a language classroom.

Assessment in education

While the term *assessment* has different meanings to different educators (Earl, 2003), many scholars distinguish between summative, diagnostic, and formative assessment. Summative assessment measures proficiency, certifies knowledge in various fields, and ranks students' performance against a set criterion (Brown & Abeywickrama, 2010; Yorke, 2008). Diagnostic assessment is typically carried out at the beginning of courses to evaluate learners' strengths, weaknesses, and areas for improvement (Wallace, 2015). It highlights the state of learners' knowledge and skills and informs learning objectives, lesson planning, and instructional activities. An identical diagnostic assessment at the end of the course establishes whether the course objectives have been met.

Unlike diagnostic assessment, formative assessment happens during instruction or in response to assignments. It provides students with current feedback on their academic progress, is ongoing, amalgamated with learning, and is proven to improve learning outcomes (Brown & Abeywickrama, 2010; Astin & Antonio, 2012; Gibbs & Simpson; 2005; Yorke, 2003). Studies have shown that formative evaluation benefits education more than summative measures because it allows instructors to identify and address learning problems several times during the course while students can use the feedback for additional practice and improvement (Astin & Antonio, 2012; Fu et al., 2018; Lipnevich & Smith, 2009; Yorke, 2003).

An alternative classification of assessment in relation to its impact on learning distinguishes assessment *of* learning, assessment *for* learning, and assessment *as* learning. Assessment of learning is summative; its results are recorded and become public, whereas assessment for and as learning is formative. The former includes personalized descriptive feedback from the teacher, enabling teachers to adjust their instruction and students to adjust their learning (Earl, 2003). In assessment as learning, Earl (2003) views the role of students "as active, engaged, and critical assessors" who "can make sense of information, relate it to prior knowledge, and master the skills involved" (p. 47).

Characteristics of quality assessment vary depending on its type and purpose. Thus, a successful summative assessment has to ensure a clear understanding of all intended learning outcomes, a variety of assessment procedures, the presence of instructional relevance, a representative sample of each student's performance, comprehensive grading, the specification of criteria for judging, feedback to students that emphasizes strengths and weaknesses, and fairness which is achieved by eliminating irrelevant difficulties, ambiguous tasks, and bias (Gronlund & Cameron, 2004). Brown and Abeywickrama (2010) argue that student perception of fair assessment may be increased if testing is well-constructed and reasonably challenging, contains items that have been practiced during the course, and can be completed within an assigned time limit.

A successful formative assessment operates on different criteria. Earl (2003) considers formative assessment to be effective if it

> empowers students to ask reflective questions and consider a range of strategies for learning and acting ... students move forward in their learning when they can use their personal knowledge to construct meaning, have skills of self-monitoring to realize that they don't understand something, and have ways of deciding what to do next.
>
> *(p. 25)*

While test designers attempt to create objective, valid, and reliable assessment tools, language tests have their constraints: "When we design a test, we cannot incorporate all the possible factors that affect performance" (Bachman, 1990, p. 31). Indeed, "in measuring language abilities, we are never able to observe or elicit an individual's total performance in a given language" (Bachman, 1990, p. 34). Furthermore, from a social constructivists' perspective that "highlights subjective and intersubjective social knowledge" (Hershberg, 2014, p. 185), no judgment can be free of bias. Therefore, human-created tests are liable to be subjective; they reflect their creators' own views regarding the object and the means of evaluation. Hence, "a test score should be interpreted as a reflection of a given test developer's section of the abilities included in a given syllabus or theory" (Bachman, 1990, p. 37).

Critical feminist pedagogy and assessment

Feminist assessment is a relatively unknown concept that synthesizes the ideas of assessment and critical feminist pedagogy. While the latter lacks a unified definition, feminist educators agree upon common themes, namely, empowering and caring, creating nonhierarchical cooperative classroom communities, respecting individual voices and experiences, reforming the teacher-student relationship through power-sharing in the classroom, and challenging the traditional pedagogical notion that teaching and knowledge can be value-free or purely subjective (English, & Irving, 2015; Monchinski, 2010; Webb et al., 2002).

The themes of creating community, giving a voice to everyone, and caring are closely related. By encouraging a commitment to social responsibility and nurturing the bonds of caring between learners, feminist educators teach students how to view themselves as members of a community (Novek, 1999). According to the feminist educator and activist bell hooks (1994),

> The exciting aspect of creating a classroom community where there is respect for individual voices is that there is infinitely more feedback because students do feel free to talk – and talk back. And, yes, often this feedback is critical.
>
> (p. 42)

The themes of empowering students and reforming and balancing the teacher-student relationship are also interconnected. The analysis of the classroom power dynamics reveals that feminist educators strive to empower their students by creating a learning environment where power and control are shared between teachers and students, and an individual's status does not determine their worth (Ropers-Huilman, 2009; Webb et al., 2002; Woodlock, 1995). Feminist pedagogues "consider values to be socially constructed and education to be political" (Monchinski, 2010) making a traditional pedagogical notion of value-free knowledge "open to question and change" in the feminist classroom (Webb et al., 2002, p. 71).

Feminist pedagogy definition and the theoretical analyses of its main principles and praxis have been at the center of scholarly debate. An important topic of feminist assessment, however, is often absent from academic discussions and is chronically under-theorized. The few inquiries into feminist assessment focus almost exclusively on women's studies programs, neglecting other disciplines, including FL teaching. Feminist pedagogues admit that assessment of students' knowledge, particularly grading, is the main source of the power imbalance between students and teachers (hooks, 1994; Luke, 1996; Shackelford, 1992); however, they do not specify how to reduce the disparity caused by traditional assessment and what form feminist assessment in a democratic classroom should take. For instance, hooks (1994), while providing an honest analysis of her teaching experience in academia and criticizing the existing grading system, does not give a detailed description of her own assessment practices in her women's studies classes. In fact, hooks offers a very general view of feminist assessment: it allows for considerable flexibility, adheres to high but not absolute standards, and provides an opportunity for students to control their grades by their labor.

Similar to hooks (1994), Schniedewind (1981) shares her experience as a women's studies professor. To avoid grades, she established the complete/incomplete grading for one of her courses; those students who needed a grade were provided with a highly specific rubric describing what assignments they needed to complete to achieve a certain grade. At first glance, this approach to assessment and grading seems to empower students because "each student decides the grade she wants to earn and does the appropriate work" (Schniedewind, 1981, p. 27). However, "appropriate work" is a vague criterion; it is unclear how to determine the degree of "appropriateness" of students' efforts.

The value of formative assessment is emphasized by Accardi (2013) who describes how rigid and patriarchal assessment methods were made "more feminist by adding an element of self-assessment and personal reflection to them" (p. 85). She does not explicitly indicate the purposes of the knowledge tests she developed for her library instruction course but provides a sample test and lists other feminist assessment methods that feature multiple choice questions, paraphrasing, and summaries. While there is no indication whether her knowledge tests are formative or summative, whether grading is involved, or what grading criteria are, Accardi (2013) admits that formative assessment is a preferable evaluation type in a feminist class.

Other feminist educators believe that summative assessment is important; by avoiding grading or assigning all students high grades, "feminist pedagogy can fall into permissive teaching that unintentionally produces a form of covert discrimination" (Akyea & Sandoval, 2005, para. 1). Akyea and Sandoval (2005) believe that no-grading approach to teaching "can be especially devastating for poor, minority, and first-generation college students" (para. 2). The feminist concern for academically disadvantaged students' self-esteem rather than their learning process shifts the focus away from their educational needs and creates a feeling of complacency. The authors argue for the value of standardized tests and grading that facilitates effective learning and empowers students by offering them a chance for success in today's world (Akyea & Sandoval, 2005).

Accardi (2013) attributes the gap in the literature on feminist assessment to possible assumptions that "assessment is somehow anti-feminist because it is counter to the learner-centered, consciousness-raising focus of feminist pedagogy" (p. 75). More than any other aspect of education, assessment "embodies a power relationship between the institution and its students, with tutors as custodians of the institution's rules and practices" (Reynolds & Trehan, 2000, p. 268). To quote *Akyea and* Sandoval (2005), "Too few feminist scholars discuss how they assess students' knowledge and products. Without a clear discussion of how feminist scholars assess students, their suggestion to share power with students leads to confusion" (para. 12). This chapter aims to address the apparent incongruity between the notions of feminism and assessment in FL classes, which necessitates the development of assessment strategies compatible with the main principles of feminist pedagogy. By looking at traditional forms of FL assessment through a feminist lens, I hope to align evaluation with feminist pedagogy to facilitate a positive learning environment where students are active agents in their education.

The study

Being a proponent of critical feminist pedagogy, I investigated the assessment practices in German and Russian language classes to determine whether they align with feminist pedagogy principles. The study was carried out in the

2016–2017 academic year at a major Canadian research university and posed the following research questions:

1. What forms of language assessment comply with critical feminist pedagogy principles?
2. What assessment-related tensions exist for instructors?
3. How can feminist reconceptualization of assessment address these tensions?

(Chitnev, 2019)

This chapter focuses on the findings relevant to elementary-level German and Russian language courses.

Methodology and procedure

The nature of the study, which required data collection and comprehensive analysis through human interaction and interpretation, dictated a qualitative methodology. The case study approach is considered to be "particularly useful to employ when there is a need to obtain an in-depth appreciation of an issue, event or phenomenon of interest, in its natural real-life context" (Crowe et al., 2011, p. 1). Also, a close investigation of cases "provides insight into an issue or refinement to a theory" (Stake, 1994, p. 237).

In addition to myself (a researcher/participant), six colleagues from my department volunteered to participate in the study. Seven participants (five female and two male instructors aged 40 to 65) appeared sufficient for identifying meaningful patterns in the data. Four participants taught elementary German or Russian courses during the time of the study, whereas three instructors had taught elementary FLs in the past.

My data collection tools included interviews,[1] my teacher journal, and student course evaluations. The teacher journal contained autoethnographic data: field notes on my pedagogical practices, my thoughts on past teaching, occasional emails from students and colleagues, and still images of students' assignments and teaching materials. While elementary courses serve as prerequisites for upper-level courses, I consider them the backbone of language programs, as students tend to make their decision to stay or withdraw from an FL program as early as the beginners' courses (Martin & Jansen, 2012). I believe feminist assessment to be particularly important for beginning language courses, and my journal focused on first-year classes.

The autoethnography format allowed me to refine my understanding of a wide range of practical assessment issues and helped me develop meaningful open-ended questions for semi-structured interviews with the participants for the next stage of the study[1]). Since I wanted to avoid imposing my own view of "feminist assessment" on the participants, my questions targeted general assessment practices without explicit reference to feminist pedagogy. The interviews lasted from 15 to 56 minutes (201 minutes total); after receiving interviewees' approval for recording, all interviews were recorded and transcribed. To protect the confidentiality of the participants, all data is anonymous in this study.

Results and discussion

In qualitative research, the data examination and interpretation are interconnected. I analyzed my teacher journal and the interview scripts to identify themes in the data using a cluster analytic approach and interpreted them by applying the principles of feminist pedagogy identified earlier. The qualitative data software program *NVivo 11* was used to perform a data-driven analysis, the results of which were then synthesized.

The data clustered around two distinct categories: *Reported assessment practices* and *Pressures, tension, and discontent*. The former was further divided into four subcategories that participants reported as the most effective assessments for their students' learning: summative, formative, complete/incomplete grading, as well as less commonly used forms of evaluation that included peer, self-, and diagnostic assessment. Participants' views on the essential qualities of assessment practices were grouped into the subcategory *Essential aspects of assessment*.

Reported assessment practices

This section presents the study data as several interrelated categories, each of which is analyzed through a feminist lens.

Summative assessment

All respondents valued summative assessment in combination with extensive written feedback. Five out of seven participants used modified forms of summative assessment. Two respondents allowed students to send drafts for instructor feedback before submitting their final work for grading. One instructor expressed satisfaction with the validity and reliability of the summative assessment tools used in her elementary classes. Her tests were based on recent language assessment research and had been developed collaboratively with other program faculty members. She considered the tests to be objective because the scoring criteria were specific and unambiguous. For example, a given number of missing endings would result in deducting an equal number of points in every case. The instructor also valued the test's capacity to assess different linguistic skills (listening comprehension, writing, speaking, and reading).

Two participants also emphasized the importance of assessing a variety of skills in their summative assessment because it allowed a teacher a relatively unbiased view of students' knowledge. Three instructors thought that fairness and objectivity could be achieved by anonymous grading, i.e., by concealing student names from graders on the university learning management system or by grading their colleagues' students rather than their own. This, they thought, was a positive feature of their summative assessment practices.

One participant considered summative assessment to be the best motivator for learning, saying, "I believe students need to be pushed somehow, and this is the way we push them. Otherwise, I don't think they will be studying." She believed that strictly graded summative assessment surpasses other motivators: "It is still the mark that [students] care about. Without this motivator, honestly, I do not see how we could motivate them enough to study under such difficult conditions." Another participant included participation in her summative assessment. At the very beginning of every course, students are informed that their mark depends on their active class participation "rather than on the correctness of their answers"; the level of individual student participation is recorded after every class. If the instructor felt that a shy student did not participate in group discussions, she assigned them to different groups.

Summative assessment through a feminist lens

From a feminist perspective, summative assessment increases a teacher-student power imbalance. Armed with summative assessment, instructors not only control student acquisition of knowledge but also determine their grades. The importance of grades for college students' funding and future careers underscores the role of summative assessment in power-imbalanced assessment approaches. Furthermore, the objectivity of summative graded tests is questionable because of the subjective decisions of the human test developer concerning its length and difficulty. Also, tests noticeably privilege those who excel at test-taking, regardless of their depth of knowledge. Thus, in my beginner language classes, senior students tend to outperform freshmen because of their extensive experience in test-taking.

Summative assessment of participation violates some core principles of feminist pedagogy as well. Including a participation score in a student's final grade raises such important issues as the subjectivity of grading, accuracy of recording, and disadvantaging shy students who may feel singled out when reassigned to different discussion groups. Moreover, unequal participation may be exacerbated by gender issues. Female student participation is known to decrease in classes where they are outnumbered by male students, whereas male participation is not affected by the number of female students in the class (Tatum et al., 2013). Considering these findings, the inclusion of participation scores in the final grade significantly compromises the fairness of summative assessment.

Finally, the participant's claim that graded summative assessment is the best motivator for student learning is neither in line with the feminist approach nor supported by evidence. According to Behling et al. (2017), graded summative assessment motivates students to outcompete their peers and avoid embarrassment rather than to learn. Research shows that motivation and academic engagement is positively influenced by the perceived enjoyment of learning the subject, the importance of the subject to the student's sense of identity, self-worth, and accomplishment, as well as its relevance to a student's personal life rather than grades (Harackiewicz et al., 2015).

Formative assessment

All of participants considered formative assessment to be important for improving student learning. One instructor described her attempts to provide comments that are both sensitive and specific. She comments on strong and weak aspects of students' performance and indicates areas of improvement. However, she admitted that such feedback is time- and effort consuming as it requires carefully tracking students' progress and developing a relationship with them.

The instructor described her practice of combining numerical grades with comprehensive verbal feedback on students' compositions as less successful than she expected. Students' attention was mostly consumed by grades. Indeed, the next test results indicated that students disregarded her feedback, which often took her hours to write. Therefore, she abandoned the practice of combining grades with feedback, commenting instead on the strengths of student writing and suggesting areas to review.

Another instructor provided formative feedback in her elementary language classes as preparation for essay writing. Before writing a graded essay, students submit several drafts. The instructor provides corrections and feedback on syntactic complexity and word choice without grading the essay. She found pre-essay assignments valuable for helping students develop self-confidence and learn about the instructor's requirements. She relies on comments and ungraded feedback to decrease the amount of grading and believes the individual feedback to be the most beneficial in her practice.

One of the instructors confessed that her formative assessment of students' pronunciation in a class of over 30 students was not as effective as she expected. Students seem to be dissatisfied with a lack of individual feedback on every person's pronunciation, as evidenced by the following comment from a course evaluation survey:

> If anything, I think [the instructor] just needs to be a bit "meaner" about our pronunciation when we speak as a whole class, because there were definitely things we mumbled through that she wouldn't pronounce herself and would leave me unaware of how a word really sounded.

Two reported that they used ongoing formative assessment by involving students in class activities and offering questions to engage every student. One of them preferred to provide collective rather than individualized personal feedback during her classes. She addressed the whole class by identifying and explaining common mistakes in class. She never singled out students who made those mistakes.

Formative assessment through a feminist lens

Feminist assessment facilitates learning ultimately leading to student success (Akyea & Sandoval, 2005). While research suggests that formative assessment advances learning (Astin & Antonio; 2012; Yorke, 2003), reducing grading for the sake of ungraded feedback not only improves teaching and learning but also helps decrease the power imbalance in class. The observation of the instructor who found formative feedback to be more effective than feedback/grade combination is consistent with Lipnevich and Smith's (2009) conclusion that detailed, descriptive feedback in the absence of a grade is more effective than similar feedback accompanied by a grade.

While feminist feedback is empowering, sensitive, and caring, some students may take a teacher's comments on their work personally and be discouraged from learning (Yorke, 2003, 2005). Furthermore, after receiving "tough" feedback from a teacher, some students feel disrespected, experience confusion, and report "that their agency or authority had been usurped rather than when productive collaboration, negotiation, and integration of new perspective occurred" (Rupiper et al., 2017, p. 1).

Examples provided by participants who favored ongoing feedback during class activities show that instructors largely focus on students' errors – in other words, on their linguistic weaknesses rather than strengths, thus contradicting the main principle of critical feminist pedagogy of empowerment and care. Also, Kerr (2020) claims that feedback on correct answers is more effective than on errors and recommends balancing positive and negative feedback in a language classroom. Moreover, relying on collective rather than personalized feedback may hinder learning because common mistakes do not apply to all students. Indeed, in large language courses, it is often unfeasible to provide individuals with caring and detailed personalized feedback during class instruction. Written formative feedback imposes problems as well because instructors lack time to focus on individual student progress or deficiencies.

Less commonly used forms of assessment

In this study, complete/incomplete grading, diagnostic, peer and self-assessment are considered less commonly used forms of assessment. Five participants used complete/incomplete grading, but only for attendance and home assignments. One instructor reported collecting home assignments every class and providing students with brief comments. Another participant reported that participation, presentation, and group discussions were graded as complete/incomplete in one of her elementary classes. She stated, "The good thing is, it really helps to get students involved, but on the other hand, it pushes your averages up."

Only one educator conducted diagnostic assessment. She asked students to write a short essay on any topic to identify their German language proficiency level. Similarly, only one instructor reported using self-assessment. She gave students test-like home assignments with answer keys so that they could grade themselves if they wanted. Each question referenced specific learning material so that students knew what to review if a particular question was problematic. These tests were submitted as regular home assignments and graded as complete/incomplete regardless of performance. After the first assignment, many students said that they found this kind of assessment useful and requested similar self-graded tests after each module. The same instructor used a combination of feedback and peer assessment to evaluate students' pronunciation. After reviewing pronunciation rules and discussing common difficulties, students read aloud in groups and provided feedback to each other before reporting their progress to the class. As reinforcement, students recorded several audio assignments at home that were graded as complete/incomplete. They also received detailed feedback on both positive aspects of their performance and areas that needed improvement.

Less commonly used forms of assessment through a feminist lens

From a feminist perspective, complete/incomplete grading presents a valuable evaluation option because it reduces stress and eliminates student competition and ranking in class. Complete/incomplete grading in combination with instructor feedback appears a successful strategy for focusing on learning, developing relationships with students, and raising students' confidence.

Diagnostic, peer, and self-assessment are effective tools for identifying students' strengths and weaknesses in language programs (Doe, 2014). Students "as active, engaged, and critical assessors" become the center of the self- and peer-assessment process when they "can make sense of information, relate it to prior knowledge, and master the skills involved" (Earl, 2003, p. 47). Formative peer- and self-assessment activities can increase learner involvement and responsibility while encouraging students to better control their learning.

I find the practice of diagnostic assessment to align with feminist pedagogy because it allows instructors to identify learners' prior knowledge and individualize their teaching by focusing on their students' backgrounds and valuing their experiences. Particularly beneficial is the inclusion of verbal feedback as it provides an opportunity for students to interpret the instructor's response and use it in their learning. A diagnostic assessment score may prepare students for an upcoming test and build their self-esteem; however, it becomes a summative assessment when counted toward a student's final grade.

Essential aspects of assessment

The subcategory *Essential aspects of assessment* includes the data applicable to all forms of assessment rather than to specific assessment practices. Of particular importance here are participants' comments explaining essential or desirable features of assessment. Five participants emphasized that assessment should facilitate student learning. One participant stated that he viewed assessment as "the learning experience," which should create opportunities for students to "learn and benefit from it." Another instructor emphasized the importance of student learning in addition to receiving grades as a purpose of assessment. One participant added "materials that students find interesting" as another essential feature of assessment. He claimed that students learn better when assessment tasks such as essays, presentations, and group discussions are based on topics relevant to students' backgrounds and interests. However, the challenge of individualized assessment is exacerbated by the diversity of the student body. Every class is different, and the relevance of assessment tasks and topics may differ between classes.

Two participants noted the increased quality of assessment in smaller classes. One instructor expressed appreciation for his own learning experience at a community college in the late seventies. He considered his small German language class of only ten students to be the best he ever had saying that as a learner, he particularly valued self-assessment: videotaping and analyzing their German performance made students appreciate their progress.

Essential aspects of assessment through a feminist lens

The study participants regard facilitation of student learning, relevant materials, and small class size as essential aspects of assessment. While the two latter attributes comply with feminist pedagogy principles as they empower students by prioritizing their personal experiences and providing more opportunities for discussion, connectedness, and sharing (Manicom, 1992), facilitation of learning has not been mentioned among the principles of critical feminist pedagogy. And yet, feminist assessment facilitates learning because it shares similar characteristics with innovative assessment practices, which are educationally meaningful for students. The only difference between the two is that innovative practices are shaped by practical concerns, whereas feminist practices are shaped by feminist theory and values (Hutchings, 1992). These shared characteristics make assessment an educational process rather than an administrative task and include the following:

1. Focus on student experience
2. Focus on using gathered information for the improvement of programs rather than for external proof

3. Use of multiple methods when gathering information in order to obtain the fullest picture of what students have learned
4. Organizing discussions of the assessment results with faculty members, administrators, and students

(Hutchings, 1992)

Pressures, tension, and discontent

The *Pressures, tension, and discontent* category describes assessment challenges in elementary language classes. The subcategory *Discontent with grading* includes two interconnected subcategories, *Discontent with students' values* and *attitudes* and *Pressure from the administration*.

Discontent with grading

When asked about their perspectives on grading, all participants described assignment of grades as a substantial source of frustration, tension, and discontent stemming from such attributes of grading as ranking students, harming learning, and feeling stressed while grading. One instructor contrasted the university grading system with gradeless evaluation in a noncredit, continuing studies elementary FL course to express her extreme satisfaction with the latter's assessment practices. Students were highly motivated, among other things, by a desire to learn the native language of their domestic partner or by their plans to go abroad. She commented that "[Students] just come to learn the language" rather than to get credits or boost their GPA and suggested that "we should go in this direction," i.e., nongrade evaluation.

All participants were dissatisfied with the university policy of establishing a "recommended" class average grade to combat grade inflation and setting a lower unofficial grade ceiling for elementary courses than for upper-level courses. One participant reported a mismatch between her pedagogical philosophy and the university assessment and evaluation policy:

> There are three aspects of it: political, business, and pedagogical. Political and business aspects – the university has to have certain standards in order to have a good reputation and not to be a lightweight university to get a lot of good students. But pedagogically I don't like it at all because it discourages things that I like, for example, participation marks or ungraded assignments.

The instructor also expressed concern about the administrative pressure in relation to grades. She stated that the combination of complete/incomplete grading and detailed feedback on students' essays increased her class average grade: "That's the frustrating part. I create more work for myself to help my students improve. Then I get higher averages, and then I'm getting punished again."

Two participants articulated an intense frustration with students' values and attitudes toward learning. One instructor stated that academic competitiveness was particularly strong in her elementary language courses with students comparing their scores to the class average and worrying about who received the highest grade rather than focusing on their learning progress. Students' competitiveness was a serious obstacle for peer assessment and support in her beginning classes.

Four instructors were dissatisfied with some students' preoccupation with grades rather than learning. One participant described a first-year female student who demanded 100% on all tests and graded assignments, monopolized the instructor's office hours, and literally pressured her for higher grades. None of the instructor's attempts to shift the student's values to learning seemed to work. The same instructor expressed her discontent with academic dishonesty during open-book tests with an unlimited number of attempts. These tests seemed to be the most promising "assessment as learning" tools that would allow students to improve their results and receive full marks with sufficient practice. Unfortunately, however, multiple test attempts created opportunities for cheating. As each attempt involved the same version of the test, students could save correct answers generated by the previous attempt and use them in the next iteration of the test, thus achieving a perfect test score.

Grading through a feminist lens

Percentage grading presents a serious challenge to feminist pedagogy. The grading system's potential to exacerbate the power imbalance between students and teachers makes it one of the most acute discrepancies between feminist pedagogy and teaching praxis. Moreover, bell-curve grading increases competition and hinders community building and mutual support in the classroom. As for instructors' discontent with students' fixation on grades, the blame cannot be laid entirely on students, as one needs to consider the context that led learners to value grades more than learning. There is widespread evidence that students experience a high level of stress in their academic pursuits (Durand-Bush et al., 2015). By focusing on grades, students may merely try to get through the stresses of a heavy course load and the pressure of being graded on a curve.

I believe that grading causes some students to cheat. Numerous empirical investigations of cheating indicate that performance goals are positively associated with cheating (McCabe et al., 2012). Thus, it was discovered that 65% of North American university students admitted to at least one incident of cheating for want of a higher grade (McCabe et al., 2012). The prevalence of graded classes may explain these findings.

Limitations of the study and suggestions for future research

A valuable form of research, the case study method permitted an in-depth analysis of assessment methods and the participants' attitudes toward them. However, the results of this study should be interpreted with caution. First, the scope of the study could be widened to include data on different assessment practices in various universities, particularly those that implement alternative assessment policies. For example, Brown University has a unique evaluation system that is more student-focused than traditional assessment and evaluation policies. The university students have the option of getting "full-letter grades A, B, or C (without plusses and minuses) or S (for Satisfactory). There is no D grade, and failing grades are not recorded" (Brown University, n.d., para. 1). The university does not calculate grade point averages, and online portfolios created by students serve as qualitative evidence of students' knowledge and skills (Brown University, n.d.). Collecting data from FL instructors at Brown and other institutions with similar approaches to evaluation may provide valuable data on feminist assessment.

Second, this study data were limited to the instructors' perspective; the analysis of the students' outlook on evaluation may yield important insight into feminist assessment in language classes. Students' years of experience in learning, observing assessment, and being evaluated can provide valuable feedback for researchers and instructors. Ultimately, creating assessment that respects students' voices and experiences may lead to improved language courses and learning outcomes.

Classroom implications

This study's findings show that among the various assessment methods used in elementary FL classes, only formative assessment and complete/incomplete grading align with critical feminist pedagogy. Assigning fewer grades, using complete/incomplete grading as well as formative, diagnostic, self- and peer assessment may reduce the need for summative assessment. These alternative forms of assessment should be supplemented by feminist feedback, which is sensitive, motivational, caring, respectful of personal experience, and encourages students to improve their own personal best rather than compete against each other.

Since starting my teacher diary in 2016, I have been making every effort to integrate feminist pedagogy and assessment into my teaching. I believe that since then, my assessment methods and pedagogy have improved in general and have become more meaningful. By providing feminist feedback and diminishing grading, I establish a more balanced power relationship between students and myself. Since there is no measurement scale of power balance in classroom relationships, I use student evaluations as a gauge. Overall, my attempts to become a feminist educator received a positive response from the students who describe my assessment and evaluation practices as communicating "clear expectations"; "helpful"; "receptive"; "respectful"; "rigorous, with assignments due each lecture, but also very effective"; and provide "a good level of feedback throughout the course"; etc.

Conclusion

As feminist theory concerns itself with issues of power, politics, and pedagogy, it provides a critical lens for perceiving the values and uses of assessment practices in FL programs. Integrating principles of critical feminist pedagogy into assessment of language skills can increase student-centeredness and improve beginning-level learning experience thus helping to retain students in the language program. Ungraded formative, diagnostic, peer- and self-assessment formats align with feminist principles and are considered innovative evaluation practices that facilitate learning. Feminist assessment reduces competition between students and restores the balance of power between teachers and students. Sadly, the current practice of graded summative assessment is inconsistent with feminist pedagogy. Out of all graded assessment and evaluation formats, only the complete/incomplete grading approach exhibits feminist qualities, as it reduces class competition in contrast to letter or numerical grading.

I strongly believe that decreasing grading and offering narrative feedback can more effectively track learning progress and provide students with better opportunities for improvement than summative assessment. Instructors who adopt feminist assessment strive to engage their students in learning and stimulate their interest in the language. They teach with passion, creativity, inspiration, and a belief that pedagogy is more than methodology: "As a craft and art, pedagogy is seduction and performance: we cajole, humor, invite, persuade, and convince in efforts to 'seduce' students into the knowledge we embody" (Luke, 1996, p. 288). By deploying feminist assessment instructors can empower students with knowledge, promote a participatory classroom community, and emphasize the process of learning rather than the end results.

Note

Part of the research presented in this chapter is based on the dissertation submitted in partial fulfillment of the requirements for the doctoral degree in the Department of Curriculum and Instruction, University of Victoria.

Note

1 See "The Interview Questions" at https://tinyurl.com/22n582v4.

References

Accardi, M. T. (2013). *Feminist pedagogy for library instruction*. Library Juice Press.
Akyea, S. G., & Sandoval, P. (2005). A feminist perspective on student assessment: An epistemology of caring and concern. *Radical Pedagogy*, 6(2). http://radicalpedagogy.icaap.org/content/issue6_2/akyea-sandoval.html

American Council on the Teaching of Foreign Languages. (2012). *ACTFL proficiency guidelines*. www.actfl.org/sites/default/files/pdfs/ACTFLProficiencyGuidelines2012_FINAL.pdf

Astin, A. W., & Antonio, A. L. (2012). *Assessment for excellence: The philosophy and practice of assessment and evaluation in higher education*. Rowman & Littlefield.

Bachman, L. F. (1990). *Fundamental considerations in language testing*. Oxford University Press.

Behling, K. C., Gentile, M. M., & Lopez, O. J. (2017). The effect of graded assessment on medical student performance in TBL exercises. *Medical Science Educator, 27*(3), 451–455.

Bloxham, S., & Boyd, P. (2007). *Developing effective assessment in higher education: A practical guide*. Open University Press.

Brown, D., & Abeywickrama, P. (2010). *Language assessment: Principles and classroom practices*. Pearson Education.

Brown University. (n.d.). *Brown's grading system*. https://www.brown.edu/campus-life/support/careerlab/employers/employer-resources/browns-grading-system

Cephe, P. T., & Toprak, T. E. (2014). The common European framework of reference for languages: Insights for language testing. *Journal of Language and Linguistic Studies, 10*(1), 79–88.

Chitnev, V. (2019). *University assessment practices through a lens of feminist pedagogy* [Doctoral dissertation, University of Victoria]. http://dspace.library.uvic.ca/bitstream/handle/1828/11338/Chitnev_Veta_PhD_2019.pdf

Council of Europe. (2001). *Common European framework of reference for languages: Learning, teaching, assessment*. Press Syndicate of the University of Cambridge.

Crabtree, R., Sapp, D., & Licona, A. (2009). Introduction: The passion and the praxis of feminist pedagogy. In R. Crabtree, D. Sapp, & A. Licona (Eds.), *Feminist pedagogy: Looking back to move forward* (pp. 1–20). The Johns Hopkins University Press.

Crowe, S., Cresswell, K., Robertson, A., Huby, G., Avery, A., & Sheikh, A. (2011). The case study approach. *BMC Medical Research Methodology, 11*, 1–9.

Doe, C. (2014). *Diagnostic English language needs assessment (DELNA)*. SAGE.

Durand-Bush, N., McNeill, K., Harding, M., & Dobransky, J. (2015). Investigating stress, psychological well-being, mental health functioning, and self-regulation capacity among university undergraduate students: Is this population optimally functioning? *Canadian Journal of Counselling and Psychotherapy, 49*(3), 253–274.

Earl, L. (2003). *Assessment as learning: Using classroom assessment to maximize student learning*. Corwin Press.

English L. M., & Irving, C. J. (2015). *Feminism in community: Adult education for transformation*. Sense Publishers.

Fu, H., Hopper, T., & Sanford, K. (2018). New BC curriculum and communicating student learning in an age of assessment for learning. *Alberta Journal of Educational Research, 64*(3), 264–286.

Gibbs, G., & Simpson, C. (2005). Conditions under which assessment supports students' learning. *Learning and Teaching in Higher Education, 1*(1), 3–31.

Gronlund, N. E., & Cameron, I. J. (2004). *Assessment of student achievement*. Pearson.

Harackiewicz, J., Canning, E., & Tibbetts, Y. (2015). Academic motivation and performance: Task value interventions. In J. D. Wright (Ed.), *International encyclopedia of the social & behavioral sciences* (2nd ed., pp. 37–42). Elsevier.

Hershberg, R. M. (2014). Constructivism. In D. Coghlan, & M. Brydon-Miller (Eds.), *The SAGE encyclopedia of action research* (pp. 183–187). SAGE.

Hoidn, S., & Klemenčič, M. (2020). Introduction and overview. In S. Hoidn, & M. Klemenčič (Eds.), *The Routledge international handbook of student-centred learning and teaching in higher education*. (pp. 1–13). Routledge.

hooks, B. (1994). *Teaching to transgress: Education as the practice of freedom*. Routledge.

Hutchings, P. (1992). The assessment movement and feminism: Connection or collision? In C. M. Musil (Ed.), *Students at the center: Feminist assessment* (pp. 17–28). Association of American Colleges.

Kerr, P. (2020). *Giving feedback to language learners*. Part of the Cambridge papers in ELT series. Cambridge University. cambridge.org/cambridge-papers-elt

Lipnevich, A. A., & Smith, J. K. (2009). Effects of differential feedback on students' examination performance. *Journal of Experimental Psychology, 15*(4), 319–333.

Luke, C. (1996). Feminist pedagogy theory: Reflections on power and authority. *Educational Theory, 46*(3), 283–302.

Manicom, A. (1992). Feminist pedagogy: Transformations, standpoints, and politics. *Canadian Journal of Education, 17*(3), 365–389.

Martin, M., & Jansen, L. (2012). Identifying possible causes for high and low retention rates in language and culture programs at the Australian National University: A characterization of three groups of students crucial for understanding student attrition. In J. Hajek, C. Nettelbeck, & A. Woods (Eds.), *Languages & Cultures Network for Australian Universities Colloquium (LCNAU 2011)* (pp. 175–219). Languages & Cultures Network for Australian Universities.

McCabe, D. L., Butterfield, K. D., & Trevino, L. K. (2012). *Cheating in college: Why students do it and what educators can do about it*. The Johns Hopkins University Press.

Monchinski, T. (2010). *Education in hope: Critical pedagogies and the ethic of care*. Peter Lang.

Novek, E. (1999). Service-learning is a feminist issue: Transforming communication pedagogy. *Women's Studies in Communication, 2*(2), 230–240.

Reynolds, M., & Trehan, K. (2000). Assessment: A critical perspective. *Studies in Higher Education, 25*(3), 267–278.

Ropers-Huilman, R. (2009). Scholarship on the other side: Power and caring in feminist education. In R. Crabtree, D. Sapp, & A. Licona (Eds.), *Feminist pedagogy: Looking back to move forward* (40–56). The Johns Hopkins University Press.

Rupiper Taggart, A., & Laughlin, M. (2017). Affect matters: When writing feedback leads to negative feeling. *International Journal for the Scholarship of Teaching and Learning, 11*(2). https://doi.org/10.20429/ijsotl.2017.110213

Schinske, J., & Tanner, K. (2014). Teaching more by grading less (or differently). *CBE Life Sciences Education, 13*(2), 159–166.

Schniedewind, N. (1981). Feminist values: Guidelines for teaching methodology in women's studies. *The Radical Teacher, 18*, 25–28.

Shackelford, J. (1992). Feminist pedagogy: A means for bringing critical thinking and creativity to the economics classroom. *American Economic Review, 82*(2), 570–576.

Stake, R. (1994). Case studies. In N. K. Denzin, & Y. S. Lincoln (Eds.), *Handbook of qualitative research* (pp. 236–247). SAGE.

Tatum, H. E., Schwartz, B. M., Schimmoeller, P. A., & Perry, N. (2013). Classroom participation and student-faculty interactions: Does gender matter? *The Journal of Higher Education, 84*(6), 745–768.

Wallace, S. (Ed.) (2015). *A dictionary of education* (2nd ed.). Oxford University Press.

Webb, L. M., Allen, M. W., & Walker, K. L. (2002). Feminist pedagogy: Identifying basic principles. *Academic Exchange Quarterly, 6*(1), 67–72.

Wong, M., & Saunders, L. (2020). *Instruction in libraries and information centers: An introduction*. Windsor & Downs Press.

Woodlock, C. (1995). Looking at feminist pedagogies: What is seen in the literature and what is seen in an art education studio/classroom. *Marilyn Zurmuehlen Working Papers in Art Education, 13*(1), 4–10. http://ir.uiowa.edu/mzwp/vol13/iss1/3

Yorke, M. (2003). Formative assessment in higher education: Moves towards theory and the enhancement of pedagogic practice. *Higher Education, 45*(4), 477–501.

Yorke, M. (2005). Formative assessment in higher education: Its significance for employability, and steps towards its enhancement. *Tertiary Education and Management, 11*(3), 219–238.

Yorke, M. (2008). *Grading student achievement in higher education: Signals and shortcomings*. Routledge.

16
ASSESSMENT OF THE RELATIONSHIP BETWEEN DERIVATIONAL MORPHOLOGICAL AWARENESS AND SECOND LANGUAGE READING COMPREHENSION

Anna Shur

Learning a second language (L2) is a nuanced process involving many complexities and possible obstacles. At the time individuals begin learning an L2, it is implied they already know at least one language. The prior knowledge of a first language (L1) can both advantage and disadvantage L2 learners whose existing linguistic knowledge and understanding can incite inaccurate assumptions about the L2 mechanisms and thus cause errors that L1 learners would not make (Lightbown & Spada, 2013).

The native language may influence one's attainment of L2 phonology, morphology, syntax, semantics, and lexicon (Kuo & Anderson, 2008). Among the aspects of L2 acquisition, morphology remains a critical research topic because of semantic, phonological, and syntactic properties of morphemes which affect the development of reading skills at many levels (Mahony et al., 2000). Morphemes represent the smallest lexical units and recur consistently in word formations (e.g., -ceive in "conceive" and "receive"). Inflection, derivation, and compounding are the main word formation processes. Inflection modifies the word form to provide grammatical information, e.g., play + -s to denote third-person singular form of the English verb. Derivation changes the meaning or the lexical category of the base morpheme by adding an affix (e.g., dis + connect = disconnect, predict + able = predictable). An individual's ability "to reflect upon and manipulate morphemes and to control word formation processes" is referred to as morphological awareness (Kuo & Anderson, 2008, p. 47). This study is focused on derivational morphological awareness (DMA) and its impact on L2 reading comprehension.

Myriad studies explored morphological awareness with reference to reading (Deacon et al., 2007; Kieffer & Box, 2013; McCutchen & Stull, 2015; Seymour, 1999; Tyler & Nagy, 1989). However, most of these studies examined English

DOI: 10.4324/9781003058441-20

language learners acquiring English as a second (ESL) or foreign (EFL) language in the U.S. or outside of the country and facing challenges trying to achieve high levels of reading proficiency required to comprehend the content. Therefore, understanding the process of reading comprehension in a second/foreign language at the beginning level and the factors that influence it remains an important research topic for the field of literacy.

Literature review

Many studies found evidence for a strong connection between L2 reading comprehension and L2 vocabulary (e.g., Droop & Verhoeven, 2003; Proctor et al., 2005). As Kieffer and Lesaux (2008) stated, the existing research often employs "a single, global measure of vocabulary and does not shed light on the complex, multi-dimensional nature of vocabulary development nor on the relationships of its various dimensions to reading comprehension" (p. 784). Morphological awareness as an ability to recognize and manipulate the morphemic structure of words (Carlislie, 1995) and, particularly, DMA, is one such dimension of vocabulary acquisition that contributes to reading comprehension (Zhang & Koda, 2012). DMA refers to the ability to recognize morphological relationships between different word forms and derive and manipulate new words (Amirjalili & Jabbari, 2018). Morphological awareness is crucial for increasing vocabulary knowledge, because morphologically complex words commonly occur in English (Anglin, 1993); nearly 80% of the new vocabulary acquired by elementary school-aged children consists of multimorphemic words (Anglin, 1993; Nagy & Anderson, 1984). Thus, distinguishing the type of morphological awareness and assessing its relationship to vocabulary knowledge based on the morphological distinctions that are most relevant for learners' first and second languages is essential for the development of their reading skills.

Languages differ in types of morphology and the role the morphemic organization of words or the word structure plays in the linguistic system (Sparks & Deacon, 2015). Previous research (e.g., Anglin, 1993; Ku & Anderson, 2003; McBride-Chang et al., 2008) showed that a person's L1 influences the type of morphological awareness that later predicts the development of reading skills in L2. For example, compounding (a word formation process that creates a new word from free morphemes, e.g., boy + friend = boyfriend) mattered in the studies that examined the transfer of morphological awareness from Chinese to English (Wang et al., 2009; Zhang et al., 2010; Zhang et al., 2012; Zhang, 2013; Zhang & Koda, 2013). Zhang et al. (2012) showed that Chinese participants performed better than their English-speaking counterparts on most English compound structures, with $F(1, 685) = 48.79$, $p < .01$, $\eta^2 = 0.06$ in the study.

Studies that investigated the transfer of morphological awareness from Spanish to English (e.g., Ramirez et al., 2010), from Korean to English (e.g., Jeon, 2011), and from Arabic to English (Kahn-Horwitz & Saba, 2018) revealed that DMA produced a significant effect on the development of English reading comprehension. Ramirez et al. (2010) demonstrated how Spanish derivational awareness implicitly affected English reading comprehension via English morphological awareness and English lexical cognates. Jeon (2011) proved that morphological awareness improves reading comprehension skills even across orthographically different languages such as English and Korean. The Kahn-Horwitz and Saba's (2018) study also showed that DMA contributed to word recognition and predicted EFL reading comprehension.

The relationship between the transfer of morphological awareness and such word formation process as compounding or derivation is explained by typological differences and similarities between languages. Thus, Desrochers et al. (2018) analyzed data from French, Greek, and English-speaking children to conclude that readers of languages with transparent orthographies, i.e., clear phonemic sound-symbol correspondences (Greek) do not rely on morphological awareness as much as those of opaque languages with inconsistent word spellings (French and English) who must activate their knowledge of morphology to decode irregular orthography. Luo et al. (2018) suggest that morphological features of the language determine the type of morphological awareness prevalent in that language. In their study, structurally different English and Chinese conditioned different types of morphological awareness: derivational and inflectional awareness in English and compound awareness in Chinese. Conversely, the Indo-European languages in Desrochers et al. (2018) study displayed the same derivational and inflectional awareness.

The study

While languages employ a wide variety of morphological systems, studies examining DMA transfer from a native language to English are still relatively rare and mainly analyze children's literacy. The purpose of this study is to examine the crosslinguistic transfer of derivational morphological awareness in L1 German and Russian adult beginning learners of English and assess DMA influence on their English reading comprehension through English vocabulary knowledge. Thus, vocabulary knowledge was also assessed because it served as the link between DMA and L2 reading comprehension. The following research questions guided this investigation:

RQ1. What is the unique contribution of DMA to L2 (English) reading comprehension in relation to vocabulary knowledge in each group of English learners (L1 German and Russian)?

RQ2. What is the role of crosslinguistic transfer in L2 reading comprehension in each group of learners?

Method

This study investigates the crosslinguistic DMA transfer and its role in the development of L2 reading comprehension. Examining crosslinguistic transfer required the assessment of DMA in both participants' L1 (German or Russian) and their L2 (English). This study also assessed English vocabulary knowledge since vocabulary mediates the relation between DMA and reading comprehension (Carlisle, 2000; Droop & Verhoeven, 2003). Thus, all participants took a vocabulary test (Nation, 1990). The final part of the assessment was an English reading comprehension test (Gough, 2011).

The language tasks were distributed to participants via *Qualtrics* (Version 5.2021). Five tests were used: general English proficiency, native language DMA, English as a second language derivational morphological knowledge, English vocabulary knowledge, and English reading comprehension. These units were distributed in one-week intervals, allowing participants one week to complete each test.

Participants

All participants were adult native speakers of German or Russian who studied EFL in their home countries. All were undergraduate students; their L2 proficiency level ranged from advanced beginning to low-intermediate. To determine if the study participants possessed the minimum level of English proficiency necessary for completing the test tasks to demonstrate their English morphological awareness, vocabulary knowledge, and reading comprehension, the English Placement Test was administered. This study employed an online test commonly used by intensive English programs at universities to assess students' knowledge of English grammar and vocabulary (e.g., https://www.englishtestsonline.com/english-placement-test-online-with-answers/). It estimates an individual's proficiency level compared to international English exams and the Council of Europe (2001) language assessment scale. The test includes 90 multiple-choice questions assessing various aspects of English grammar, vocabulary, and usage.

Initially, 29 German and 35 Russian students began participation in the study; after eliminating those who did not complete all five tests, the final sample size was 51: 23 participants were native speakers of German (three male, 20 female), and 28 were native speakers of Russian (two male, 26 female). The results of a *t*-test analysis of the English general proficiency test demonstrated no significant difference in the general proficiency scores across German ($M = 87.74$, $SD = 6.07$) and Russian participants ($M = 86.32$, $SD = 7.27$); $t(49) = 0.75$, $p = 0.46$. This result ensured equal conditions for the assessment of second language literacies in both groups because participants possessed equivalent beginning levels of general English proficiency.

Context

The two locations for data collection were outside of the U.S. Russian participants attended a large public university in western Russia. The university contains 24 academic programs. Foreign language courses are mandatory in all programs; the length of language study depends on the program of study and ranges from one to four years. English is one of the foreign languages offered at the university.

German participants studied in one of the largest public universities for applied sciences in southern Germany which offers a wide range of undergraduate and graduate programs including English and English Studies. Foreign language courses are mandatory for both graduate and undergraduate students in all programs. Similar to its Russian counterpart, the German university offers language classes, including English, that last from one to four years depending on the student's major program.

Research design

This research was a correlational study. Three independent variables were investigated as predictors of the outcome variable, EFL reading comprehension: native language (German or Russian) DMA, English DMA, and English vocabulary knowledge. An online test was administered to measure each of the variables. Participants received links to tests and had one week to complete each. Only data from participants who completed all four tests were analyzed in the study.

Instruments

The study employed a total of five assessment measures: general proficiency, one each for native language DMA (Russian or German), English DMA, English vocabulary knowledge (Nation, 1990), and English reading comprehension (Gough, 2011). The numbers of items in general proficiency test, reading comprehension test, native language DMA test, English DMA test, and vocabulary knowledge test were 90, 40, 74, 74, and 120, respectively.

The researcher's assessment of DMA was based on the premise that it is a multifaceted construct involving complex relational, syntactic, and distributional knowledge (Tyler & Nagy, 1989). Relational knowledge describes the ability to distinguish the base, stem, and affixes in morphologically complex words and recognize the relationships between morphemes. Syntactic knowledge is defined as the understanding of the use of derivational affixes and the ways they change the part of speech. Distributional knowledge refers to the perception of constraints imposed by syntactic categories of the bases on affix attachment.

To assess L2 (English) DMA, the set of morphological instruments was adopted from Carlisle's (2000) study. To assess relational knowledge, the decomposition task was included; it consisted of 28 real-word segmentation questions asking participants to isolate the base in a derived word. To address the distributional knowledge of L2 DMA, the task suggested by Schmitt and Meara (1997) was used. It required producing derived words for the nine prompt words with the suffixes presented in alphabetic order. The assessment of the syntactic component of L2 DMA used in the current study was adopted from the work of Nagy et al. (1993). The task consisted of nine sentences in which an underlined derived word needed to be judged as grammatical or ungrammatical.

The design of native language DMA assessment measures presented challenges as the existing morphological tests for adults in Russia and Germany are markedly different from tests of English DMA that were used in this study. Thus, the researcher developed and validated German and Russian morphological tests that were better aligned with the English tests used in this study. The German and Russian equivalent tests were created in accordance with the specific features possessed by the morphological systems of these two languages. For example, both tests required the use of inflectional morphology, with the Russian measures including many more inflections than the German tasks. This limitation appeared to be inevitable due to the structure of the Russian language whose rich inflectional system expresses relationships between words in sentences. The final versions of the German and Russian DMA measures were aligned with the English tests. Similar to the English version, each of them included 74 items that were divided according to relational, distributional, and syntactic aspects. Thus, both L1 and L2 DMA tests aimed at the same aspects and included equal numbers of items.

To ensure the validity of the German and Russian tests, the researcher conducted a pilot study with native speakers of German and Russian enrolled as international students at a U.S. university. Participants took both their L1 and English tests. In total, there were five participants for each pair of the pilot tests, German-English and Russian-English; they were not included in the sample described in the current study. The pilot test results indicated that the L1 tests targeted the same level of proficiency of the students, as the average number of errors observed across German and Russian tests was consistent with the number of errors noted in the English test. The researcher also noticed that participants tended to make errors within the same aspect of tasks (e.g., distributional knowledge) in both their L1 and English tests.

As vocabulary knowledge is considered one of the predictors of reading comprehension (Choi, 2015; Kuo & Anderson, 2006), its assessment was essential for data collection process. This study employed the Vocabulary Levels Test) (Nation, 1990) to measure participants' English vocabulary knowledge.

The reading component of the International English Language Testing System (General Training Test; Gough, 2011) was administered to assess participants' English reading comprehension skills. The three-section reading test consists of 40 questions that target (1) reading for gist, (2) reading for main ideas and details, and (3) understanding logical argument.

Data collection

The study materials were administered online in two universities located in Germany and Russia. English instructors were requested to distribute the tests among their students via email. A brief cover letter explained the purpose of the given inquiry.

This study used *Qualtrics* (Version 5.2021) survey software to allow participants access to each of the tests: general language proficiency, first language DMA, English DMA, vocabulary knowledge, and reading comprehension. Consequently, data collection was divided into five phases according to the tests: general English proficiency, native language DMA, English DMA, English vocabulary knowledge, and English reading comprehension. Each phase lasted for one week.

Data analysis

Descriptive statistics of the participants' performance on all the tests are shown in Table 16.1. Means and standard deviations are provided in proportion to correct choice of items. The researcher ran a multiple regression analysis of the data using *IBM SPSS Statistics* (Version 24). To address the first research question about the unique contribution of DMA to L2 (English) reading comprehension in relation to vocabulary knowledge in each group of learners, a regression analysis was performed with reading comprehension as the outcome variable and vocabulary knowledge and DMA in both native languages and English as predictors. This analysis identified the independent variables that best predicted the dependent variable in each group.

To answer the second research question which targeted the role of cross-linguistic transfer in L2 reading comprehension in each group of learners, a simple regression analysis was performed in each participant group to determine if native language DMA predicted English DMA. A *t*-test was used to compare reading comprehension scores between German and Russian participants.

Results

The correct answer percentage on each test was calculated for use in the statistical analyses (Table 16.1).

Research question 1

In answer to RQ1, what is the unique contribution of DMA to L2 (English) reading comprehension in relation to vocabulary knowledge in each group of English learners (L1 German and Russian), it was found that in the German group, none of the independent variables (L1 DMA, L2 DMA, vocabulary

TABLE 16.1 Test results in German and Russian participant groups

	German participants (n = 23)		Russian participants (n = 28)	
	M	SD	M	SD
General proficiency	87.74	6.07	86.32	7.27
L2 Reading comprehension	76.35	11.73	82.04	10.23
L1 DMA	91.91	3.80	89.68	3.95
L2 DMA	82.87	7.16	88.75	4.73
L2 Vocabulary knowledge	81.52	8.53	89.07	7.77

Note: on a scale of 0–100.

knowledge) predicted reading comprehension with statistical significance $F (3, 19) = 1.24$, $p > 0.05$, $R^2 = 0.16$. All three independent variables were constant. The stepwise multiple regression test run to confirm these findings did not show any statistically significant results regardless of the entry order of independent variables.

The results in the Russian group were different (Table 16.2). A stepwise multiple regression analyses was conducted to evaluate whether all the independent variables (L1 DMA, L2 DMA, and vocabulary knowledge) predicted reading comprehension among Russian-speaking participants. In total, three regression analyses were conducted with different sequences of entering the independent variables.

The Russian language DMA did not yield statistically significant results regardless of the entry order of predictors, $t (26) = -0.70$, $p > 0.05$. Vocabulary knowledge entered into the regression equation was significantly correlated to reading comprehension, $F (1, 26) = 12.52$, $p < 0.05$, contributing 33% ($R^2 = 0.33$). Combined with English DMA, the contribution of vocabulary knowledge to reading comprehension increased by 14%, $F (2, 25) = 10.94$, $p < 0.05$.

TABLE 16.2 Summary of predictors of reading comprehension in the L1 Russian group

		B	SE	β	t	p
Model 1	Vocabulary knowledge	0.75	0.21	0.57	3.54	0.00
	R^2		0.33			
	F		12.52			
Model 2	Vocabulary knowledge	0.63	0.20	0.48	3.18	0.00
	English DMA	0.84	0.33	0.39	2.58	0.02
	R^2		0.47			
	R^2 Change		0.14			
	F		10.94			

Note: n = 28.

Research question 2

RQ 2 investigated the role of crosslinguistic transfer in L2 reading comprehension in each group of learners (L1 German and Russian). The simple regression analysis performed in the German participant group (Table 16.3) showed that the prediction model was statistically significant, $F(1, 21) = 4.51$, $p < 0.05$, meaning that the level of English DMA can be predicted by the level of German DMA. The model accounted for approximately 18% of the variance ($R^2 = 0.18$) meaning there is a strong relationship between these two variables. For every 1-unit increase of German DMA, it is expected that participants' English DMA will increase by 0.79.

The results of the simple regression analysis in the L1 Russian group revealed that the prediction model was statistically insignificant, $F(1, 26) = 0.08$, $p > 0.05$. Thus, the level of Russian DMA does not predict the level of English DMA, nor does DMA transfer from Russian to English for Russian learners of English.

An independent-samples t-test was conducted to compare reading comprehension test results for the groups of German and Russian learners of English. There was no significant difference in the reading comprehension scores between Germans ($M = 76.35$, $SD = 11.73$) and Russians ($M = 82.04$, $SD = 10.23$); $t(49) = -1.85$, $p > 0.05$. These results suggest that the participants' first language did not influence their reading comprehension scores.

Stepwise multiple regression analyses were run in each group to see if either L1 or L2 DMA contributed to vocabulary knowledge. As mentioned earlier, vocabulary knowledge affected reading comprehension in the Russian group but not in the German group. Thus, it was important to see if vocabulary knowledge served as the link between DMA and reading comprehension, although derivational morphological awareness did not directly influence reading comprehension.

It was also important to establish the relation between DMA and vocabulary knowledge in the German group. Since German DMA contributed to English derivational awareness, it was assumed that the latter would contribute to vocabulary knowledge. In each group, two stepwise multiple regression analyses were performed using L1 and L2 DMA as independent variables. None of these

TABLE 16.3 Summary of simple regression analysis predicting English DMA in the German group

Model		B	SE B	β	P
1	Constant	10.07	34.32		0.77
	German DMA	0.79	0.37	0.42	0.04
	R^2		0.18		
	F		4.51		

Note: $n = 23$. Dependent variable – English DMA; predictor – German DMA.

analyses showed statistically significant results ($p > 0.05$). Thus, it was concluded that neither L1 nor L2 DMA add to vocabulary knowledge in any of the groups.

Discussion

This study investigated DMA of native speakers of German and Russian in their L1 and L2 (English) and assessed their vocabulary knowledge and reading comprehension.

The influence of DMA on L2 reading comprehension in relation to vocabulary knowledge was analyzed using a stepwise multiple regression analysis in each participant group. There was one dependent variable of L2 reading comprehension and three predictors (L1 DMA, L2 DMA, and L2 vocabulary knowledge). The latter variable was introduced because that awareness of derivational affixes as well as knowledge of base words promotes better inference of meanings in unfamiliar lexical items (Baumann et al., 2003; Bowers & Kirby, 2010).

The results of the multiple regression analysis in each participant group indicated statistically significant results only for the Russian group. However, only two out of three independent variables appeared to serve as predictors of the development of L2 reading comprehension, namely, L2 DMA and vocabulary knowledge, while native language (Russian) DMA did not have any statistically significant relationship with the outcome variable. The multiple regression analysis in the German group indicated that there were no statistically significant correlations among predictors and the outcome variable. The results in the Russian participant group are confirmed by previous research: L2 DMA along with vocabulary knowledge were significant predictors of reading comprehension (Kuo & Anderson, 2008; Zhang & Koda, 2012). The Russian participants confirmed this finding through the demonstrated statistically significant correlation between their vocabulary knowledge combined with L2 DMA and reading comprehension, although the L1 DMA did not have any statistically significant relationship with L2 reading comprehension.

There is scarce research on the influence of Russian DMA on reading comprehension skills in any language including Russian among native speakers of Russian. However, some studies conducted in Russia (Kornev et al., 2010; Rakhlin et al., 2014) offer empirical evidence of the statistically significant correlation between morphological awareness and word recognition among native speakers of Russian. At the same time, Kornev et al. (2010) provides many examples of inconsistency and irregularity of Russian morphology that can complicate the development of morphological awareness and word knowledge. This inconsistency can be explained by language typology: Russian is a fusional language that expresses multiple grammatical categories, e.g., case, number, and gender in a single morpheme.

In the German group, none of the independent variables (L1 DMA, L2 DMA, vocabulary knowledge) were significantly correlated to reading comprehension.

Unlike the findings in the Russian group, these results appeared to be unexpected and contradictory to the existing pattern of morphological awareness facilitating reading comprehension that has been established by research (Kahn-Horwitz & Saba, 2018; Zhang et al., 2012). However, DMA does not always augment L2 reading comprehension. For example, the results of Qian's (1999) study of Chinese and Korean learners of English did not show any correlation between DMA and L2 reading comprehension.

The statistically insignificant relation between vocabulary knowledge and reading comprehension in the German group seems to be incongruous since many previous studies (e.g., Ku & Anderson, 2003; Nagy et al., 2006) provide evidence of vocabulary knowledge reinforcing reading comprehension. Also, an extensive background knowledge of the text topic and associated vocabulary advances reading comprehension (Anderson & Pearson, 1984). However, readers often fail to connect their L2 vocabulary to the topic and content of reading, even when their word knowledge relates to the information presented in the text. Hirsh (2003) noted that knowledge about the topic of the text can be sufficient for reading comprehension as readers integrate the ideas presented in the text and generate inferences using their background knowledge. Thus, the German participants could use their prior knowledge of the topics they found in the reading comprehension test to make inferences about the content without relying on their vocabulary knowledge.

Also, the researcher hypothesized that the DMA transfer from German to English would be a significant predictor of reading comprehension. However, since German and English have typologically similar grammatical structures, L1 grammatical knowledge may also contribute to reading comprehension in the German participant group. Further research is needed to gain insight into factors affecting the development of English reading comprehension in conjunction with learners' L1.

The study showed statistically significant results for transferring DMA only in the German group. This finding is congruent with the initial assumption that DMA transfer would be easier for native speakers of German than for native speakers of Russian. This assumption stems from the fact that German and English use the Latin script and are typologically closer to each other than Russian and English. The results of the regression analyses confirmed this idea. However, there was no statistically significant difference in the reading comprehension scores between Germans and Russians. The researcher interpreted this finding as evidence that the crosslinguistic transfer of DMA had no influence on the development of L2 reading comprehension. This conclusion needs confirmation by further research with larger participant samples.

The comparison of the English, German, and Russian morphological systems and word formation mechanisms revealed similarities across all three languages. The features common to all three languages are semantic changes and the shift of word class resulting from derivation. The derivational affixes in all three languages also demonstrate similarities. For example, suffixes may signal the part of speech of the word they are attached to (e.g., the English -ment, the Russian -shshik, and the German -heit are nominal suffixes). The structural similarity means that participants' perceptions of the derivational processes in their L1 and English could not be dramatically different since the nature of these processes implies the same kind of alterations: semantic changes and shift from one part of speech to another. Thus, the statistically significant result of the assessment of the DMA transfer occurring only in the German group does not indicate that the crosslinguistic transfer cannot happen among Russian learners of English. Further research can shed light on the DMA transfer between different languages.

Limitations of the study

The major limitation of this study is a small participant number: only 23 individuals in the German group and 28 people in the Russian group. Thus, further research with a larger participant sample is required to investigate the relationship between DMA and L2 reading comprehension among native speakers of both German and Russian. The need for further investigation exists also because German and Russian are morphologically complex languages (Zeller et al., 2013) with rich derivational systems that involve all parts of speech and frequently transform one part of speech into another. This complexity requires a high level of DMA that facilitates inferencing of meaning of complex words during reading.

Classroom implications

The results of this study suggest that DMA can be successfully used in the language classroom for the development of vocabulary knowledge and reading comprehension skills. Learners with well-developed DMA may be more efficient at deducing meanings of such complex words as "encampment," "classification," and "despicable" and understanding their relationships with the monomorphemic words "camp," "class," and "speak." Consequently, a better understanding of word meanings would contribute to learners' reading comprehension. Thus, explicit teaching of morphology should become part of vocabulary instruction. Classroom activities should include recognition of word parts (e.g., roots, suffixes, and prefixes) and how they can be utilized to transform words. Also, instructors could demonstrate examples of true cognates – words with similar spelling and meaning in students' L1 and L2 – to improve reading comprehension skills. To develop their students' DMA, teachers could employ a variety of techniques (e.g., puzzles, word maps, matching games).

The use of word (semantic) maps is a morphological analysis strategy that helps students learn words by providing a systematic approach to deconstructing words into their meaningful parts (roots, prefixes, and suffixes). Students can figure out meanings of even unfamiliar words using a graphic that shows a word, its morphemes, and words that include these same morphemes. A teacher can use semantic maps either before or after reading texts. A think-aloud (a strategy requiring students to verbalize their thought process during an activity) can be used along with a semantic map to analyze the word and determine its meaning. Then students can be asked to select other words with the given morphemes in the text and analyze meanings of these words.

Puzzles and crosswords are another way of teaching students to identify morphemes and analyze the ways they can modify words. For example, one can teach specifically Latin and Greek roots, prefixes, and suffixes providing students with definitions of words and asking them to fill in a crossword by using words that include Latin or Greek morphemes. Charts with these morphemes can be shown in class to give students hints at the right answers.

Morphemes can also be taught in an entertaining activity using a mix-and-match game. A teacher prepares cards that contain either the whole word, prefix, suffix, root, or the definition. After the cards are distributed to the class, students move around the classroom trying to find the match to the card they have. For example, if a student's card contains a definition, they should find a classmate whose card shows a morpheme included in the defined word. A student who has a card with a morpheme can look for a card that shows a word that includes the morpheme on their card. These activities help students learn to recognize parts of words and understand how to build words using morphemes.

Conclusion

The purpose of this study was to describe crosslinguistic transfer of DMA in groups of German and Russian adult learners of English and assess how it contributed to their reading comprehension in English. The study demonstrated unexpected results in the German group where none of the predictors was significantly correlated with reading comprehension despite the evidence of crosslinguistic transfer of DMA. However, German participants' reading comprehension score was not different from the reading score in the Russian group, which showed no evidence of the crosslinguistic DMA transfer. Russian DMA was not significantly correlated with reading comprehension, although the other independent variables (English DMA and vocabulary knowledge) were found to predict reading comprehension.

This study will benefit researchers and educators of ESL/EFL because it broadens the range of participants' first languages. A better understanding of the development of English literacy skills among native speakers of German and Russian provides new perspectives on the theory and practice of ESL/EFL teaching and assessment. Implementing similar research with other languages, including non-Indo-European, will allow researchers and educators to investigate correlations between DMA, vocabulary knowledge, and reading comprehension and to shed light on the development of literacy skills in other world languages as well.

References

Amirjalili, F., & Jabbari, A. A. (2018). The impact of morphological instruction on morphological awareness and reading comprehension of EFL learners. *Cogent Education*, *5*(1), 1–30.

Anderson, R. C., & Pearson, P. D. (1984). A schema-theoretic view of basic processes in reading. In P. D. Pearson (Ed.), *Handbook of reading research* (pp. 255–291). Longman.

Anglin, J. M. (1993). Vocabulary development: A morphological analysis. *Monographs of the Society for Research in Child Development*, *58*(10), i–186. https://doi.org/10.2307/1166112

Baumann, J. F., Edwards, E. C., Boland, E. M., Olejnik, S., & Keme'enui, E. (2003). Vocabulary tricks: Effects of instruction in morphology and context on fifth-grade students' ability to derive and infer word meaning. *American Educational Research Journal*, *40*, 447–494.

Bowers, P. N., & Kirby, J. R. (2010). Effects of morphological instruction on vocabulary acquisition. *Reading and Writing: Interdisciplinary Journal*, *12*, 169–190.

Carlisle, J. F. (1995). Morphological awareness and early reading achievement. In L. B. Feldman (Ed.), *Morphological aspects of language processing* (pp. 189–209). Lawrence Erlbaum.

Carlisle, J. F. (2000). Awareness of the structure and meaning or morphologically complex words: Impact on reading. *Reading and Writing: Interdisciplinary Journal*, *12*, 169–190.

Choi, Y. H. (2015). Roles of L1 and L2 derivational morphological awareness in L2 reading through the mediation of L2 vocabulary knowledge. *The Journal of Asia TEFL*, *12*(3), 81–114.

Council of Europe. (2001). *Common European framework of reference for languages: Learning, teaching, assessment*. Cambridge University Press.

Deacon, S. H., Wade-Woolley, L., & Kirby, J. (2007). Crossover: The role of morphological awareness in French immersion children's reading. *Developmental Psychology*, *43*(3), 732–746.

Desrochers, A., Manolitsis, G., Gaudreau, P., & Georgiou, G. (2018). Early contribution of morphological awareness to literacy skills across languages varying in orthographic consistency. *Reading and Writing*, *31*, 1695–1719. https://doi.org/10.1007/s11145-017-9772-y

Droop, M., & Verhoeven, L. (2003). Language proficiency and reading ability in first- and second-language learners. *Reading Research Quarterly*, *38*, 78–103.

Gough, C. (2011). *IELTS target 5.0: Preparation for IELTS general training: Leading to IELTS academic*. Garnet Publishing.

Hirsh, E. D., Jr. (2003). Reading comprehension requires knowledge – Of words and the world. *American Educator*, *27*(1), 10–44.

Jeon, E. H. (2011). Contribution of morphological awareness to second-language reading comprehension. *The Modern Language Reading*, *95*(2), 217–235.

Kahn-Horwitz, J., & Saba, M. (2018). Weak English foreign language readers: The cross-linguistic impact of morphological awareness. *Reading and Writing*, *31*, 1843–1868.

Kieffer, M. J., & Box, C. D. (2013). Derivational morphological awareness, academic vocabulary, and reading comprehension in linguistically diverse sixth graders. *Learning and Individual Differences*, *24*, 168–175.

Kieffer, M. J., & Lesaux, N. K. (2008). The role of derivational morphological awareness in the reading comprehension of Spanish-speaking English language learners. *Reading and Writing: Interdisciplinary Journal, 21,* 783–804.

Kornev, A. N., Rakhlin, N., & Grigorenko, E. L. (2010). Dyslexia from a cross-Linguistic and cross- cultural perspective: The case of Russian and Russia. *Learning Disabilities: A Contemporary Journal, 8*(1), 41–69.

Ku, Y. -M., & Anderson, R. C. (2003). Development of morphological awareness in Chinese and English. *Reading and Writing: Interdisciplinary Journal, 16,* 399–422.

Kuo, L., & Anderson, R. C. (2006). Morphological awareness and learning to read: A cross-language perspective. *Educational Psychologist, 41,* 161–180.

Kuo, L., & Anderson, R. C. (2008). Conceptual and methodological issues in comparing metalinguistic awareness across languages. In K. Koda, & A. M. Zehler (Eds.), *Learning to read across languages: Cross-linguistic relationships in first- and second-language literacy development* (pp. 39–67). Routledge.

Lightbown, P. M., & Spada, N. (2013). *How languages are learned.* Oxford University Press.

Luo, Y. C., Koh, P. W., Deacon, S. H., & Chen, X. (2018). The roles of metalinguistic skills in Chinese–English biliteracy development. *Reading and Writing, 31,* 1721–1740. https://doi.org/10.1007/s11145-017-9778-5

Mahony, D., Singson, M., & Mann, V. (2000). Reading ability and sensitivity to morphological relations. *Reading and Writing: Interdisciplinary Journal, 12,* 191–218.

McBride-Chang, C., Tardif, T., Cho, J.-R., Shu, H., Fletcher, P., Strokers, S. F., & Leung, K. (2008). What's in a word? Morphological awareness and vocabulary knowledge in three languages. *Applied Psycholinguistics, 29,* 437–462.

McCutchen, D., & Stull, S. (2015). Morphological awareness and children's writing: Accuracy, error, and invention. *Reading and Writing, 28,* 271–289.

Nagy, W., & Anderson, R. C. (1984). How many words are there in printed school English? *Reading Research Quarterly, 19,* 304–330.

Nagy, W., Berninger, V. W., & Abbott, R. D. (2006). Contributions of morphology beyond phonology to literacy outcomes of upper elementary and middle-school students. *Journal of Educational Psychology, 98,* 134–147.

Nagy, W. E., Diakidoy, I.-A. N., & Anderson, R. C. (1993). The acquisition of morphology: Learning the contribution of suffixes to the meanings of derivatives. *Journal of Reading Behavior, 25*(2), 155–170.

Nation, I. S. P. (1990). *Teaching and learning vocabulary.* Heinle and Heinle.

Proctor, C. P., Carlo, M., August, D., & Snow, C. E. (2005). Native Spanish-speaking children reading in English: Toward a model of comprehension. *Journal of Educational Psychology, 97,* 246–256.

Qian, D. D. (1999). Assessing the roles of depth and breadth of vocabulary knowledge in reading comprehension. *Canadian Modern Language Review/La revue canadienne des langues vivantes, 56*(2), 282–308.

Rakhlin, N., Cardoso-Martins, C., & Grigorenko, E. L. (2014). Phonemic awareness is a more important predictor of orthographic processing than rapid serial naming: Evidence from Russian. *Scientific Studies of Reading, 18,* 395–414.

Ramirez, G., Chen, X., Geva, E., & Kiefer, H. (2010). Morphological awareness in Spanish-speaking English language learners: Within and cross-language effects on word reading. *Reading and Writing: Interdisciplinary Journal, 23,* 337–358.

Seymour, P. H. K. (1999). Cognitive architecture of early reading. In I. Lundberg, F. E. Tennessen, & I. Austad (Eds.), *Learning to spell* (pp. 319–337). Erlbaum.

Schmitt, N., & Meara, P. (1997). Researching vocabulary through a word knowledge framework: Word association and verbal suffixes. *Studies in Second Language Acquisition*, *20*, 17–36.

Sparks, E., & Deacon, H. (2015). Morphological awareness and vocabulary acquisition: A longitudinal examination of their relationship in English-speaking children. *Applied Psycholinguistics*, *36*, 299–321.

Tyler, A., & Nagy, W. E. (1989). The acquisition of English derivational morphology. *Journal of Memory and Language*, *28*, 649–667.

Wang, M, Yang, C., & Cheng, C. (2009). The contributions of phonology, morphology, and orthography in Chinese–English biliteracy acquisition. *Applied Psycholinguistics*, *30*, 291–314.

Zeller, B., Snajder, J., & Pado, S. (2013, August). *DErivBase: Inducing and evaluating a derivational morphology resource for German* [Conference presentation]. Association for Computational Linguistics, Sofia, Bulgaria. http://libguides.scu.edu.au/c.php?g=356657&p=2408473

Zhang, D. (2013). Linguistic distance effect on cross-linguistic transfer of morphological awareness. *Applied Psycholinguistics*, *34*, 917–942.

Zhang, D., & Koda, K. (2012). Contribution of morphological awareness and lexical inferencing ability to L2 vocabulary knowledge and reading comprehension: Testing direct and indirect effects. *Reading and Writing: Interdisciplinary Journal*, *25*, 1195–1215.

Zhang, D., & Koda, K. (2013). Morphological awareness and reading comprehension in foreign language: A study of young Chinese EFL learners. *System*, *41*, 901–913.

Zhang, J., Anderson, R. C., Li, H., Dong, Q., Yu, X., & Zhang, Y. (2010). Cross-language transfer of insights into the structure of compound words. *Reading and Writing: Interdisciplinary Journal*, *23*, 311–336.

Zhang, J., Anderson, R. C., Wang, Q., & Packard, J. (2012). Insight into the structure of compound words among speakers of Chinese and English. *Applied Psycholinguistics*, *33*(4), 1–27.

INDEX

activities: collaborative 151, 171, 172; communicative 31, 37–38, 42–44; cultural 22, 35, 81, 89, 102–108; extracurricular 106–108, 170; group 51–55; Internet-based 156; speaking 217; task-based 150, 162, 172; telecollaborative 149, 162; vocabulary 104, 195; writing 22, 35, 104, 171, 172
affordances 152; educational 153, 161; of task-based instruction 60; pedagogical 151, 155, 161; social 153, 154, 159; taxonomy of 159
American Council on the Teaching of Foreign Languages (ACTFL) 3, 30, 68, 83, 149, 150, 155, 235
anxiety 35, 43, 134, 155, 167, 176, 180, 203, 217, 229
assessment 180, 235–239; alternative 235, 239; diagnostic 236, 245, 250; formative 108, 125, 126, 236, 239, 243–244, 249, 250; grade-based 235; learning-oriented (LOA) 217–219; less commonly used 244–255; measures 181, 258; peer 245, 248, 250; proficiency-based 235; reliability of 230; self- 172, 239, 245, 246, 250; summative 126, 236–239, 241–243, 249, 250; tools 185, 196, 237; writing 217, 218
authentic materials 22, 66, 71, 78, 79
automatic use of language 28, 29, 38
autonomy 2, 6, 45, 61, 116, 120–121, 154, 167, 179, 186, 201–202

Big C and little c culture 80–82, 89, 96, 105
blended learning 77–81, 85, 89–91, 167–171, 173, 179, 181, 197
Bloom's taxonomy 44
Byram, M. 60, 63, 68, 77, 78, 80, 81, 96–98, 104, 114, 125, 131

Common European framework of reference for languages 3, 131, 136, 149, 188
communication 14, 37, 42, 44, 58, 80, 118, 122, 150, 152–153, 156, 159, 171, 204; asynchronous 158; authentic 11, 13, 24, 65–66, 171; computer-mediated (CMC) 59, 78, 151, 154; intercultural 12, 60, 131, 132, 136; Internet 155, 157; interpersonal 67; meaning-based 151, 155; nonverbal 119, 123; objectives 161; second language (L2) 12, 29, 161, 171; skills 171–171; spoken/oral 11, 133, 17, 19, 20, 22, 23, 30, 160, 172; three modes of 58, 62, 66, 68, 72; virtual 203; *see also* activities
competence: communicative 42, 58, 77, 170, 172; cultural 22, 60, 62, 72, 132, 136; intercultural 68, 95–113, 131, 150, 203; grammar 46; literacy 17; reading and writing 11; strategic 159; translingual and transcultural 113–114

Index **271**

comprehension 47–50, 52, 55, 209; listening 66, 134, 135, 241, 253; of TL culture 132; reading 135, 171, 172, 254–266; vocabulary 135
concordance 186, 188–189, 195
constructivist 80, 202, 237
corpus linguistics 27, 186–187, 194
curriculum xi, 6, 12, 15, 29, 39, 107, 109, 114, 117; blended 85, 91; comprehensive skills 11; flipped 127; L2 culture in 77–95, 98–99, 104, 108, 118–123, 126; objectives 218

Deardorff, D. K. 62, 109, 123, 125, 131
Dörnyei, Z. 11–13, 22, 26

Ellis, N. C. 27, 28, 38, 42, 150
Ellis, R. 38, 43, 44, 58–61, 67, 150
English as a foreign language (EFL) 43, 45, 59, 79, 134, 150, 203
English as a second language 12, 198, 257

feedback 3, 47, 65, 70, 119, 125, 153, 168, 188, 190, 196, 209, 218, 235–250; corrective 59, 60, 71; immediate 206; peer 63, 71; targeted 38
flipped learning 42–44, 48–54, 117, 127; see also curriculum
foreign languages: Chinese 11–23, 30, 42–55, 78–90, 150, 196, 204, 255, 256, 264; German 30, 51, 78, 117, 150, 168, 188, 195, 196, 209, 210, 239, 240, 245, 246, 256–266; French 11–23, 30, 32, 51, 59, 158, 160, 168, 188, 195, 196, 204, 209, 256; Korean 13, 86, 217–231, 255, 256, 264; Russian 27–41, 150–162, 191, 195, 197, 200–211, 239–253; Spanish 11–23, 27, 30, 32–35, 46, 51, 58–72, 79, 116–119, 126, 168, 191, 195, 196, 204, 210, 255, 256; Ukrainian 167–173; world xii, 2, 99, 109, 117, 267

grammar 18, 28–30, 37, 42–55, 59–63, 66, 70, 78, 96, 108, 114, 131, 135, 158, 160, 172, 191, 210, 257; accuracy 229; acquisition of 42, 46, 208; cognitive 27, 28; construction 27; explicit instruction of 44; practice 102, 117; presentation of 171; skills 195, 204; traditional instruction of 42, 44; see also competence; pedagogical approaches

independent learning 88, 90, 171, 179, 180
intercultural sensitivity 63, 95, 96, 98, 99, 109
International English Language Testing system (IELTS) 106, 259
Internet 142, 151, 153, 154, 156, 157, 178, 186, 210, 225; see also activities

Kramsch, C. 77, 80–82, 86, 97, 124, 132

learning management system (LMS) 47, 62, 84, 190, 242
learning outcomes x–xii, 12, 29, 30, 36, 45, 52, 67, 99, 115, 121, 126, 168, 180, 186, 203, 236, 249
Liddicoat, A. J. 97–98, 105, 107
literacy 13, 23, 152, 204, 255; children's 256; digital 11, 14, 21; information 152; L2 14, 151, 157, 162; media 152; technical 210; traditional 151, 156; see also competence
Long, M. 43, 59, 157

motivation: learner xi–xii, 11–24, 32, 36, 45, 48, 54, 60, 90, 135, 149, 155, 159, 161, 178, 197, 201, 203, 207–211, 219, 222, 243; resultative 26; dynamics of 34

online learning 65, 69, 71, 167, 186, 171; see also blended learning; flipped learning

pedagogical approaches: communicative language teaching (CLT) 42, 56, 96, 170; culture learning in a blended environment (CLBC) 78–90; ethnographic 79, 81; focus on form 29, 43–44, 58, 60, 70–71; focus on forms 43; four-skill-integrated 62, 64, 72; "grammar + vocabulary" 36, 39; Presentation, Practice, Production (PPP) 59; "skill before content" 77; task-based instruction 58–72; usage-based instruction (UBI) 26–39

reflection 47, 54, 68, 85, 97, 103, 105–108, 115, 125, 132, 162, 225, 228, 237, 239; cultural 105, 120; journal 31, 159; paper 84, 86, 120

scaffolding 61–63, 70, 71, 80, 151, 155, 157, 161, 171, 190, 219, 220
second language acquisition 27, 45, 58
SMART goals 38
social media 21, 23, 24, 149, 151, 154–156, 158–160, 178
strategies 61, 67, 155, 176, 219; assessment 239; for cultural instruction 108; instructional 1, 4, 38, 135; knowledge-acquisition 134; learning 54, 135, 237; mapping 135; negotiating of meaning 150; orthographic 23; self-efficacy and self-regulation 134

telecollaboration 78, 149–151, 153–156; *see also* blended learning; flipped learning; online learning
textbooks xi, xii, 26, 150, 171, 172, 187, 188, 190, 207–209, 211, 222, 225, 228; explanations 29, 36; to teach culture 102, 104–106, 108, 114, 115, 117, 118, 126, 132, 137, 138
textbook-based course 27; curriculum 39
translanguaging 108

VanPatten, B. 26, 42, 150, 217
vocabulary 18, 21–23, 36–39, 59, 61–62, 78, 114, 131, 135, 142, 156, 157–160, 186, 196, 203–204, 220, 225–269; accuracy 229; lack of 24, 139–141, 155, 160; lists 29, 66; practice 102; materials 108; presentation of 171; usage 192; *see also* activities
Vygotsky, L. S. 80, 219
Vygotsky's socio-cultural theory 72, 202, 219

writing 13, 15, 18, 23, 67, 83, 113, 115, 118–120, 141, 150–151, 160, 162, 169, 171, 172, 185, 189, 195, 220, 223; accuracy of 60, 229; blogs 60; collaborative 157, 217–231; digital 12–24, 162; essay 243; journal 31, 35; pen 12–23; performance 203; practice 81, 172; process 150, 219, 226; reflective 125; samples 190–194; social media 23, 156–157; system 3, 12, 217; *see also* activities; assessment; competence